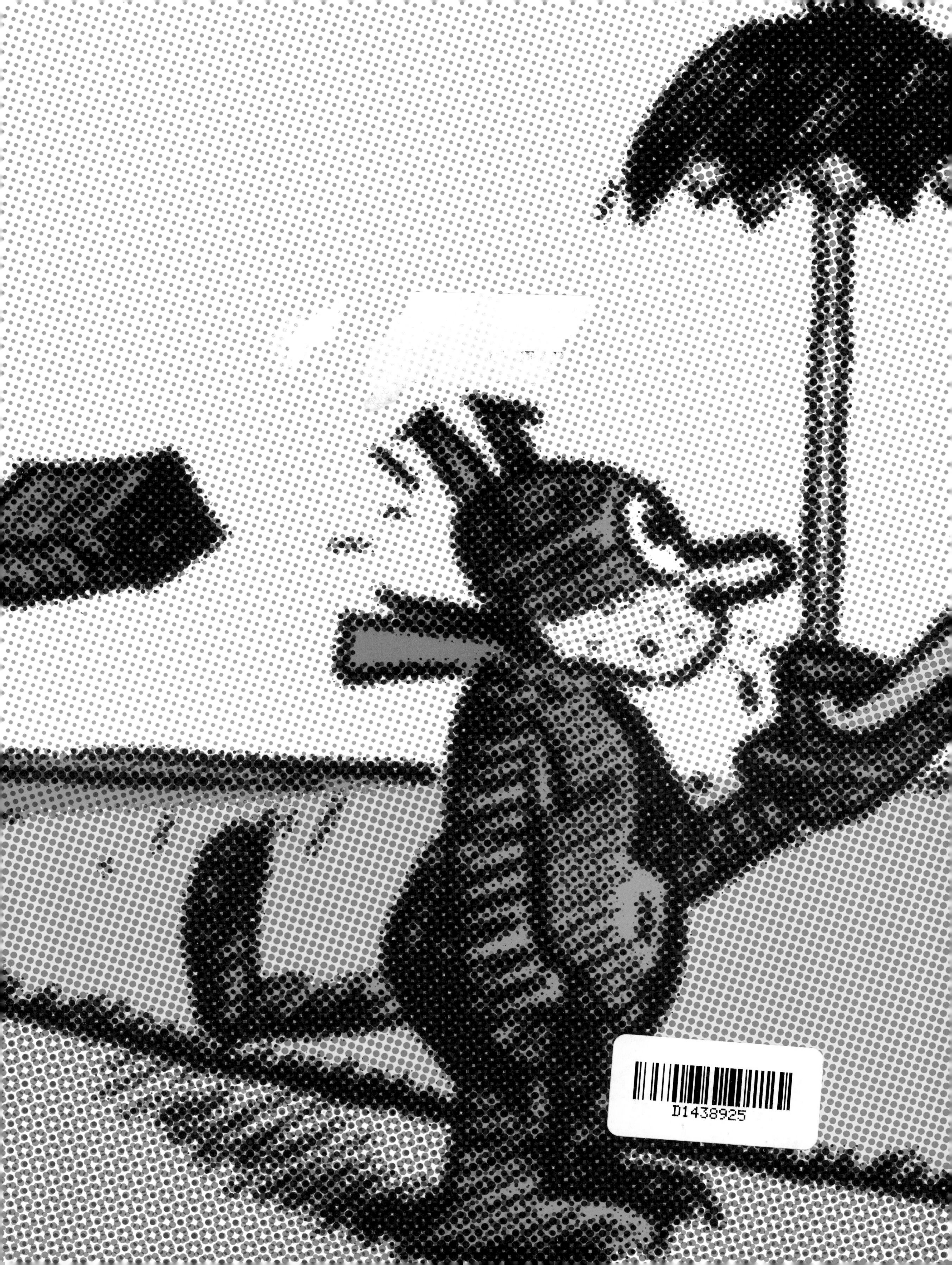

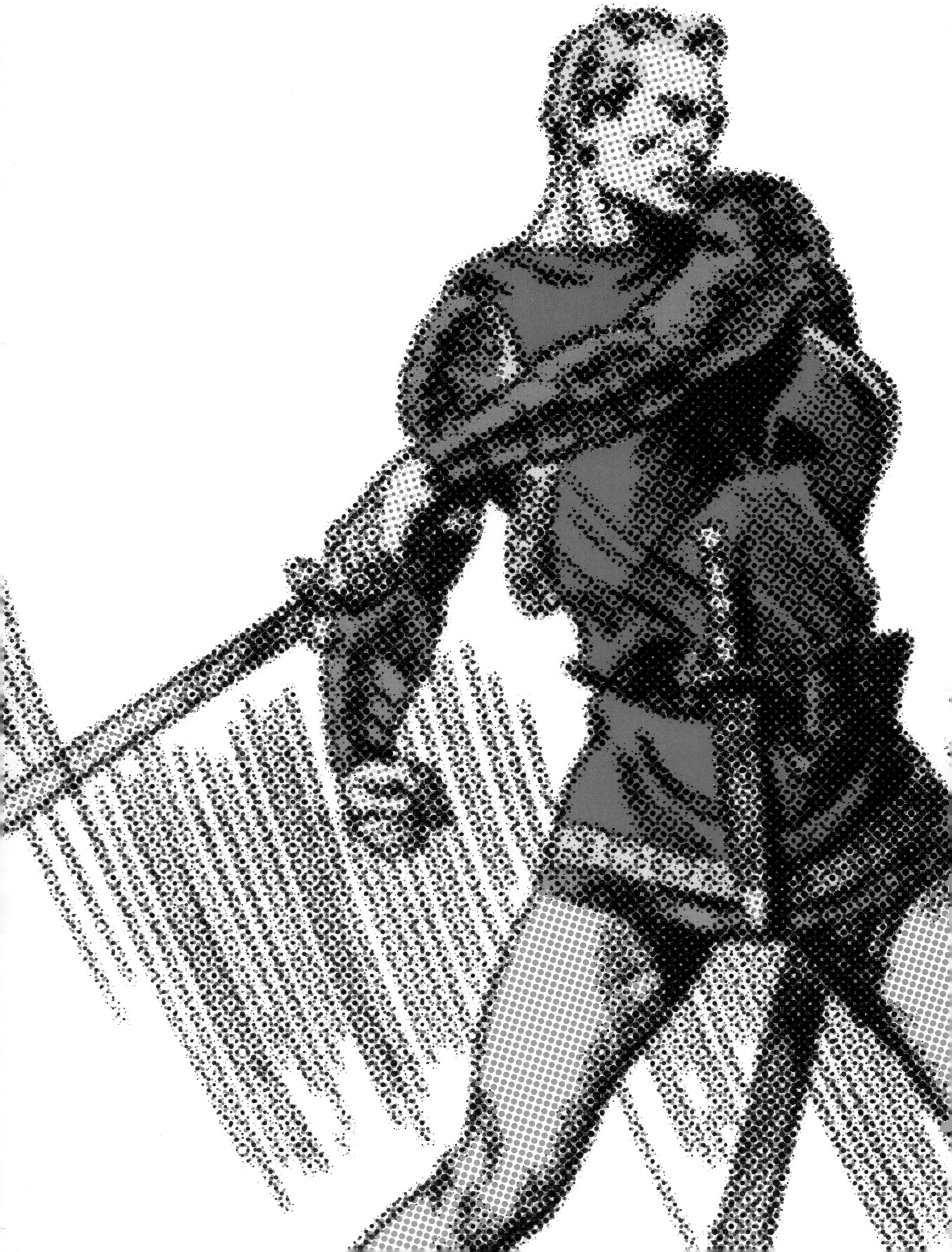

the comics

the comics
BEFORE 1945

BRIAN WALKER

HARRY N. ABRAMS, INC. PUBLISHERS

Dedicated to the passionate preservationists who rescued this priceless artwork from oblivion.

Editor: Richard Slovak
Designer: Carole Goodman / Blue Anchor Design
Production Manager: Justine Keefe

Library of Congress Cataloging-in-Publication Data

Walker, Brian.
  The comics before 1945 / Brian Walker.
        p. cm.
  A companion volume to The comics since 1945.
  Includes bibliographical references and index.
  ISBN 0-8109-4970-9
  1. Comic books, strips, etc.—United States—History and criticism.
  I. Walker, Brian. Comics since 1945. II. Title.

  PN6725.W23 2004
  741.5'0973'09041—dc22

                                        2004009514

Copyright © 2004 Brian Walker

Published in 2004 by Harry N. Abrams, Incorporated, New York.

Printed and bound in China

10   9   8   7   6   5   4   3   2   1

Harry N. Abrams, Inc.
100 Fifth Avenue
New York, NY 10011
www.abramsbooks.com

Abrams is a subsidiary of LA MARTINIÈRE

contents

THE TOAST MASTER—*Yellow Kid original watercolor presentation piece by Richard F. Outcault.* September 2, 1897.
Courtesy of Marty Goldman and the Barnum Museum

Little Rosilia McGraw: No; we won't come and play with youz, Delia Costigan. Our rejuced means may temporary necessitate our residin' in a rear tenement, but we're jist as exclusive as when we lived on the first floor front and papa had charge of the pound in the Department of Canine Captivity!

FEUDAL PRIDE IN HOGAN'S ALLEY—The first appearance of the Yellow Kid by Richard F. Outcault. June 2, 1894, Truth magazine.
Courtesy of Richard D. Olson

introduction

IT ALL BEGAN WITH THE YELLOW KID. OR DID IT? Richard Felton Outcault's bald-headed, flap-eared, buck-toothed street urchin, who made his first appearance in *Truth* magazine on June 2, 1894, is often described as "the kid who started the comics." Coulton Waugh's landmark history, *The Comics* (1947), describes a scene from a "February day of 1896" when Charles Saalburg, "foreman of the *New York World's* tint-laying Ben Day machines," used the kid's nightshirt to experiment with a faster-drying yellow ink. When Outcault's "The Great Dog Show in M'Googan Avenue" appeared in the newspaper on February 16, the bright hue made a "vivid bulls-eye in the whole big page." The Yellow Kid, as he soon became known, "caught the fancy of hundreds of thousands of readers." Waugh claimed, "A new form of communication was about to be built on this foundation." In subsequent years, this story has been repeated so many times that it is widely accepted as the official account of the birth of the art form.

The truth is, almost every aspect of Waugh's tale is a myth. The *Chicago Inter-Ocean* was the first American news-paper to install a high-speed rotary color press, in September 1892, and was publishing color comics in a small insert format by 1893. In the spring of 1894, a new weekly supplement for kids, the *Inter-Ocean Jr.,* was introduced with a regular color comic series starring *The Ting Ling Kids* by Charles Saalburg

on the cover. By 1896, Saalburg was working for the *New York World* as a cartoonist and art director—not as a press foreman. The *World,* following the lead of the *Inter-Ocean,* had purchased a four-color rotary press from R. Hoe and Company and published its first color comics on May 21, 1893. The cartoon on the cover of this supplement, by Walt McDougall, featured bright yellow hues.

In June 1893, *American Pressman* published an article, "Working Colors on Each Other," that described an inquiry from an anxious printer: "He worked his yellow first, after striking his key-form; then he put on his red and ran that off. These two colors seemed to go all right, and to 'stay put': but when he got on his blue the trouble showed itself. The impression showed up with a fatty or mottled look, especially after it had lain for some time; and the color wasn't true." The writer suggested an easy remedy for the pressman's problems: dusting the sheets with powdered magnesia would keep the inks from amalgamating. Surviving comic sections from the era provide proof that most of the problems with color printing had been worked out long before February 1896.

Roy McCardell, who was on the staff of the *New York World* in the early 1890s, claimed in his 1905 article, "Opper, Outcault and Company," that he had the original idea to publish a color comic section and suggested it to his managing editor,

Ballard Smith, in 1891. Three years later, McCardell recommended Outcault to Morrill Goddard, editor of the *Sunday World,* who was hiring artists for his new weekly comic supplement.

The first appearance of the Yellow Kid in the *New York World,* on February 17, 1895, was a black-and-white reprint of an Outcault cartoon from *Truth.* In the first color episode, on May 5, 1895, the Kid's nightshirt was blue. It was yellow on November 24, 1895, and red with black polka dots on December 15, 1895, before permanently changing back to yellow on January 5, 1896. All of these developments had taken place before Waugh's alleged pressroom incident.

In fact, Richard F. Outcault's *Hogan's Alley,* starring the Yellow Kid, did not introduce any of the important elements we now associate with newspaper comics: speech balloons, sequential narrative, recurring characters, regularly titled series, color printing, adaptation to other media, and product licensing. Speech balloons had been combined with graphic images for centuries, and sequential narrative was well established in many forms. American newspapers had been publishing cartoons since the late 1860s, and Sunday sections were printed in color before the Yellow Kid made his debut. Recurring characters, regularly titled series, and the successful merchandising of cartoon "stars" had been pioneered by other artists.

Then why is the Yellow Kid universally regarded as the poster boy for the birth of the comics? The answer lies in

the long evolution of the art form and the ultimate convergence of numerous historical trends.

The first cartoonists were probably cave dwellers. Although it is tempting to imagine a dramatic scene in which a bearskin-clad creator discovered the power of pictures in a single burst of inspiration, the historical record suggests that visual storytelling evolved gradually. Egyptian hieroglyphics, Greek friezes, Roman carvings, and medieval tapestries provide evidence of this long progression.

During the Middle Ages, illuminated manuscripts combined calligraphy and illustration in extended narratives. When movable-type printing was introduced in the fifteenth century, words and images were increasingly separated, due to the different techniques used to reproduce drawings and set type. Single printed pages, known as "broadsides" or "broadsheets," were the most common medium for graphic expression; although they often contained speech balloons, they were not "comics" in the modern sense. Broadsheets initially concentrated on religious themes, but by the seventeenth and eighteenth centuries, scenes from daily life, as well as political and social satire, predominated.

The technological progress of the industrial age created an acceleration in the evolution of graphic communication. As printing and distribution methods became mechanized, periodicals and newspapers replaced broadsheets as the prime vehicles for

ARMED HEROES—British Prime Minister Henry Addington faces off against Napoleon Bonaparte in this cartoon by James Gillray. May 18, 1803

cartoons and illustration. Circulation climbed as literacy increased and as publishers discovered that entertainment sold better than enlightenment. It was during the nineteenth century that the comic strip took its present form.

In 1809, the English caricaturist Thomas Rowlandson introduced Dr. Syntax, a pedantic schoolmaster who appeared in a series of satirical prints in *Poetical Magazine.* When these cartoons were collected in book form, the popularity of Rowlandson's character took off. Dr. Syntax hats, coats, mugs, and plates were peddled in the shops of London. Charles Ross and Marie Duval's *Ally Sloper,* which debuted in Britain's *Judy* on August 14, 1867, and Palmer Cox's *Brownies,* which first appeared in America's *St. Nicholas* in February 1883, were later examples of popular cartoon "stars" that appeared regularly in periodicals and were merchandised successfully.

Speech balloons were still common in American political and satirical prints during the first part of the nineteenth century. This began to change with the launching of a string of successful humor magazines modeled after the British *Punch,* which began in 1841. *Yankee Doodle* (1846), *Frank Leslie's Illustrated Newspaper* (1855), *Harper's Weekly* (1857), *Wild Oats* (1870), *Puck* (1877), *Judge* (1881), and *Life* (1883) established the new standard format for "cartoons," a term introduced in 1843. The comic weeklies abandoned speech balloons in favor of a style of cartooning that placed the text below the drawings. Many of the single-panel social vignettes in these publications were conversational exchanges of the "he said, she said" variety. Although multi-panel comics and cartoons with

speech balloons could also be found in the humor magazines, it was not until the turn of the century that newspaper cartoonists "revived" these centuries-old devices.

One of the pioneers of newspaper comics, Jimmy Swinnerton, started as a sketch artist on the *San Francisco Examiner* in 1892 and created a recurring comic feature, *Little Bears,* for that paper in late 1893. In an interview published in 1934, "Swin" reminisced about the transition from magazine cartoons to newspaper comics: "In those days we swore by [cartoonist Eugene] Zimmerman and [cartoonist Frederick Burr] Opper, and the others of the grotesque school who illustrated printed jokes. It was not the fashion to have balloons showing what the characters were saying, as that was supposed to have been buried with the English [caricaturist George] Cruikshank, but along came the comic supplements, and with Dick Outcault's Yellow Kid the balloons came back and literally filled the sky."

The eighteenth-century English artist William Hogarth had explored the storytelling potential of multi-image cartoons in such popular print series as *A Harlot's Progress* (1732), but Rodolphe Töpffer is widely regarded as the father of sequential comics. In 1827, the Swiss artist, writer, and teacher produced the first of his "picture novels"—multi-panel illustrated stories with the text below the drawings. Töpffer later described his discovery in an essay on aesthetic theory: "The drawings, without their text, would have only a vague meaning; the text, without the drawings, would have no meaning at all. The combination makes up a kind of novel, all the more unique

| Mr. Oldbuck's first sight of his ladye-love. | He beholds her vanishing in the distance. |

THE ADVENTURES OF MR. OBADIAH OLDBUCK—Two panels from the earliest known American comic book, by Rodolphe Töpffer, translated from the French edition and published by Wilson and Company. September 14, 1842. Courtesy of Robert L. Beerbohm

in that it is no more like a novel than it is like anything else." Töpffer's stories were translated from the original French and reprinted in pirated editions in other countries (as there were no international copyright laws). Many scholars consider one of his graphic novels, the forty-page *Adventures of Obadiah Oldbuck,* published by Wilson and Company of New York in September 1842, to be the earliest known example of an American comic book.

The German artist Wilhelm Busch refined the art of graphic narrative in his first picture stories, published in the 1860s. *Max und Moritz,* the most famous of these *Bilderbogen,* starred two mischievous pranksters and directly influenced the American newspaper cartoonist Rudolph Dirks, who created *The Katzenjammer Kids* for William Randolph Hearst's *New York Journal* in 1897.

The first American daily newspaper to use cartoons on a regular basis was James Gordon Bennett's *New York Evening Telegram,* starting in 1867. The four-page pink sheet, which sold for two cents, showcased a large front-page political cartoon by Charles Green Bush every Friday. On March 4, 1873, a group of engravers, encouraged by advances in halftone photo-reproduction, launched the *New York Daily Graphic.* This fully illustrated newspaper featured cartoons by many of the leading artists of the day, including A. B. Frost, E. W. Kemble, and

THE BOOM IN JOURNALISM—Cartoon by Charles Green Bush.
October 25, 1883, Life magazine. Courtesy of the International Museum of Cartoon Art

Frederick B. Opper. These experiments provided the incentive for other New York City papers, including the *World* and the *Herald,* to increase their use of pictures. On September 23, 1889, unable to keep up with the competition, the *Daily Graphic* ceased publication.

After Joseph Pulitzer purchased the *New York World* in 1883, he expanded the Sunday supplement from four pages to twenty, offering a mix of sensational news, literary features, and illustrations. By 1887, the circulation of the *Sunday World* had reached 250,000. A comic supplement, modeled after successful humor magazines like *Puck* and *Judge,* was added in 1889. Many of the artists who had been working for these publications eventually found themselves drawing cartoons for the new Sunday newspaper supplements.

The newspaper business was going through a radical transformation in the latter half of the nineteenth century. Between 1870 and 1900, while the population of the United States doubled and that of city dwellers tripled, the number of English-language daily newspapers increased from 489 to 1,967. The total circulation of these publications rose, in the same period, from 2.6 million copies to 15 million. Metropolitan newspapers installed high-speed presses, subscribed to services that relayed news rapidly by telegraph, and published multiple daily editions of twenty-four to thirty-six pages. Prices dropped to as little as a penny per issue as competition became fierce.

By the mid-1890s, all of the important innovations in comic strip format and publishing were in place. Speech balloons, though temporarily out of vogue, were still familiar to most cartoonists as an effective method of incorporating dialogue into their drawings. Multi-panel cartoons with extended narrative sequences could be found in both newspapers and magazines of the time. Palmer Cox's Brownies were at the peak of their

Max und Moritz

Schnupdiwup! there goes, O   Schnupdiwup! da wird nach oben
Jeminy!   Schon ein Huhn heraufgehoben.

MAX UND MORITZ—Drawing from the picture story by Wilhelm Busch, first published in 1865. *Courtesy of Dover Publications*

popularity, dramatically showing how cartoon characters could be promoted and merchandised to consumers around the world. Newspaper publishers were adding color comic sections to their rapidly growing Sunday supplements. Richard F. Outcault was in the right place at the right time.

In 1890, Outcault was on the staff of *Electrical World* magazine. He also sold freelance cartoons to the comic weeklies. On June 2, 1894, a single-panel drawing by him, entitled "Feudal Pride in Hogan's Alley," appeared in *Truth* magazine. In the cartoon, a small, bald-headed boy in a nightshirt can be seen peering around the corner of "Hogan's Alley" and "Ryan's Arcade." This was the first appearance of the character who was to become the Yellow Kid. In late 1894, Outcault was hired by Morrill Goddard, editor of the *New York Sunday World*. Four more single-panel drawings featuring the curious-looking Irish slum urchin ran in *Truth* before his newspaper debut in the *New York World*, on February 17, 1895: "Fourth Ward Brownies" was a reprint of a cartoon from eight days earlier in *Truth*.

The earliest of Outcault's *Hogan's Alley* cartoons were not comic strips at all, but single-panel city scenes with cavorting slum kids. Accompanying text appeared either outside the drawings or on signs and surfaces within the compositions. The January 5, 1896, episode, "Golf—The Great Society Sport as Played in Hogan's Alley," featured the Kid (he was not officially named "Mickey Dugan" until June 7 of that year), in a yellow nightshirt, gravitating toward the center of the teeming tableau. The Kid began to speak, in the form of crude, grammatically incorrect writing pinned to his nightshirt, on April 12, 1896, in the "First Championship Game of the Hogan's Alley Baseball Team."

In the meantime, William Randolph Hearst had been stirring the pot of Park Row publishing. The son of a California silver miner who struck it rich in the Comstock Lode, Will had used the family fortune to transform the *San Francisco Examiner* into a successful West Coast version of Pulitzer's *World*. After his father died in 1891, he persuaded his mother to use a portion of the profits from the sale of their interest in the Anaconda copper mines to finance his newspaper career. Will Hearst then set his sights on New York City.

On October 10, 1895, *The Fourth Estate* (later renamed *Editor & Publisher*) announced the thirty-two-year-old's arrival from San Francisco and his purchase of the *New York Journal*: "He has money and he is not afraid of spending it. New York is the field of his ambitions and with the resources of almost unlimited capital and absolutely exhaustless courage he has entered the fight."

Hearst soon made good on the predictions about him. He dropped the price of the struggling morning paper to one cent, and in four months its circulation soared from 20,000 to 150,000. To compete, Pulitzer was forced to sell his *New*

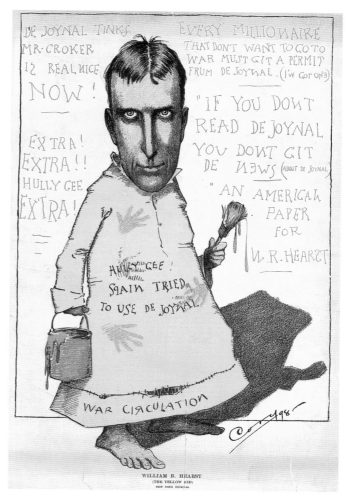

WILLIAM RANDOLPH HEARST—Cartoon by J. Campbell Cory. The Yellow Kid became an icon for "yellow journalism." June 8, 1898, The Bee magazine. Courtesy of Mark Johnson

York World for a penny. Then, in January 1896, Hearst began raiding Pulitzer's ranks by hiring Goddard, the *Sunday World* editor, along with eleven members of Goddard's staff. Solomon Solis Carvalho resigned as the *World*'s publisher on March 19 and went to work for Hearst on March 31. The *New York Evening Journal* debuted on September 28 and soon passed a circulation mark of 175,000. By that time, the morning *Journal* was moving an average of 425,000 copies a day.

After installing a new high-speed multicolor press, Hearst acquired the services of Pulitzer's most popular cartoonist, Richard F. Outcault. With his Yellow Kid as the star attraction, the *American Humorist,* an eight-page color comic supplement in the *Sunday Journal,* debuted on October 18, 1896. Hearst sold 375,000 copies of that edition, in spite of an increase in price from three to five cents. In the meantime, Pulitzer hired George Luks to continue *Hogan's Alley* in the *World*. Although Roy McCardell reported in 1905 that "there were lawsuits for breaking of contracts and for infringement of copyright brought by both papers," there are no known court records of a legal decision regarding ownership of the Yellow Kid.

On October 25, 1896, one week after Outcault's first cartoon was published in the *Journal,* he combined sequential

THE YELLOW KID—This half-page cartoon by Richard F. Outcault was the first Yellow Kid episode to incorporate speech balloons and sequential panels.
October 25, 1896, New York Journal. Courtesy of Denis Kitchen

drawings and speech balloons for the first time. In "The Yellow Kid and His New Phonograph," dialogue could be seen emanating from Edison's invention in the form of a speech balloon. The final picture of the five-drawing composition revealed that the source of the sound was a parrot that had been concealed within the base of the device. The Yellow Kid, falling over backward, remarked, "De phonograph is a great invention— NIT! I don't tink—wait till I git dat foolish bird home I won't do a ting te him well say!" The Kid's words were contained inside a speech balloon with the tail pointing to his mouth. Newspaper readers probably chuckled and turned the page, unaware of the historic importance of this cartoon.

During the next fifteen months, Outcault repeated this multi-panel layout approximately eighteen times, in half-page cartoons done as a secondary feature to the full-page Yellow Kid episodes on the cover of the comic section. Speech balloons and multiple panels added a new dimension to Outcault's comics. When dialogue was placed within speech balloons in the drawings, the characters appeared to speak with greater immediacy than when text was placed below the illustrations. Balloons transformed two-dimensional performers into personalities with thoughts and emotions, who could speak and move simultaneously like real people. Sequential drawings created the illusion of time. The space between two successive images could represent seconds, minutes, days, or years. A progression of pictures told a story with a beginning, a middle, and an end. The combination of speech balloons and sequential

panels increased the potential for more effective character development and storytelling in comics.

Rudolph Dirks and Frederick B. Opper institutionalized Outcault's innovations. Dirks's *Katzenjammer Kids,* which debuted on December 12, 1897, was one of the first newspaper comics to use sequential panels on a regular basis, although initially the text was set in type below the pictures. Opper's *Happy Hooligan* made standard use of both panels and speech balloons soon after its debut on March 11, 1900, and it can be regarded as the first definitive modern American newspaper comic strip.

Not all comics historians agree on the significance of these developments. Doug Wheeler, an expert in nineteenth-century comics, has published numerous examples of cartoons from the late 1700s to the mid-1890s that meet the same qualifications as Outcault's historic strip. In an article announcing his discoveries, he claimed, "One of my projects has been gathering evidence that the long-held claim that the first publication of a multi-panel, sequential comic strip told entirely via word balloons or in-panel dialogue was 'The Yellow Kid and His New Phonograph' by Richard Outcault on October 25, 1896, is *wrong.*" He concluded, "Our history books are flawed." Wheeler is part of a growing number of researchers into the Victorian era who argue that Outcault and the Yellow Kid should be relegated to a footnote in comics history.

The roots of this disagreement lie in the varying criteria for defining the term *comic strip.* There is no consensus among the leading comics scholars on a basic definition.

Bill Blackbeard, the founder of the San Francisco Academy of Comic Art, believes that a comic strip "may be defined as a serially published, episodic, open-ended dramatic narrative or series of linked anecdotes featuring recurrent named characters. The successive drawings regularly include ballooned dialogue that is crucial to the telling of the story."

Doug Wheeler challenges the stipulation that comic strips must contain continuing characters as "ludicrous." "Characters are story elements, the same as plot and dialogue," Wheeler maintains. "They are not the medium in which the story is told."

Pascal Lefevre and Charles Dierick, the editors of *Forging a New Medium: The Comic Strip in the Nineteenth Century,* propose that comics are a "juxtaposition of fixed (mostly drawn) pictures on a support as a communicative act." In this "prototypical definition," certain examples need not be excluded if they lack one or two of the criteria (such as speech balloons or a paper support).

Robert C. Harvey, the author of *The Art of the Funnies,* feels that definitions like this are "simply too broad to be useful as anything except a springboard to further discussion." In Harvey's view, "comics consist of pictorial narratives or expositions in which words (often lettered into the picture area within speech balloons) usually contribute to the meaning of the picture and vice versa. A pictorial narrative uses a sequence of pictures (i.e., a 'strip' of pictures); a pictorial exposition may do the same—or may not (as in single-panel cartoons—political cartoons as well as magazine-type gag cartoons)." Harvey's "visual-verbal blending" definition excludes such well-known newspaper features as *Prince Valiant* and *Tarzan,* in which the text is separate from the illustrations.

Belgian comic strip theorist Thierry Smolderen takes a unique point of view. "I'm a complete relativist about comics," claims Smolderen. "For me, there exists no absolute definition of comics: different social groups (editors, artists, readers, censors, printers, teachers, etc.) participating in the existence of the medium will forge different working definitions, by selecting and generalizing the traits that are pertinent to their way of participating in it."

All of these interpretations have merit, but the relativist approach is probably the most realistic. Cartoonists do not concern themselves with definitions. They are commercial artists and, in most cases, are hired by editors and paid by publishers. The space they work in and the audience they are entertaining are determined by the nature of the publication in which their cartoons appear. Within these boundaries, a wide range of creative expression is possible. Cartoonists make use of many tools, including speech balloons, recurring characters, and sequential narrative, and are constantly breaking rules and experimenting with the art form. Although there are cartoonists who jump from one medium to another, the parameters of

each commercial venue are distinct. Trying to impose a universal definition on this multifaceted and ever-changing graphic enterprise is virtually impossible.

Newspaper comic strips, or the "funnies," have been familiar to the American public for more than a century. They have changed considerably in size and content over the years, yet most comics still have speech balloons, panel borders, a regular cast of characters, and jokes or stories (or both). Almost all American newspapers have daily comic pages and color Sunday sections, and the most famous funnies stars, such as Little Orphan Annie, Popeye, Dick Tracy, Snoopy, and Garfield, are recognizable to readers of all ages. The Yellow Kid was the direct ancestor of these characters, and Richard F. Outcault's *Hogan's Alley* was the first successful newspaper comic feature— no more, no less.

In 1905, Roy McCardell recounted the events leading up to the Yellow Kid's debut. "The [*New York World* comic] supplement was a success from the start [May 21, 1893]," he remembered, "but it was not until a year and a half later its success became enormous. Then Outcault made his first 'hit.' Ninety-nine times out of a hundred a paper's 'hit' is accidental—caused by a picture or series of pictures that strikes the public fancy. A 'hit' is the making of the most moribund of papers; it can well be imagined how one is sought and striven for by even a successful paper. Outcault's first 'hit' was with the 'Yellow Kid.'"

As early as November 1, 1896, just a week after the "The Yellow Kid and His New Phonograph" was published, *Ev'ry Month* magazine reported, "Mr. Outcault is now having his day. His 'Yellow Kid' is familiar to a vast and applausive metropolis. His work is being bid for by the great metropolitan dailies, and at the music halls in Broadway you can see a travesty which has in it, a band of typical East Side children from the quarter which he discovered and called *Hogan's Alley.* There is a *Hogan's Alley* comedy on the road, and there are *Hogan's Alley* songs on the market. Through it all Mr. Outcault's exceedingly clever drawings depicting life in *Hogan's Alley* are appearing in a great paper every Sunday, and Mr. Outcault is making money. What else could one add to make success?"

The colorful posters that were plastered all over New York City during the height of the battle between Hearst and Pulitzer and the hundreds of products inspired by Outcault's creation were further proof that the Yellow Kid was a hit. The success of the Yellow Kid is not simply a myth created by subsequent generations of comics historians. It is a pivotal chapter in the long history of the art form.

On September 7, 1896, Outcault formally applied for copyright registration by sending a letter with a drawing of "The Yellow Dugan Kid" to the Library of Congress. Although many historians claim that Outcault obtained legal ownership

NEW YORK JOURNAL POSTER—Published at the peak of the competition between the Journal **and the** New York World, **with art by Archie Gunn and Richard F. Outcault.** October 1896. Courtesy of Craig Koste

of the Yellow Kid, records at the Library of Congress indicate that his request was never officially granted, due to an irregularity in the application process. Consequently, he was never able to prevent widespread exploitation of his character by other artists and manufacturers of Yellow Kid products.

The phrase "yellow journalism" is another aspect of this story that comics scholars have disputed. Roy McCardell wrote in 1905 that "the rivalry between the *World* and the *Journal* caused the papers without the attractions of Mr. Outcault's work and Mr. Luks's work to describe those papers as 'Yellow Kid journals,' and then, by dropping the monosyllable, to call them simply 'yellow journals.'" According to recent research by Mark Winchester, one of the earliest appearances of the term, used specifically to denounce the type of sensational journalism that Hearst and Pulitzer practiced, was in the *New York Times* on March 12, 1897. Bill Blackbeard argues, in his definitive history of the Yellow Kid, that the phrase can be traced to the "*Journal-Examiner* Yellow Fellow Transcontinental Bicycle Relay" sponsored by Hearst in the summer of 1896. Other writers have attempted to associate "yellow journalism" with "yellow peril" fears stemming from the First Sino-Japanese War of 1894–95, or with the "yellow-backed pamphleteering" of lurid novels in the mid-nineteenth century. Regardless of the derivation, most historians agree that the term came into wide acceptance after the sinking of the battleship *Maine*

on February 15, 1898. During the Spanish-American War, which soon followed this incident, the Yellow Kid frequently appeared as an icon of "yellow journalism" in political cartoons that were critical of the sensational and jingoistic coverage of the conflict by the New York press.

By that time, ironically, neither of the competing Yellow Kid comic features by Richard F. Outcault and George Luks was appearing any longer in the *Journal* or the *World*. Presumably, the negative association between his creation and the journalism practiced by Hearst and Pulitzer had become an embarrassment to Outcault.

In "How the Yellow Kid Was Born, " published in the *New York World* on May 1, 1898, Outcault looked back on his success with little affection. "Now, it is more than six years [Outcault had his dates wrong] since my pen first traced the outlines of Mickey Dugan on paper," he recalled. "In that time I suppose I have myself made twenty thousand Yellow Kids, and when the million buttons, the innumerable toys and cigarette boxes and labels and what not are taken into consideration, some idea can be gleaned of how tired I am of him.

"I have but one request to make, and that is, when I die," Outcault concluded, "don't wear yellow crepe, don't let them put a Yellow Kid on my tombstone and don't allow the Yellow Kid himself to come to my funeral. Make him stay on the East Side, where he belongs."

A HOT POLITICAL CONVENTION IN HOGAN'S ALLEY—Original pen-and-ink Sunday page by Richard F. Outcault. *July 12, 1896, New York World. Courtesy of Marty Goldman*

After his death on September 25, 1928, the *Los Angeles Herald* wrote, "If the 'Yellow Kid' could come back out of the past today, he would bow his head in mourning for his creator, Richard Felton Outcault, 'father of the comic strips.'" The obituary in the *New York World* offered a more qualified eulogy: "To say the late R. F. Outcault was the inventor of the comic supplement is of course to ignore the social factors that lead up to all inventions." The controversy surrounding the origin of comics and the role of Richard F. Outcault's Yellow Kid will never die.

THE ARTWORK

The comics reproduced in this book reflect the evolution of the art form during the first half of the twentieth century. In the early years of the funnies, cartoonists experimented with many different layouts and panel arrangements, limited only by the dimensions of a newspaper page. By the 1920s, syndicates had standardized the formats for most newspaper comics, which were produced as black-and-white daily strips or panels and color Sunday pages. During the 1930s, Sunday pages were also being offered in half-page configurations.

The original drawings for both daily and Sunday features were usually done with a pen or brush and India ink on heavy illustration board, but cartoonists frequently experimented with a variety of techniques and tools to produce distinctive shading and special effects. Artists often colored a few panels of their originals as guides for the printers; eventually, however, overlays done on transparent paper replaced this method. On occasion, cartoonists also completely hand-colored their original art to give to their friends and admirers as presentation pieces.

Newspaper comics were printed much larger than they are today, but the quality of reproduction varied considerably. The color on surviving newsprint pages can be quite brilliant, although the interior pages of many early comic sections were often printed in only two colors. Comics on newsprint, in both daily and Sunday papers, can also be faded, incomplete, or out of registration. Only a small sampling of these newspaper sections have survived the ravages of time.

The comics on the following pages were obtained from many different sources. Original artwork from private collectors and public institutions was photographed, scanned, or photocopied to provide the sharpest images. Color photographs of black-and-white or partially colored strips often reveal pencil lines, margin notations, and deterioration of the paper. High-contrast black-and-white reproductions of pen-and-ink pieces show the strips the way they were intended to be seen. In some cases, original artwork was not available, so syndicate proofs and newspaper pages were used for source material. A select group of Sunday pages was also digitally restored by American Color, the company that currently prepares comics for all of the major syndicates, using original artwork and printed pages as color guides.

It is the author's intention to present these historical examples with the fidelity of the original artwork preserved as much as possible. For the sake of comparison, it is interesting to look at continuous tone images of the original pieces, but daily strips and panels were intended to be reproduced in high-contrast black and white. Digital color restoration of the Sunday pages corrects for the limitations of high-speed presses and cheap newsprint, but it is also important to see the Sunday funnies the way they looked to newspaper readers at the time. It is hoped that the variety of source material and the different reproduction methods used in this book will provide a comprehensive appreciation for the art of the comics during this period.

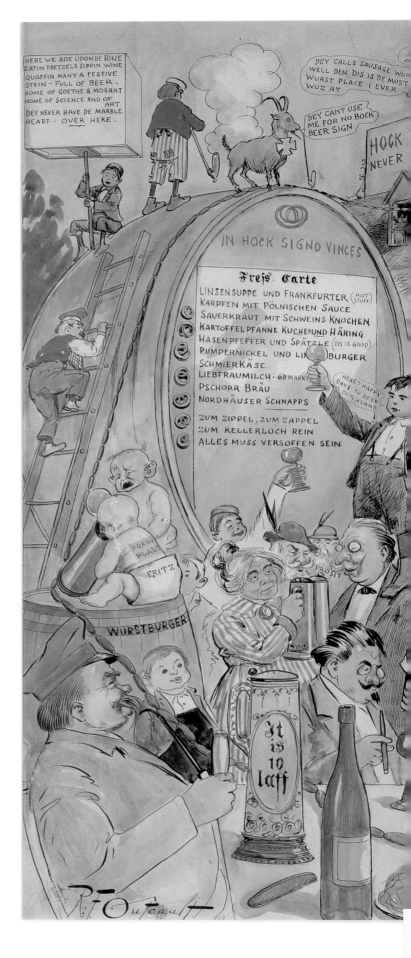

THE YELLOW KID INVADES GERMANY—Original hand-colored Sunday page by Richard F. Outcault. From January 17 to May 30, 1897, the Yellow Kid went on a world tour. *April 4, 1897, New York Journal. Courtesy of the International Museum of Cartoon Art*

TRAINING FOR THE FOOTBALL CHAMPIONSHIP GAME IN HOGAN'S ALLEY.

HOGAN'S ALLEY Sunday page by George B. Luks. The artist, whom Joseph Pulitzer hired as Outcault's successor, was a member of the "Ashcan School" of painters. *October 11, 1896, New York World. Courtesy of Denis Kitchen*

the turn of the century

"Stonehammer is an enterprising fellow, isn't he?"
"What's he doing now?"
"He's starting what he calls a 'newspaper.' He's going to get out a copy every year."

OUR ANTEDILUVIAN ANCESTORS cartoon by Frederick B. Opper. 1901, New York Journal. Courtesy of Editor & Publisher

——— IF ———
THE INAUGURAL DINNER AT THE WHITE HOUSE.

IF—THE INAUGURAL DINNER AT THE WHITE HOUSE—J. S. Pughe pictures in this lithograph what it might have looked like if William Randolph Hearst had been elected president of the United States. June 29, 1904, Puck magazine. Courtesy of Periodyssey/Richard Samuel West Collection

IT HAS BEEN CALLED THE AGE OF OPTIMISM, THE AGE OF CONFIDENCE, AND THE AGE OF INNOCENCE. THE FIRST DECADE OF THE TWENTIETH CENTURY WAS ALSO A GOLDEN AGE OF MASS ENTERTAINMENT. NICKELODEONS, NIGHTCLUBS, DANCE HALLS, MOVIE THEATERS, VAUDEVILLE HOUSES, SPORTS STADIUMS, AMUSEMENT PARKS, WORLD'S FAIR MIDWAYS, PHONOGRAPH PARLORS, AND PENNY ARCADES ATTRACTED MILLIONS OF PATRONS, EAGER TO PART WITH THEIR HARD-EARNED SPENDING MONEY.

Commercial entertainment was, for the most part, an urban enterprise. In 1900, New York City boasted more movie theaters and playhouses than any metropolis in the world and, by the end of the decade, had a combined seating capacity of more than two million. Tin Pan Alley composers, who wrote many of the songs for the stage shows, sold two billion copies of sheet music in 1910. The first nickelodeon—a small, dark room where customers watched short films projected on a screen—opened in 1905. Within three years, there were ten thousand nickelodeons drawing an estimated ten million customers a week. Professional baseball held its first World Series in 1903, and boxing, tennis, college football, golf, horse racing, and the Olympics (held in St. Louis in 1904) all thrilled American sports fans. The success of the 1893 Chicago World's Fair, which drew fourteen million visitors, was followed by

expositions in Atlanta (1895), Nashville (1897), Omaha (1898), Buffalo (1901), and St. Louis (1904). More than twenty million people, from every corner of the earth, took the trolley car ride to the Coney Island amusement parks in 1909.

Many factors contributed to this explosion in the consumption of popular culture. Although the average worker in 1910 toiled ten hours a day, six days a week, for an annual income ranging between $418 and $575, Americans had more leisure time than ever before. As the nation shifted from an agricultural to an industrial economy, labor became less skilled and more regimented. White- and blue-collar wage earners alike sought relief from their daily drudgery. Entrepreneurs and entertainers profited handsomely by providing fun seekers with a dizzying variety of ways to spend their off-hours. Telephones, phonographs, cameras, and other modern devices also made staying at home more enjoyable.

Americans were reading more. Between 1876 and 1915, illiteracy decreased from 20 percent to 6 percent. The immediate beneficiaries of this trend were magazine, book, and newspaper publishers. *The Saturday Evening Post,* which claimed weekly sales of more than two million by 1913, was the most widely read periodical in the world. *The Ladies' Home Journal, Collier's, Munsey's, McClure's,* and *Cosmopolitan* were among the many magazines that exerted a powerful influence on the social life and buying habits of the American consumer. The first "best-seller list" was published in *The Bookman* in 1895, and readers' tastes were soon being documented on a regular basis. In 1900, more than two thousand new fiction titles were issued, one-quarter of which were romance novels marketed to female readers.

Newspapers provided a daily diversion for the harried city worker. In addition to news, the metropolitan press offered sports pages, advice columns, human-interest stories, women's features, and comics. Joseph Pulitzer's *New York World* and William Randolph Hearst's *New York Journal* each passed the one million mark in circulation after the sinking of the American battleship *Maine* in Havana's harbor in 1898. The total circulation of daily newspapers throughout the United States doubled between 1892 and 1914.

The success of the Sunday newspaper was even more dramatic. *Editor & Publisher* reported on April 5, 1902, "Year by year it has grown, until today its size is formidable. The regular issues contain from 32 to 86 pages, and the specials, such as those of Christmas and Easter, from 100 to 130 pages." The comic supplement, it added, had "caught the fancy of the public, and now every illustrated Sunday newspaper has one printed in colors."

The Yellow Kid dramatically demonstrated the selling power of a popular comic character. Following Richard F. Outcault's departure from the *New York Journal* in 1898, *The Katzenjammer Kids* by Rudolph Dirks became the anchor of Hearst's flagship *American Humorist* comic section. "Katzenjammer," which means "cats' yowling" in German, was a popular colloquialism for "hangover." Dirks's pranksters, Hans and Fritz, were soon joined by the long-suffering Mama, as well as the rotund mariner, Der Captain (1902), and his trusty sidekick, Der Inspector (1905), establishing the core cast of the strip. In the first few years, Dirks rarely used speech balloons, preferring either pantomime or text beneath the panels.

Frederick B. Opper joined the Hearst staff in 1899 and was put to work drawing single-panel cartoons for the Sunday supplement. On March 11, 1900, Opper introduced his first newspaper comic feature, *Happy Hooligan,* which starred an irrepressible Irish hobo with a tin can balanced on his head. From the beginning, Opper incorporated speech balloons into his *Happy Hooligan* episodes. Cartoonists around the country were soon imitating the successful formula that Outcault, Dirks, and Opper pioneered. The unique combination of recurring characters, sequential panels, speech balloons, and bright colors eventually came to be known as the "Sunday funnies."

STOKES' COMIC JUVENILES

Foxy Grandpa and the Boys
Foxy Grandpa's Triumphs
Foxy Grandpa's Frolics
Foxy Grandpa's Surprises
Foxy Grandpa Up-to-date
Jimmy and His Scrapes
Little Sammy Sneeze
The Trials of Lulu and Leander
Sam and His Laugh
Handy Happy Hooligan
Happy Hooligan Home Again
Happy Hooligan's Travels
Maud the Mirthful Mule
Maud the Matchless
Maud

HERE WE ARE AGAIN.

Outcault's Buster, Mary Jane and Tige
Outcault's Buster Brown and Company
Buster Brown's Antics
Buster Brown's Pranks
Buster Brown, His Dog Tige and Their Troubles
Buster Brown and His Resolutions
Willie Westinghouse Edison Smith
The Komical Katzenjammers
The Cruise of the Katzenjammer Kids
The Tricks of the Katzenjammer Kids
The Three Funmakers: (Hooligan, Maud and the Katzenjammer Kids)

STOKES ADVERTISEMENT—In 1908, this comic book publisher had twenty-seven titles in print, featuring the most popular Sunday funnies stars.
Courtesy of Doug Wheeler

HAPPY HOOLIGAN—*Frederick B. Opper's immortal Irish tramp. Original drawing for a* **Boston Sunday American** *premium. 1906. Courtesy of Richard Marschall*

Although the majority of creations introduced during the first decade featured interchangeable characters and predictable humor, some newspapers developed durable comic stars to compete with the Hearst lineup. Foxy Grandpa, Buster Brown, and Little Nemo debuted in the *New York Herald* between 1900 and 1905, the Newlyweds and their baby Snookums first appeared in the *New York World* in 1904, Hairbreadth Harry was a headliner in the *Philadelphia Press* starting in 1906, and Slim Jim became the most popular character in the World Color Printing Company stable beginning in 1910.

Newspaper chains and syndicates helped to facilitate the rapid spread of the comics. The *New York Herald* began selling its features to other papers as early as 1895. Pulitzer published the same lineup of comics in both of his newspapers, the *New York World* and the *St. Louis Post-Dispatch,* beginning in 1897. In 1900, there were eight newspaper chains, the largest being

the Scripps group of nine papers. Hearst owned six papers by 1903 and was distributing his comics to more than seventeen other clients.

Syndicates had grown steadily since the Civil War, but now, in addition to text features, they began selling color comics. The McClure Syndicate and the World Color Printing Company of St. Louis offered comic features to newspapers that were not serviced directly by the chains. The *Philadelphia North American,* the *Philadelphia Inquirer,* and the *Boston Globe* were among the many newspapers that developed their own comic talent.

In less than a decade, the Sunday funnies had grown from a local phenomenon in New York City to a nationwide mass medium. The most popular characters were familiar to millions of readers in cities across the country. By 1908, 75 percent of American Sunday newspapers were publishing comics. Three organizations—Hearst, McClure, and World Color—serviced three-quarters of this market.

With success came criticism. Religious groups had been protesting the publication of newspapers on the Christian Sabbath since the *New York Courier* issued its first Sunday edition on March 20, 1825. Seventy years later, when comics were being added to the growing Sunday supplements, these attacks continued with renewed vigor. "The Sunday newspaper is the most potent influence in our midst for the destruction of the Lord's Day as a day of rest and worship," wrote a group of Pennsylvania clergymen, known as the Sabbath Association, in July 1894. "There will ever be bigots and fanatics," responded *The Fourth Estate* in defense, "but their whole force cannot stop the progress of that engine of modern civilization—the newspaper."

A decade later, the funnies were under siege for both aesthetic and moral reasons. In June 1906, M. J. Darby, the newly elected president of the National Association of Newspaper Circulation Managers, gave an address to the organization entitled "Is the Comic Supplement a Desirable Feature?" Lamenting a decline in artistic quality, Darby said, "The crude coloring, slap-dash drawing, and very cheap and obvious funniness of the comic supplement cannot fail to debase the taste of readers and render them to a certain extent incapable of appreciating the finer forms of art."

The *Boston Herald* dropped its entire comic section in 1908, as well as its failing syndicate operation. The paper defended its decision, stating in an editorial, "The comic supplement has had its day. We discard it as we would throw aside any mechanism that has reached the end of its usefulness." The writer added, "Most discerning persons throw them aside without inspection, experience having taught them that there is no hope for improvement in these gaudy sheets." A number of prominent newspapers, including the *Milwaukee Journal,* the *Indianapolis Star,* and the *New York Tribune,* followed the lead of the *Boston Herald* and briefly discontinued their Sunday comics.

Even the father of the funnies predicted the passing of the comics. "One bunch of comic artists has been supplying all of the colored supplement pictures for the past twelve or fifteen years," wrote Outcault on January 16, 1909. "No new men in this field have appeared to startle the editors or the public. It seems only natural at the rate comics have been turned out for the last decade that the supply of ideas should become exhausted. Also the public."

Other protests, with the support of prominent religious leaders, social workers, and educators, focused on the detrimental effect that comics supposedly had on children. Maud Adams of Cincinnati, in an address to the Playground Association of America in September 1908, lamented that instead of showing proper behavior, strips like *Buster Brown* taught youngsters that "it is cunning to throw water from an upper window upon an old person and to outwit an infirm old man."

In 1909, *The Ladies' Home Journal* joined the movement, calling comics "a crime against American children." Edith Kingman Kent, chairman of the Committee for the Suppression of the Comic Supplement, warned in 1910, "The avidity with which many children seize this pernicious sheet, with its grotesque figures and vivid and crude coloring, amounts to a passion, which wise parents should regard with alarm and take steps to prevent."

In April 1911, Dr. Percival Chubb, a prominent New York educator and religious leader, presided over a meeting of the League for the Improvement of the Children's Comic Supplement. Representatives of that group and the Federation of Child Study, the International Kindergarten Union, and the Child Welfare League, as well as the president of the Academy of Design, reached a consensus that the comics needed to be reformed, not eliminated. By 1915, most of the newspapers that had dropped their color supplements had reinstated them. The crusade against comics lost its momentum. The funnies continued to grow in popularity.

There was a grain of truth in some of the criticism. Newspaper publishers promoted Sunday supplements as family entertainment. Many comic sections often included a feature designed especially for children, another primarily for adults, and several others for readers of all ages. Juvenile characters such as Little Jimmy appeared in the same pages as philanderers like Mr. Jack. Although nudity, foul language, deviant behavior, and religious comment were taboo in comics from the beginning, bad manners, sexual innuendo, and mindless violence were rampant in the early years.

Between 1900 and 1910, approximately nine million immigrants arrived on American shores, and the majority of these

SOME BITS OF AMERICAN SCENERY—Ethnic caricatures by James Montgomery Flagg in a double-page spread. April 1904, Life *magazine*

newcomers settled in the nation's largest cities. The early comics were not consciously directed toward a specific target audience, but there is little doubt that the colorful graphics appealed to immigrants, and the content of the Sunday funnies reflected this readership.

Newspaper cartoonists continued many of the traditions of slapstick and ethnic humor that had been established during the nineteenth century in minstrel shows, vaudeville acts, and comic publications. Violence, pratfalls, puns, and stereotypes were the defining characteristics of this homegrown American humor. Both on the stage and in the comics, all non-natives were fair game; Englishmen wore monocles and were uppity, pugnacious Irishmen ate corned beef and cabbage, mustached Frenchmen were overly polite and hopelessly romantic, Germans were overweight and prone to fits of temper, towheaded Swedes were naive and stubborn, and blacks ate watermelon, rolled dice, and were lazy and superstitious. Immigrants responded to these stereotypes, both positively and negatively, and recognized their fellow city dwellers in the graphic melting pot on the funnies pages.

The reformers who attacked the comics were mostly upper- and middle-class, white, native-born Americans. They were shocked by the rough-and-tumble humor of the Sunday funnies and found the characters to be vulgar, brash, and disrespectful. Immigrants and children loved the comics for the same reasons

that the ruling classes abhorred them: they celebrated anarchy, rebellion, and the triumph of the underdog.

The funnies never outgrew the bad reputation of their obstreperous youth. In 1906, the literary critic Ralph Bergengren, writing in the *Atlantic Monthly,* complained that in the comics, "Respect for property, respect for parents, for law, for decency, for truth, for beauty, for kindliness, for dignity, or for honor, are killed, without mercy." This negative attitude by self-appointed arbiters of public taste toward the "low art" of the comics has persisted ever since.

In 1905, Roy McCardell summed up the rowdy appeal of the comic supplement: "Its humor is strenuous, not to say brutal; the knock-about comedians of the old time music-halls might easily have posed for most of the pictures that the supplement has printed in its ten years of life. The characters are thrown out of windows, clubbed, kicked, knocked down and out, laid flat by trucks dropped upon them; but they turn up smilingly the next Sunday to go through the same operations in other forms."

Many of the early comics featured visual punch lines that were recycled over and over again. Maud the mule habitually gave her victims a swift kick. Everett True ended each episode by violently dispatching the source of his frustration. Scary William was forever frightened, and Willie Westinghouse Edison Smith's inventions always backfired. Cartoonists would milk these one-note gag strips for as long as they could

CLARENCE THE COP—Charles W. Kahles's popular policeman, who starred in Pulitzer's World from 1900 to 1908, sees himself in the funnies.
September 12, 1908. Courtesy of Bill Blackbeard

and then move on to another gimmick. Hundreds of short-lived titles, which often told readers all they needed to know about the main characters, appeared and disappeared in the formative years of the Sunday funnies.

Charles William Kahles was a prolific pioneer who created twenty-three different comic features during his thirty-three-year career. In the first decade of the century, he did strips for the McClure Syndicate as well as the *Philadelphia North American* and the *Philadelphia Press*. In 1905, he was producing eight different titles simultaneously: *Clarence the Cop, Billy Bounce, The Teasers, Mr. Buttin, Doubting Thomas, Pretending Percy, Fun in the Zoo,* and *The Terrible Twins*. His most successful creation, *Hairbreadth Harry,* was one of the first serial story strips, and it ran from October 21, 1906, to January 17, 1940. (Franklin Osborne Alexander continued it after Kahles's death on January 21, 1931.)

George Herriman, remembered today as the creator of *Krazy Kat,* was also active during this era of experimentation. Among the many short-lived features Herriman introduced before launching his first successful strip, *The Dingbat Family,* in 1910 were *Handy Andy, Tattered Tim, Professor Otto, Acrobatic Archie, Musical Mose, Major Ozone, Mr. Proones the Plunger,* and *Baron Mooch.*

Carl "Bunny" Schultze's *Foxy Grandpa,* which debuted in the *New York Herald* on January 7, 1900, was one of the most enduring of the one-note gag strips. Schultze reversed the formula of Dirks's *Katzenjammer Kids:* at the end of each Sunday page, clever Grandpa inevitably outwitted the two mischievous tykes who were trying to trick him. Schultze's feature lasted for more than eighteen years, and there were *Foxy Grandpa* plays, films, books, and toys.

Two of the most memorable strips of the era, *Buster Brown* and *Little Nemo,* also built successfully on a simple premise that was repeated in each installment. They were widely imitated, profitably merchandised, and universally praised as classic creations.

After Outcault left the *New York Journal* in 1898, he worked briefly for the *New York World* and sold freelance cartoons to *Life* and *Judge*. In 1901, he produced a feature for the *New York Herald, Pore Li'l Mose,* which starred a little black boy and his animal friends. Outcault struck gold again when he introduced *Buster Brown* in the *Herald* on May 4, 1902. A genteel version of Mickey Dugan (a.k.a. the Yellow Kid), Buster wore Little Lord Fauntleroy suits and lived in a respectable middle-class home. In each episode, this attractive and intelligent ten-year-old would initiate some form of mayhem—pulling down curtains, spilling food, breaking dishes, crashing his bicycle—with devilish naughtiness. In the end, Buster was usually spanked or otherwise punished, and he repented in the form of handwritten resolutions. The following week, he would be back to create new mischief.

BUSTER BROWN AND TIGE—The stars of Richard F. Outcault's second "hit" creation, in a special drawing for **The Bookman.** *November 1902. Courtesy of Robert C. Harvey*

The rest of the cast—Tige the bulldog, Mrs. Brown, and girl-friend Mary Jane—were modeled after Outcault's own dog, wife, and daughter.

Once again, Outcault's timing was perfect. *Buster Brown* was distributed to papers across the country, and its star became a national celebrity. Middle-class readers, who had been repelled by the urban squalor of *Hogan's Alley,* were pleasantly titillated by the polite shenanigans of Buster's suburban setting. Outcault was quick to seize on the commercial potential for marketing his character and was intent on not losing control of this creation, as he had with the Yellow Kid.

Outcault's contract with the *Herald* expired on December 31, 1905. After entertaining an offer from the *Denver Post* to draw *Buster Brown* for a yearly salary of $10,000, Outcault decided to sign with Hearst. The *Herald* continued to publish *Buster Brown,* drawn by other artists, while Outcault was producing his creation for the Hearst papers. According to *Editor & Publisher* on February 17, 1906, "as many as five papers containing *Buster Brown* pictures were recently on sale in Detroit on the same Sunday."

Outcault initiated legal action to prevent the *Herald* from releasing the competing version. The *Herald* responded by copyrighting *Buster Brown* in Washington, D.C., and, on February 6, 1906, filing a countersuit with the U.S. District Court in New York. The attorney for the *Herald* argued that because his client had invested large sums of money in promoting the feature, it was entitled to legal ownership.

Both cases were tried in the same court by the same judge. The *Herald* was awarded the right to the title, *Buster Brown,* and given clearance to continue releasing the feature. The Star Company, the Hearst-owned publisher of the *New York American* and the *Journal,* was also granted permission to produce new episodes but was not allowed to use the title.

Fortunately for Outcault, this decision applied only to control of the drawings. He had reserved the right to "dramatize" his creation and had written agreements to that effect, signed by the *Herald.* A later court case granted him all ancillary rights to the character. In the ensuing years, the Outcault Advertising Agency initiated more than thirty lawsuits against companies for illegally using *Buster Brown* artwork. There were also numerous court battles over theatrical rights. One of these stage shows earned Outcault $44,000 in royalties over a four-year period.

Buster Brown was the first comic strip character to be used as a brand name. In 1904, Outcault attended the St. Louis World's Fair and granted licenses to the Brown Shoe Company and the watch manufacturer Robert Ingersoll; they worked out a cooperative promotion, packaging shoes and watches together. Before long, Buster was endorsing a wide range of products, including textiles, dolls, toys, games, coffee, soft drinks, flour, bread, apples, suits, hosiery, and pianos.

"Buster Brown was the crucial link between comic strips and the development of a visual culture of consumption in America," explained Ian Gordon in *Comic Strips and Consumer Culture.* "Indeed 'Buster Brown' cannot be understood solely as a comic strip. All of his incarnations contributed to the makeup of his character, and each reinforced or advertised the others." In the coming years, other cartoon characters, including Popeye, Mickey Mouse, and Snoopy, would be marketed with the same synergistic techniques that Outcault pioneered with Buster Brown.

Winsor McCay's *Little Nemo in Slumberland,* which debuted in the *New York Herald* on October 15, 1905, was also based on a recurring scenario: Nemo falls asleep, dreams, and wakes up in the last panel, tumbling out of bed. From this starting point, McCay explored a world of graphic fantasy that stretched the limits of the imagination.

In 1891, McCay (who was born sometime between 1867 and 1871) started working at the Vine Street Dime Museum in Cincinnati, where he illustrated scenery, posters, and signs. This early experience in the colorful atmosphere of sideshows and carnival amusements provided inspiration for many of his later creations. After four years on the art staff of the *Cincinnati Enquirer,* McCay relocated to New York and, in 1903, was hired by James Gordon Bennett to draw cartoons for the *Telegram* and the *Herald.* Among the many features he created for these papers were *Little Sammy*

NEMO AND FRIENDS—Promotional drawing by Winsor McCay for the **Baltimore Sun,** featuring the characters from LITTLE NEMO IN SLUMBERLAND. *c. 1910*

GERTIE THE DINOSAUR—Poster advertising the release of Winsor McCay's historic animated film. November 1914. Courtesy of Ray Winsor Moniz

Sneeze, about a boy whose uncontrollable outbursts inevitably led to chaos, and *Hungry Henrietta,* which starred a girl with an insatiable appetite.

Although McCay never acknowledged the influence of Sigmund Freud, who had published *The Interpretation of Dreams* in 1900, a fascination with human psychology is evident in much of his work. McCay's most adult-oriented creation, *Dream of the Rarebit Fiend,* explored the obsessions of the subconscious. In each episode, after eating a rich meal of Welsh rarebit, the main character had a graphic nightmare about a deep fear, such as suffocation, weightlessness, or drowning.

Little Nemo in Slumberland was, without question, McCay's masterpiece. Between 1905 and 1911, he put on a virtuoso performance in the pages of the *New York Herald.* Majestic architecture, fanciful creatures, and evocative scenery were rendered with graphic precision. He experimented with innovative page layouts, using tall panels to suggest height and panoramas to provide breadth. Successive action sequences anticipated later experiments in film animation. His use of color took full advantage of the *Herald*'s presses, which were reputed to be the best in the business. He developed continuing story lines, chronicling Nemo's extended adventures in Befuddle Hall, Shanty Town, and across North America in an airship.

McCay was modest about his abilities. In Clare Briggs's 1926 book, *How to Draw Cartoons,* he shared with aspiring artists some of the lessons he had learned: "The greatest contributing factor to my success was an absolute craving to draw pictures all the time." "I don't think I had any more talent for drawing than other kids had, but I think it was the interest I had in drawing and the fun I had in making them that brought out what perfection I have." "The cartoonist must create, he must see in his mind a situation, maybe full of life and comedy, maybe still or dramatic or tragic."

Other cartoonists explored fantasy in the funnies, but *Little Nemo* was the most acclaimed strip in the genre. Critics of lowbrow humor praised the high artistic and moral qualities of McCay's creation, and other cartoonists were quick to imitate his successful formula. Among the many fantasy strips of the era were *Wee Willie Winkie's World* and *The Kin-der-Kids* (both 1906) by Lyonel Feininger, *Nibsy, the Newsboy, in Funny Fairyland* (1906) by George McManus, *Danny Dreamer* (1907) by Clare Briggs, *The Explorigator* (1908) by Harry Grant Dart, *Mr. Twee Deedle* (1911) by Johnny Gruelle, and *Bobby Make Believe* (1915) by Frank King.

During his long career, McCay pursued many interests. In 1906, he took his act on the road and performed "chalk talks" on the vaudeville circuit. He was a pioneer in the field of animation, and his 1914 film, *Gertie the Dinosaur,* which he cleverly incorporated into his stage show, was the first animated cartoon to feature a character with a convincing personality.

He went to work for Hearst in 1911 and was an influential political cartoonist throughout the 1920s.

McCay died of a cerebral hemorrhage on July 26, 1934. He was respected among his peers as one of the greatest cartoonists in America. "His distinction was built on unsurpassed technique, seemingly unlimited imagination, unsparing insistence on detail and inventive genius," stated one obituary.

In *The Art of the Funnies,* Robert C. Harvey summed up McCay's unique place in the history of the art form: "He was so far ahead of his time that many of his innovations were beyond the abilities of his contemporaries: what he had discovered and demonstrated about the capacities of each medium had to be rediscovered decades later by the next generation of cartoonists."

In the first years of the twentieth century, comics began to appear in daily newspapers as well as Sunday supplements. Strips and panels could be found scattered throughout the morning and evening editions, often on the sports pages. The readers of the dailies were mostly male workers, on their way to and from work. The content of many early efforts, such as *Mr. Jack, The Hall Room Boys, E. Z. Mark,* and *The Outbursts of Everett True,* reflected the tastes of this audience. Rube Goldberg, George Herriman, Jimmy Swinnerton, Gus Mager, and TAD Dorgan were among the cartoonists who paid their dues during the formative years of the funnies and went on to attain fame in the coming decades.

Bud Fisher was a sports cartoonist on the *San Francisco Chronicle* in 1907. One day he decided to try something new with his drawing. "In selecting the strip form for the picture,"

BUD FISHER—Self-caricature from **The Mutt and Jeff Cartoons,** *the first book collection of Fisher's strip, produced by the Ball Publishing Company.* 1910. *Courtesy of the International Museum of Cartoon Art*

MUTT AND JEFF WISH EVERYBODY A MERRY CHRISTMAS—Special drawing by Bud Fisher for the New York American. *1913. Courtesy of Editor & Publisher*

Fisher remembered, "I thought I would get a prominent position across the top of the page, which I did, and that pleased my vanity. I also thought the cartoon would be easy to read in this form. It was."

The strip, *Mr. A. Mutt Starts in to Play the Races,* appeared on November 15, 1907, and starred a chinless racetrack gambler. After "absorbing a little of the 'inside infor,'" Mutt placed three ten-dollar bets on "Proper," "Money Muss," and "Blondy." These were names of real horses that were running across the bay at the Emeryville racetrack. The last panel of Fisher's drawing invited readers to "See what Mr. Mutt does for himself in tomorrow's '*Chronicle.*'" It was a clever new use of the "cliffhanger," a well-known plot device popular in serialized fiction and stage melodramas of the era.

From this simple beginning, the first successful daily comic strip was born. Fisher's readers returned—day after day—to learn the results of Mutt's wagers. Many actually believed that they were legitimate tips and raced to the betting windows to put their money on the horses mentioned in the strip.

For the next few months, Mutt's daily activities revolved around gathering information for his next bet, raising money, placing wagers, and watching races, which he would lose, more often than not. After that, the whole cycle would begin again. When Mutt's horse did come in, he never held on to his winnings for long.

In 1908, Fisher's feature veered off in a new direction. In a rambling continuity, Mutt was arrested for petty thievery, tried, convicted, and sent to an insane asylum. Fisher dabbled in political commentary during the trial, using the names of real San Francisco bigwigs who were embroiled in a local corruption scandal. Somehow, during all this, Mutt still managed to place bets at the racetrack. On March 27, while in the "bughouse," Mutt met a short, bald, deluded fellow who intro-

duced himself as the famous boxing champion James Jeffries, or "Jeff" for short. Gradually the two developed a friendship, but it was not until 1910, when the first book collection, *The Mutt and Jeff Cartoons,* was published, that they officially became a team. The title of the strip remained *A. Mutt* until September 15, 1916.

The addition of Jeff raised the level of humor in Fisher's feature. Mutt's plans were now eternally doomed to failure by Jeff's ineptitude. Although Mutt would take his frustrations out on his bumbling sidekick in the form of kicks, punches, and thrown objects, Jeff never held a grudge. Together the lanky opportunist and the diminutive fall guy became a universal archetype: the mismatched pair. *Mutt and Jeff* survived for more than seventy-five years, until the strip was canceled in 1983. They remained friends to the end.

Less than a month after *A. Mutt* debuted in the *San Francisco Chronicle,* Hearst, the publisher of the *San Francisco Examiner,* hired Fisher for $45 a week, double his previous salary. With uncanny foresight Fisher wrote, "Copyright 1907, H. C. Fisher," in the last strip he submitted to the *Chronicle* and the first two he drew for the *Examiner.* He later registered the copyright in Washington, D.C. After Fisher went to work for Hearst, the *Chronicle* directed Russ Westover (who later created *Tillie the Toiler*) to draw *A. Mutt.* Fisher challenged the *Chronicle*'s right to continue his creation, and on June 7, 1908, the newspaper gave in and ceased publication of the strip. Fisher was the first cartoonist to successfully establish ownership of his creation.

In the next decade, Bud Fisher, the highest-paid cartoonist in the comics business, faced off against William Randolph Hearst, the nation's most powerful publisher, in a prolonged court battle. At stake was legal and financial control of a pen-and-ink property that Fisher had guided to success. It would be a landmark decision.

richard f. outcault

THE "FATHER OF THE NEWSPAPER COMIC STRIP" flaunted his success by sporting a natty hunter's cap, a waxed mustache, and a walking stick when he appeared in public, but he was modest about his abilities. "I am the worst artist along Park Row," he told a reporter in 1896. In a later interview, he summed up his career by claiming, "*The Yellow Kid,* my first conception, and *Buster Brown,* my last, are but mediums for the same kind of epigrammatical humor of a strain that I look on peculiarly as my own."

Richard Felton Outcault was born in Lancaster, Ohio, on January 14, 1863. His German ancestors, who arrived in America in 1720, originally spelled their name "Altgelt." Richard's father, Jesse, was a modestly successful cabinetmaker and encouraged his son's artistic interests. After attending public school, R. F. studied at McMicken College (which later became the Art Academy of Cincinnati) for three years and then found employment painting scenes on strongboxes for the Hall Safe and Lock Company.

In 1888, Edison Laboratories mounted an exhibition of electrical illumination at the Centennial Exposition of the Ohio Valley and Mid-Atlantic States in Cincinnati. Outcault was hired for the sum of $400 to provide illustrations of the display for *Electrical World* magazine, and eventually he joined the Edison company as a full-time employee, moving to its headquarters in West Orange, New Jersey. In 1889, he traveled to France as the official draftsman for the Edison exhibit at the International Exposition in Paris and studied art in the Latin Quarter.

When Outcault returned to New York in 1890, he supplemented his work for *Electrical World* by selling cartoons to *Truth, Life,* and *Judge* magazines. Some of these single-panel drawings featured scenes of tenement life, a popular subject of the era. When Joseph Pulitzer launched his new colored comic section on May 21, 1893, freelance artists like Outcault were his primary recruits, since many of the top cartoonists were already under contract to the comic weeklies. Outcault's first cartoon for the *Sunday World* was a six-panel sequence entitled "Uncle Eben's Ignorance of City Ways Prevents His Keeping an Engagement with His Wife," which appeared on September 16, 1894.

Outcault also continued to draw cartoons for *Truth,* and on February 17, 1895, the *Sunday World* reprinted one of these panels. "Fourth Ward Brownies" was the first appearance in Pulitzer's paper of the bald-headed street urchin who was to become the Yellow Kid.

Years later, Outcault described the original inspiration for his curious creation. "When I used to go about the slums on newspaper assignments," he remembered, "I would encounter

RICHARD F. OUTCAULT—Caricature by William Shields. *February 9, 1908,* San Francisco Examiner

him often, wandering out of doorways or sitting down on dirty doorsteps. I always loved the Kid. He had a sweet character and a sunny disposition, and was generous to a fault. Malice, envy or selfishness were not traits of his, and he never lost his temper."

The success of the Yellow Kid brought Outcault wealth and fame, but after less than three years he was ready to move on. He drew his last regular Yellow Kid episode for William Randolph Hearst's *New York Journal* on February 6, 1898, although his famous ragamuffin made a few guest appearances in some of his subsequent features. Outcault went back to work for Pulitzer between February 1898 and July 1900, creating a number of short-lived comics series. He then joined James Gordon Bennett's *New York Herald* and introduced *Buster Brown* on May 4, 1902.

Although Outcault was adept at rendering comedic action in his drawings, his style was more typical of the realistic illustration found in nineteenth-century humor magazines than the raucous exaggerations being pioneered in the newspaper comic sections in the first decade of the twentieth century. As the funnies evolved, Outcault's detailed cross-hatching and elegant line work began to look dated. After 1910, Outcault produced new episodes of *Buster Brown* on a semi-regular basis as he became increasingly involved in the Outcault Advertising Agency, which managed the numerous Buster Brown licensing accounts.

The last episode of *Buster Brown,* syndicated by Hearst, appeared on December 11, 1921; reprints were published until 1926. Outcault spent his retirement years traveling, lecturing, and painting, and he died at his suburban mansion in Flushing, New York, on September 25, 1928.

HOGAN'S ALLEY Sunday page by Richard F. Outcault. The last Yellow Kid page by Outcault published in Pulitzer's paper. October 4, 1896, New York World.
Courtesy of Denis Kitchen

MCFADDEN'S ROW OF FLATS proof sheet by Richard F. Outcault. When he moved to the Journal, Outcault's version of HOGAN'S ALLEY appeared under this new title. *October 25, 1896, New York Journal. Richard D. Olson Collection, The Ohio State University Cartoon Research Library. Courtesy of the Frye Art Museum, Seattle. Photo credit: Susan Dirk/Under the Light*

BUSTER BROWN original hand-colored Sunday page by Richard F. Outcault. August 30, 1903, New York Herald. Courtesy of the International Museum of Cartoon Art

THE YELLOW KID HE MEETS TIGE AND MARY JANE AND BUSTER BROWN—*Original hand-colored Sunday page by Richard F. Outcault.*
July 7, 1907, American Examiner. Courtesy of the Art Wood Collection of Cartoon and Caricature, Prints and Photographs Division, Library of Congress

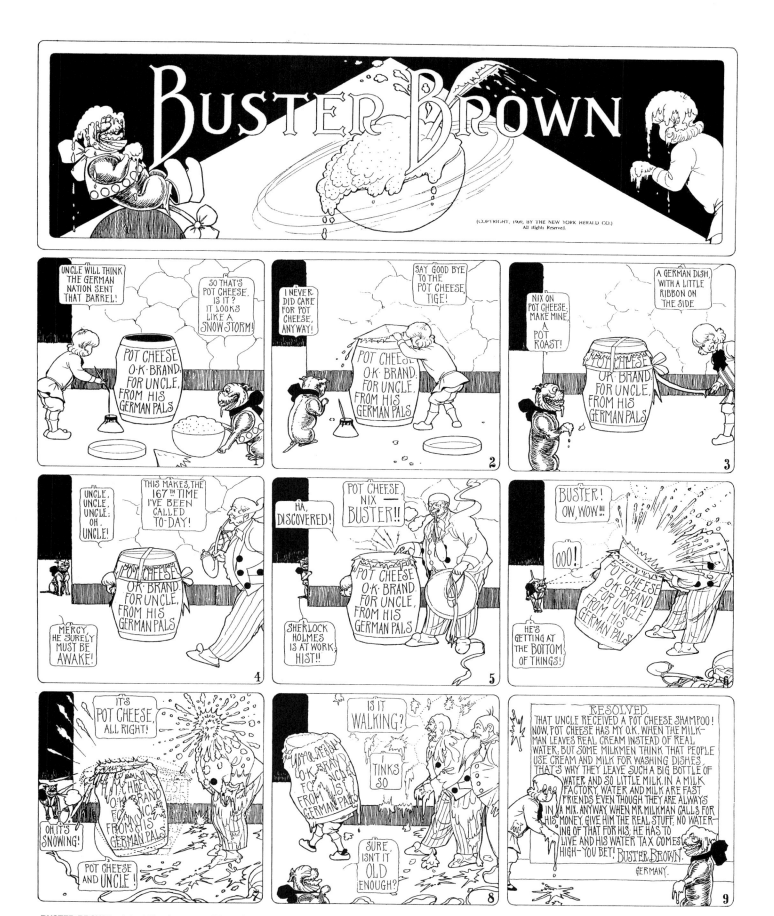

BUSTER BROWN original Sunday page. After Richard F. Outcault left the *Herald* to work for the *Hearst* newspapers in 1906, a number of artists continued his feature for that paper. This artist is unknown, although the page looks as if it may have been done by Winsor McCay, who was working for the *Herald* at this time. *1909, New York Herald. Courtesy of Illustration House*

rudolph dirks

RUDOLPH DIRKS—Self-caricature from Comics and Their Creators. 1942

THE CREATOR of the longest-surviving feature in comics history was a newcomer to the field when he was hired by William Randolph Hearst in 1897. His immortal mischief-makers—dark-haired, bow-tied Hans and fair-haired, lace-collared Fritz—appeared in two separate, competing features for sixty-five years and still star in a weekly version syndicated by King Features.

Rudolph Dirks was born in 1877 in Heinde, Germany, and immigrated to Chicago when he was seven years old. He began selling cartoons to *Judge* and *Life* in 1894 and three years later went to work for the *New York Journal*.

According to Hearst family legend, young Willie picked up a copy of Wilhelm Busch's picture-story book *Max und Moritz* while touring Europe with his mother. Dirks himself, however, did not credit Hearst with the idea to create a comic strip based on Busch's *Bilderbogen*. On December 12, 1897, at the suggestion of his comic editor, Rudolph Block, Dirks introduced a multi-panel sequence in which three boys grappled with a gardener and his hose.

The following week, the cast had been reduced to a pair of pranksters. In the early episodes, "The Katzies" rebelled against their Mama, but in the next few years, Der Captain, a shipwrecked sailor who acted as their surrogate father, and Der Inspector, a truant officer, became the primary victims of the boys' practical jokes.

It was obvious to readers from the beginning, by the clothing and the setting, that the Katzenjammers were German, although it was not until a few years later, when Dirks started using speech balloons on a regular basis, that the unique dialect of the characters became apparent. "Mitt dose kids, society is nix," a trademark phrase perpetually bellowed by Der Inspector, was typical of the mispronounced English spoken in the strip.

The success of Dirks's feature spawned many imitations, the foremost being *The Fineheimer Twins* by Harold Knerr, which began running in the *Philadelphia Inquirer* on February 15, 1903. When Dirks parted ways with Hearst in 1912, Knerr took over as the new artist on *The Original Katzenjammer Kids*, which was relaunched in the Hearst newspapers on November 29, 1914. In June of that same year, Pulitzer began publishing Dirks's continuation of his creation, which was retitled *The Captain and the Kids* in 1918 due to anti-German sentiment during World War I. (Knerr's feature was renamed *The Shenanigan Kids* for the same reason.)

Although he was only an adequate draftsman, Dirks pioneered the use of many comic devices that eventually became part of the art form's visual language. Parallel lines and dust clouds to indicate speed, dotted lines to represent eye contact, and sweat beads to suggest fear or nervousness were among the many forms of graphic communication that appeared regularly in the panels of *The Katzenjammer Kids*. Dirks was more of an innovator than Knerr, who drew in a polished "big-foot" style (featuring characters with oversized feet, heads, and noses) and was considered to be the more gifted of the two artistically.

In *America's Great Comic-Strip Artists,* Richard Marschall summed up this pioneer's legacy: "Dirks took the young art form's basic formula—peace, scheming, mayhem, exposure, punishment—and made it appeal to all ages and types of readers, expressed through a new vocabulary appropriate to comic strips alone. Hans and Fritz's endless explosions and chases may have seemed trivial, yet they endure. After almost a century, *The Katzenjammer Kids* can be read as a virtual 'dod-gasted' blueprint of what a comic strip is."

YELLOW KID? ACH, NO! IT'S ONLY THE KATZENJAMMER KID—
(And His "Brudder.")

THE KATZENJAMMER KIDS Sunday page by Rudolph Dirks. This artist's Kids took over as the headliners in the Hearst comic sections after Outcault moved on. March 27, 1898, New York Journal. Courtesy of Peter Maresca

MAMA KATZENJAMMER CROSSES A BRIDGE—Sunday half-page by Rudolph Dirks. *1900,* San Francisco Examiner.
Courtesy of Peter Maresca

MAMA KATZENJAMMER ISS SO STRONG! ACH, YES!—Sunday half-page by Rudolph Dirks. April 21, 1901, St. Louis Daily Globe-Democrat.
Courtesy of Mark Johnson

My! But the Katzenjammers Are Rich !

THE KATZENJAMMER KIDS *original hand-colored Sunday page by Rudolph Dirks. This page was Exhibit No. 11 in the 1913 trial between the Press Publishing Company, representing Dirks, and Hearst's Star Company. Part of Dirks's breach-of-contract suit was based on his complaint that Hearst's editor, Rudolph Block, instructed him to put the Katzenjammers into high-society situations. Dirks made two or three attempts to satisfy this request before he gave up, claiming that this was not the type of humor he was comfortable doing.* June 2, 1912, New York Sunday American. *Courtesy of Eugene J. Walter Jr.*

THE SHENANIGAN KIDS original hand-colored Sunday page by Harold Knerr. The Katzenjammers changed their name during World War I due to anti-German sentiment. *December 28, 1919. Courtesy of the International Museum of Cartoon Art*

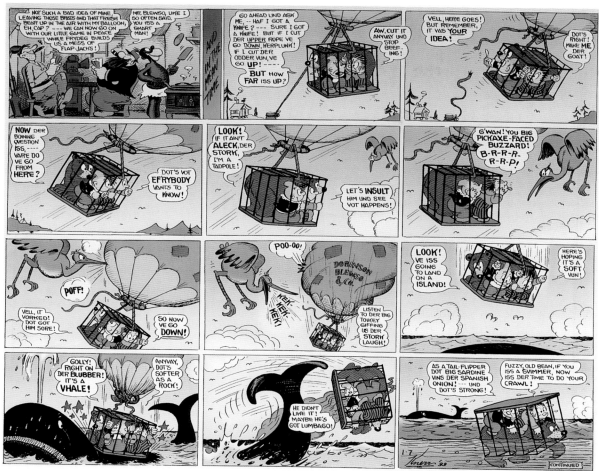

THE KATZENJAMMER KIDS original artwork with color overlays of a two-page sequence by Harold Knerr. An aviation enthusiast, Knerr frequently incorporated flying contraptions into his stories. © January 7 and 14, 1933, King Features Syndicate, Inc. Courtesy of Bruce Hamilton

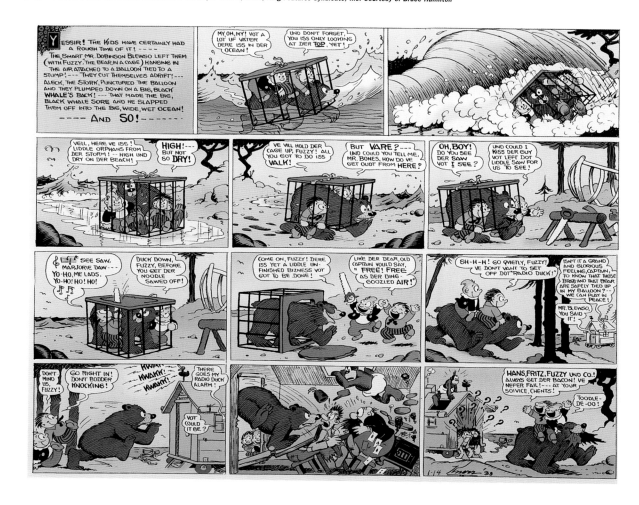

frederick b. opper

F. Opper. AT WORK

THE "DEAN OF AMERICAN CARTOONISTS" was a leading artist in the humor magazines of the nineteenth century, a pioneer in the early years of the newspaper comic strip, and an influential political cartoonist for more than two decades before he retired in 1932. Five years later, when he passed away at the age of eighty, his friend Russ Westover, creator of *Tillie the Toiler,* eulogized him in a memorial radio broadcast: "Mr. Opper did with his comic characters in print what Will Rogers did on the screen and over the air—broke that tension—made people laugh and forget their troubles for awhile at least."

Frederick Burr Opper was born on January 2, 1857, in Madison, Ohio, the son of an Austrian immigrant. He dropped out of school at the age of fourteen to work for the local newspaper, and two years later he left for New York to seek his fortune as an artist. His first known published cartoon appeared in *Wild Oats* in 1876; a year later, he joined the staff of *Frank Leslie's Illustrated Newspaper.* He moved to *Puck* magazine in 1881, where he produced black-and-white cartoons and spot illustrations, as well as color lithographs, for eighteen years until he was recruited by William Randolph Hearst in 1899. The veteran cartoonist brought respectability to the press lord's "yellow journal."

In the first decade of the new century, Opper launched a string of classic newspaper comic strips in the pages of the *New York Journal* and *American,* including *Happy Hooligan* (March 11, 1900), *Our Antediluvian Ancestors* (January 20, 1901), *Alphonse and Gaston* (September 22, 1901), *And Her Name was Maud* (June 24, 1904), and *Howson Lott* (April 25, 1909).

Opper's "trust-busting" political cartoons were also widely distributed and featured such immortal graphic icons as Willie (McKinley), Teddy (Roosevelt), Nursie (Mark Hanna), Papa (the fat-bellied Trust), and Mr. Common Man. A remarkably prolific artist, Opper illustrated books by Bill Nye, Mark Twain, Eugene Field, and Finley Peter Dunne.

An interviewer who visited the famous cartoonist at his house in New Rochelle, New York, in October 1929 observed that he worked in a modest second-floor room, which had a window that overlooked the backyard. It was equipped with a small drawing board, two bottles of India ink, and a box of crayons. A rolltop desk, a bookcase, several stuffed chairs, and a select group of drawings and photographs given to him by his fellow artists completed the Spartan surroundings.

"I have done hundreds of series in my time," Opper told the reporter. "Some of them have been popular for a time, and some haven't. You can never tell when the public's fancy is going to be tickled. All a comic artist can do is to set out to amuse and entertain whoever will look at his work. If he's got the stuff, he can do it; if he hasn't, he can't."

Opper turned from the interviewer to his drawing board and began coloring the printer's guide for his next *Happy Hooligan* strip. "Comic art is a wonderful business if the artist has the particular kind of ability it takes," he continued. "I still do enough to keep me busy but I can't work as fast as I used to."

At that time, he was turning out a Sunday page and three editorial cartoons a week. He had been a professional cartoonist for fifty-three years. Although his eyesight was failing, Fred Opper still had the right stuff.

ALPHONSE AND GASTON panel from a Sunday page by Frederick B. Opper. 1903

HAPPY HOOLIGAN *original hand-colored Sunday page by Frederick B. Opper. Happy often traveled with his brothers, Gloomy Gus and Lord Montmorency.*
© April 9, 1905, American-Journal-Examiner. Courtesy of Angelo Nobile

HAPPY HOOLIGAN original hand-colored Sunday page by Frederick B. Opper. Happy began his long courtship with Suzanne in 1908, which finally culminated on June 18, 1916, in their marriage. c. 1910, New York American. Courtesy of Illustration House

AND HER NAME WAS MAUD.

AND HER NAME WAS MAUD *Sunday page by Frederick B. Opper. A variation on a recurring theme, as farmer Si Slocum and Maud are upended by a motor* **car.** *© February 27, 1921, King Features Syndicate, Inc. Courtesy of Russ Cochran*

jimmy swinnerton

THE GRAND OLD MAN of cartooning is often overlooked as a pioneer of the art form. His newspaper career began before the introduction of the Sunday funnies and lasted for more than sixty years.

James Guilford Swinnerton was born in Eureka, California, on November 13, 1875, the son of a judge who was also the founder of the *Humboldt Star,* a weekly newspaper. After studying at the California Art School in San Francisco, the sixteen-year-old towhead landed a job at William Randolph Hearst's *Examiner* in 1892.

Years later, Swinnerton looked back on his early days as a newspaper cartoonist: "The artist of that date had to go to all sorts of happenings that are now covered by the staff photographers, as photographs were not yet produced successfully on news pages. A typical day was spent covering, say, a flower show or trial in the morning, a baseball game in the afternoon with, maybe, an art opening and a murder or two at night. One had to be ready to draw anything at a moment's notice. Those of us who had a comic turn in our work would try to crowd a comic drawing in whenever we could and, in so doing, our editors began to find out that a good cartoon, or comic drawing, drew more notice from readers; in that way the comic drawing in the newspaper world gradually came into its own."

The young cartoonist's talents came to the attention of his boss in 1893 when he drew a realistic illustration of Monarch, a grizzly bear Hearst had captured and put on display in San Francisco as a publicity stunt. "Swin" was asked to do a daily drawing of the state mascot, and his humorous, roly-poly version of Baby Monarch became a fixture in the paper beginning in October 1893. This continuing feature, which eventually included a full cast of little bears and human tykes, was not a comic strip as many historians have claimed, but it was one of the first examples of repeated appearances by popular characters in an American newspaper.

Little Bears became *The Journal Tigers* (inspired by the Tammany tiger, representing the Democratic Party political machine in New York) when Swinnerton went to work for the *New York Journal* in 1897. Mr. Jack, a philandering feline

JIMMY SWINNERTON—Self-caricature. April 1923, Circulation magazine

with a straw hat and cane, emerged from the pack to star in his own strip beginning in 1903. One of the little tykes also got his own Sunday page, which debuted on February 14, 1904. *Little Jimmy* was Swinnerton's most enduring creation, running almost continuously until 1958.

During his brief stay in New York City, Swinnerton went through a failed marriage, suffered a nervous breakdown, and was diagnosed with tuberculosis; the doctors gave him only two weeks to live. "If I remained much longer in New York, I would have passed on," he claimed. In the summer of 1906, Hearst put his artist friend on a train bound for Colton, California, a refuge for TB patients. Swinnerton spent the rest of his life in California and Arizona. "I arrived in pretty good condition and fell headlong, head over heels in love with the grand Arizona desert and sunsets," he remembered. "In fact I liked the place so much I forgot to die." He survived to the ripe old age of ninety-eight.

OUR TIGERS GO ABROAD—*Original hand-colored Sunday page by Jimmy Swinnerton. After he came to New York in 1897, Swinnerton's LITTLE BEARS became THE JOURNAL TIGERS.* c. 1900. Courtesy of Illustration House

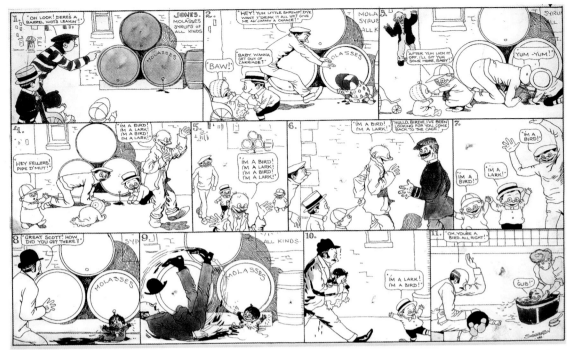

LITTLE JIMMY *original Sunday half-page by Jimmy Swinnerton. Jimmy Thompson, the star of Swinnerton's long-running feature, had an innocent curiosity about the world around him and was often punished by his parents for his distractions.* 1909. Courtesy of Illustration House

MR. JACK *daily strip by Jimmy Swinnerton.* 1919. Courtesy of Rob Stolzer

MR. JACK *daily strip by Jimmy Swinnerton. A womanizing cat-about-town, Mr. Jack, who first appeared in the Sunday funnies in 1903, was given his own daily strip nine years later.* 1914. Courtesy of Russ Cochran

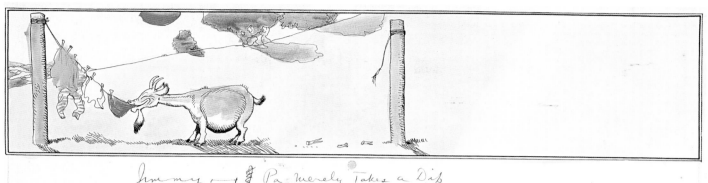

PA MERELY TAKES A DIP—Original hand-colored *LITTLE JIMMY* Sunday page by Jimmy Swinnerton. *July 5, 1914. Collection of the Cartoon Art Museum, San Francisco. Photo courtesy of the Frye Art Museum, Seattle. Photo credit: Susan Dirk/Under the Light*

CARTOON PIONEERS

In addition to Outcault, Dirks, Opper, and Swinnerton, many other talented creators contributed to the development of the art form during the early years of the century. On the following pages are newspaper comics by a sampling of these innovators, some of whom also did work for the weekly humor magazines.

LATEST NEWS FROM BUGVILLE original hand-colored half-page by Gus Dirks. In 1903, Rudolph's younger brother, who was also a regular contributor to *Judge* magazine, committed suicide. *c. 1902. Courtesy of Illustration House*

LEANDER AND CHARLEY MEET ON THE FIELD OF HONOR—Sunday half-page by F. M. Howarth. A frequent contributor of sequential comics to the weekly humor magazines of the late nineteenth century, Howarth created *LULU AND LEANDER* in 1902 for the Hearst newspapers. *© August 13, 1905, American-Journal-Examiner. Courtesy of Mark Johnson*

FOXY GRANDPA ON THE BEACH.

COPYRIGHT 1901 BY THE NEW YORK HERALD CO.

BOYS—AH! HERE'S GRANDPA TAKING A SUN BATH. LET'S ROLL THE BARREL ON HIM.

BOYS—LOOK OUT. GRANDPA, SOMETHING'S COMING.

GRANDPA—HERE! WHAT'S THIS!

WHY, BOYS, IS THIS YOUR

BARREL?

WELL, THE BARREL'S ON YOU THIS TIME, BOYS.

FOXY GRANDPA Sunday half-page by Carl "Bunny" Schultze. Grandpa always outwitted his two tormentors, who were never given names.
1901, New York Herald. *Courtesy of Peter Maresca*

THE UPSIDE-DOWNS OF LITTLE LADY LOVEKINS AND OLD MAN MUFFAROO THE THRILLING ADVENTURE of THE DRAGON

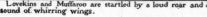

Lovekins and Muffaroo are startled by a loud roar and a sound of whirring wings.

It is a terrible Dragon that comes swooping down on them. Muffaroo escapes, but little Lady Lovekins gets caught.

She tries to stab the monster, but his scales are very hard, and he just flies along without feeling the knife at all. For two days and two nights they travel thus, until at last the Dragon begins to feel hungry!

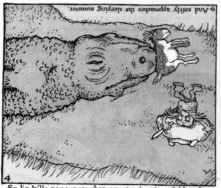

So he kills some goats that are grazing in a field, and eats them, watching Lovekins all the while. But he eats too much and with one goat still in his mouth he falls asleep.

Then Lovekins steals quietly away and hides herself in some woods. Suddenly she hears something tramping over the leaves toward her.

It turns out to be Old Man Muffaroo who has been following along the ground in the direction taken by the big Dragon. Lovekins wants to go home with him at once.

THE UPSIDE DOWNS Sunday half-page by Gustave Verbeck. This clever feature was designed to be read right side up and then turned upside down to complete the story. May 8, 1904, New York Herald. *Courtesy of Peter Maresca*

BILLY BOUNCE *Sunday page by Charles W. Kahles. An early Kahles creation, Billy was one of the first comic characters with superpowers.*
1905, McClure Syndicate, Inc. Courtesy of Peter Maresca

BROWNIE CLOWN OF BROWNIE TOWN Sunday page by Palmer Cox. The Brownies, who first appeared in St. Nicholas magazine in 1883, also had a short career as newspaper comics stars, beginning in 1903. October 20, 1907, Detroit News Tribune. Courtesy of Mark Johnson

SPARE RIBS AND GRAVY *Sunday page by George McManus. This feature, by the creator of* BRINGING UP FATHER, *ran in the World from January 28, 1912, to February 8, 1914, and revolved around the exploits of two bumbling explorers and a tribe of African natives.* c. 1912, New York World. Courtesy of Craig Englund

RACIAL CARICATURE

Ethnic stereotypes appeared in many of the early comics, but they gradually fell out of favor as the syndicates began marketing their features to a more diverse audience. Offensive black caricatures persisted much longer and were still relatively common in newspaper comics until World War II. Although racial stereotyping still exists today, it is no longer considered an acceptable form of graphic representation.

Certain distinguishing characteristics were common to most black caricatures. E. C. Matthews, in his 1928 instruction book, *How to Draw Funny Pictures,* advised that "the wide nose, heavy lips and fuzzy hair are all as important to a colored cartoon character as the dark complexion." Black dialect was also used to accentuate their ignorant or foolish behavior. In terms of subject matter, Matthews observed that "the cartoonist usually plays on the colored man's love of loud clothes, water-melon, chicken, crap-shooting, fear of ghosts, etc."

During the first part of the century, black characters were almost always cast in subservient roles as maids, butlers,

janitors, or stable boys. Sunshine in *Barney Google,* Mushmouth in *Moon Mullins,* Rachel in *Gasoline Alley,* and Smokey in *Joe Palooka* were typical of the black supporting players in popular strips of the 1920s and 1930s.

A comprehensive overview of newspaper comics before 1945 would be incomplete without including many of these characters. The images of black people shown here, and in subsequent chapters, must be evaluated in the historical context of the era. Important lessons can be learned by studying the visual record of racial intolerance, and hopefully these past transgressions can be avoided.

Today, cartoonists are more sensitive to their black readers and no longer rely on simplistic caricatures and clichés. Fully developed African-American characters are still a minority on the funnies pages, however. A great deal of progress needs to be made before blacks receive fair and equal treatment in the comic sections of American newspapers.

SAMBO AND HIS FUNNY NOISES Sunday page by Billy Marriner. One of the first features to star a black character, albeit a "pickaninny" with "dumb luck," Marriner's strip was syndicated from April 2, 1905, to March 21, 1915, by the McClure Syndicate. *March 22, 1908, San Francisco Chronicle. Courtesy of Mark Johnson*

winsor mccay

WINSOR MCCAY—Caricature by Cliff Sterrett. February 10, 1907, New York Herald

UNIVERSALLY PRAISED as the finest draftsman ever to work in the comics medium, this inspired and dedicated artist was also a pioneer in the field of film animation and an influential graphic commentator for the Hearst newspapers later in his career.

Zenas Winsor McCay was born in 1867, 1869, or 1871, according to varying accounts. A fire in his boyhood town of Spring Lake, Michigan, destroyed all of the town's records, so there is no definitive date of his birth. Winsor's parents encouraged his compulsive urge to draw, and an art teacher at the Michigan State Normal School, John Goodison, taught him important lessons in perspective, composition, and color, which he put to use throughout the rest of his life.

McCay's two most important comic strip creations, *Dream of the Rarebit Fiend* (September 10, 1904) and *Little Nemo in Slumberland* (October 15, 1905), both relied on a similar formula. Each episode would begin with a subconscious fantasy already in progress and would build to the climactic panel in which the character would awaken. Readers were conditioned by McCay's brilliant visualization techniques to instantly perceive the change between a character's internal and external point of view.

John Canemaker, McCay's biographer, eloquently described the magical charms of his masterpiece: "*Little Nemo in Slumberland* offers an extraordinary array of ravishing images that stay in the mind like remembered dreams. McCay's virtuoso draftsmanship is irresistible, as when butterflies seek shelter from the rain under an 'umbrella tree,' or the open mouth of a giant dragon becomes a traveling coach, or when a walking, talking icicle exhorts us up the cold staircase of Jack Frost's palace."

McCay's life was riddled with contradictions. Though possessed of an imagination that bordered on the bizarre, he led a conventional middle-class existence and was often pictured at his drawing board wearing a coat, a hat, and a tie. He was relatively shy, yet he had no fear of performing on a vaudeville stage. His art was hand-drawn, but he was a pioneer in the technology of film animation. He earned a fortune during his lifetime but left very little for his family when he died.

In 1909, according to McCay, his son showed him a book of drawings that appeared to move when the pages were flipped. The child's amusement inspired him to begin experimenting with moving pictures projected on a screen. He produced four thousand drawings on rice paper, photographed each one at the Vitagraph Studio near his home in Sheepshead Bay, New York, hand-colored the 35mm frames, and incorporated the final short subject into his stage show. Between 1911 and 1921, McCay produced ten animated films.

William Randolph Hearst, who hired McCay in 1911, became disenchanted with these extracurricular activities and ordered his star cartoonist to focus exclusively on newspaper work. During the 1920s, to honor his contract, McCay cut back on public performances, film experiments, and comic strips. He turned out hundreds of detailed drawings for the Hearst papers to illustrate the editorials of Arthur Brisbane. Although some historians argue that Hearst stifled McCay's brilliant imagination, his "sermons in line" were powerful graphic statements of universal themes, which transcended Brisbane's pompous pronouncements.

"As fantasist, draftsman, observer, and reporter, satirist, innovator, and developer of new forms of communication," writes Canemaker, "McCay must be ranked among the greatest figures of twentieth-century popular art." No cartoonist has ever surpassed his achievements.

DREAM OF THE RAREBIT FIEND comic page by Winsor McCay. The artist used the pen name "Silas" on his first successful feature, which ran several days a week in the Telegram. In this episode, he gets a "big head" listening to compliments about his vaudeville stage act. *c. 1906,* New York Evening Telegram *(New York Herald Company). Courtesy of Craig Yoe.*

DREAM OF THE RAREBIT FIEND comic page by Winsor McCay. An artist struggles with changing scenery. 1906, New York Evening Telegram (New York Herald Company). Courtesy of Jack Gilbert

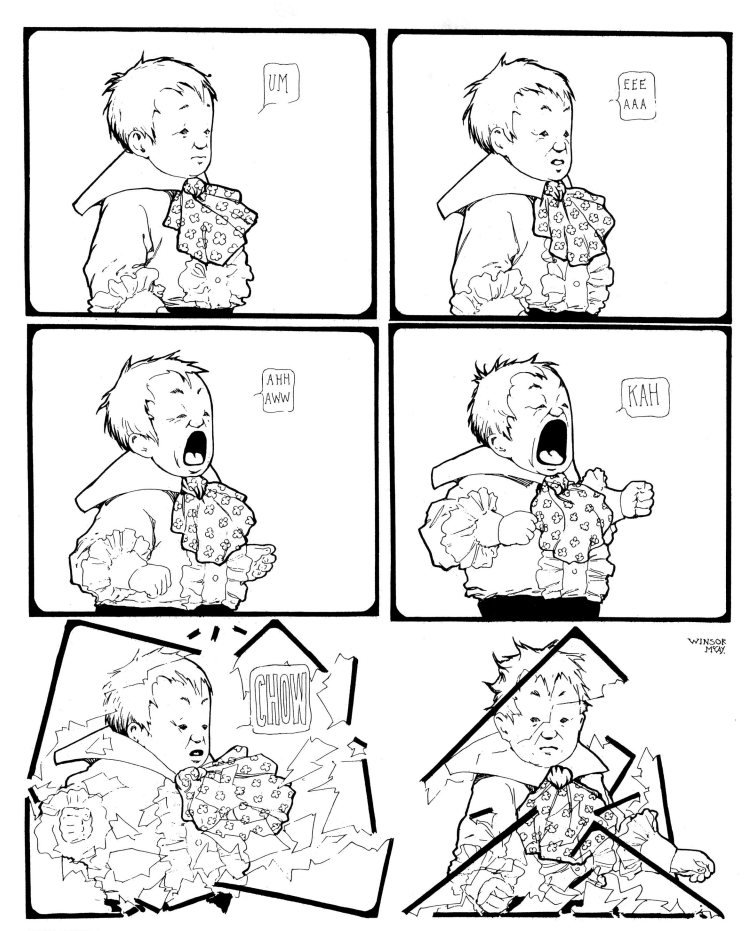

LITTLE SAMMY SNEEZE comic page by Winsor McCay. Sammy shatters the panel borders with a powerful "kah-chow." *September 24, 1905, New York Herald.*
Courtesy of Ray Moniz

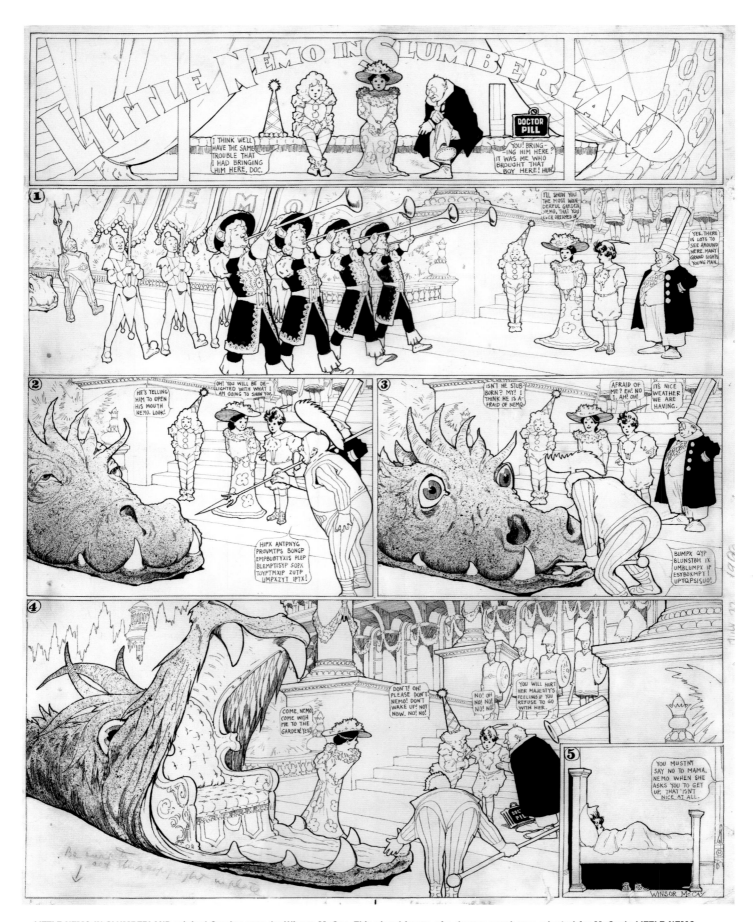

LITTLE NEMO IN SLUMBERLAND original Sunday page by Winsor McCay. This visual image of a dragon coach was adapted for McCay's LITTLE NEMO animated film, which was completed in 1911. *July 22, 1906, New York Herald. Courtesy of Ricardo Martinez*

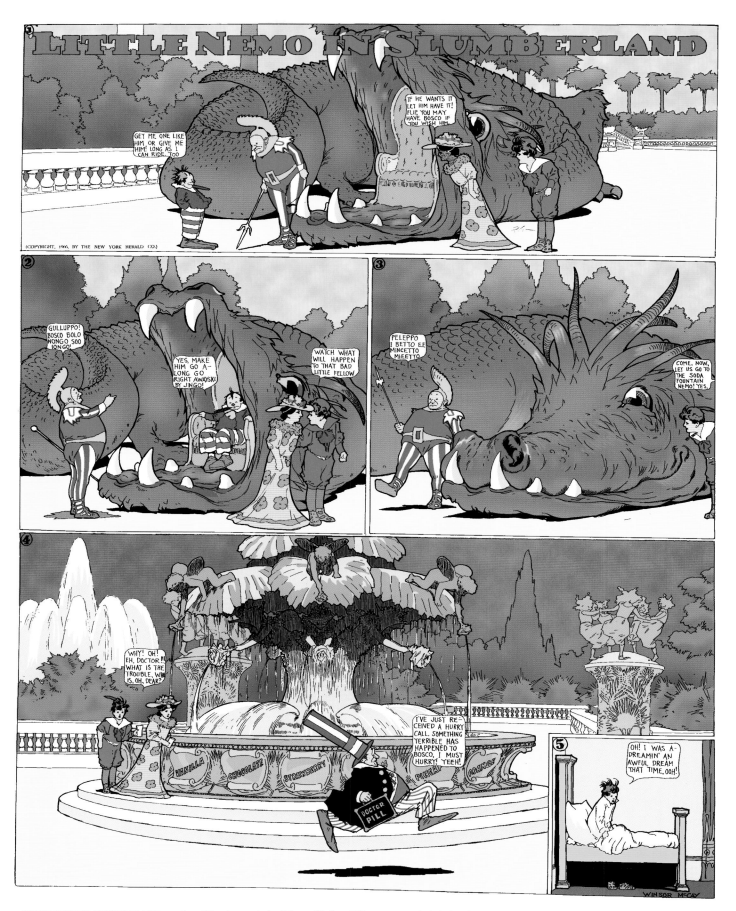

LITTLE NEMO IN SLUMBERLAND recolored Sunday page by Winsor McCay. This page concluded the three-part sequence with the dragon coach.
August 5, 1906, New York Herald. Courtesy of Illustration House and American Color

FANTASY IN THE FUNNIES

The success of Winsor McCay's *Little Nemo in Slumberland* inspired other cartoonists to create comic features that explored the world of childhood dreams and imagination.

NIBSY, THE NEWSBOY, IN FUNNY FAIRYLAND Sunday page by George McManus. Nibsy is hawking Sunday editions of the "Funny Side," the New York World's comic section, in this classic episode of McManus's fantasy creation. May 20, 1906, New York World. Courtesy of Mark Johnson

Wee Willie Winkies World

1 Willie Winkie had a fine walk in the country the other day and met with lots of strange and interesting things. Right in the beginning he saw from afar on the road two giant poplars, like sentinels, with arms held forbiddingly on high. A bit farther on a whole regiment of cherry trees peered curiously down at the little fellow to see how he would manage about passing the poplars. It was rather intimidating, especially as there were some big clouds in the sky, who certainly looked queer. "To the courageous belong the world," thought Willie, and pushed bravely on. So he passed the poplars and even stuck his tongue in his cheek at the clouds.

2 After a while he came to a field on the side of the hill, where the sheaves of wheat resembled a crowd of little, old grannies plodding along to town.

3 Then suddenly he stood before a jolly-looking culvert with a black, open mouth and a mane of grass, which made him look like a lion.

4 Wow! What was that? Willie Winkie stood quite still in amazement. He found himself face to face with an elephant, and out of the tree-tops of the neighboring wood he saw a screaming eagle and a grinning-jawed crocodile arise. But all of a sudden he laughed out aloud! "I was really fooled that time!" The elephant really is nothing but an old tree trunk and the eagle and the crocodile only tops of trees.

5 But the great event of the walk was the old freight locomotive, who stood puffing and groaning on the curve of the railway. "What are you grumbling about?" asked Willie Winkie. "If I were a locomotive I'd run around all day and pull ever so many cars and never complain!" And then he showed the locomotive how to move, waving his arms in a circle and saying "Choo! choo!"

Your Uncle Feininger 1906

6 As the sun went lower Willie went over the fields where the little river flows, and, climbing a hillock, sat down to rest a moment. There he saw a procession of trees, which seemed to be hurrying onward. They were such funny trees, lean and skimpy, and Willie thought they must be anxious to get home before night, so as to have supper. A queer little house stood alone in the middle of the field, squinting sadly at the patched up brickwork down its face. And then Willie Winkie went home on a scamper and dreamt lots of funny things, about which I'll tell you next time, perhaps.

WEE WILLIE WINKIE'S WORLD color proof sheet for the Sunday page by Lyonel Feininger. Between April 29, 1906, and January 20, 1907, this German-American artist, who later became a famous painter, created two short-lived features, THE KIN-DER-KIDS and WEE WILLIE WINKIE'S WORLD, for the Tribune. September 30, 1906, Chicago Sunday Tribune. Courtesy of Prints and Photographs Division, Library of Congress

THE EXPLORIGATOR Sunday page by Harry Grant Dart. A superbly illustrated page that had a brief life in the New York World *from May 3 to August 9, 1908.*
Courtesy of Peter Maresca

DANNY DREAMER Sunday page by Clare Briggs. Danny meets Teddy Roosevelt in an episode of Briggs's first successful creation, which ran from December 1, 1907, to February 23, 1913, in the Tribune. March 1, 1908, Chicago Sunday Tribune. *Courtesy of Mark Johnson*

MR. TWEE DEEDLE Sunday page by Johnny Gruelle. This charming feature followed *LITTLE NEMO* in the Herald *and was written and illustrated by the creator of RAGGEDY ANN AND ANDY.* June 28, 1914, New York Herald. Courtesy of Peter Maresca

the teens

THE THRILL THAT COMES ONCE IN A LIFETIME daily panel by H. T. Webster. The artist looks back nostalgically on the early days of the funnies. © 1923 Press Publishing Company. Courtesy of the San Francisco Academy of Comic Art

THE CARTOONIST MAKES PEOPLE SEE THINGS!

THE CARTOONIST MAKES PEOPLE SEE THINGS—A powerful anti-German cartoon by James Montgomery Flagg. *c. 1918*

THE OPTIMISM AND INNOCENCE OF THE TURN OF THE CENTURY GRADUALLY FADED BETWEEN 1910 AND 1920. A RAPID SUCCESSION OF DRAMATIC EVENTS FORCED AMERICANS TO FACE THE REALITIES OF UNREGULATED INDUSTRIALIZATION, SOCIAL INEQUALITY, AND GLOBAL CONFLICT.

The Triangle Shirtwaist Company fire on March 25, 1911, resulted in the deaths of 146 people, most of whom were immigrant seamstresses, and led directly to long-overdue labor reform laws in New York City. When the *Titanic* went down in the frigid North Atlantic on April 14–15, 1912, and 1,513 souls were lost, questions were raised about the fallibility of the vessel's designers and the much higher survival rate of its upper-class passengers. The first Model T to roll off Henry Ford's new assembly line in Highland Park, Michigan, in 1914 ushered in the modern era of mass production. In April 1914, labor unrest intensified nationwide after the Colorado state militia opened fire on striking miners, who were seeking recognition for the United Mine Workers union. The assassination of Archduke Franz Ferdinand, heir to the Austro-Hungarian throne, in Sarajevo on June 28, 1914, led directly to the disastrous "war to end all wars," which the United States entered almost three years later. D. W. Griffith's epic film *The Birth of a*

Nation opened on March 3, 1915, and sparked controversy for its sympathetic portrayal of the Ku Klux Klan. The shooting of Czar Nicholas II and his family on July 16, 1918, marked the climax of the Russian Revolution and the corresponding growth of the American socialist movement. The influenza epidemic, which started in the spring of 1918 and quickly spread across six continents, claimed more than twenty-one million victims in one year. In 1919, the United States ratified the Eighteenth Amendment, prohibiting "the manufacture, sale, or transportation of intoxicating liquors," and Congress passed the Nineteenth Amendment, stating that the "right of citizens . . . to vote shall not be denied . . . on account of sex." Eight members of the Chicago White Sox, who lost the 1919 World Series to the Cincinnati Reds, were later indicted for accepting bribes from professional gamblers to "throw" the games.

It was a time of disillusionment and uncertainty. Events were unfolding at an unprecedented pace, and Americans had an insatiable desire to keep themselves informed. Business had never been better for newspaper publishers.

In 1913, the number of daily newspapers in America reached a peak of 2,622, with a combined circulation of more than twenty-eight million. After the outbreak of World War I in 1914, metropolitan evening papers experienced a 25 percent increase in sales due to the time difference between Europe and New York; frontline dispatches were quickly added to the night editions, and the large city papers often featured five to eight pages of war news at the end of the day. As the hostilities spread, however, newsprint shortages put a halt to this growth. Paper prices rose by more than one-third between 1914 and 1917, and the total number of weekly, semiweekly, and daily publications in the United States decreased as marginal papers struggled to survive. In the postwar era of consolidation, large newspaper chains swallowed up their competitors.

The number of cities with more than one newspaper also peaked before World War I. Exclusive stories, sensational headlines, popular columnists, and powerful editorials fueled the competition between city papers. But as editors increasingly relied on the wire services—the Associated Press (AP), United Press Associations (UPA), and International News Service (INS)—for their national and international news, uniformity set in. The same reports could be found in any paper that subscribed to these services. Conversely, comics were sold on an exclusive territorial basis, so competing newspapers did not have access to the same strips and panels. Consequently, the funnies became one of the few unique features that a paper could offer to its readers. By the end of the decade, signing up one of the top strips, like *Mutt and Jeff* or *The Gumps,* could make or break a newspaper.

The syndicates that sold the most popular comic features grew in size and stature. The Newspaper Enterprise Association began servicing the Scripps chain in 1902; Joseph Pulitzer launched his Press Publishing Syndicate in 1905; and Moses Koenigsberg, a Hearst executive, established the Newspaper Feature Syndicate in 1913 and King Features two years later. Among the other organizations that joined the ranks of long-established syndicates were the George Matthew Adams Syndicate (1907), the Central Press Association (1910), Associated Newspapers (1912), the Wheeler Syndicate (1913), and the Ledger Syndicate (1918). The Chicago Tribune Syndicate, which had been distributing comics since 1901, became the Chicago Tribune–New York News Syndicate in 1919.

The syndicates gradually transformed the content of the comics. Urban, ethnic, and slapstick humor was complemented by more family-friendly fare. Although many of the creations from the first decade of the century, including *Happy Hooligan, The Katzenjammer Kids,* and *Buster Brown,* continued to be among the most popular strips, new titles released in the

FONTAINE FOX—Self-caricature by the successful syndicated cartoonist. February 11, 1928, The Saturday Evening Post. *Courtesy of the International Museum of Cartoon Art*

second decade provided a broader spectrum of choices for urban, suburban, and rural readers. Syndicate editors were aware of the objections raised by the anti-comics crusaders, but they were more concerned about the entertainment value of their features. Comics designed specifically for children, such as *The Teenie Weenies* (1914), *Uncle Wiggily's Adventures* (1919), and *Peter Rabbit* (1920), were launched, but the reform movement did little to change the industry.

As the syndicates became more powerful, they were able to attract the best talent. Homegrown artists who achieved local renown were quickly snapped up by the big distributors. The top cartoonists began earning huge salaries. They were also free to work where and when they wanted, as well as to entertain better offers from competing syndicates. To protect their investments, the syndicates signed artists to long-term contracts and secured the copyrights to the features they distributed.

Fontaine Fox, who had been producing a weekly panel on suburban life for the *Chicago Post* since 1908, signed a lucrative contract with the Wheeler Syndicate in 1913 to produce *Toonerville Folks.* Fox was grateful for the increased exposure and income that this arrangement made possible. "I feel toward the syndicates as Henry Ford should feel toward the man who first thought of applying the conveyor-belt system to factories and made mass production possible," Fox explained. "In drawing for many scattered newspapers, instead of one published in the city in which I lived, I had to alter the type of work I had been doing. I realized the need of identifying myself in the minds of my following with a series of characters, so as to make each cartoon's appeal as sure in San Francisco as in New York."

Will Lawler, writing in *Editor & Publisher* on February 21, 1914, summed up the role of cartoonists as circulation producers at that time: "The comic artist of today is a power in newspaperdom and in most cases is paid well, and in some handsomely, because his work when good is what attracts readers and readers make circulation. His work not only appears in the paper that pays him his salary but is syndicated in many papers throughout the United States, thus enabling the publisher to not only pay the artists good salaries but also make a profit on their labor."

In 1912, George McManus, creator of *The Newlyweds,* quit the *New York World* to work for the Hearst organization. "Mr. McManus, when approached cautiously the other evening in Louis Martin's Cafe and asked why the change, rubbed his thumb and forefinger together," observed a New York reporter. "Judging from the cracked ice he wears in his scarf, the *Journal* must have offered him a million dollars a picture. George takes his good fortune with characteristic aplomb."

According to *American Magazine,* Bud Fisher was making $78,000 a year drawing *Mutt and Jeff* in 1916; when the earnings from vaudeville lectures, animated cartoons, and novelty products were added, his annual income approached $150,000. Rube Goldberg was also reportedly making $100,000 a year from his combined *New York Mail* salary and movie royalties.

As their salaries rose and syndicates competed for their services, cartoonists became increasingly aware of their importance. Two of the top creators of this period, Rudolph Dirks and Fisher, rebelled against the control of "the Chief," William Randolph Hearst. Both disputes ended up in court.

LITTLE TRAGEDIES OF A NEWSPAPER OFFICE—Jimmy Murphy, creator of **TOOTS AND CASPER**, gets an offer that is too good to be true. December 18, 1919, Editor & Publisher

RUDOLPH DIRKS—Early self-caricature of the legendary pioneer. June 1905, Everybody's Magazine

According to comics legend, Dirks's defection began when he decided to take an unprecedented vacation in 1912. John Dirks recounted his father's story for *Cartoonist PROfiles* in 1974:

He'd been working for 15 years on the *Katzenjammers* and he wanted a rest. When Hearst's *New York Journal,* for whom Dirks was doing the feature, heard of the cartoonist's plans, they told him to work up a year's worth of pages in advance before leaving. Dirks started on this herculean project and continued it for some months but difficulties developed. Dirks felt that his contract had been breached so he and Mrs. Dirks sailed for Europe. The *Journal* sent cables and Rudy did send some pages to them from overseas. At this point, Joseph Pulitzer's *New York World* got into the act and made vigorous efforts to get Dirks to work for them. They landed him and it was agreed between Dirks and Pulitzer that the page would be suspended until the legal aspects of his *Journal* contract were straightened out. The case went to court and became a very well-publicized affair. The final decision decreed that Rudy could draw his original characters, under a different title for the *World,* and that the *Journal* owned the original title and could produce a strip with the original characters.

This often-retold story may not be entirely accurate. Dirks had gone on sabbaticals before and frequently took time off to paint, so the vacation could not have been the only point of contention. The cause for the break was also the result of his relationship with comic editor Rudolph Block. Many artists chafed under Block's harsh supervision, and when the *World* made Dirks a tempting financial offer, he decided to leave.

Hearst hired Harold Knerr to continue *The Katzenjammer Kids* for the *Journal* in 1914, and Dirks went on to produce an identical feature for the *World*. Dirks's version started in June 1914 and was titled *Hans und Fritz* beginning on May 23, 1915— and renamed *The Captain and the Kids* in 1918, after the United States entered the war against Germany. Including rip-offs and reprints, at one time there were five different comic strips starring mischievous twins appearing simultaneously in the nation's newspapers.

On June 13, 1914, *Editor & Publisher* ran an interview with Mama Katzenjammer about the bewildering situation she now found herself in. "I haff been to court, unt der court says Rudolph vas der varder of der kits," explained Mrs. Katzenjammer. "Den dot other mans, he say, 'Nit—I vas der vater of der kits—' unt he makes dem do stunts yust der same as Rudolph."

"Yes it must be a very distressing situation for a lady to be placed in," responded the interviewer. "Sure—it vas makin' me unt Hans unt Fritz unt der Captain vork overtime. But vat can ve do?" she sighed. "Der kits now haff two varders unt two pages efery Sountay."

Both features continued to run opposite each other, in competing newspapers, until United Feature Syndicate finally pulled the plug on *The Captain and the Kids* in 1979. King Features still distributes *The Katzenjammer Kids* to a small list of subscribers, mostly in foreign countries.

The dispute between Fisher and Hearst's Star Company lasted more than six years and culminated at the U.S. Supreme Court. In 1910, Fisher signed a five-year contract with the Star Company, publishers of the *New York American*, to draw the Mutt and Jeff strip for a salary that escalated from $200 to $300 a week. Before this contract expired in 1915, Fisher entered into a three-year agreement with John Wheeler to produce his feature exclusively for a $1,000-per-week guarantee. The Star Company responded by copyrighting the title *Mutt and Jeff* and arranging for other artists to continue the feature.

Three legal actions were then initiated. The Star Company first sought an injunction to prevent the Wheeler Syndicate from using the title and the characters. The other two suits were brought by Wheeler to prevent the Star Company from producing imitations of Fisher's creation. The judge in the original trial, as well as judges in the appeals courts, ruled in favor of Fisher in all three suits. The case ultimately

WELL, WELL! LOOK WHO'S HERE!—Caricature of Bud Fisher and his two stars published at the time he signed his new contract with the Wheeler Syndicate and began his long court battle with Hearst's Star Company. August 7, 1915, Editor & Publisher

reached the U.S. Supreme Court in November 1921. The high court refused to overrule the previous decisions of the lower courts, throwing out the appeal of the Star Company. Fisher was granted exclusive rights to reproduce his characters and legal protection from competitive imitations.

In "Confessions of a Cartoonist," published in *The Saturday Evening Post* on August 4, 1928, Fisher claimed, "I am as proud of this achievement as anything I ever did, since the whole contention of the Hearst legal forces was that they had the rights to the characters because of the popularity they had given them through publication. Our contention was that I had originated the strip on another paper where it was published before it appeared in any Hearst newspaper, and to prove it we produced the copies of the *San Francisco Chronicle* in which the drawings I had copyrighted away back in 1907 were published."

Wheeler, who started all the ruckus back in 1915, summed up Fisher's legacy in his 1961 memoir, *I've Got News for You:* "He probably did more to make the cartoon business for his more cowardly confreres than anyone else who has ever been in it." Fisher had taken on the Chief and won.

Fisher was not the only San Francisco sports cartoonist to make it big in New York. Thomas Aloysius "TAD" Dorgan

INDOOR SPORTS daily panel by TAD Dorgan. TAD, who invented the term "hot dog" (among other expressions), makes a humorous comment on the news of the day. © December 12, 1920s, King Features Syndicate, Inc. Courtesy of the International Museum of Cartoon Art

was working at the *San Francisco Bulletin* when he attracted the attention of Arthur Brisbane, the editor of the *New York Journal,* in 1904. After coming East, TAD became the highest-paid sports cartoonist in the business. He also created three canine characters—Silk Hat Harry, a carousing dog-about-town; Curlock Holmes, a bulldog detective; and Judge Rummy, a monocled mutt—who starred in variously titled strips beginning in 1910. TAD's best-known panels were *Indoor Sports* and *Outdoor Sports,* which lampooned prizefights, ball games, and horse races, as well as office politics and home life. He also did a domestic Sunday-page feature, *For Better or Worse,* during the 1920s.

TAD is remembered today as one of the most prolific contributors to the "slanguage of America." He popularized the lingo of the speakeasies, racetracks, and smoke-filled rooms of his day and penned many of his own unique phrases, including "Yes, we have no bananas," "Half the world are squirrels and the other half are nuts," and "23-skiddoo." His description of the dachshund-like sausages being served at Coney Island in 1913 (which allegedly contained canine ingredients) as "hot dogs" has now become the accepted designation for that popular foodstuff.

Rube Goldberg replaced TAD as the sports cartoonist on the *San Francisco Bulletin* in 1905. Two years later he moved to New York and got a job at the *Evening Mail.* In addition to sports cartoons, Goldberg turned out an endless stream of clever human-interest panels, including such pun-laden classics

as *Foolish Questions, Mike and Ike—They Look Alike,* and *I'm the Guy.* One of these creations, which appeared on an irregular basis, featured *The Inventions of Professor Lucifer G. Butts.* This satirical spoof of technological progress would prove to be the cartoonist's most enduring legacy. A "Rube Goldberg device" has become the dictionary term for a wildly complicated contraption designed to accomplish the simplest of tasks.

A restless genius, Goldberg produced many comic features during his long, prolific career, including *Boob McNutt* (1915), *Bobo Baxter* (1927), *Doc Wright* (1934), *Lala Palooza* (1936), and *Rube Goldberg's Sideshow* (1938). He was also a Pulitzer Prize–winning political cartoonist, an accomplished sculptor, and one of the founders of the National Cartoonists Society.

The graphic jesters of the daily comics, much like the early pioneers of the Sunday funnies, experimented constantly. They alternated titles, casts, and situations at their whim. In addition to TAD and Rube, Gus Mager, T. E. Powers, Maurice Ketten, Harry Hershfield, Jimmy Swinnerton, and Tom McNamara were among the stars of the New York publishing world during these formative years.

The fame and fortune of American cartoonists were also fueled by the growing film industry. Newspaper comics and cinema evolved at the same time and had a close relationship in the early years. Many of the first short, live-action films borrowed sight gags familiar to readers of the funnies. A film based on Opper's *Happy Hooligan* was released by Thomas

MEETING THEDA BARA—*Promotional poster for one of the MUTT AND JEFF animated films produced by Bud Fisher and distributed by William Fox. June 23, 1918. Courtesy of Bruce Hershenson*

Krazy Kat, Silk Hat Harry, Jerry on the Job, and *Little Jimmy* had been produced.

Many of the leading cartoonists also pursued opportunities in the film business. In 1916, Goldberg was commissioned to create an animated newsreel spoof for Pathé, *The Boob Weekly,* and he reportedly earned $75,000 for his efforts. After leaving the Hearst organization, Fisher teamed up with the Barré-Bowers studio and produced a series of four-minute *Mutt and Jeff* cartoons in 1916. A year later, when he returned from military service, he set up his own operation, Bud Fisher Films Corporation, and released the studio's first series of fifteen cartoons on June 9, 1917. Fisher signed a lucrative deal with Fox to distribute his films, and fifty-two *Mutt and Jeff* cartoons were made every year until 1922. Although Fisher claimed in interviews that he personally drew all of his cartoons, he was rarely seen around the studio.

Animated adaptations of comic strip creations continued to be produced throughout the silent-film era, but Felix the Cat and Mickey Mouse were to become the major cartoon movie stars during the next two decades. These film personalities also appeared in their own newspaper comic strips.

Stories about the top-earning cartoonists, which appeared regularly in newspapers and magazines, inspired the next generation of creators. Fledgling artists, who dreamed of becoming the next Bud Fisher or Rube Goldberg, mailed in their hard-earned dollars (usually about $25 for twenty-five lessons) to the numerous cartoon correspondence schools that were established during the decade. The three most popular were the C. N. Landon, W. L. Evans, and Federal programs. Gene Byrnes (*Reg'lar Fellers*), Merrill Blosser (*Freckles and His Friends*), Edwina Dumm (*Cap Stubbs and Tippie*), Martin Branner (*Winnie Winkle*), Roy Crane (*Wash Tubbs*), and Milton Caniff (*Terry and the Pirates*) were all Landon graduates. Chester Gould (*Dick Tracy*) and Elzie Crisler Segar (*Popeye*) provided testimonials in advertisements for the W. L. Evans course as former students. Clare Briggs, Fontaine Fox, Frank King, Winsor McCay, and Sidney Smith were among the many established luminaries who served on the advisory board of the Federal School.

As the funnies were more widely distributed, new types of features began to appear. George McManus's *Bringing Up Father,* which officially began on January 2, 1913, represented an important transition in the thematic evolution of the comics. It featured ethnic caricatures, a repetitive gag formula, and an urban setting—common characteristics of strips from the first decade. But it also explored topics that were echoed in many

Edison's company in 1900, soon followed by adaptations of *Foxy Grandpa* (1902) and *The Katzenjammer Kids* (1903). Richard F. Outcault signed a contract with his old employer, Edison, for a series of eight *Buster Brown* films in 1903. One of the most notable productions of this period was Edwin S. Porter's 1906 *Dream of the Rarebit Fiend,* inspired by Winsor McCay's strip in the *New York Evening Telegram.* These were all live-action productions, however, and it was not until McCay's 1911 film of *Little Nemo in Slumberland* that the arduous task of hand-drawn animation of comic strip characters was attempted.

After McCay showed the way, animated cartoons based on popular comic strips proliferated. Emile Cohl produced thirteen *Newlywed* films between 1913 and 1914. Hearst founded the International Film Service in 1915, and by the following year, cartoons starring his funny-paper stars were screened with the Hearst Vitagraph Newsreel. By the time the studio closed in July 1918, animated adaptations of *Happy Hooligan, The Katzenjammer Kids, Bringing Up Father,* features from the second wave of creations: family relationships and a desperate striving for social status and financial success. At the peak of its popularity, *Bringing Up Father* claimed eighty million readers in five hundred newspapers from forty-six countries and was translated into sixteen languages. McManus earned an estimated $12 million in the forty years he produced the strip.

Like many of his contemporaries, McManus experimented with numerous comic features before he hit the jackpot with his most well-known creation. Among the many short-lived titles he introduced while at the *New York World* were *Panhandle Pete* (1904), *Nibsy, the Newsboy, in Funny Fairyland* (1906), and *Spareribs and Gravy* (1912). *The Newlyweds* (1904) was the most successful feature he produced for Pulitzer's paper. Baby Snookums, who arrived in the strip on May 19, 1907, eventually stole the spotlight from the young lovebirds.

When Hearst hired him in 1912, McManus continued *The Newlyweds* under a new title, *Their Only Child,* and introduced a string of other generic family features. It was out of this revolving cycle of domestic comedies that his immortal bickering couple, Maggie and Jiggs, emerged.

The genesis of *Bringing Up Father* began in 1895 when McManus attended a performance of *The Rising Generation.* This stage production featured a nightly card game in which a former Irish laborer, played by Billy Barry, complained to his friends. He had become rich overnight and now lived on Fifth Avenue with his wife and daughter. They hoped to be accepted by their new upper-class neighbors and were mortified by his uncouth behavior. He had no desire to fit in and schemed to thwart the family's efforts to civilize him by sneaking off to play poker. McManus later adapted this plot to his new feature and milked the scenario in endlessly clever ways.

In the strip, Jiggs's wife, Maggie, and their haughty daughter, Nora, tried without success to turn him into a respectable social climber. Much to their chagrin, Jiggs's sole ambition in life was to rejoin his old working-class cronies for a plate of corned beef and cabbage and a game of cards at Dinty Moore's tavern. He would go to incredible lengths— crawling out windows, walking on ledges, hanging on wires— to achieve his goal.

McManus illustrated the costumes, interiors, and scenery in *Bringing Up Father* with a stylishly elegant line that suggested the influence of Art Deco. He was also adept at drawing hilariously caricatured secondary characters, violently hurled crockery, and voluptuously proportioned females. Zeke Zekley was McManus's assistant beginning in the mid-1930s and had a hand in the artwork for the next two decades.

In the 1920s and 1930s, McManus explored continuing plotlines that went beyond the daily domestic doings that characterized the formative years of the feature. Maggie and

GEORGE MCMANUS—Self-caricature for an article, "Jiggs, The Globe Trotter." *May 1926, World Traveler magazine. Courtesy of the International Museum of Cartoon Art*

Jiggs sailed off on a European tour in 1920, returned to a life of poverty after going bust in Hollywood in 1923, traveled to Japan in 1927, and, from December 1939 to July 1940, made an epic journey across the United States.

McManus, who bore a striking resemblance to his main character, told *Collier's* magazine in 1952, "I am not Jiggs. Maggie is not my wife. I have no daughter." "Yet I think I may have become Jiggs," he added. "Or, if you like, Jiggs may have become me. They say if you live long enough with a person you come to look and act as he does, and Jiggs and I have lived together for 40 years—through 85,000 drawings of the comic strip *Bringing Up Father*." McManus passed away two years later, but Jiggs survived on the funnies pages for another four decades.

The success of *Bringing Up Father* encouraged other cartoonists and their distributors to explore the fertile field of domestic comedy. They discovered that the ethnic slang, racial stereotypes, and urban settings of the early Sunday funnies did not play as well to Middle America. The syndicates increasingly regarded their comics as marketable commodities and consciously developed them to appeal to the largest demographic.

THE GUMPS—*The main cast of Sidney Smith's popular comic strip, from a Chicago Tribune Syndicate advertisement. February 22, 1919, Editor & Publisher*

Agent (1914), Harry Tuthill's *The Bungle Family* (1918), and Jimmy Murphy's *Toots and Casper* (1918) were among the early family-oriented strips that incorporated one or more of these thematic elements. Sidney Smith's *The Gumps* (1917) was the quintessential creation in the emerging genre.

Joseph Medill Patterson, copublisher of the *Chicago Tribune*, had the idea to create a comic strip that would realistically reflect American family life, and he recruited one of the *Tribune*'s cartoonists, Sidney Smith, to produce it. The name that the Captain (as Patterson was called) chose for the new strip, *The Gumps*, which debuted on February 12, 1917, was derived from a Patterson family term used to describe pompous blowhards.

Andy Gump, the unattractive star of Smith's feature, had a long nose and no chin. His wife, Minerva, was a plain woman, and his son, Chester, was well-mannered and energetic. Andy's wealthy Uncle Bim rounded out the cast. Minerva was the brains of the family, and when the helpless Andy found himself in a jam, he would plead for his wife's assistance with a desperate cry of "Oh Min!"

The Gumps was a "talky" strip. Andy's long-winded lectures on the cost of living, taxes, and other concerns filled his speech balloons to the bursting point, and the family discussions would go on for days. In the first few years, the story lines involved fairly conventional domestic dilemmas, such as Min's overspending, Andy's New Year's Eve hangover, and predictable mother-in-law problems. Beginning in 1920, Smith's plots became more adventurous as the Gumps found themselves entwined in Bim's marital romance, Andy's political campaign, and Chester's treasure hunt. *The Gumps* evolved into what could be considered the first "soap opera strip." It was not the first feature to use continuing stories, but it was certainly the most successful one to employ the cliffhanger approach.

Patterson's instincts had been correct. The public loved *The Gumps*. The Captain seemed to sense what the average American comic strip reader wanted and knew how to give it to them. Patterson would play a pivotal role in guiding the funnies business during the next two decades.

Kid strips, which had always been popular, fit nicely into the syndicates' new marketing strategy. Wholesome humor, youthful ambition, and innocent shenanigans were just what newspaper editors and readers were looking for, and features starring juvenile protagonists proliferated. Among the many notable debuts during the decade were *Us Boys* (1912) by Tom McNamara, *Jerry on the Job* (1913) by Walter Hoban, *Bobby Make-Believe* (1915) by Frank King, *Freckles and His Friends* (1915) by Merrill Blosser, *Just Boy* (1916) by A. C. Fera, *Cap Stubbs and Tippie* (1918) by Edwina Dumm, and *Harold Teen* (1919) by Carl Ed.

Most of the new family strips featured a combination of soon-to-be predictable character types. There was often a pretty girl, a bumbling father, an all-knowing mother, a precocious younger sibling, and a troublemaking pet. The parents dreamed of financial success and were acutely aware of their social status, while the kids pursued more frivolous activities. Story lines revolved around get-rich-quick schemes, employment opportunities, and other money-related issues.

Charles Wellington's *Pa's Son in Law* (1911), Cliff Sterrett's *Polly and Her Pals* (1912), Harry Hershfield's *Abie the*

Another emerging genre was the "slice-of-life" panel. John McCutcheon, who was the political cartoonist for the *Chicago Tribune* from 1903 to 1946, started the trend with occasional drawings on domestic doings in rural America. Clare Briggs, who knew McCutcheon from his years on the *Tribune* between 1907 and 1914, was influenced by his mentor and developed a panel for the *New York Tribune* in 1914 that used a rotating series of titles. *The Days of Real Sport, When a Feller Needs a Friend,* and *Ain't It a Grand and Glorious Feeling?* were among the many headings for Briggs's cartoons, which evoked nostalgia for a simpler time.

H. T. Webster, often called the "Mark Twain of the Comics," took a similar path, although his subjects were more oriented toward the suburban experience. Among Webster's most memorable titles were *The Thrill That Comes Once in a Lifetime, Life's Darkest Moments,* and *The Timid Soul,* starring Caspar Milquetoast. Fontaine Fox's *Toonerville Folks* (1908) and Clare Dwiggins's *School Days* (1909) were also outstanding newspaper panel cartoons that started during this period and focused on everyday life.

One creation that did not fit neatly into any of these categories was George Herriman's *Krazy Kat.* It has always been regarded by art critics and intellectuals as something of an anomaly on the funnies pages.

"A person with a fancy for the comic section is ordinarily prone to be ashamed of it," wrote Summerfield Baldwin in the June 1917 issue of *Cartoons* magazine. "The shame and the excuses are right and natural, save in this single instance. For to follow the adventures of Mr. Herriman's fantastic animals is a delight which no one should underestimate or fail to enjoy."

Herriman's masterpiece was based on a deceptively simple set of role reversals among his main trio of performers. Instead of chasing the mouse, Krazy Kat adores Ignatz. Instead of fleeing in fear from the cat, Ignatz attacks the lovesick feline with a brick. Instead of bullying the cat, Officer Pupp protects Krazy from Ignatz. Or, as the poet e. e. cummings put it in the introduction to a *Krazy Kat* collection published in 1946, "Dog hates mouse and worships 'cat,' mouse despises 'cat' and hates dog, 'cat' hates no one and loves mouse."

It started inauspiciously in Herriman's *The Dingbat Family* during the summer of 1910. The cat who was to become Krazy first appeared as the Dingbats' pet on June 24, and on July 10 an unnamed mouse hurled a missile at the cat's skull in the lower portion of the strip. This was the beginning of a historic game of cat and mouse. Over the course of the next month, Herriman changed the name of his feature to *The Family Upstairs* and created a separate world for the cat and mouse in panels below the main action. This strip-beneath-a-strip ran regularly until October 28, 1913, when it finally became an independent daily feature. The first full-page *Krazy Kat* appeared

GEORGE HERRIMAN—Self-portrait of the shy cartoonist. October 21, 1922, Judge magazine

in black-and-white on April 23, 1916, in the Hearst weekly *City Life* section. Except for a brief experiment with color, between January 7 and March 11, 1922, Herriman's page appeared only in black-and-white until it began running as a color tabloid page in 1935.

Hearst was Herriman's biggest fan. According to comic legend, the Chief once demanded that Herriman be given a raise. Herriman sent the money back, modestly claiming that he did not deserve extra compensation because it took so little time to produce the strip. Although *Krazy Kat* was never a financial success, Herriman was able to live comfortably—his salary was reported as $750 a week during the Depression— and he had a guaranteed lifetime contract with King Features. When Herriman died in 1944, *Krazy Kat* was appearing in only thirty-five newspapers.

The unpretentiousness of Herriman's creation left it wide open to interpretation. Many saw it as an allegory for unrequited love. Others read it is a mythic struggle between good and evil. In more recent years, some scholars have argued that because Herriman was a mulatto and Krazy Kat is black, the strip represents the artist's confusion about his own racial identity.

Herriman's message was made even more inscrutable by the fact that he never identified Krazy Kat's gender. After considering the question, Herriman explained, "I realized Krazy was something of a sprite, an elf. They have no sex. So that Kat can't be a he or a she."

The brick that Ignatz perpetually bounced off Krazy's bean has also been described symbolically. In *America's Great Comic-Strip Artists*, Richard Marschall explained, "The brick in Coconino was like the apple in Eden, an agent of both disruptive and bonding impulses."

The setting for the strip was equally significant. In *Krazy Kat: The Comic Art of George Herriman*, the authors claimed, "There can be no true understanding of George Herriman, and only a limited understanding of *Krazy Kat*, without some knowledge of the Navajo country, which includes the settlement of Kayenta as well as Monument Valley and straddles Arizona and Utah." Herriman spent many of the happiest days of his life in this part of the United States, and the cacti, mesas, buttes, and desert sky became the distinguishing characteristics of Krazy Kat's Coconino County. The constantly changing backgrounds of Herriman's pages mirrored the shifting light patterns he observed in the southwestern landscape.

Herriman was dedicated to his craft and became a master of the art form. His scratchy scribblings were remarkably expressive, and the characters moved with quirky energy, coming alive on the page. He loved to play with lines and shapes, colors and sounds, and the scenery was evocative and surreal. A graphic poet of words and images, Herriman created scripts that read like fables, and the dialogue had a syncopated rhythm that was laced with street slang, foreign accents, and clever phrasing. Each episode was an experi-

ment in composition; in later years, Herriman introduced a simpler design with customized, hand-drawn logos and bold, abstract layouts.

In *The Seven Lively Arts*, published in 1924, Gilbert Seldes declared, "*Krazy Kat*, the daily comic strip of George Herriman is, to me, the most amusing and fantastic and satisfactory work of art produced in America to-day."

"Such is the work which America can pride itself on having produced," Seldes concluded in his famous essay. "It is rich with something we have too little of—fantasy. It is wise with pitying irony; it has delicacy, sensitiveness, and an unearthly beauty. The strange, unnerving, distorted trees, the language inhuman, un-animal, the events so logical, so wild, are all magic carpets and faery foam—all charged with unreality. Through them wanders Krazy, the most foolish of creatures, a gentle monster of our new mythology."

Herriman responded to Seldes in a letter that "now I've got an inflated 'mouse'—a 'kop' busting with Ego—and a 'kat' gone clean Kookoo—on my hands. . . . Gilbert being just weaklings guess they can't hold their good fortune—and I don't blame them—you said some nice things—werra—werra nice things—"

An extremely modest man, Herriman was uncomfortable with praise. He would never have accepted his place as the most universally revered cartoonist of all time. In his mind he was just drawing a comic strip about a cat, a mouse, and a dog.

KRAZY KAT, OFFICER PUPP, AND IGNATZ—*Original hand-colored postcard that Herriman drew for a friend in the 1930s.* Courtesy of Jack Gilbert

bud fisher

THE FIRST MILLIONAIRE CARTOONIST was a colorful character who traveled with Pancho Villa in Mexico, married Countess de Beaumont on a luxury liner bound for Europe, bred racehorses, and mingled in high society. He is credited with starting the first successful daily comic strip and was one of the few artists to establish ownership of his creation, in an era when syndicates controlled the rights to all of the features.

Harry Conway "Bud" Fisher was born in Chicago on April 3, 1885. He dropped out of the University of Chicago after three months and was hired as a sports cartoonist for the *San Francisco Chronicle* in 1905. It was here that he introduced his horse-racing strip, *A. Mutt,* which began running daily on November 15, 1907. Less than a month later, Fisher switched to Hearst's *San Francisco Examiner,* and then he joined the staff of the *New York American* in 1909.

Shortly before his contract with Hearst expired in 1915, he signed a lucrative deal with the Wheeler Syndicate. A prolonged court battle over the ownership of the strip ensued, and the case was not resolved until 1921. Fisher, who emerged victorious, reaped the profits from *Mutt and Jeff* newspaper sales as well as animated cartoons, stage shows, and licensed products based on the characters, and he was reportedly earning an annual salary approaching $250,000 in the early 1920s.

John Wheeler, who first met Fisher in 1913, described him as "a dapper, cocky little guy." He was also an egotistical showman who cultivated his image as a celebrity. He was often photographed in his Rolls-Royce, and he hobnobbed with celebrities and showgirls. A hard-drinking playboy, he squandered his fortune on bad investments and two failed marriages.

By the 1920s, Fisher was spending less and less time at his drawing board. He hired Ed Mack, the artist who briefly did a competing version of his strip for Hearst in 1915, as his assistant. After Mack's death in 1932, Al Smith continued to produce *Mutt and Jeff,* with only minimal input from his boss.

Tragically, Fisher spent his final years alone and forgotten. In the early 1950s, Rube Goldberg, George McManus, and Bob Dunn visited the aging cartoonist at his Park Avenue apartment. "It was like stepping back into the year 1925," remembered Dunn. "If the rest of the apartment looked shabby genteel, the bedroom looked like the corner of Skid Row and Tobacco Road. No carpeting or rug. Cigarette butts all over the parquet floor.

BUD FISHER—This caricature of the famous cartoonist shows him arriving at Saratoga carrying trophies from his victories in other horse races. c. 1920s

"I couldn't believe what we were seeing," he added. "The big bed had no sheet on it. Just the bare mattress. And two beaten up old pillows without pillowcases. Propped up on an elbow was the legendary creator of *Mutt and Jeff.* He hadn't shaved in at least a week."

Fisher tried to keep up professional appearances by complaining to his fellow cartoonists about getting behind with his deadlines, but they all knew he had not drawn the strip for many years. He died of cancer not long after this visit, on September 7, 1954, at the age of sixty-nine. John Wheeler summed up Fisher's demise in his 1961 autobiography, *I've Got News for You:* "He squandered his own life and was a very unhappy man." It was a tragic end for a talented artist who fought courageously for his creative independence and achieved the highest levels of success in his chosen field.

MUTT AND JEFF daily strip by Bud Fisher. Mutt takes advantage of Jeff in a game of billiards in this early example of Fisher's strip.
© 1910 H. C. Fisher. Courtesy of Jim Scancarelli

MUTT AND JEFF daily strip by Bud Fisher. Jeff is in Turkey getting the Istan-bull from three street vendors. © 1913 H. C. Fisher. Courtesy of Bruce Hamilton

MUTT AND JEFF daily strip by Bud Fisher. The boys get orders from a Prussian prince in this episode from World War I. © 1915 H. C. Fisher. Courtesy of Bruce Hamilton

MUTT AND JEFF daily strip by Bud Fisher. The famous cartoonist can't please all of his readers. © 1919 H. C. Fisher. Courtesy of Craig Yoe

MUTT AND JEFF daily strip by Bud Fisher. Although Fisher is pictured at the drawing board in panel no. 4, the strip was drawn by Ed Mack throughout the 1920s. © July 30, 1923, H. C. Fisher. Courtesy of the Cartoon Art Museum, San Francisco

MUTT AND JEFF daily strip by Bud Fisher. Mutt and Jeff shave and pose as child actors in Hollywood. © 1925 H. C. Fisher. Courtesy of Bruce Hamilton

MUTT AND JEFF daily strip by Bud Fisher. The boys try to sign up King Alfonso of Spain for their vaudeville act. © 1926 H. C. Fisher. Courtesy of Bruce Hamilton

MUTT AND JEFF daily strip by Bud Fisher. A delegation of Jeffs nominates Jeff for president. On the previous day, the Mutt convention selected Mutt as its candidate. © July 26, 1932, H. C. Fisher. Courtesy of Bruce Hamilton

MUTT AND JEFF original hand-colored Sunday page by Bud Fisher. Jeff asks his creator for a special favor. © *November 25, 1928, H. C. Fisher. Courtesy of Jack Gilbert and the Barnum Museum*

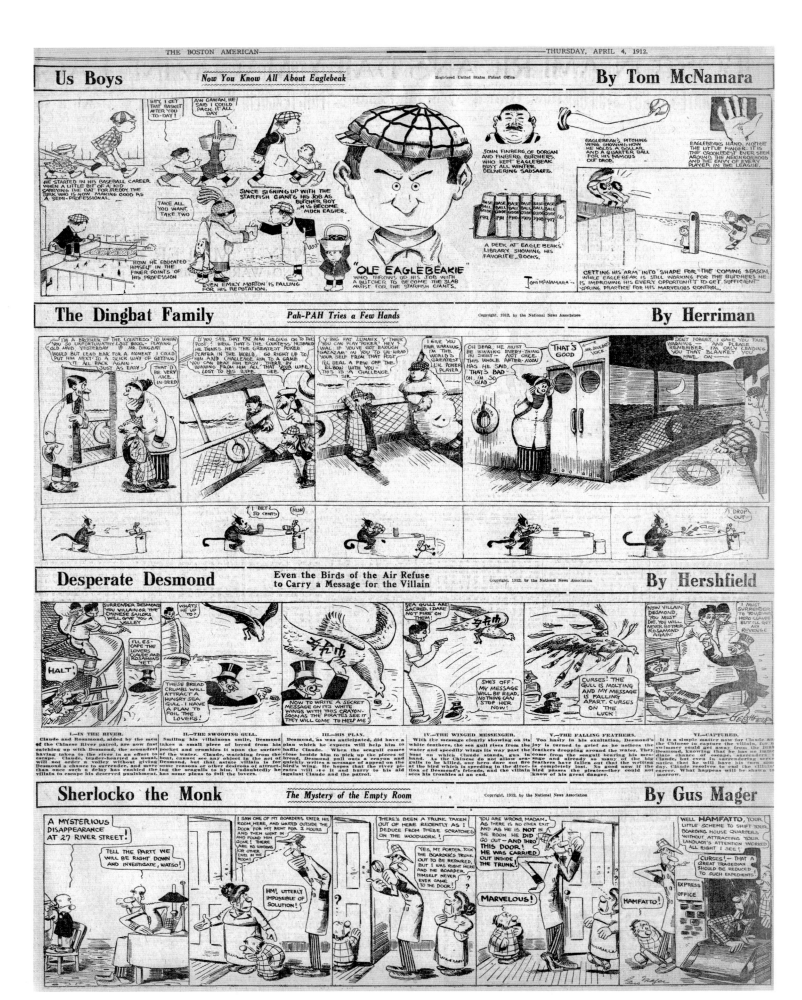

COMICS PAGE—This lineup from the Hearst-owned *Boston American* is an early example of daily strips being grouped together on the same page.
April 4, 1912. Courtesy of Mark Johnson

THE HALL ROOM BOYS comic feature by Harold Arthur McGill. This strip, which revolved around the exploits of two social pretenders, Percy and Ferdie, first appeared during the week in the New York American in 1904, before a Sunday feature was introduced in 1916 in the New York Herald. *May 30, 1909.*
Courtesy of Richard Marschall

DAILY DOSE In the first decade of the century, newspapers published comics during the week on an irregular basis. Features would typically appear two to four days a week on the editorial and sports pages or buried amid the classified ads in the back of the afternoon editions. Between 1910 and 1915, comics that ran six days a week became more common. The Hearst papers were among the first to group these features together on the same page. Most of the daily strips were designed to appeal to city workers commuting back and forth to their jobs, so their content dealt mostly with urban and suburban themes. A sampling of some of these early creations is featured here and on the following pages.

THE OUTBURSTS OF EVERETT TRUE comic feature by A. D. Condo. One of the earliest weekday features syndicated by the Newspaper Enterprise Association, beginning on July 22, 1905, Condo's vertical-format strip starred a cranky middle-aged man with an explosive temper. *c. 1920, NEA Service. Courtesy of the Art Wood Collection of Cartoon and Caricature, Prints and Photographs Division, Library of Congress*

JERRY ON THE JOB daily strip by Walter Hoban. This long-running feature debuted in the *New York Journal* on *December 29, 1913*. After trying a variety of occupations, Jerry Flannigan was hired in 1915 by a railroad. The "flop" in the final panel was a signature Hoban visual device. *Courtesy of Jim Scancarelli*

AUTO OTTO daily strip by Gene Ahearn. The artist drew a strip about a devoted car enthusiast for the Newspaper Enterprise Association before creating his most successful feature, *OUR BOARDING HOUSE*, in 1921. *Courtesy of the International Museum of Cartoon Art*

FRECKLES AND HIS FRIENDS daily strip by Merrill Blosser. A graduate of the Landon School, Blosser launched his popular kid strip on September 20, 1915. Freckles grew from a ten-year-old to a teenager and outlived his creator, ending his comic career in 1973. *Courtesy of the International Museum of Cartoon Art*

HAROLD TEEN daily strip by Carl Ed. Captain Joseph Medill Patterson bought this feature for the Tribune Syndicate in 1919. Harold reached the peak of his popularity during the Roaring Twenties and continued to appear until 1959. *Courtesy of Jim Scancarelli*

DESPERATE DESMOND daily strip. *1911. Courtesy of Gary Ernest Smith*

DESPERATE DESMOND portrait by Harry Hershfield.
Courtesy of Rob Stolzer

HARRY HERSHFIELD This pioneer of daily comics launched two important features in the *New York Evening Journal* during the teens. *Desperate Desmond* (above), which debuted in 1910, was a continuity strip that burlesqued melodramas, similar to Charles W. Kahles's earlier creation, *Hairbreadth Harry*. *Abie the Agent* (right), which began in 1914, starred a middle-class Jewish businessman and ran, off and on, until 1940.

ABIE THE AGENT daily strip. *1917. Courtesy of Sandy Schechter*

TAD DORGAN Variously titled *Judge Rummy's Court, Old Judge Rumhauser,* and *Silk Hat Harry's Divorce Suit,* Thomas Aloysius Dorgan's longest-running feature, which started around 1910 in the *New York Evening Journal,* featured a cast of carousing canines. TAD also produced a daily panel, which ran in the 1910s and 1920s in the *Evening Journal.* It alternated between scenes of professional and amateur sporting events, such as baseball, boxing, and golf, and situations set in the workplace or at home.

JUDGE RUMMY—Panel and daily strips by TAD Dorgan. *1910s. Courtesy of the International Museum of Cartoon Art (top), Rob Stolzer (middle), and Illustration House (bottom)*

OUTDOOR SPORTS daily panel by TAD Dorgan. 1920s. Courtesy of the International Museum of Cartoon Art

INDOOR SPORTS daily panel by TAD Dorgan. 1920s. Courtesy of the San Francisco Academy of Comic Art

THE INVENTIONS OF PROFESSOR LUCIFER G. BUTTS *daily panel by Rube Goldberg.* c. 1910s. Courtesy of George George

RUBE GOLDBERG

The original "Rube Goldberg device" was invented by Professor Lucifer G. Butts (above), who first appeared about 1914. *I'm the Guy, Mike and Ike—They Look Alike,* and *Foolish Questions* were among the many panels Goldberg produced for the *New York Evening Mail* from 1907 to 1915, after which his work was distributed by the McNaught Syndicate.

THE INVENTIONS OF PROFESSOR LUCIFER G. BUTTS *daily panel by Rube Goldberg.* c. 1910s. Courtesy of the Art Wood Collection of Cartoon and Caricature, Prints and Photographs Division, Library of Congress

THE WEEKLY MEETING OF THE TUESDAY'S LADIES CLUB and MIKE AND IKE—THEY LOOK ALIKE *daily panel (with two titles running side by side) by Rube Goldberg.* c. 1910s. Courtesy of the Art Wood Collection of Cartoon and Caricature, Prints and Photographs Division, Library of Congress

BOOB MCNUTT Sunday page by Rube Goldberg. The longest-running comic strip feature by Goldberg debuted in the New York Evening Mail *on May 15, 1915, and was later distributed, until 1934, by the McNaught Syndicate. December 15, 1918, Boston Sunday Advertiser and American. Courtesy of Mark Johnson*

MONK FAMILY daily strips by Gus Mager. c. 1910s. Courtesy of Illustration
House (top left), Rob Stolzer (top right), and Editor & Publisher (bottom)

GUS MAGER After he was hired by Hearst
in 1904, this self-taught artist displayed an affinity
for drawing simians with monikers that defined
their personalities, such as Tightwaddo the Monk,
Coldfeeto the Monk, and Groucho the Monk. Mager,
who was credited with giving the Marx Brothers
their names, eventually came up with Sherlocko the
Monk, a human sleuth who starred in a Sunday-
page feature from 1910 to 1913. After that, Sherlocko
became Hawkshaw the Detective and appeared in
various forms until the late 1940s.

Sherlocko the Monk

By Gus Mager
Copyright, 1912, National News Association.

The Adventure of the Vanishing Fish.

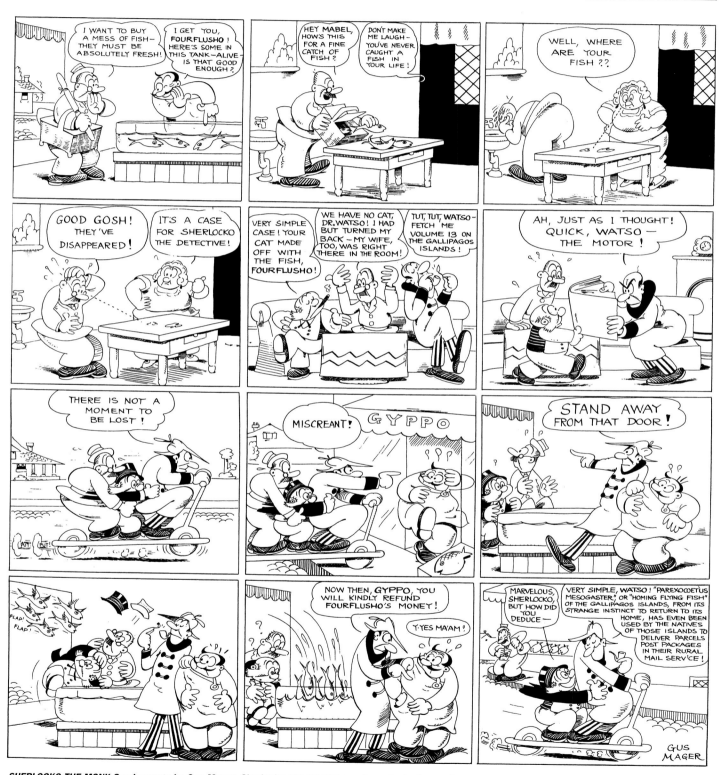

SHERLOCKO THE MONK Sunday page by Gus Mager. Sherlocko and Dr. Watso solve a typically mundane mystery.
© 1912 National News Association. Courtesy of Russ Cochran

george herriman

THE
JOE WELCH

HOW'S THE
GORDON
GAWG ?

OH, YOU
LOWSE

"ORTICHOKE JOE"

GEORGE HERRIMAN—Caricature by TAD Dorgan

EARLY IN HIS CAREER, the graphic poet of the comics pages enjoyed the playful camaraderie of TAD Dorgan, Harry Hershfield, Gus Mager, and Tom McNamara in the art department of the *New York Journal* and was often seen out on the town after hours. In his later years, he lived reclusively with his daughter, thirteen stray cats, and five Scottie dogs in the hills of Hollywood. He always wore a hat, even while working at his drawing board, and was extremely modest about his artistic abilities.

George Joseph Herriman was born in New Orleans on August 22, 1880. During his lifetime, Herriman kept his background a secret. His parents were designated as "mulattos" on federal census records, and George's birth certificate listed him as "colored," although on his 1944 death certificate he is identified as "Caucasian." Herriman reportedly once told a close associate that he was "Creole" and had kinky hair because he thought he had some "Negro blood."

In light of this information, a number of contemporary writers have categorized him as "African American" and attempted to analyze his work in the context of his race. Thomas Inge, in a 1996 article, "Was Krazy Kat Black?" observed, "If Herriman thought he had 'Negro blood,' it did not seem to have much direct influence on his early art.

"People should be allowed to create their own identities beyond the traditional identifications of race and ethnicity," argued Inge. "Perhaps we should allow George Herriman that liberty."

Herriman's family moved to Los Angeles in the mid-1880s, and he grew up in a multiethnic community. At the age of

twenty, like many of his contemporaries, he hopped an eastbound freight train to see if he could break into the New York cartoon market. After selling single-panel drawings to *Judge* magazine, as well as numerous one-shot comic features to some of the fledgling syndicates, Herriman landed his first regular job as a sports cartoonist on William Randolph Hearst's *New York American* in the spring of 1904.

By August 1906, he was back in Los Angeles working for Hearst's *Los Angeles Examiner.* While at that paper, Herriman tried out more short-lived strip ideas, including *Mr. Proones the Plunger* (December 10, 1907), *Baron Mooch* (November 1, 1909), *Mary's Home from College* (December 20, 1909), and *Gooseberry Sprig* (December 23, 1909), in addition to producing daily political and sports cartoons.

Herriman was summoned back to New York, where he launched his first successful strip, *The Dingbat Family,* on June 20, 1910. It was in the panels of this feature that his famous cat and mouse were introduced. *Krazy Kat* debuted as an independent daily strip on October 28, 1913, and as a full-page feature on April 23, 1916.

Herriman also continued to experiment with other comic creations, all of which starred human characters. A mooching aristocrat, who resembled Bud Fisher's Mutt, was the star of *Baron Bean,* a daily strip that ran from January 5, 1916, to January 22, 1919. *Now Listen Mabel* (April 23 to December 18, 1919) revolved around a doomed romantic courtship, and *Us Husbands* (January 16 to December 18, 1926) featured standard domestic comedy. *Stumble Inn,* which was a daily strip from October 30, 1922, to May 12, 1923, and a color Sunday page from December 9, 1922, to January 9, 1926, took place in a boardinghouse. Herriman became the artist on the King Features gag panel *Embarrassing Moments* on April 28, 1928; introduced a regular character, Bernie Burns; and continued it until December 3, 1932. From that date until his death on April 25, 1944, he concentrated exclusively on *Krazy Kat.*

Herriman moved to California in 1922 and returned to New York only once, embarking on a cross-country trip with Tom McNamara in 1924. He lost his wife in 1934 and his first daughter five years later, and he lived with his second daughter at his Spanish-style mansion in Hollywood. He managed to continue working, in spite of arthritis and migraine headaches, right up until he died.

At the funeral, his old cartoonist friend Harry Hershfield said, "If ever there was a saint on earth, it was George Herriman." His ashes were scattered in his beloved Monument Valley.

MAJOR OZONE'S FRESH AIR CRUSADE Sunday half-page by George Herriman. One of Herriman's early syndicated features. *May 6, 1906, World Color Printing Company.*
Courtesy of Bill Blackbeard

BARON MOOCH daily strip by George Herriman. The artist's first "dingbat" was Gooseberry Sprig, who can be seen in the far-right-hand corner of this short-lived strip. *December 14, 1909, Los Angeles Examiner. Courtesy of Art Wood*

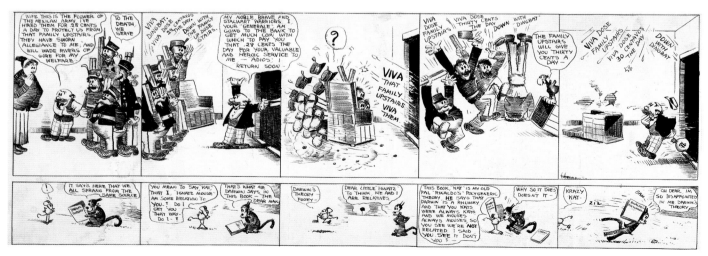

THE FAMILY UPSTAIRS daily strip by George Herriman. Krazy Kat and Ignatz the mouse debuted in this Herriman domestic feature and eventually got their own space in panels below the main strip. *1912, New York Journal. Courtesy of Gary Ernest Smith*

KRAZY KAT *original hand-colored Sunday page by George Herriman. The artist gave this page to Rudolph Dirks's sister.* December 3, 1916. Courtesy of Jack Gilbert

Krazy Kat

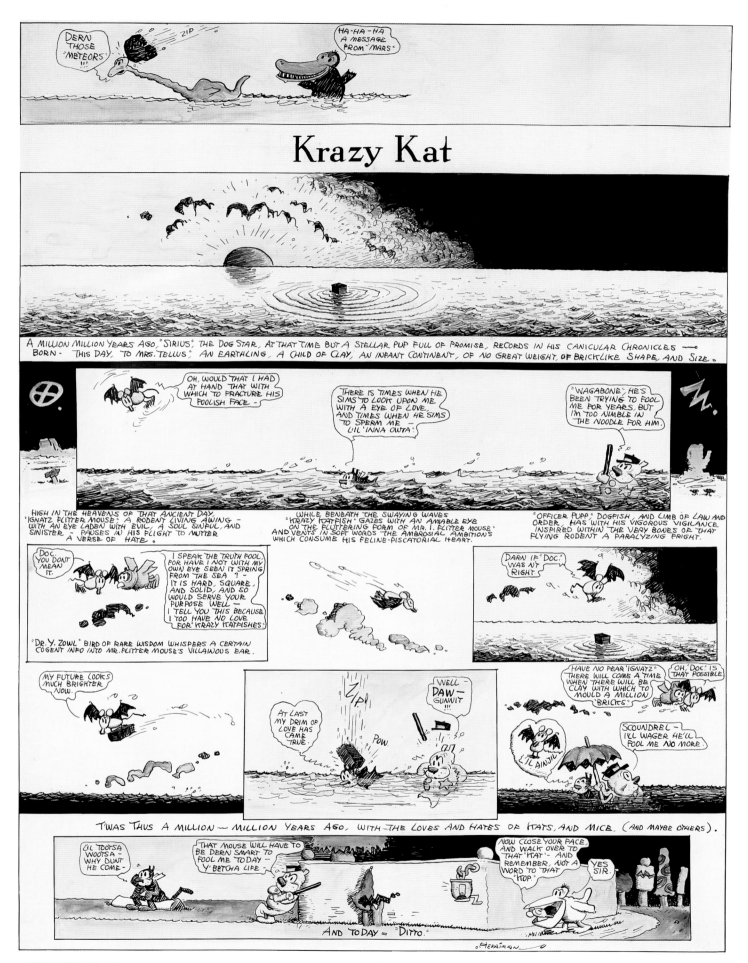

KRAZY KAT original hand-colored Sunday page by George Herriman. One of only two surviving original pages from a ten-week period in 1922 during which Herriman's feature was printed in color. It tells the story of the origins of Krazy's universe. *February 25, 1922. Courtesy of Bruce Hamilton*

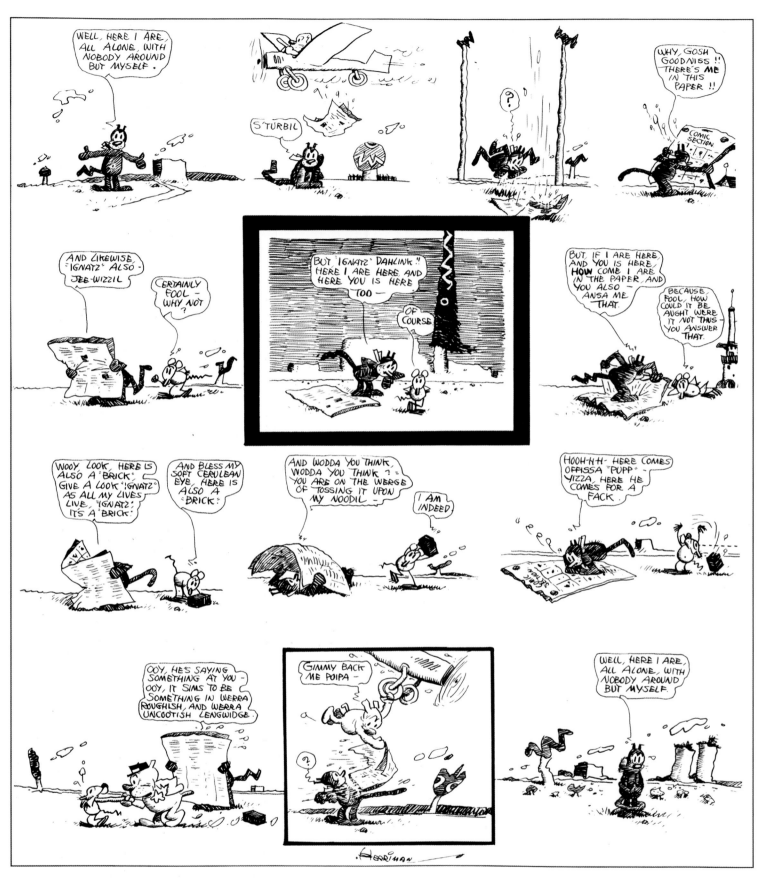

KRAZY KAT *original pen-and-ink Sunday page by George Herriman. The funnies are delivered to Coconino, and the Kat puzzles over the concept of illusion versus reality.* April 16, 1922. *Courtesy of Craig Yoe.*

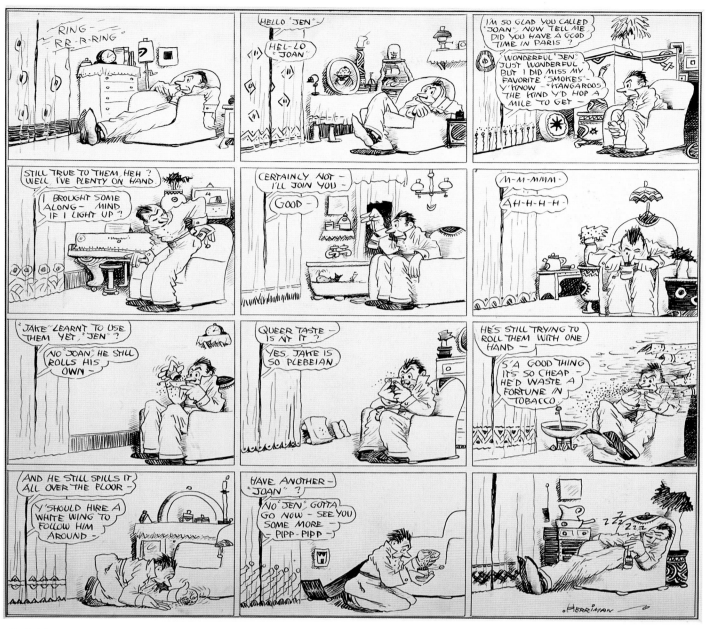

US HUSBANDS Sunday page by George Herriman. Although more conventional in theme and design than KRAZY KAT, this short-lived domestic feature still had elements of Herrimanesque inspiration. 1926. Courtesy of Jack Gilbert

BARON BEAN daily strip by George Herriman. This aristocratic pretender starred in a daily comic strip from January 5, 1916, to January 22, 1919, syndicated by Hearst's International Feature Service. c. 1917. Courtesy of Illustration House

KRAZY KAT daily strip by George Herriman. January 17, 1918. Courtesy of Jack Gilbert

DAILY KOMICS
Although Herriman's Sunday pages receive the most praise for their innovative layouts, the daily strip, which ran from 1913 to 1944, also featured expressive art and clever writing.

KRAZY KAT hand-colored daily strip by George Herriman. © April 19, 1922, International Feature Service, Inc. Courtesy of Jack Gilbert and the Barnum Museum

KRAZY KAT daily strip by George Herriman. © November 10, 1934, King Features Syndicate, Inc. Courtesy of Mort Walker

KRAZY KAT daily strip by George Herriman. © October 11, 1939, King Features Syndicate, Inc. Courtesy of Bruce Hamilton

KRAZY KAT recolored Sunday page by George Herriman. This feature began appearing as a color tabloid page in the Hearst papers on June 1, 1935.
© June 11, 1939, King Features Syndicate, Inc. Courtesy of Russ Cochran and American Color

george mcmanus

GEORGE MC MANUS—*Caricature drawn by his assistant Zeke Zekley. 1954*

THE CREATOR OF THE MOST henpecked father in the funnies was a neatly dressed, corpulent fellow of Irish descent who smoked cigars and loved a good joke. He insisted that any resemblance to his lead character was purely coincidental.

George McManus was born on January 23, 1884, in St. Louis, where his father was the manager of the Grand Opera House. In his second year of high school, thirteen-year-old George Jr. was caught doodling in class by his English teacher. She sent him home with a note, complaining about the objectionable drawings. When his father saw his son's handiwork, he took the boy down to the art department of the *St. Louis Republic* and got him a job. A year later, McManus's first comic strip effort, *Alma and Oliver,* appeared in the paper. "It was a terrible mess," he later admitted.

Another tale the jovial cartoonist loved to relate involved a racing tip he received from a shoeshine boy. He took the advice and placed $100 on Hamburg Belle at 30-to-1 odds. To his surprise, the horse won the race, and he used the $3,000 payoff to buy a train ticket to New York City and start his career. The day his money ran out, he landed a job with the *New York World.* In addition to talent, the young cartoonist had the luck of the Irish.

A decade later, after a string of comic creations that included *Panhandle Pete* (February 21, 1904), *The Newlyweds* (April 10, 1904), *Nibsy, the Newsboy, in Funny Fairyland* (May 20, 1906), and *Spareribs and Gravy* (January 28, 1912), he launched his most famous feature. *Bringing Up Father,* which debuted on January 2, 1913, would make McManus a millionaire.

The life story of Jiggs was as real to him as his own anecdotal history. "He was born in Ireland, you know, and

came to this country, expecting to find the streets paved with gold," McManus told a reporter in 1926. "But they were paved with bricks and cobblestones instead. So he became a hod-carrier. Romance came into his life when he met Maggie slinging dishes in a beanery, and they were married. He threw away the hod and began to sell bricks on commission. Then he went into the brickmaking business and manufactured a brick especially designed for throwing purposes. It was much harder than the ordinary building brick and sold year around."

His rags-to-riches yarn did not end there. "Then Maggie became a social climber," McManus continued. "Wealth changed her viewpoint. Society, dukes, counts and college professors came into her life. She forgot the old crowd. But Jiggs has stuck to his clay pipe and his corned beef and cabbage. He is still as good as any other man in Dinty Moore's and willing to prove it."

There was more to the marriage than bickering and fighting, McManus pointed out: "Maggie is going to make a gentleman of Jiggs if she breaks every Ming vase in America doing it. So Maggie continues to lead her own life and Jiggs continues to lead what he can of his. Deep down in their hearts they love each other, as was demonstrated when Jiggs temporarily lost his money and had to go to work. And being Irish, they will live 'happily ever after'—at least as long as I draw them."

The story of Maggie and Jiggs was the realization of the American dream, rendered in pen-and-ink and told in daily installments. It was a reflection of George McManus's own rise to success. In the world of comics, *Bringing Up Father* is a classic example of art imitating life.

JIGGS—*Portrait by George McManus.* April 1923, Circulation *magazine*

THE NEWLYWEDS—THEIR BABY Sunday page by George McManus. Snookums, who recognizes his creator at the top of this page, takes his parents on a noisy trip to Coney Island. *August 11, 1907, Denver Sunday News-Times. Courtesy of Mark Johnson*

BRINGING UP FATHER daily strip by George McManus. c. 1918. Courtesy of Illustration House

BRINGING UP FATHER daily strip by George McManus. c. 1916. Courtesy of Sandy Schechter

BRINGING UP FATHER daily strip by George McManus. c. 1919. Courtesy of Craig Englund

BRINGING UP FATHER original hand-colored Sunday page by George McManus. The Sunday version of McManus's feature debuted on April 4, 1918. This is the earliest known original example. May 19, 1918. Courtesy of Craig Englund and Illustration House

BRINGING UP FATHER daily strips by George McManus. Maggie and Jiggs travel to Japan in this sequence from 1927. © March 28, April 5 and 12, and May 9, 1927, International Feature Service, Inc. Courtesy of the Art Wood Collection of Cartoon and Caricature, Prints and Photographs Division, Library of Congress

BRINGING UP FATHER recolored Sunday page by George McManus. Maggie and Jiggs return to the neighborhood from their epic cross-country journey.
© July 7, 1940, King Features Syndicate, Inc. Courtesy of Russ Cochran and American Color

MAMA'S ANGEL CHILD original hand-colored Sunday page by Penny Ross. A former assistant to Richard F. Outcault, Ross created a female Buster Brown named Esther for his ornately illustrated feature, which ran from March 1, 1908, to October 17, 1920. *c. 1918. Courtesy of Bill Janocha*

COMICS FOR KIDS Although the anti-comics crusaders were unsuccessful in putting an end to the Sunday funnies, a number of features that appealed to children were introduced during the decade. Many of these creations starred cute kids and funny animals and provided an alternative to the more adult-oriented strips in the color comic sections.

DIMPLES original hand-colored Sunday page by Grace Drayton. Best known as the originator of the *Campbell Soup Kids*, Drayton created many features starring cute, dimpled tykes, including DOLLY DINGLE, which began in 1908, and DIMPLES, starting in 1914. *1913/14. Courtesy of Jack Gilbert and the Barnum Museum*

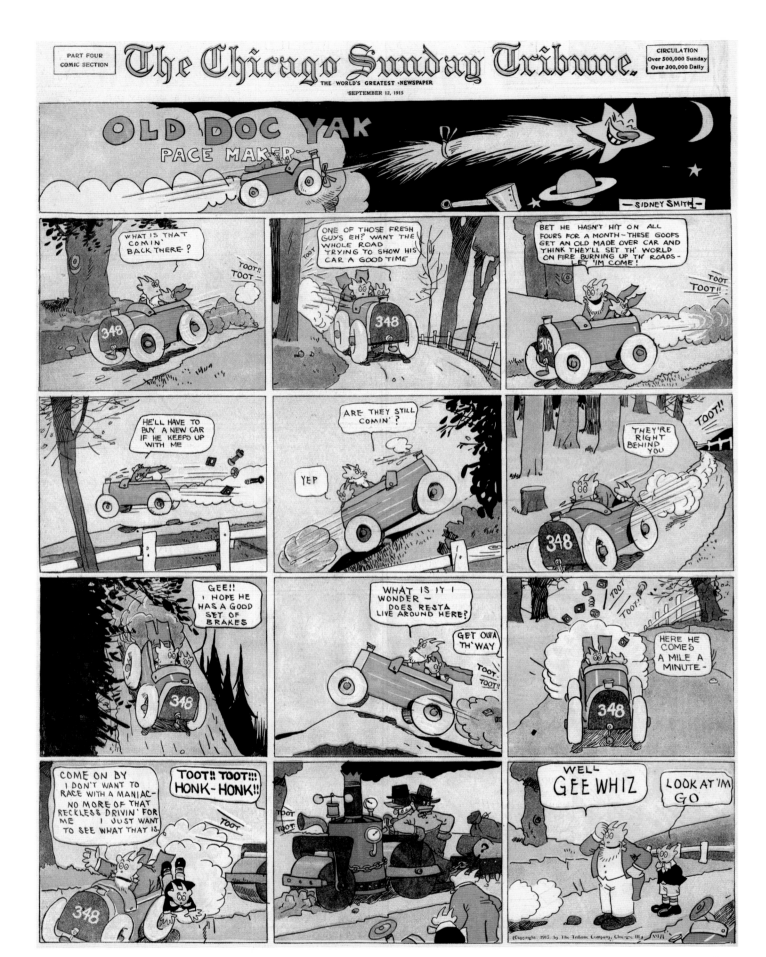

OLD DOC YAK Sunday page by Sidney Smith. Before launching THE GUMPS in 1917, Smith drew a humorous animal feature starring an anthropomorphic goat. It was called BUCK NIX when it debuted as a daily strip in 1908 and OLD DOC YAK after 1912. September 12, 1915, Chicago Sunday Tribune. Courtesy of Mark Johnson

SLIM JIM AND THE FORCE Sunday page by Stanley Armstrong. The most popular star in the World Color Printing Company's stable, Slim Jim was chased by virtually the same trio of policemen from 1910 to 1937. The feature was drawn by three different artists: George Frink (1910), Raymond Crawford Ewer (1911–14), and Stanley Armstrong (1914–37). *1920, Arizona Daily Star. Courtesy of Mark Johnson*

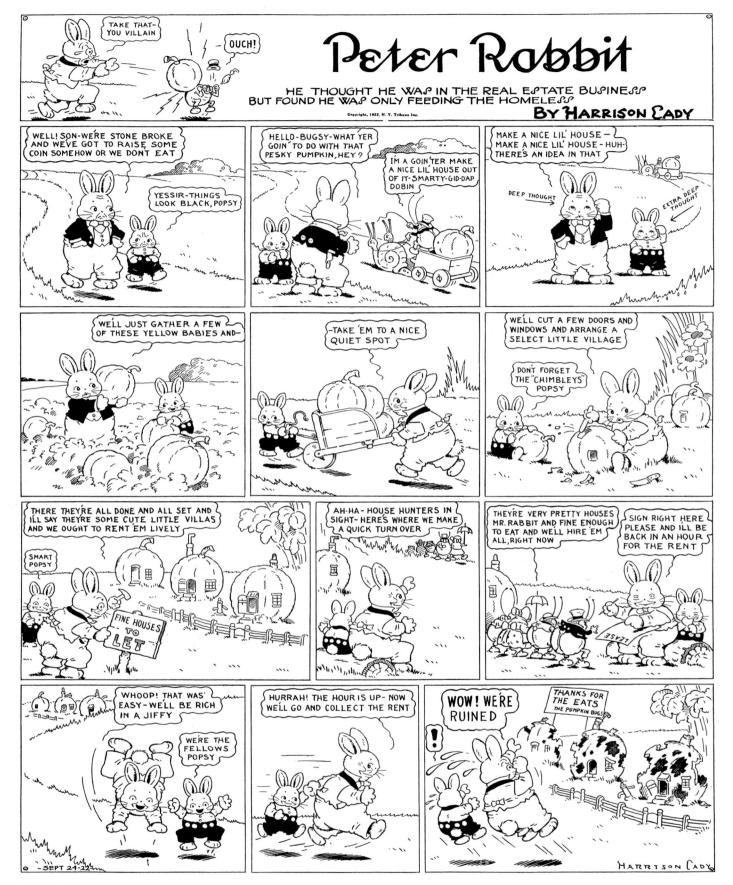

PETER RABBIT Sunday page by Harrison Cady. This funny bunny originally appeared in Thornton Burgess's children's stories, which Cady illustrated. Peter starred in a comic strip adaptation beginning in 1920. © September 24, 1922, New York Tribune, Inc. Courtesy of Bill Janocha.

THE TEENIE WEENIES *Sunday page by William Donahey. This band of little people, who lived in a normal-sized world, was created exclusively for the Chicago Tribune in 1914. After ten years, the full-page feature went into national syndication.* 1916. Courtesy of Mark Johnson

BOBBY MAKE-BELIEVE *original Sunday page by Frank King. Before he launched* GASOLINE ALLEY, *Frank King drew this visually innovative boyhood fantasy strip, which ran from January 31, 1915, to December 7, 1919, in the* **Chicago Tribune.** *c. 1918, Chicago Tribune. Courtesy of the Art Wood Collection of Cartoon and Caricature, Prints and Photographs Division, Library of Congress*

the twenties

DAYS OF REAL SPORT daily panel by Clare Briggs. The comics were useful for more than just wrapping fish. ©1927 New York Tribune, Inc. Courtesy of Editor & Publisher

MERELY MARGY *panel from a daily strip by John Held Jr.* © *September 6, 1927, King Features Syndicate, Inc. Courtesy of Rob Stolzer*

THE JAZZ AGE ROARED WITH THE SOUNDS OF PROSPERITY, PLEASURE, AND REBELLION. ANXIOUS FOR A "RETURN TO NORMALCY" AFTER THE HORRORS OF WORLD WAR I, AMERICANS TOSSED OFF THE STRICT MORAL CODES OF VICTORIAN SOCIETY AND DANCED THE CHARLESTON, DRANK BOOTLEG LIQUOR, FOLLOWED THE LATEST FADS, AND SPECULATED RECKLESSLY IN THE STOCK MARKET. POPULAR CULTURE, FUELED BY THE MASS PRODUCTION OF CONSUMER GOODS AND THE GROWING PERVASIVENESS OF THE MEDIA, UNITED THE NATION IN THE EBULLIENT PURSUIT OF GOOD TIMES.

In 1925, President Calvin Coolidge made his famous declaration that "the business of America is business." It was a characteristic understatement by the tight-lipped chief executive. Between 1920 and 1929, the gross national product grew from $74 billion to $104.4 billion. In 1923, unemployment reached a new low of 2.4 percent. From 1913 to 1927, the buying power of a skilled laborer increased 50 percent. Americans showed their unquestioning faith in economic progress by embracing materialism and borrowing money on easy credit terms. The unshakable optimism of Wall Street investors encouraged middle-class wage earners to buy stocks on margin, paying only a fraction of the purchase price to their brokers. Volume on the New York Stock Exchange went from 227 million shares in 1920 to 920 million in 1928.

Prohibition of alcohol, which became law on January 16, 1920, was widely disregarded, as average citizens became common criminals by concealing illegal hooch in hip flasks. The thirteen-year "noble experiment" was a total failure, resulting in an increase in liquor consumption and the growth of organized crime. Stills, speakeasies, and rumrunners proliferated as federal agents found it easier to take bribes than arrest violators. Drinking was glamorized in movies and magazines, and a spirit of rebelliousness grew among the nation's youth.

Women voted for the first time in a national election on November 2, 1920, helping to put the handsome and affable, but incompetent, Warren Harding in the White House. Improved opportunities in the workplace made financial independence possible and encouraged more daring behavior among the fairer sex. The younger generation flaunted its newfound freedom by drinking, smoking, and swearing in public and dressing in more provocative clothing. The flapper—with her short, flimsy dress, bobbed hair, flat chest, and rolled-up silk stockings—became the icon of the Jazz Age. Youth culture flourished as shebas necked with their sheiks in the back of jalopies and shimmied to the beat of the latest hit songs.

Americans embraced a seemingly endless parade of pastimes with obsessive enthusiasm. Among the many popular fads of the era were mah-jongg, crossword puzzles, contract bridge, yo-yos, roller skating, flagpole sitting, dance marathons, and endurance races. Historic events, ranging from the first Miss America Pageant in 1921 to Charles Lindbergh's transatlantic airplane flight in 1927, grabbed headlines and captivated the nation. It was also the "Golden Age of Sport," as Babe Ruth, Jack Dempsey, Red Grange, and Bobby Jones were among the many heroes who were revered for their athletic accomplishments.

In 1926, F. Scott Fitzgerald, in describing the giddy mood of the era, wrote, "The restlessness approached hysteria. The parties were bigger. The pace was faster, the shows were broader, the buildings were higher, the morals were looser, and the liquor was cheaper; but all these benefits did not really minister to much delight. Young people wore out early—they were hard and languid at twenty-one."

Columnist Walter Lippmann summed up this trend in 1929 when he observed, "What most distinguishes the generation who have approached maturity since the debacle of idealism at the end of the War is not their rebellion against the moral code of their parents, but their disillusionment with their own rebellion. It is common for young men and women to rebel, but that they should rebel sadly and without faith in their rebellion, that they should distrust the new freedom no less than the old certainties—that is something of a novelty."

A new style of "jazz journalism" emerged during the 1920s, which mirrored the sensational tenor of the times. Although newspapers had been printed in a half-page size before, three papers, all published in New York, pioneered the modern "tabloid" format. The trend began with the *Illustrated Daily News*, which first hit the newsstands on June 26, 1919.

Inspired by the success of Alfred Hamsworth's *London Daily Mirror*, Joseph Medill Patterson, copublisher of the *Chicago Tribune*, decided to launch a tabloid paper in New York. The smaller size was easier for readers to handle traveling to work on the crowded subways, Patterson reasoned, and short articles and photographs took less time to digest. Five years later, the *Daily News* (the title was shortened during the first year), with a circulation of 750,000, was the most successful newspaper in the United States.

On June 24, 1924, William Randolph Hearst launched the *New York Daily Mirror*; three months later, Bernarr Macfadden began publication of the *Daily Graphic*. All three of these tabloid papers featured sensational headlines, lurid crime stories, and celebrity gossip, but the *Daily Graphic* outdid the competition when it came to "gutter journalism." Typical *Graphic* headlines screamed "I Know Who Killed My Brother" and "For 36 Hours I Lived Another Woman's Love Life." Fake pictures, known as "composographs," were created by superimposing speech balloons and faces on staged pictures.

By 1930, the editorial policy of the *Daily News* was changing. "The people's major interest is not in the playboy, Broadway, and divorces," Patterson told his staff, "but in how they're going to eat; and from this time forward, we'll pay attention to the struggle for existence that's just beginning." This approach proved successful and the *Daily News* continued to grow, reaching a circulation peak of 2.4 million daily readers and 4.5 million Sunday customers by 1947. The *Graphic*, which died in 1932, and the *Mirror*, which folded in 1963, never earned a profit for their publishers.

A new medium began challenging newspapers in the 1920s. One of the first independent commercial radio stations, KDKA in Pittsburgh, broadcast the results of the Harding-Cox presidential election in 1920. The number of radio households grew from 60,000 in 1922 to 13,750,000 in 1930. There were 618 stations in operation by the end of the decade.

The first newspaper-owned station was set up in the *Detroit News* building on August 20, 1920. By 1927, forty-eight newspapers owned stations, sixty-nine sponsored programs,

THE RADIO BUGGS daily strip by Walt McDougall. c. 1920. Courtesy of the International Museum of Cartoon Art

and ninety-seven provided news shows. Newspaper people were cautious about radio, however. On April 22, 1922, George Miller, editor of the *Detroit News*, claimed that "the broadcasting station never will supplant to any material extent the daily newspaper as the source of popular information."

An article in *Editor & Publisher* on February 9, 1924, pointed out the perceived shortcomings of radio among members of the newspaper fraternity: "The organized press has never shown excitement over any threatening aspect of radio, because no matter how much it may be controlled and commercialized, it possesses physical difficulties which, in general terms, makes it a poor competitor for the established newspaper. These difficulties include the impossibility of exercise of the selective process of the reader—he sits at his radio and takes what is being sent, whether he likes it or not, and he takes the full dose."

In addition to news and music, radio began to offer entertainment programs. Freeman Gosden and Charles Correll created one of the most successful shows in broadcast history when they adapted to radio their blackface vaudeville routine about a taxicab driver and his lazy partner. *Amos and Andy* debuted on Chicago's WMAQ in March 1928 and within a year was reaching forty million listeners on the NBC network. Late in 1928, an *Amos and Andy* comic strip, linked to the radio show, debuted. It was syndicated by the *Chicago Daily News*, the owner of WMAQ. By the 1930s, the crossover influence was going in the other direction, as radio programs based on the comic strips *Buck Rogers, Little Orphan Annie, Dick Tracy,* and *Terry and the Pirates* became some of the most popular programs on the airwaves.

Despite competition from radio, the newspaper business continued to thrive. The combined circulation of American newspapers reached forty million by the end of the decade, and advertising revenue totaled $860 million. *Editor & Publisher* reported in 1927 that there were eighty syndicates distributing more than two thousand different features to newspapers around the world. "Among the thousands of different types of syndicate offerings now available, the so-called 'funnies,' comic strips and cartoons, continue well in the lead as far as numbers are concerned," the magazine claimed. "Nearly 150 artists are earning their livelihood by catering to this peculiar American taste, now popular even in the Orient and South American countries."

Cartoonists' salaries increased accordingly. In 1922, Sidney Smith, creator of *The Gumps,* signed a well-publicized million-dollar contract with the Chicago Tribune–New York News Syndicate. The ten-year deal provided Smith with an annual salary of $100,000 and a new Rolls-Royce every third year. The Bell Syndicate was paying Bud Fisher a minimum of $3,000 a week for *Mutt and Jeff* in 1928, and creators of many

of the other top features were earning between $50,000 and $100,000 a year.

The artists were also supplementing their incomes with advertising work. In 1927, more than thirty-five top cartoonists were each getting between $10 and $2,000 a drawing from advertising clients. Fontaine Fox, creator of *Toonerville Folks,* was producing cartoons for the Cooper and Brass Research Institute featuring the "Terrible-Tempered Mr. Bang," and Clare Briggs was lending his talents to a campaign for Old Gold cigarettes.

"I think that it is a big mistake for syndicate artists, whose work is being paid for as an exclusive feature by newspapers, to make an advertising drawing exactly similar in size, shape and appearance to his regular newspaper feature," admitted Fox. "If, however, the artist makes a drawing that is not exactly like his regular cartoon, but is plainly an illustration or advertisement, I do not admit any harm is done."

The syndicates distributing the work of Fox and Briggs did not see it that way, however, and in March 1928, the two artists announced that they would no longer illustrate ads for newspapers. "Mr. Fox has agreed with us," claimed Henry Snevily of the Bell Syndicate, "that to make advertising drawings in practically the same physical form as the feature cartoons and using the same characters is a bad policy, confusing to the readers." Newspaper editors, who were paying the syndicates for the exclusive right to publish these features in their market territory, had complained that competing papers could offer the same material to their readers simply by running the ads. The cartoonists were permitted to continue illustrating advertisements, but only for magazine publication.

The increasing power of the syndicates was made evident by a survey presented to the American Society of Newspaper Editors in May 1924. Although the twenty-nine editors who responded to the questionnaire admitted that most of their dealings with syndicates were positive, the overall sentiment was that they felt intimidated. "We seem all to be extravagant and cowardly in dealing with syndicates and their features," wrote one New York editor. "I am quite sure always when a feature of some merit comes to me, if I don't take it, one of my newspaper competitors will."

Among the many complaints the editors voiced in the survey were that too many features were being offered, the prices were exorbitant, unethical sales methods were often employed, the importance of features in building circulation was exaggerated, the size of exclusive territories denied them access to certain popular features, and large papers had unfair competitive advantages over smaller ones. The general consensus was in favor of home editing, using staff writers and artists, as opposed to assembling newspapers from syndicated material.

The syndicates responded to these charges in a report delivered in January 1925. They blamed newspaper editors for buying features they did not need, paying too much for the most desirable features, pressuring salesmen for unfair advantages over their competitors, driving hard bargains, breaking contracts, patronizing fly-by-night syndicates, and refusing to take risks with unproven talent.

One syndicate manager took a more compromising approach: "It seems to me that the relation between newspapers and syndicates should be one of selective cooperation. I think that syndicates do not spend enough time or thought acquainting themselves with what editors actually need in advance of trying to fill their requirements." This executive proposed that syndicates could save a lot of money by consulting newspaper editors before signing and promoting expensive talent.

Cartoonists and syndicates learned, through a long process of trial and error, what newspaper readers liked and disliked. "The comic-cartoon series has become a commodity, produced and marketed much like any other commodity, and it is just as bad business to release a comic strip with an objectionable feature as to sell complexion soap with grit in it," wrote Amram Schoenfeld in a February 1, 1930, article in *The Saturday Evening Post* entitled "The Laugh Industry."

The larger the market for comics became, the more universal the strips had to be in terms of content. Cartoonists were under increasing pressure to entertain this mass audience without offending anyone. A curious double standard developed. Newspaper readers were more sensitive about perceived transgressions in their favorite comics than they were about the same references in movies, plays, and books.

The funnies business gradually adopted a strict code of self-censorship. Among the many unwritten taboos on the comics pages were the following: Female characters should not be shown drinking, smoking, swearing, or even kissing a man who was not their spouse. Married couples were to remain eternally faithful and could never get divorced, although they were allowed to complain profusely about their relationship. A wife could physically abuse her husband, but a man could never strike a woman. Comments that might directly offend any ethnic group, nationality, religion, political persuasion, or profession were to be avoided at all costs. A long list of expletives, including "hell" and "damn," was forbidden, and comic characters were not permitted to use the Lord's name in vain. Antisocial behavior, including drunkenness, vandalism, and criminality, was not tolerated, except by villains. Readers were particularly sensitive to any activity that endangered the life of a comic strip child. References to death and disease were, in most cases, frowned upon.

There were exceptions to these rules, of course. It was acceptable for Harry Hershfield, a Jewish cartoonist, to make fun of his own people in his strip *Abie the Agent*. The same was true of George McManus, an Irishman, and his autobiographical creation, *Bringing Up Father*. Conversely, if a comic strip featured a black character in any but the most menial of roles (maids, butlers, janitors, porters, and stable boys), complaints from southern readers were inevitable.

TABOOS—Cartoonist Ken Kling used the word "diabetes" in the second panel of this WINDY RILEY comic strip, but the syndicate changed it to an imaginary disease, "haliobetis." © 1929 McNaught Syndicate, Inc. Courtesy of Robert C. Harvey

Although cartoonists often broke these taboos, they became increasingly conditioned to avoid the wrath of editors, who might cancel strips that offended readers too often. Termination meant the loss of income, and in the end, the profit motive was the bottom line.

Gilbert Seldes, in his landmark 1924 survey, *The Seven Lively Arts,* included a chapter on "The 'Vulgar' Comic Strip." Seldes put a positive spin on the challenges that cartoonists faced. "The enormous circulation [the comic strip] achieves imposes certain limitations," he wrote. "It cannot be too local, since it is syndicated throughout the country; it must avoid political and social questions because the same strip appears in papers of divergent editorial opinions; there is no room in it for acute racial caricature, although no group is immune from its mockery." Seldes concluded, "These and other restrictions have gradually made of the comic strip a changing picture of American life—and by compensation it provides us with the freest American fantasy."

During the 1920s, no individual in the comics business understood the tastes of the average newspaper reader better than Joseph Medill Patterson. As the head of the Chicago Tribune–New York News Syndicate, he launched a string of comic strips that were enormously popular during the decade. Although these features were each unique creations, they shared one important quality: readers of Patterson's strips were given a compelling reason to return each day to see what new adventures awaited the characters. They had to find out if Uncle Bim was going to marry the Widow Zander, or when Daddy Warbucks would rescue Annie, or what Winnie Winkle was wearing. They were hooked, and no day was complete without a visit with their favorite funnies friends.

Patterson and his cousin Robert McCormick became coeditors and copublishers of the *Chicago Tribune* in 1914.

Although the grandsons of the paper's founder had very different views—McCormick was a conservative and Patterson leaned toward socialism—their friendship and mutual respect fostered a cooperative relationship. For the most part, McCormick focused his attention on the business side of the operation while Patterson devoted his talents to the content of the newspaper. During World War I, Patterson enlisted as a private in the army and rose to the rank of captain in the artillery, earning him his lifelong nickname.

After returning from Europe in 1919, Patterson launched the *Illustrated Daily News* in New York, although he continued to live in Chicago until 1926. *The Gumps* ran on page 15 of the first issue, on June 26, 1919, and the comics would be an essential element of the tabloid from then on. When an eight-page color comic section was introduced on February 12, 1923, circulation jumped by sixty-five thousand.

Patterson took an active role in nurturing the syndicate's comics. He had regular meetings with his cartoonists and made crucial changes, particularly in the early developmental stages of new features. His prescient suggestions are part of comics legend. Patterson once summed up his basic formula: "Youngsters for kid appeal, a handsome guy for muscle work and love interest, a succession of pretty girls, a mysterious locale or a totally familiar one."

The Gumps was the feature that built the syndicate, and during the early 1920s the *Chicago Tribune* became known as "the Gump paper." Although Sidney Smith often took credit for the original inspiration, the strip was Patterson's brainchild from the beginning. After its debut in 1917, *The Gumps* evolved into the prototypical soap opera strip, as it chronicled the trials and tribulations of a lower-middle-class family who represented, in Patterson's view, the typical *Tribune* reader.

In 1923, the Minneapolis Board of Trade momentarily halted business so that brokers could run to the newsstands

THE GUMPS GASOLINE ALEY MOON MULLINS WINNIE WINKLE *The bread winner* HAROLD TEEN LITTLE ORPHAN ANNIE SMITTY

CAPTAIN PATTERSON'S ALL-STAR LINE-UP—The Chicago Tribune–New York News Syndicate launched a string of successful strips during the late teens and early twenties. (GASOLINE ALLEY was misspelled in the original ad.) *Courtesy of Editor & Publisher*

HAROLD TEEN AND LILLUMS LOVEWELL—Special drawing by Carl Ed from the Editor & Publisher series ALL IN THE DAY'S WORK. November 1, 1924. *Courtesy of Editor & Publisher*

to find out if Andy Gump's rich Uncle Bim had finally succumbed to the machinations of the conniving Widow Zander. When the brokenhearted Mary Gold died on April 30, 1929, there was an outpouring of sympathy as the nation mourned the pen-and-ink character as if she were flesh and blood. Smith had become a master of manipulating the emotions of his faithful fans and was famously rewarded for his efforts.

The next strip Patterson launched was Carl Ed's *The Love Life of Harold Teen,* on May 4, 1919. Harold came along just in time for the youth movement of the Roaring Twenties, sporting such fashions as toreador trousers, sloppy socks, and whoopee hats and popularizing phrases like "cute canary," "dim bulb," and "kissable kid." It provided a sanitized picture of a Jazz Age teenager, suitable for family viewing.

Winnie Winkle was not the first strip to star a working girl; that distinction belonged to A. E. Hayward's *Somebody's Stenog,* which began in 1916. When Martin Branner's creation debuted on September 20, 1920, women were about to vote for the first time in a national election and the era of emancipation was just getting into full swing. Winnie held down a job as a stenographer and supported her family—deadbeat dad Rip, well-meaning Ma, and precocious brother Perry. She managed to dress fashionably by making her own clothes and changed outfits on a daily basis. Branner's strip helped earned the *Daily News* its reputation as "the Stenographer's Gazette."

The original cast of *Gasoline Alley*—Walt Wallet, Bill, Doc, and Avery—was first shown tinkering on a flivver in the corner quadrant of Frank King's Sunday page, *The Rectangle,* on November 24, 1918. *Gasoline Alley* became a daily feature

on August 24, 1919, but a year and a half later, Patterson felt it needed more feminine appeal and told King to "get a baby in the story fast." On Valentine's Day of 1921, Walt—who was a bachelor—found an infant on his doorstep; he later named the baby Skeezix. King's creation earned the distinction of being the first strip in which the characters aged in real time. Over the course of eight decades, *Gasoline Alley* has chronicled middle-class family life in small-town America with gentle humor and quiet drama.

The next cartoonist Patterson helped to get started was Walter Berndt, a former office boy at the *New York Journal.* Following the Captain's orders, Berndt changed the name of his creation from *Bill the Office Boy,* a strip that ran for two weeks in the *New York World* in 1922, to *Smitty,* after randomly opening up a telephone book to a page of Smiths. A year after the strip was launched on November 27, 1922, Patterson directed Berndt to "put a little pathos in the *Smitty* strip" by having the boy's boss, Mr. Bailey, fire him unjustly for petty thievery. Berndt, who also became an unofficial talent scout for Patterson, took this advice well and continued to provide lighthearted suspense in the strip for the next five decades.

In 1923, the Captain was looking for a feature to compete with the roughneck appeal of King Features' *Barney Google.* He found the perfect artist to accomplish this goal in Frank Willard, a friend and former assistant of Barney's creator, Billy DeBeck. *Moon Mullins* debuted on June 19, 1923, and, after an initial period of experimentation with various locales, settled on a suburban boardinghouse, inhabited by a motley assortment of social pretenders and lowlifes. The colorful cast included Moonshine Mullins, an unrepentant con man, as well as landlady Emmy Schmaltz, the pompous Lord and Lady Plushbottom, rotund Uncle Willie, Mamie the maid, and kid brother Kayo. In characteristic fashion, Patterson named the

SMITTY—Special drawing by Walter Berndt from the Editor & Publisher series ALL IN THE DAY'S WORK. July 26, 1924. Courtesy of Editor & Publisher

lead character himself, adapting the Prohibition term for illegally distilled spirits.

The brightest new star of Patterson's stable during the 1920s was Harold Gray's Little Orphan Annie, who made her first appearance on August 5, 1924. Gray, who had worked as Sidney Smith's assistant on *The Gumps* for five years, began submitting numerous ideas for his own strip. According to syndicate legend, when the Captain saw Gray's latest effort, *Little Orphan Otto,* he exclaimed, "He looks like a pansy. Put a skirt on the kid and we'll call it *Little Orphan Annie.*" Under Patterson's direction, Gray developed a unique blend of adventure, pathos, humor, and social comment. A syndicate advertisement from December 20, 1924, summed up the initial marketing pitch for *Little Orphan Annie:* "It is the comic strip Cinderella, the great child story of the ages—the story of the little girl who accepts the frowns of fortune with fortitude and the smiles of fortune with grace and kindliness."

In the first continuity, eleven-year-old Annie slugged a boy who was teasing her, displaying the feisty independence that won over the hearts of readers. Nearly two months later, she would meet a wealthy munitions manufacturer named Daddy Warbucks, and in January 1925, Annie adopted her faithful canine sidekick, Sandy. This triumvirate became the core cast of the strip. Together they faced adversity with a self-reliant determination that mirrored Harold Gray's personal philosophy.

The comic strip lineup of the Chicago Tribune–New York News Syndicate represented, in many ways, the major thematic genres of the decade. Some of these creations helped to define previously established trends, while others pioneered new ideas. Success inspired imitation in the highly competitive world of newspaper syndication.

Family strips like *The Nebbs* and *The Bungle Family* copied the proven formula of *The Gumps. Smitty* resembled King Features' *Jerry on the Job,* which started in 1913. King Features' *Tillie the Toiler* followed *Winnie Winkle* into the workplace. *Moon Mullins* was Patterson's answer to Hearst's *Barney Google. Etta Kett* spoke to the same audience as *Harold Teen. Ella Cinders* and *Little Annie Rooney* borrowed elements from *Little Orphan Annie.* Only *Gasoline Alley* seemed immune from the cloning process.

In assessing the historical contributions of the decade, Ron Goulart, in *The Funnies: 100 Years of American Comic Strips,* observed, "There was not, however, a Lost Generation of comic artists and the twenties produced no examples of disillusionment, nihilism or sexual revolution in the comic strip format." Cartoonist John Held Jr.'s wispy flapper, who starred in the comic strip *Merely Margy,* was widely regarded as a graphic icon of the era. But there was no voice comparable to F. Scott Fitzgerald in the comics medium.

BARNEY GOOGLE panel from a daily strip by Billy DeBeck. This pop-eyed con man broke the world's record for flagpole sitting when he hung on for twenty-one days in 1927. © June 17, 1927, King Features Syndicate, Inc. Courtesy of the San Francisco Academy of Comic Art

The frivolity of the Roaring Twenties was not entirely absent on the funnies pages, however. The excitement of baseball stadiums, racetracks, and boxing rings, the aromas of speakeasies and flophouses, and the sound of Dixieland and Tin Pan Alley were all captured by Billy DeBeck in *Barney Google*. His comic strip alter ego was the Everyman of the Jazz Age. Barney mixed "Google High Balls" in his kitchen the same month the Volstead Act was passed. He swam across the English Channel in 1926 and sat on top of a flag-pole for twenty-one days in 1927. DeBeck's rags-to-riches tales reflected the happy-go-lucky spirit of the times.

The most significant new development in the comics medium during the 1920s was the emergence of the adventure strip. Episodic continuity had been featured in newspaper comics almost from the beginning. The Yellow Kid went on an eighteen-week around-the-world tour in 1897, and Frederick B. Opper used the words "to be continued" in a three-episode sequence of *Alphonse and Gaston* in 1903. The cliffhanger approach, requiring readers to wait until the next installment to see how a story played out, was a key device employed by Charles W. Kahles in *Hairbreadth Harry* (1906) and Bud Fisher in *Mutt and Jeff* (1907). Ed Wheelan's *Midget Movies,* which first appeared with that title in 1918 and continued as *Minute Movies* in 1921, parodied narrative elements from film melodramas. "Wheelan Pictures Ink" employed a regular troupe of actors who performed western, detective, aviation, and sports scripts, anticipating the major adventure genres of the 1930s. By the 1920s, the majority of humor strips featured loosely constructed stories that could last a few days or ramble on for months.

A new breed of comic, one that added the element of physical danger to storytelling, came on the scene in the mid-1920s. Many of these strips featured juvenile heroes and exotic locales. Although Little Orphan Annie frequently found herself in dangerous situations, it was not until the 1930s that life-threatening violence—the defining characteristic of the modern adventure strip—became part of Gray's narrative blend.

Meanwhile, between February 1 and July 12, 1925, Chester Gump, the seven-year-old son of Andy and Min Gump,

BOBBY THATCHER promotional drawing by George Storm. An advertise-ment for the "original boy adventure strip" promised "detectives, fisticuffs and skullduggery at sea." © September 2, 1933, McClure Syndicate, Inc. Courtesy of Editor & Publisher

embarked on an exciting South Sea adventure in a Sunday-only continuity written by Brandon Walsh and illustrated by Stanley Link. In one of these episodes, Chester, who was aided by his faithful Chinese servant Ching Chow, fired at a native chieftain with a gun and apparently killed him (it was implied that the bullet hit its target outside of the panel border). According to comics historian Bill Blackbeard, this was "the first blood-letting in combat ever encountered in a comic strip." Over the course of the next four years, Chester would go off on two more extended adventures.

Violent gunplay was also depicted in *Phil Hardy,* a short-lived daily strip created by Jay Jerome Williams (under the pen name Edwin Alger) and George Storm in November 1925. In the opening sequence, Phil, who was shanghaied on a steamer bound for South Africa, found himself in a shoot-out between the mutinous crew and its officers. The fifteen-year-old boy was shown wielding a revolver in the bloody battle. Storm went on to launch another juvenile adventure strip, *Bobby Thatcher,* which ran for ten years beginning in 1927.

Roy Crane's *Wash Tubbs,* which debuted on April 21, 1924, was the most influential of these early adventure strips. Crane started out doing a humorous feature starring a

PHIL HARDY daily strip by George Storm. Guns were blazing in the opening sequence of Storm's first feature. © December 17, 1925, Bell Syndicate, Inc. Courtesy of the San Francisco Academy of Comic Art

WASH TUBBS *daily strip by Roy Crane. Wash and Easy are shipwrecked on an island in one of their early adventures together.*
© 1930 NEA Service, Inc. Courtesy of Howard Lowery

spectacled grocery clerk named Washington Tubbs III, but he quickly tired of writing daily gags about his lead character's amorous affairs and sent him off on a treasure hunt to the South Pacific. For the next five years, Crane's diminutive hero scampered around the globe, gaining and losing riches, chasing girls, and fighting his way out of jams. Violence and danger increasingly entered the story lines as Wash picked up a partner, Gozy Gallup, in 1927 and ran afoul of the roguish Bull Dawson in 1928. The transformation of Crane's creation was almost complete.

On May 6, 1929, Wash encountered a wandering soldier of fortune in the dungeons of Kandelabra, a fictitious European kingdom. Captain Easy provided the element that the rollicking adventure strip was lacking: an adult hero. The two-fisted, square-jawed adventurer showed his stuff by punching his way out of the jail. From then on, Wash and Easy were inseparable—except, of course, when the plot required otherwise.

Robert C. Harvey, in *The Art of the Funnies,* claimed, "It is impossible to overestimate the impact of this character on those who wrote and drew adventure strips in the thirties." A direct lineage can be traced from Captain Easy to Pat Ryan, the costar of Milton Caniff's *Terry and the Pirates,* as well as to Clark Kent (Superman) and Bruce Wayne (Batman) in comic books. Easy was the prototype of the flawed hero: he was just as capable of failure as triumph and had a sensitive side to his prickly personality. In 1933, Crane retitled his Sunday page *Captain Easy—Soldier of Fortune,* and he did some of his finest work in these separate continuities.

Lindbergh's daring solo flight across the Atlantic in May 1927 inspired another adventure genre: the aviation strip. *Tailspin Tommy* (July 19, 1928) by Glenn Chaffin and Hal Forrest, *Tim Tyler's Luck* (August 13, 1928) by Lyman Young, and *Skyroads* (May 27, 1929) by Lester Maitland and Dick Calkins were among the numerous creations that appeared not long after Lucky Lindy landed in Paris. All three strips initially featured young male heroes and, of course, airplanes.

In many comics histories, January 7, 1929, is recorded as the exact date when the adventure strip was born. On that day, both *Buck Rogers,* often regarded as the first science fiction strip, and *Tarzan,* one of the earliest features to be drawn in a

TARZAN *special art by Hal Foster of the famous jungle hero and his simian sidekick.* © 1933 United Feature Syndicate, Inc. Courtesy of Jack Gilbert

LITTLE ORPHAN ANNIE *daily strip by Harold Gray. This episode appeared less than a month after the stock market crash.*

realistic, illustrative style, made their debut appearance. Although the big bang theory rarely applies to developments in the comics medium, an important transition was taking place. Within a relatively short time, "blood and thunder" strips were competing for space with the previously dominant "big-foot" humor genre. This shift would be the major story in the comics industry during the next decade.

The stock market crash that began on "Black Thursday," October 24, 1929, would also have a major impact on the newspaper business. *Editor & Publisher* reported on November 2, 1929, "As the figures in the stock tables receded, the figures in [newspaper] circulation charts soared to gratifying peaks and in some instances passed World Series and national election records. In New York during the first day of the crash, newsstands resembled trading posts on the Stock Exchange

floor with clamoring crowds waiting for each new edition with its heartbreaking news."

While newspaper circulation continued to remain relatively high throughout the Great Depression, advertising dropped off at an alarming rate. There was a 15 percent loss in newspaper ad revenue in 1930, 24 percent in 1931, 40 percent in 1932, and 45 percent in 1933. Although the business started to recover by the second half of the decade, many struggling publications died.

Comics continued to be among the most dependable features the newspapers had to offer to their readers in these troubled times. Cartoonists rose to the challenge and created some of the most memorable strips in comics history. The funnies helped America survive the Depression.

THE GUMPS daily strip by Sidney Smith. The original cast. © 1917. Courtesy of the San Francisco Academy of Comic Art

FAMILY LIFE

Sidney Smith's continuing saga of the Gump clan debuted in 1917 and was one of the most popular features of the 1920s. Other notable creations in the emerging family strip genre were *Polly and Her Pals* (1912), *Keeping Up with the Joneses* (1913), *The Bungle Family* (1918), *Toots and Casper* (1918), *Gasoline Alley* (1919), and *The Nebbs* (1923).

THE GUMPS daily strip by Sidney Smith. Andy gets his wife's attention with his soon-to-be famous exclamation. © 1917. Courtesy of Illustration House

THE GUMPS daily strip by Sidney Smith. Golf season has arrived, but Andy has family responsibilities. © 1921. Courtesy of Bill Janocha

THE GUMPS daily strip by Sidney Smith. Andy and Uncle Bim sneak a nip in the basement and discuss marriage. © February 16, 1921. Courtesy of Rob Stolzer

THE GUMPS daily strip by Sidney Smith. Andy has a hangover on New Year's Day. © January 1, 1924. Courtesy of Rob Stolzer

THE GUMPS daily strip by Sidney Smith. Bim is returning home to Australia. © 1926. Courtesy of Jim Scancarelli

THE GUMPS daily strip by Sidney Smith. Andy ponders what to do with his newfound wealth. © 1927. Courtesy of Sandy Schechter

THE GUMPS original Sunday page by Sidney Smith. A gripping episode from Chester Gump's second adventure story, written by Brandon Walsh and illustrated by Stanley Link. © October 19, 1926. Courtesy of the Art Wood Collection of Cartoon and Caricature, Prints and Photographs Division, Library of Congress

KEEPING UP WITH THE JONESES *daily strip by Pop Momand. This strip about two competing families was based on a phrase popularized in the nineteenth* *century. March 11, 1929. Courtesy of Sandy Schechter*

THE BUNGLE FAMILY *daily strip by Harry Tuthill. George Bungle talks to himself about the ups and downs of Wall Street investing. October 28, 1920s.* *Courtesy of Rob Stolzer*

TOOTS AND CASPER *daily strip by Jimmy Murphy. Inspired by the success of THE GUMPS, Murphy introduced melodrama into his domestic comedy strip in* *the mid-1920s. © 1927 King Features Syndicate, Inc. Courtesy of Richard Marschall*

THE NEBBS *introductory strip by Sol Hess (writer) and W. A. Carlson (artist). A successful businessman, Hess contributed ideas to Sidney Smith before* *starting his own family strip. © 1923 Bell Syndicate, Inc. Courtesy of Mark Johnson*

TOOTS AND CASPER and IT'S PAPA WHO PAYS! Sunday page proof by Jimmy Murphy. In January 1926, King Features Syndicate came up with a new marketing gimmick: two comics for the price of one. They directed many of their cartoonists to develop a companion feature to run at the top of their Sunday pages. Among the King "toppers" were ROSIE'S BEAU by George McManus, PARLOR, BEDROOM AND SINK by Billy DeBeck, DOT AND DASH by Cliff Sterrett, and IT'S PAPA WHO PAYS! by Jimmy Murphy. In December 1930 and January 1931, the Chicago Tribune–New York News Syndicate introduced a new batch of strips that ran at the bottom of their Sunday pages, including THAT PHONEY NICKEL by Frank King, MAW GREEN by Harold Gray, and CIGARETTE SADIE by Chester Gould. Other syndicates also offered companion features as toppers, bottomers, half-pagers, or single panels within their Sunday pages.
© May 8, 1927, King Features Syndicate, Inc. Courtesy of Richard Marschall.

THE BUNGLE FAMILY original hand-colored Sunday page by Harry Tuthill. George gets locked in the coal bin. *January 23, 1927. Courtesy of the Sheldon Memorial Art Gallery, Howard Collection of American Popular Art*

frank king

ONE OF THE FEW STRIPS in which the characters aged at a relatively normal rate, *Gasoline Alley* is the *Our Town* of the comics pages, and the family history that has unfolded in its panels for more than eighty years reads like the Great American Novel. The creator of this epic chronicle was a gentle soul, who approached his craft with workmanlike devotion.

Frank King was born on June 11, 1883, in Cashton, Wisconsin, and his middle-class upbringing in the nearby town of Tomah provided him with a lifetime of inspiration. He landed his first job with the *Minneapolis Times* in 1901, and four years later he went to the Chicago Academy of Fine Arts. After completing his studies, he worked at Hearst's *Chicago American* and *Examiner* before ending up at the *Tribune* in 1909.

King's first successful feature for the *Chicago Tribune* was the charming fantasy strip *Bobby Make-Believe,* which debuted on January 31, 1915. He also produced a black-and-white Sunday page, *The Rectangle,* which was a collection of single-panel cartoons about life in Chicago and other miscellaneous topics.

GASOLINE ALLEY daily panel by Frank King. Walt Wallet gets some unsolicited advice on what to name his new baby. © 1921. Courtesy of Richard Marschall

At the suggestion of *Tribune* copublisher Robert McCormick, King incorporated a new panel, "Sunday Morning in Gasoline Alley," into this page on November 24, 1918; it starred a group of men—Walt Wallet, Doc, Avery, and Bill—who spent their spare time tinkering with old cars. Nine months later, on August 24, 1919, *Gasoline Alley* debuted as an independent feature.

When Walt found an abandoned baby on his doorstep on Valentine's Day of 1921, the dynamics of the strip changed dramatically. In 1959, King recounted the evolution of his creation: "I had started with a popular interest: automobiles. Then I hit on an interesting human situation: Walt and Skeezix. Then I stumbled on the whole idea of growing up the characters. All these points in the progress of *Gasoline Alley* illustrate that if you mirror humanity, if people see themselves in your work, they will want to follow it, to go on seeing themselves."

King developed a clean, unembellished style for the strip that perfectly matched its wholesome tone. Throughout the 1920s and 1930s, the daily episodes traced Skeezix's growth from a baby to a teenager, as well as the cycle of romances, marriages, and births involving the rest of the cast. The Sunday pages provided a showcase for King's more ambitious efforts.

One of these flights of fantasy provided a bird's-eye view of the Wallet neighborhood, with a superimposed grid of six separate scenes. Seasonal strolls through the countryside, dream sequences, holidays, vacations, and thoughtful musings gave King the opportunity to experiment with different art techniques and visual effects.

As the characters in *Gasoline Alley* grew older and changed, they seemed to become almost human. "It is really true that my people seem to act on their own; seem to want to do certain things, almost without my planning it," King claimed. "I think that is a sign that a character has come alive. He has emerged with a personality; the original creative act is over. Now, what the strip artist does is just to cook up situations, and let the strip people react to them in their own way."

A string of talented cartoonists continued to come up with new scenarios for the folks at *Gasoline Alley.* Bill Perry took over the Sunday page in 1951, and Dick Moores assumed full-time duties on the daily strip after King died in 1969. Jim Scancarelli has written and illustrated both the daily and Sunday versions since Moores passed away in 1986. King's characters are in good hands and still have a long life in front of them.

THE RECTANGLE Sunday half-page by Frank King. The **GASOLINE ALLEY** gang first appeared in this Sunday-page feature that King drew from 1918 to 1920 for the Chicago Tribune. *November 23, 1919. Courtesy of Jim Scancarelli*

PATERNAL INSTINCT—Illustrations by Frank King. In 1923, Walt fought a custody battle for Skeezix. *Courtesy of Jim Scancarelli*

GASOLINE ALLEY daily strip by Frank King. The talk in the neighborhood is divided between babies and cars. © 1921. *Courtesy of Jim Scancarelli*

GASOLINE ALLEY daily strip by Frank King. Walt and his mother ponder the identity of a mysterious benefactor. © 1922. Courtesy of Jim Scancarelli

GASOLINE ALLEY daily strip by Frank King. Skeezix learns a naughty word. © 1924. Courtesy of Mort Walker

GASOLINE ALLEY daily strip by Frank King. The artist often used silhouettes to create an evocative mood in the strip. © 1925. Courtesy of the International Museum of Cartoon Art

GASOLINE ALLEY daily strip by Frank King. On June 24, 1926, Walt married Phyllis Blossom. © 1930. Courtesy of Russ Cochran

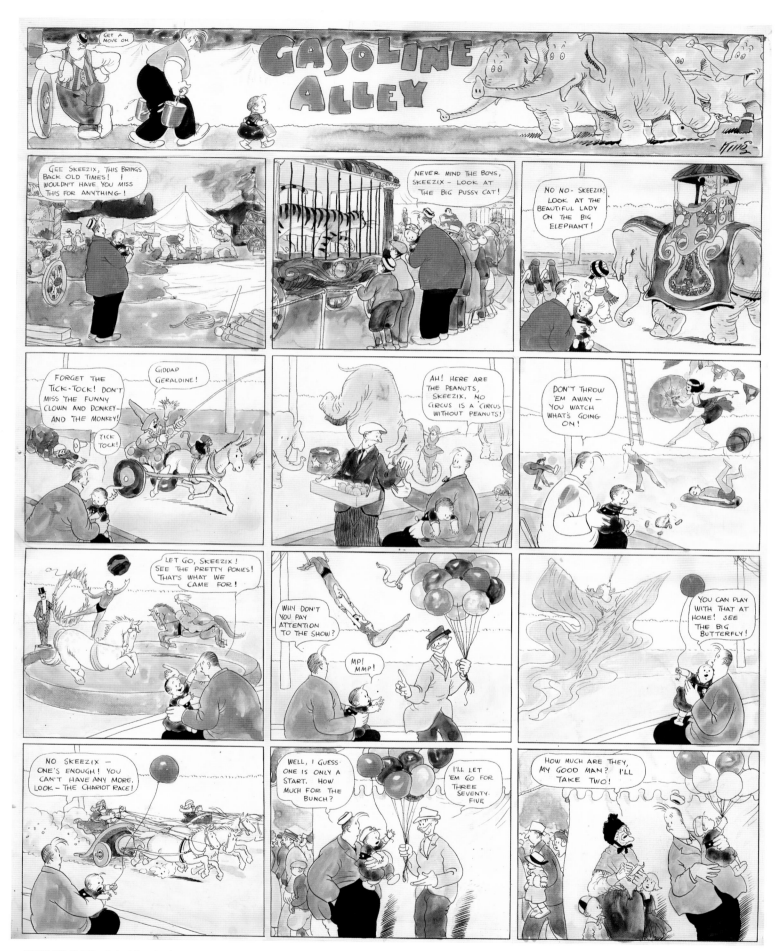

GASOLINE ALLEY original hand-colored Sunday page by Frank King. **The circus comes to town.** © June 11, 1922. Courtesy of Ricardo Martinez

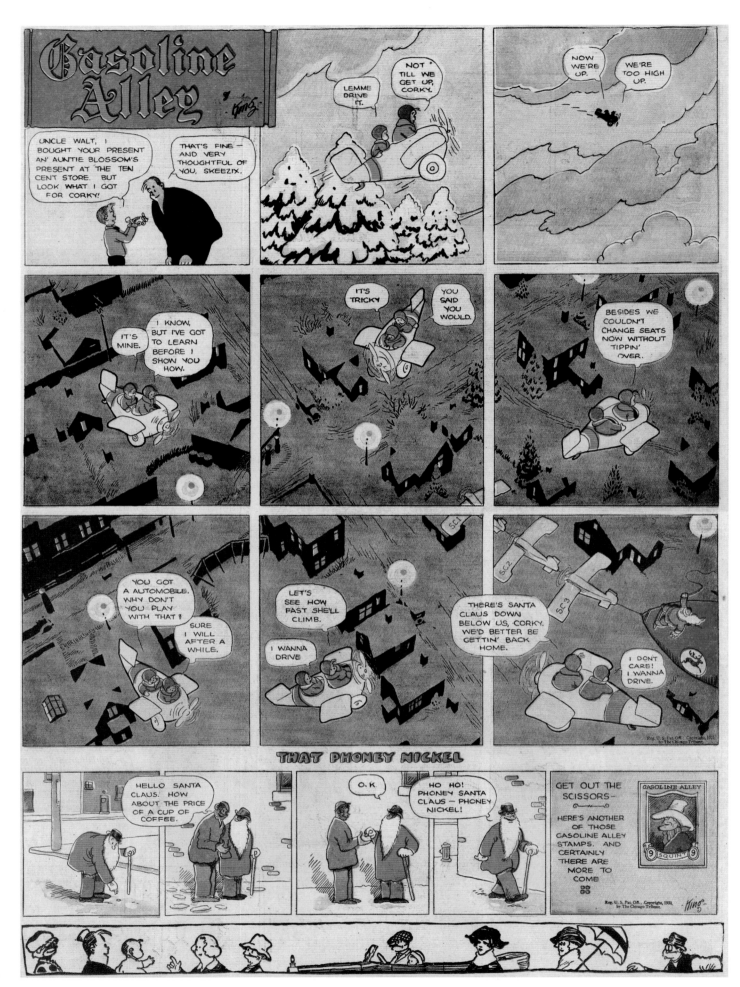

GASOLINE ALLEY Sunday page by Frank King. The artist did many of these innovative panel-within-panel layouts in his Sunday pages. © 1931. Courtesy of Peter Maresca

GASOLINE ALLEY daily strip by Frank King. This strip was done with the scratchboard technique. © August 31, 1939. Courtesy of Jim Scancarelli

GASOLINE ALLEY daily strip by Frank King. A cast portrait. © February 10, 1942. Courtesy of Jim Scancarelli

GASOLINE ALLEY daily strip by Frank King. Skeezix gets a letter from his fiancée, Nina, while serving in the army. © June 1, 1943. Courtesy of Jim Scancarelli

GASOLINE ALLEY daily strip by Frank King. Skeezix is treated after being wounded in combat during World War II. © July 7, 1943. Courtesy of Jim Scancarelli

cliff sterrett

ONE OF THE FIRST comic strips to star an independent "new woman," *Polly and Her Pals* evolved into a graphic tour de force that captured the improvisational spirit of the Jazz Age in pen-and-ink. The creator of this classic feature is one of the most overlooked and underrated geniuses in the history of the art form.

Clifford Sterrett was born into a middle-class family of Scandinavian ancestry in Fergus Falls, Minnesota, on December 12, 1883. At the age of eighteen, he studied at the Chase Art School in Manhattan, and two years later he landed his first job in the art department of the *New York Herald.*

In 1911, Sterrett created four comic strips for the *New York Evening Telegram: Ventriloquial Vag, When A Man's Married, Before and After,* and *For This We Have Daughters?.* A year later, when he switched over to the *New York Journal,* he adapted the latter idea and transformed it into *Positive Polly,* which debuted on December 4, 1912.

Sterrett's strip, soon renamed *Polly and Her Pals,* starred the college-aged Polly Perkins, her middle-aged parents, Paw and Maw, and the scene-stealing Kitty the cat. As the cast expanded to include a household full of quirky relatives, Paw became the central character as the eternally suffering patriarch of the clan. The gags in *Polly and Her Pals* revolved around the day-to-day trials and tribulations of this extended family group.

In the first decade of the feature, Sterrett's Sunday pages were densely packed short stories jammed with colloquial dialogue, background detail, and slapstick action. The daily strips began to display the distinctive angular design and innovative use of black-and-white that were to characterize the next phase of his artistic development.

The years between 1926 and 1935 are considered to be the high point in the evolution of Sterrett's style. He experimented with shapes, lines, and patterns to create compositions that were both geometrically balanced and playfully abstract. He

CLIFF STERRETT—Self-caricature from Comics and Their Creators. *1942. All Polly and Her Pals comic strips © King Features Syndicate, Inc.*

used exaggeration, distortion, and surrealism to dramatic effect. Art critics detected elements of Cubism in his work, and other cartoonists tried to incorporate "Sterrettisms"—triangular rooftops, circular flowers, checkered floors, crescent moons, and oval windows—into their strips.

The unique look of *Polly and Her Pals* has always been difficult to describe in words. Cartoonist and comic scholar Art Spiegelman made a valiant attempt in the introduction to one of the few reprint collections of the strip, published in 1990: "If comic art can be seen as a kind of picture-writing, Cliff Sterrett was its master calligrapher. His hyper-animated graceful-lined doodle-figures spout sweat drops and stars, or leave wonderful amoeba-shaped puffclouds behind them as they bounce through cheerfully dizzy and dizzying compositions at the outer edges of gravity and logic."

By the mid-1930s, Sterrett was suffering from rheumatism and had to cut back on his workload. Paul Fung took over the daily *Polly and Her Pals* strip on March 9, 1935. Sterrett continued to produce the Sunday-page episodes, with the help of assistants, until June 15, 1958. He died six years later. His legacy has yet to be fully appreciated.

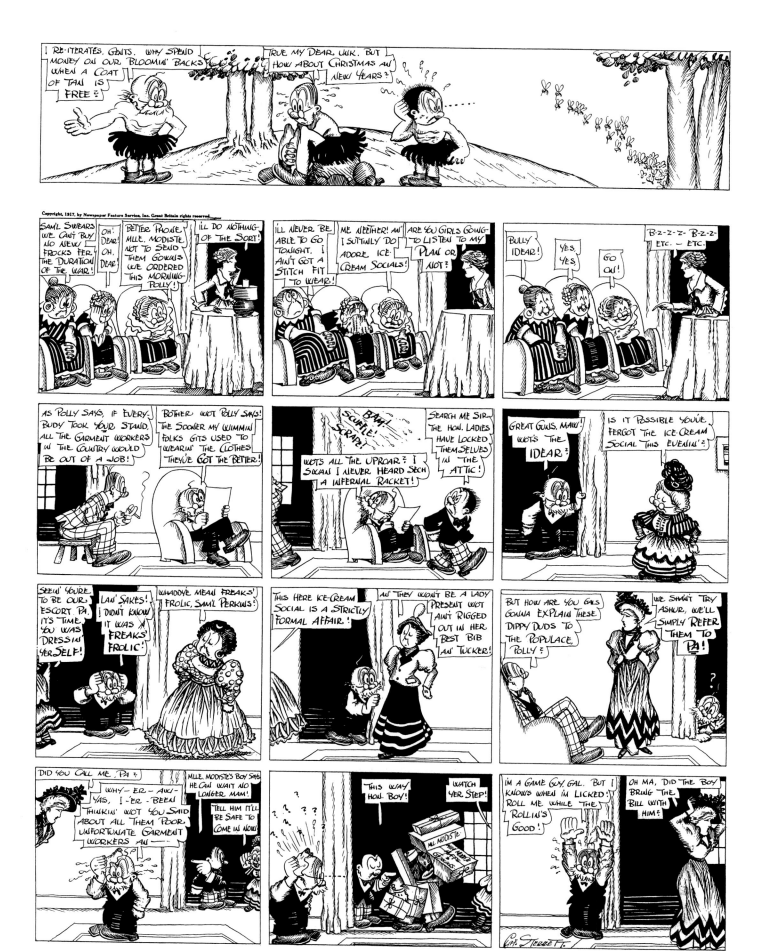

POLLY AND HER PALS Sunday page by Cliff Sterrett. Although the strip was drawn in a more conventional style in the early years, some of Sterrett's trademark design elements were beginning to emerge at this stage in his artistic development. © 1917. Courtesy of Howard Lowery

POLLY AND HER PALS recolored Sunday page by Cliff Sterrett. A classic episode from Sterrett's peak period. © March 3, 1935. Courtesy of Craig Yoe and American Color

POLLY AND HER PALS Sunday page by Cliff Sterrett. Paw's visit to an art museum gives Sterrett an opportunity to try his hand at Cubism. *May 31, 1936.*
Courtesy of the International Museum of Cartoon Art

POLLY AND HER PALS daily strip by Cliff Sterrett. Polly's appearances became less frequent as Sterrett's strip evolved. *© 1934. Courtesy of Howard Lowery*

SOMEBODY'S STENOG daily strip by A. E. Hayward. The first successful working-girl strip debuted in 1916 and starred Cam O'Flage; her boss, Sam Smithers; and coworkers Mary Doodle and Kitty Scratch. © January 10, 1930, Ledger Syndicate, Inc. Courtesy of Bill Janocha

THE FEMININE MYSTIQUE

During the 1920s, women exercised their new voting rights, looked for jobs outside the home, and expressed themselves more openly in public. These changes were reflected on the comics pages as strips starring female characters proliferated. Two distinct character types emerged: the working girl and the flapper. The more ambitious ones found employment in offices and dress shops, while others dabbled in acting or other short-term jobs that permitted enough changes to keep the stories interesting. Flapper fashions were popular with most of the female comic strip stars, and short skirts, long legs, bobbed hair, and lipstick became the accepted style. On the following pages is a selection of comic strips from this era featuring hardworking and attractive leading ladies.

WINNIE WINKLE THE BREADWINNER daily strip by Martin Branner. Winnie's father, Rip, didn't have any qualms about living off his daughter's earnings.
c. 1921. © Tribune Media Services, Inc. All rights reserved. Reprinted with permission. Courtesy of All Star Auctions

TILLIE THE TOILER daily strip by Russ Westover. The diminutive, bulb-nosed Clarence "Mac" McDougall was hopelessly in love with the leggy secretary and part-time model Tillie Jones. © 1928 King Features Syndicate, Inc. Courtesy of Sandy Schechter

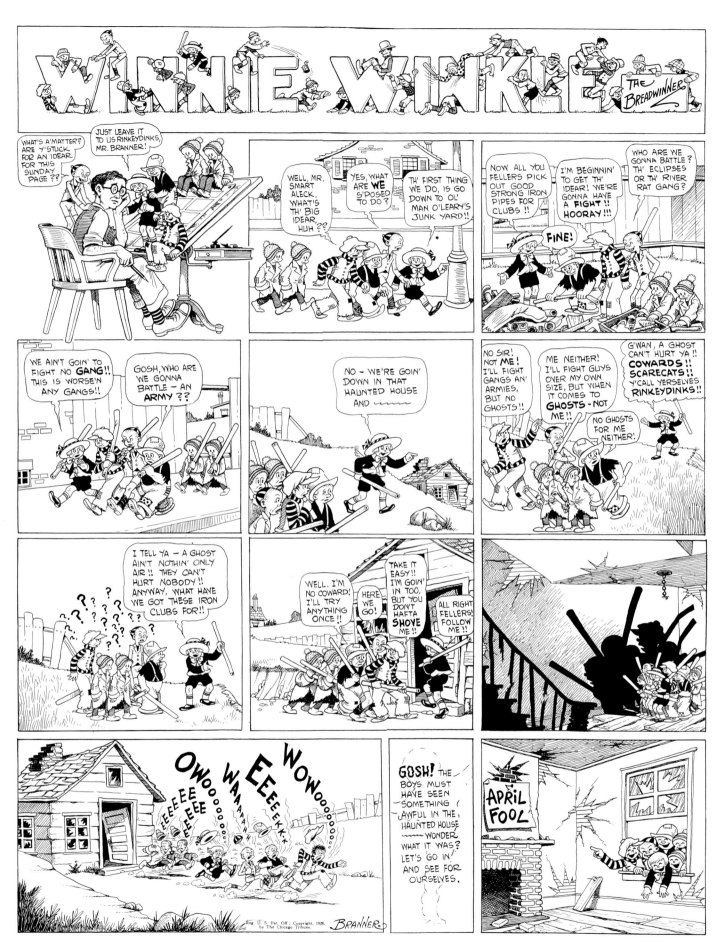

WINNIE WINKLE THE BREADWINNER *Sunday page by Martin Branner, with self-caricature. Winnie's brother Perry and his gang of friends, the Rinkeydinks,* **took over the Sunday episodes in Branner's feature.** © April 1, 1928, Tribune Media Services, Inc. All rights reserved. Reprinted with permission. *Courtesy of David Applegate.*

BOOTS AND HER BUDDIES daily strip by Edgar (Abe) Martin. Known as "the sweetheart of the comics," Boots was an attractive blonde coed who always played by the rules. © 1930 NEA Service, Inc. Courtesy of Sandy Schechter

GUS AND GUSSIE daily strip by Jack Lait (writer) and Paul Fung (artist). Gus Donnerwetter and Gussie Abadab were aspiring actors who worked a variety of odd jobs while waiting for their big break. © May 25, 1926, King Features Syndicate, Inc. Courtesy of Sandy Schechter

ELLA CINDERS daily strip by Bill Conselman (writer) and Charlie Plumb (artist). The Cinderella of the Jazz Age, Ella was a slightly older Orphan Annie who lived a similar rags-to-riches-to-rags existence. © September 15, 1930, Metropolitan Newspaper Feature Service, Inc. Courtesy of Illustration House

ETTA KETT daily strip by Paul Robinson. This leading lady was originally designed to teach proper etiquette to young people and, as a fashion-conscious flapper, continued to set a good example by remaining eternally chaste. © August 1, 1928, Central Press Association, Inc. Courtesy of Mark Johnson

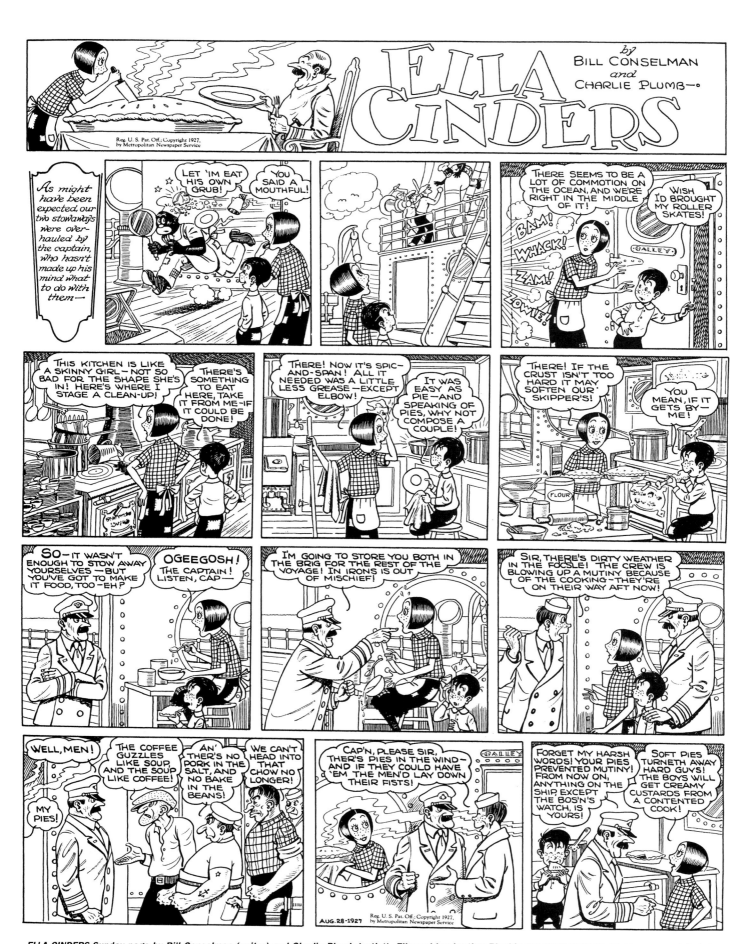

ELLA CINDERS Sunday page by Bill Conselman (writer) and Charlie Plumb (artist). Ella and her brother Blackie are stowaways on an ocean vessel during one of their out-of-luck periods. © August 28, 1927, Metropolitan Newspaper Feature Service, Inc. Courtesy of Sandy Schechter

LADY BOUNTIFUL *daily strip by Gene Carr. One of the first strips with a glamorous female lead, LADY BOUNTIFUL debuted in the New York Journal in 1902. A version was still being produced by Carr in the late 1920s. © October 18, 1928, King Features Syndicate, Inc. Courtesy of Bill Janocha*

PETEY *daily strip by C. A. Voight. Similar to Cliff Sterrett's Paw, Voight's Petey lived with his plump wife and pretty niece. c. 1920s, New York Tribune. Courtesy of the International Museum of Cartoon Art*

FRITZI RITZ *daily strip by Larry Whittington. Launched in 1922 by Whittington, FRITZI RITZ was taken over by Ernie Bushmiller in 1925. © October 13, 1925, King Features Syndicate, Inc. Courtesy of Bill Janocha*

DUMB DORA *daily strip by Chic Young. This early pretty-girl strip by the creator of BLONDIE starred a brunette flapper who wasn't as dumb as her name suggested. © February 19, 1930, Newspaper Feature Service, Inc. Courtesy of the International Museum of Cartoon Art*

BETTY original hand-colored Sunday page by C. A. Voight. Lester DePester, the hapless boyfriend of wealthy Betty Thompson, was always the fall guy in Voight's elegantly illustrated Sunday feature. © December 3, 1922, New York Tribune, Inc. Courtesy of Illustration House

MERELY MARGY Sunday page by John Held Jr. Arab was Margy's main sheik. © May 25, 1930, King Features Syndicate, Inc. Courtesy of Illustration House

MERELY MARGY daily strip by John Held Jr. *After making his mark as an illustrator in many of the leading magazines of the 1920s, Held created a flapper comic strip in 1927, but it did not survive long after the stock market crash.* © September 6, 1927, King Features Syndicate, Inc. Courtesy of Rob Stolzer

SUNNY SUE Sunday page by Nell Brinkley. The Brinkley Girl was the Gibson Girl of the Jazz Age and starred in numerous features, illustrated by Brinkley for the Hearst newspapers, from 1907 to 1937. © July 20, 1929, International Feature Service, Inc. Courtesy of the International Museum of Cartoon Art

billy debeck

THE CREATOR OF BARNEY GOOGLE, Spark Plug, and Snuffy Smith was one of the most naturally gifted cartoonists ever to work in the comics medium. He could draw gorgeous girls and goofy-looking guys and depict them in wild action and peaceful repose. He was a good letterer and a master of graphic design. Urban skylines gave his strips a sense of time and place, and mountain scenery evoked the natural beauty of Appalachia. He could be dramatic, poetic, or romantic and still be funny. As talented as he was artistically, the real secret to his success was an affinity for the common people.

William Morgan DeBeck was born on the South Side of Chicago on April 16, 1890. His parents were of French, Irish, and Welsh stock. After graduating from high school in 1908, he attended the Chicago Academy of Fine Arts and got his first job at the *Youngstown (Ohio) Telegram* in 1910. He worked briefly at the *Pittsburgh Gazette-Times* and finally landed a big-city position at the *Chicago Herald,* where he launched his first successful strip, *Married Life,* on December 9, 1915. When the *Herald* merged with the *Examiner* in May 1918, DeBeck found himself working for William Randolph Hearst.

On June 17, 1919, a new strip, *Take Barney Google, F'rinstance,* debuted in the *Chicago Herald and Examiner.* For the next three years, this henpecked, sports-loving, pop-nosed, bug-eyed character gradually diminished in height as his popularity increased. Then, on July 17, 1922, his fortunes changed. A wealthy gentleman gave Barney a sad-faced nag named Spark Plug. When the horse won the Abadaba Handicap, he became a rich man—and so did his creator.

"Spark Plug, I am happy to say, has caught on," wrote DeBeck in 1924. "All over the United States you find stuffed Spark Plugs and Spark Plug games and Spark Plug drums and Spark Plug balloons and Spark Plug tin pails. And there is a Spark Plug play on the road. The only thing that is lacking is a Spark Plug grand opera."

Throughout the rest of the 1920s and early 1930s, Barney and Spark Plug, along with Sunshine the jockey, pursued an endlessly entertaining series of humorous adventures. They entered the Comic Strip Derby, the Horshoe Handicap, and the T-Bone Stakes. They traveled across the United States, swam the English Channel, solved a murder mystery, and joined a secret society. Barney even ran for president.

And then, on November 17, 1934, a cantankerous mountain man took aim at Barney Google in the backwoods

"I'll say that's pretty tough!" says Barney

BILLY DEBECK—Self-caricature. September 1921, Circulation magazine. Courtesy of Robert Beerbohm
All Barney Google comic strips © King Features Syndicate, Inc.

of North Carolina. Snuffy Smith would eventually get equal billing in the strip, as the hillbilly and the city slicker developed a lasting friendship. The pairing brought a new source of energy and gags to the feature and helped maintain its popularity throughout the remainder of the Depression.

Billy DeBeck died of cancer on November 11, 1942, and Fred Lasswell, DeBeck's former assistant, took over the strip. *Barney Google and Snuffy Smith* had 206 clients in 1946. Forty years later, it was appearing in nearly 900 papers.

"My folks had come out of a country atmosphere, so I was very comfortable with country people," explained Lasswell. "So I started concentrating during the transition period on slowly working Barney out of there and trying to get a little more down-home feeling in the strip."

DeBeck built *Barney Google* into a solid success during his twenty-three-year tenure on the feature. Lasswell continued it for almost sixty years, until 2001 (and it is still running). He took a creation that had earned a place in comic strip history and developed it into an enduring classic.

BARNEY GOOGLE

BARNEY GOOGLE Sunday page proof by Billy DeBeck. Barney and his "sweet woman" were the stars of DeBeck's strip before Spark Plug came on the scene in 1922. This New Year's Eve episode is from the first year of the BARNEY GOOGLE Sunday page. © December 26, 1920. Courtesy of King Features Syndicate

BARNEY GOOGLE daily strip by Billy DeBeck. Barney and Spark Plug swam across the English Channel in 1926. © November 24, 1926. Courtesy of Craig Englund

BARNEY GOOGLE daily strip by Billy DeBeck. During the 1920s and early 1930s, Barney, Spark Plug, and Sunshine lived from one horse race to the next.
© May 5, 1930. Courtesy of Craig Englund

BARNEY GOOGLE daily strip by Billy DeBeck. Barney dreams of his past adventures with Spark Plug. © August 20, 1931. Courtesy of Craig Englund

BARNEY GOOGLE daily strip by Billy DeBeck. Spark Plug raced against a pint-sized look-alike named Pony Boy in the International Derby in 1931.
© September 8, 1931. Courtesy of Bill Janocha

BARNEY GOOGLE daily strip by Billy DeBeck. There were often "recap" strips to bring readers up to speed on DeBeck's fast-paced stories.
© November 23, 1931. Courtesy of Craig Englund

BARNEY GOOGLE daily strip by Billy DeBeck. The excitement of the racetracks was captured in this episode. © November 27, 1931. Courtesy of Craig Englund

BARNEY GOOGLE daily strip by Billy DeBeck. Sunshine, Barney's loyal jockey, was a major character in the strip from mid-1923 until Snuffy Smith stole the sidekick role in late 1934. © December 3, 1931. Courtesy of Craig Englund

BARNEY GOOGLE daily strip by Billy DeBeck. An outstanding example of DeBeck's free-flowing pen-and-ink style. © February 1, 1932. Courtesy of Craig Englund

BARNEY GOOGLE recolored Sunday page by Billy DeBeck. Barney ran for president twice: in the daily continuities in 1928 and in a Sunday-page series in 1932. © April 17, 1932. Original artwork courtesy of Howard Lowery and American Color

BARNEY GOOGLE daily strip by Billy DeBeck. A recap strip for one of DeBeck's mystery stories. © August 26, 1932. Courtesy of Sandy Schechter

BARNEY GOOGLE daily strip by Billy DeBeck. Snuffy and Lowizie (later spelled "Loweezy") made their first appearance in BARNEY GOOGLE on November 17, 1934. © December 26, 1935. Courtesy of Rob Stolzer

BARNEY GOOGLE *Sunday page by Billy DeBeck. The whole population of Hootin' Holler shows up to welcome Lowizie, Snuffy, and Barney back from a trip to the city. Bunky, who first appeared in the topper feature* PARLOR, BEDROOM AND SINK *in 1928, became the star of his own companion strip from* **1935 to 1948.** © April 18, 1937. Courtesy of Peter Maresca.

MOON MULLINS daily strip by Frank Willard. Moon takes a swing at boxing champion Gene Tunney. © 1926 Tribune Media Services, Inc. All rights reserved. Reprinted with permission. Courtesy of Sandy Schechter.

THE LOW LIFE

In 1924, Gilbert Seldes defended the robust vitality of what critics called the "Vulgar Comic Strip" as having "so little respect for law, order, the rights of property, the sanctity of money, the romance of marriage, and all the other foundations of American life, that if they were put into fiction the Society for the Suppression of Everything would hale them incontinently to court and our morals would be saved again." In addition to *Mutt and Jeff* and *Barney Google*, *Moon Mullins*, *Joe Jinks*, and *Joe and Asbestos* were among the strips that featured the exploits of con men, hustlers, and promoters in the world of racetracks, boxing rings, and saloons.

JOE JINKS daily strip by Vic Forsythe. Joe watches Dynamite Dunn fight Mysterious Mike, who turns out to be boxing champ Jack Dempsey. © March 23, 1929, Press Publishing Company (New York World). Courtesy of Sandy Schechter

JOE AND ASBESTOS daily strip by Ken Kling. Although Kling's feature appeared in only ten newspapers, he was among the highest-earning cartoonists in the United States, with an annual salary of $100,000. His clients paid top dollar for the "hot" racing tips that were set in type and pasted into the blank spaces in the strip. © July 6, 1930, Bell Syndicate, Inc. Courtesy of Sandy Schechter

MOON MULLINS daily strip by Frank Willard. Moon's landlady, Emmy Schmaltz, disapproves of his girlfriend, Little Egypt. © March 7, 1924, Tribune Media Services, Inc.

MOON MULLINS daily strip by Frank Willard. Lord Plushbottom, shown here with the cane, married Emmy Schmaltz in 1934. © 1925 Tribune Media Services, Inc.

MOON MULLINS daily strip by Frank Willard. Moon is in hot water again. © 1931 Tribune Media Services, Inc. All rights reserved. Reprinted with permission. Courtesy of Sandy Schechter

MOON MULLINS daily strip by Frank Willard. Moon's kid brother Kayo and his Uncle Willie were regulars in the strip. (Willard sent this strip to Mort Walker, who created BEETLE BAILEY in 1950, when Walker was a young, aspiring cartoonist in the mid-1930s.) © July 24, 1933, Tribune Media Services, Inc. All rights reserved. Reprinted with permission. Courtesy of Mort Walker

MOON MULLINS original hand-colored Sunday page by Frank Willard. The artist often featured wild slapstick and visual sight gags in his Sunday-page episodes. © 1928 Tribune Media Services, Inc. All rights reserved. Reprinted with permission. Courtesy of Gary Ernest Smith

MOON MULLINS Sunday page by Frank Willard. Kayo plays a trick on Emmy Schmaltz.
© October 25, 1931. Tribune Media Services, Inc. All rights reserved. Reprinted with permission. Courtesy of Russ Cochran

OUR BOARDING HOUSE daily panel by Gene Ahearn. The debut appearance of Ahearn's famous blowhard, Major Hoople. © January 27, 1922, NEA Service, Inc. Courtesy of Mark Johnson

OUT OUR WAY special panel by J. R. Williams with self-caricature. In 1936, Williams had 700 daily and 242 Sunday clients, the most of any syndicated feature. © December 13, 1924, NEA Service, Inc. Courtesy of Editor & Publisher

SALESMAN SAM daily strip by George Swanson. Sam Howdy worked in J. Guzzleman's general store in Swanson's screwball strip. © May 3, 1922, NEA Service, Inc. Courtesy of Frank Pauer

PACKAGE DEAL In 1901, Robert F. Paine of the *Cleveland Press* founded the Newspaper Enterprise Association. Beginning in 1909, it distributed a selection of features to its mostly small-town clients for a package price, and the papers could choose which ones to run. On the next page is a sampling of the top strips and panels that the service offered during the 1920s.

All at Sea
by Carolyn Wells
© 1927 BY NEA SERVICE INC.

SALESMAN SAM — SAM IS CANNED — By SWAN

WASHINGTON TUBBS II — By CRANE

BOOTS AND HER BUDDIES — TWO MINDS — By MARTIN

OUR BOARDING HOUSE — By AHERN   **JACK LOCKWILL AT ROCKLAKE** — By GILBERT PATTEN

JAKE IS ON HIS WAY HOME

SAINT and SINNER
by Anne Austin

FRECKLES AND HIS FRIENDS — THAT'S A FAIR QUESTION — By BLOSSER   **OUT OUR WAY** — By WILLIAMS

HEROES ARE MADE—NOT BORN.

LIFE SKETCHES
By W.E. Hill—An Artist Who Senses Spirit Of The Day

"WHAT'S WRONG WITH THE MOVIES?"

Copyright, 1922, by The Chicago Tribune

① Outside any moving picture theatre, showing a line of movie fans waiting for the second show. "Where is Your Daughter Tonight?" a tale of the underworld—is the feature.

② C. Hurlbutt Growl, assistant sub editor on the "Tri-monthly Review," is all of a-quiver over the condition of the movies. "What's wrong with the motion picture industry" is to be his contribution to the April "Tri-monthly," and maybe it isn't going to be full of withering phrases like "Degradation through sex appeal." "Low tone of morality" and "Sterility of Purpose." Everything's wrong with the movies, according to C. Hurlbutt. Perhaps C. H.'s latest returned scenario has something to do with it.

③ Mrs. St. John Ampico, clubwoman, and stationary advisor on committees of the Woman's Self Betterment League, is also dead sure that something is vitally wrong with the movies. Something very vital. And in her little address before the Thursday Club, Mrs. Ampico gave it as her opinion that financial ruin for the motion picture industry is inevitable unless producers can be made to realize that the American public frowns upon questionable sex films. "More educational features, daily incidents in the life of the mud lark, or the house fly for instance, that's the kind of subject our girls and boys really want to see."

④ The Right Reverend Whitely Black opines that something has got to be done, and done immediately, or the whole country will be flooded, nay inundated, with crime wave upon crime wave. And all because of the low moral tone of the motion picture of today. "Let us have pictures based on Bible themes," says the Right Reverend, "take the Story of Ruth and Naomi—there's material for some right minded producer!"

⑤ Mrs. Erda Mudie Mobrey, popular novelist, is of the opinion that the public will stay away from the movies unless the film magnates employ better scenario writers. You should have seen what they did to Mrs. Mobrey's magazine short story "Uphill, Downdale to Grandma Higgins," when it appeared on the screen. "Scarlet Hips," it was called and Mrs. Mobrey, who was present at the Monday matinee, had to be carried out kicking and screaming.

⑥ List to the wail of Miss Eleanor Lime Light from the speaking stage. Traveled all the way from New York to Los Angeles and back again, with nothing but a riled disposition to show for it. She didn't film as well as they hoped she would. "No place in the movies for people who can act—they want ten-year-old waitresses and nurse girls instead! That's what's the matter with the movies!"

⑦ And now meet Miss Tolita Cutely of Hollywood's most exclusive set and super-feature star of the Sex Playful Studios, Inc. Miss Cutely and her lady press agent are very very busy these days explaining to a breathless world what isn't the matter with the movies, and Hollywood in particular. "Tolita," explains the lady P. A., "is too busy being just a dear sweet trusting little girl to even think of all the frightful stories you read in the papers about the motion picture people. Next to her dear public, her mamma, and work, of course, she loves her dollies best. Look at this photo of Tolita tiptoeing away, after putting her Teddy bear and her Jackie Coogan doll to bed, and I know you will agree with me that here is a womanly little girl, full of sunshine and light, who has never lost her sense of values."

⑧ And here is a closeup of Miss Cutely in her Hollywood palace, en route to bed at 8:30 P. M., with her favorite dollies. Doesn't this change your ideas of movie people?

⑨ This is Adolph P. Crackwell, the film magnate, who made "Sex Playful Films" a household word. "The public," says he, via Mike Blood, his press agent, "does not want unhealthy sex plays. What the public wants and what we are striving to offer, are stories of clean universal appeal with a homely touch of human sweetness and simplicity. In fact, our next release will be a film version of Whittier's "Barefoot Boy."

⑩ Outside any motion picture theatre, a few weeks or months hence, showing the customary line of fans waiting for the second show. "Paths of Shame," a screen version of Whittier's "Barefoot Boy," is the current attraction. Miss Tolita Cutely, the featured player, plays the part of the vamp who lures the Barefoot Boy to the city. "The part was especially introduced by Mr. Whittier himself to suit Miss Cutely's rare personality," writes her P. A. Incidentally, the line of waiting fans extends around the corner, which may or may not tend to show that what's wrong with the movies is the public.

LIFE SKETCHES Sunday page by W. E. Hill. This long-running feature started as *AMONG US MORTALS* in the New York Tribune in 1916 and was distributed by the Chicago Tribune–New York News Syndicate beginning in 1922. Sunday Oregonian. © April 2, 1922, Chicago Tribune. Courtesy of Bill Griffith

COMMODUS
Hero of the Colesseum.
KILLED AN ELEPHANT WITH ONE BOW SHOT —
THE ARROW PASSING COMPLETELY THROUGH THE BODY OF THE ELEPHANT —

Commodus was left-handed and red-headed —

JEAN FOLEY, of Pittsburg
WROTE A LETTER OF 190 PAGES —
102,640 WORDS

GEORGE WRIGHT
(Cincinnati Red Stockings)
1869
PLAYED 52 GAMES
HIT .518
SCORED 339 RUNS
AND MADE
59
HOMERS.

Miss
DOROTHY SMITH, of Boston
CAN TOUCH HER TOE WITH HER ELBOW

ABE THE NEWSBOY
— A San Francisco lightweight
HAS FOUGHT 906 BATTLES
— and is still fighting

RIPLEY'S BELIEVE IT OR NOT original page by Robert Ripley. This fact-based, novelty feature started as a sports cartoon in the New York Globe in December 1918. © 1920s. Courtesy of Bill Janocha

WHEN A FELLER NEEDS A FRIEND daily panel by Clare Briggs. The artist often featured a small-town Tom Sawyer named "Skin-nay" in his nostalgic cartoons. © July 7, 1924, New York Tribune, Inc. Courtesy of Sandy Schechter

THE TIMID SOUL daily panel by H. T. Webster. The reticent and fussy Caspar Milquetoast was Webster's most memorable character. © April 13, 1936, New York Tribune, Inc. Courtesy of the International Museum of Cartoon Art

A SLICE OF LIFE The syndicated daily panel evolved from political, sports, and humorous cartoons done by such local favorites as John McCutcheon of the *Chicago Tribune,* TAD Dorgan of the *New York Journal,* and Rube Goldberg of the *New York Evening Mail.* During the 1920s, Clare Briggs, H. T. Webster, Fontaine Fox, J. R. Williams, and Clare Dwiggins were among the artists producing nationally distributed panels that dealt with the recurrent themes of childhood, nostalgia, idle pastimes, family relationships, home life, and the workplace.

OUR SECRET AMBITIONS daily panel by Garr Williams. The artist joined the Chicago Tribune in 1921 and took over Clare Briggs's former spot, on the front page of the second section, in 1924. © March 5, 1923, Chicago Tribune. Courtesy of Rob Stolzer

TOONERVILLE FOLKS *daily panel by Fontaine Fox. While working at the Chicago Post in 1908, Fox created a weekly panel that starred a group of small-town kids. When he signed a contract with the Wheeler Syndicate in 1913, he expanded the cast of the feature, which eventually was titled TOONERVILLE FOLKS, to include the Skipper of the Toonerville Trolley, the Powerful Katrinka, the Terrible-Tempered Mr. Bang, Aunt Eppie Hogg, and Mickey (Himself) McGuire.* © 1926 Bell Syndicate, Inc. Courtesy of Sandy Schechter

SCHOOL DAYS *daily panel by Clare Dwiggins. "Dwig" drew on his own childhood experiences for many of his creations, which included SCHOOL DAYS (1909), TOM SAWYER AND HUCK FINN (1918), and NIPPER (1931).* © McClure Syndicate, Inc. Courtesy of the International Museum of Cartoon Art

OUT OUR WAY *daily panel by J. R. Williams. This popular panel, which debuted on November 22, 1921, featured a rotating cast of graying mothers, slovenly kids, grizzly cowboys, and cantankerous machine-shop workers.* © October 10, 1924, NEA Service, Inc. Courtesy of Frank Pauer

DIFFICULT DECISIONS *daily panel by Gluyas Williams. A regular contributor to The New Yorker from its inception in 1925, Williams also did a syndicated panel that ran under different titles from the mid-1920s to the 1940s.* © November 2, 1927, Bell Syndicate, Inc. Courtesy of the International Museum of Cartoon Art

TOONERVILLE FOLKS Sunday page by Fontaine Fox. The *TOONERVILLE FOLKS* Sunday page debuted in 1918 and remained in circulation, along with the daily panel, until 1955. © McNaught Syndicate, Inc. Courtesy of Russ Cochran

SCHOOL DAYS

Now That the Flying Machine is Invented
Who Will Invent a Landing Machine?

By Dwig

SCHOOL DAYS original hand-colored Sunday page by Clare Dwiggins. The first Sunday series of Dwig's most enduring creation debuted in 1914 and was revived in 1928. © October 27, 1929, McClure Syndicate, Inc. Courtesy of Jack Gilbert and the Barnum Museum.

NIPPER daily strip by Clare Dwiggins. The last major creation by this prolific artist was set in a contemporary small town and ran from 1931 to 1937. © 1930s, Public Ledger

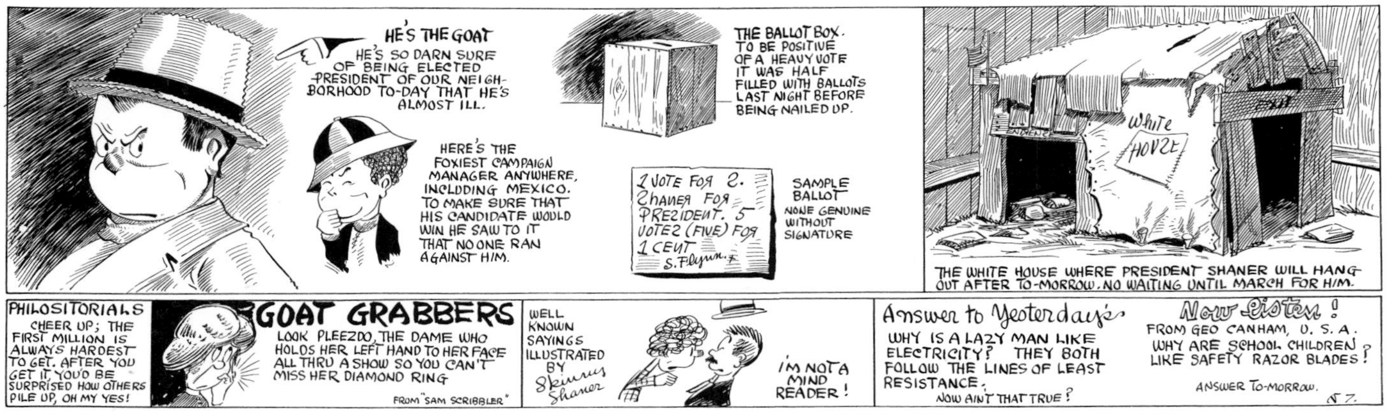
HE'S THE GOAT
HE'S SO DARN SURE OF BEING ELECTED PRESIDENT OF OUR NEIGHBORHOOD TO-DAY THAT HE'S ALMOST ILL.
HERE'S THE FOXIEST CAMPAIGN MANAGER ANYWHERE, INCLUDING MEXICO. TO MAKE SURE THAT HIS CANDIDATE WOULD WIN HE SAW TO IT THAT NO ONE RAN AGAINST HIM.
THE BALLOT BOX. TO BE POSITIVE OF A HEAVY VOTE IT WAS HALF FILLED WITH BALLOTS LAST NIGHT BEFORE BEING NAILED UP.
1 VOTE FOR 2. SHANER FOR PREZIDENT. 5 VOTEZ (FIVE) FOR 1 CENT S. Flynn.
SAMPLE BALLOT NONE GENUINE WITHOUT SIGNATURE
WHITE HOUZE
THE WHITE HOUSE WHERE PRESIDENT SHANER WILL HANG OUT AFTER TO-MORROW. NO WAITING UNTIL MARCH FOR HIM.
PHILOSITORIALS
CHEER UP; THE FIRST MILLION IS ALWAYS HARDEST TO GET. AFTER YOU GET IT, YOU'D BE SURPRISED HOW OTHERS PILE UP, OH MY YES!
GOAT GRABBERS
LOOK PLEEZDO, THE DAME WHO HOLDS HER LEFT HAND TO HER FACE ALL THRU A SHOW SO YOU CAN'T MISS HER DIAMOND RING
FROM "SAM SCRIBBLER"
WELL KNOWN SAYINGS ILLUSTRATED BY Skinny Shaner
I'M NOT A MIND READER!
Answer to Yesterday's
WHY IS A LAZY MAN LIKE ELECTRICITY? THEY BOTH FOLLOW THE LINES OF LEAST RESISTANCE.
NOW AIN'T THAT TRUE?
Now Listen!
FROM GEO CANHAM, U. S. A.
WHY ARE SCHOOL CHILDREN LIKE SAFETY RAZOR BLADES?
ANSWER TO-MORROW.

US BOYS daily strip by Tom McNamara. One of the first of the modern kid comics, US BOYS was also the inspiration for Hal Roach's OUR GANG comedies.

CHILD STARS Everyday life, viewed through the eyes of comic strip kids, was another thematic preoccupation on the funnies pages during the 1920s. The new generation was less antisocial than the mischievous pranksters of the past, and their adventures were depicted with greater authenticity and attention to detail. Adolescents and teenagers also joined the youth movement as newspapers offered something for every age group.

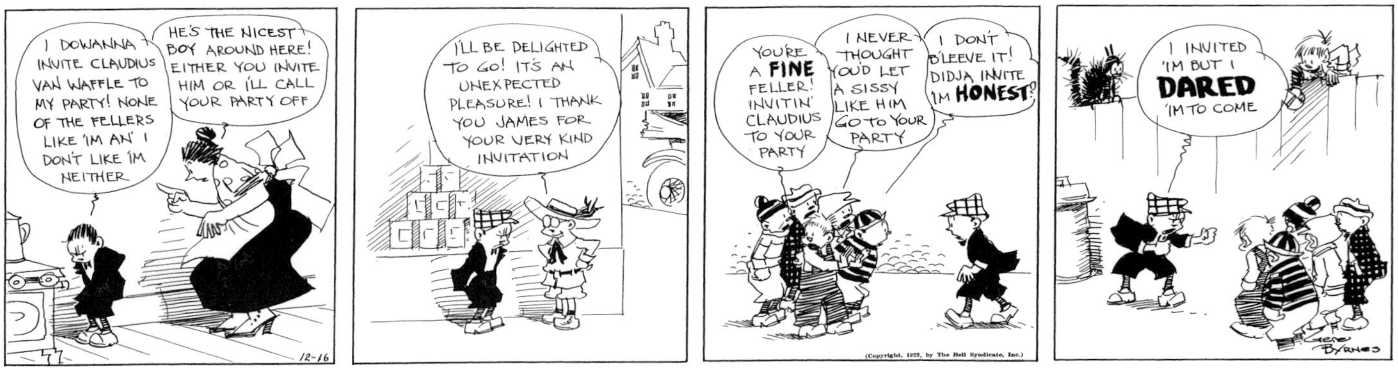
I DOWANNA INVITE CLAUDIUS VAN WAFFLE TO MY PARTY! NONE OF THE FELLERS LIKE 'IM AN' I DON'T LIKE 'IM NEITHER
HE'S THE NICEST BOY AROUND HERE! EITHER YOU INVITE HIM OR I'LL CALL YOUR PARTY OFF
I'LL BE DELIGHTED TO GO! IT'S AN UNEXPECTED PLEASURE! I THANK YOU JAMES FOR YOUR VERY KIND INVITATION
YOU'RE A FINE FELLER! INVITIN' CLAUDIUS TO YOUR PARTY
I NEVER THOUGHT YOU'D LET A SISSY LIKE HIM GO TO YOUR PARTY
I DON'T B'LEEVE IT! DIDJA INVITE 'IM HONEST?
I INVITED 'IM BUT I DARED 'IM TO COME

REG'LAR FELLERS daily strip by Gene Byrnes. This popular feature, which began as a single panel in 1917, featured a suburban gang lead by Jimmie Dugan, the lad in the checkered cap.

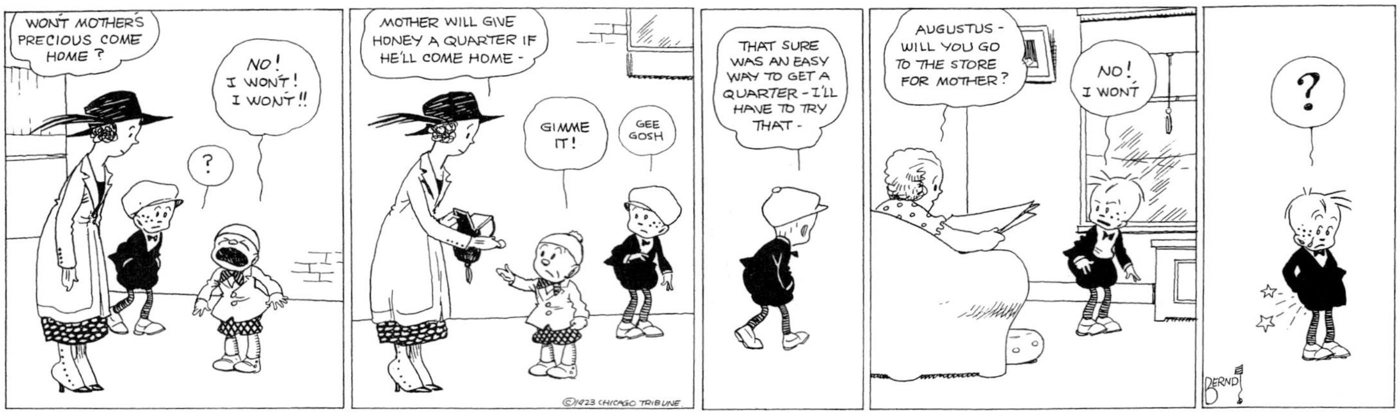
WON'T MOTHER'S PRECIOUS COME HOME?
NO! I WON'T! I WON'T!!
?
MOTHER WILL GIVE HONEY A QUARTER IF HE'LL COME HOME -
GIMME IT!
GEE GOSH
THAT SURE WAS AN EASY WAY TO GET A QUARTER - I'LL HAVE TO TRY THAT -
AUGUSTUS - WILL YOU GO TO THE STORE FOR MOTHER?
NO! I WON'T
?

SMITTY daily strip by Walter Berndt. Augustus Smith, the thirteen-year-old star of Berndt's 1922 creation, worked in Mr. Bailey's office and lived with his parents and little brother Herby.

Reg'lar Fellers
BY Gene Byrnes

MAR. 25-28-

©1928 N.Y. TRIBUNE, INC.

REG'LAR FELLERS Sunday page by Gene Byrnes. Jimmie Dugan, Puddinhead Duffy, Baggy Scanlon, and Bump Mahoney discuss life in prison while touring their suburban neighborhood. © March 25, 1928, New York Tribune, Inc. Courtesy of the International Museum of Cartoon Art

HAROLD TEEN original hand-colored Sunday page by Carl Ed. Harold goes for his first shave in this April Fool's Day episode.

SMITTY original daily strips by Walter Berndt. Lost dogs, office politics, and occasional vacations were typical of the lighthearted story lines during the fifty-two-year run of Berndt's feature. © April 16, 1930, January 29 and June 18, 1931, and February 2, 1932, Tribune Media Services, Inc. All rights reserved. Reprinted with permission. Courtesy of the Art Wood Collection of Cartoon and Caricature, Prints and Photographs Division, Library of Congress

harold gray

HAROLD GRAY AND LITTLE ORPHAN ANNIE—Photograph and drawing. *December 20, 1924. Courtesy of Editor & Publisher*
All Little Orphan Annie comic strips © Tribune Media Services, Inc. All rights reserved. Reprinted with permission. Courtesy of the Harold Gray Collection, Boston University (unless otherwise noted)

THE MASTER STORYTELLER of the comics, this deeply dedicated cartoonist was often criticized for using his strip to promote an agenda of conservative political beliefs. Undaunted, he never wavered from his unique personal vision, and for more than four decades he nurtured a creation that was among the top features in readership popularity.

Harold Gray was born on a farm near Kankakee, Illinois, on January 20, 1894. After graduating from Purdue University in 1917, he joined the staff of the *Chicago Tribune*. In 1920, he began assisting Sidney Smith on *The Gumps*, gaining valuable experience before launching his own strip on August 5, 1924.

Little Orphan Annie was initially modeled after Mary Pickford and, like the famous film star's characters, found herself in one predicament after another. It did not take long for Annie to establish lasting friendships, and by early 1925, she was teamed up with her loyal canine companion, Sandy, and her eternal benefactor, Daddy Warbucks. The story lines in the strip evolved from predictable melodramas in the 1920s, following the spunky waif's wandering encounters with an ever-changing cast of foster families, to extended adventure yarns in the 1930s, filled with intrigue, danger, and fantasy.

The little girl in the red dress was always the star attraction in the strip and won the devotion of newspaper readers, as well as radio, movie, and theater audiences. In Gray's eyes she was "tougher than hell, with a heart of gold and a fast left, who can take care of herself because she has to."

Critics described the style of the strip as "primitive," "awkward," and "mediocre," but Gray made the most of his admittedly limited artistic abilities. "In the beginning *Little Orphan Annie* appeared crude, but soon Gray's visuals were to transform themselves into a gallery of icons," wrote Richard Marschall in *America's Great Comic-Strip Artists.* "Indeed he was to become the comics' great expressionist, with every graphic element reflecting—even manifesting—moods, currents, and fears."

Gray made effective use of cross-hatching, and his liberally applied blacks and background shadings provided an ominous sense of foreboding. At times, Annie's famous empty eyes could be remarkably expressive; in other situations, readers saw the world through her vacant stare.

Frequently under fire for his conservative diatribes, often in the form of long monologues delivered by the characters in the strip, Gray had a philosophy that was personal and consistent. He hated pretension, intolerance, abuse of power, censorship, and governmental intervention. He fought against Franklin Delano Roosevelt's New Deal and the increasing power of the labor unions. His heroes were farmers, shopkeepers, and factory workers. At times he advocated vigilante justice and criminal behavior for the right cause. Above all, he was a champion of self-reliance.

The editorializing in the strip always remained secondary to the storytelling. Gray would set up a new situation quickly and then build suspense for weeks or months. His plots often ended with a climactic resolution. Each episode of *Little Orphan Annie* represented a day in the life of the characters, and some of the continuities stretched more than a year in length. He had a gift for finely woven yarns, laced with heartwarming pathos, dramatic tension, and moral rectitude.

In his final years before his death in 1968, Gray seemed increasingly out of step with the times, but he remained committed to his ideals until the end. Similar to his spirited orphan, he was fiercely independent and eternally optimistic—a true American original.

LITTLE ORPHAN ANNIE original hand-colored Sunday page by Harold Gray. This early episode shows Annie with her Mary Pickford curls.
© January 11, 1925. Courtesy of Illustration House

LITTLE ORPHAN ANNIE daily strip by Harold Gray. Daddy Warbucks and Annie meet for the first time. © *September 27, 1924*

LITTLE ORPHAN ANNIE daily strip by Harold Gray. Daddy confides his dilemma of financial success and marital failure to Annie. © *October 3, 1924*

LITTLE ORPHAN ANNIE daily strip by Harold Gray. A kind policeman helps Annie rescue a homeless mutt, who becomes her faithful sidekick, Sandy.
© *January 21, 1925*

LITTLE ORPHAN ANNIE daily strip by Harold Gray. Annie, who is living with the Silo family when a tornado destroys their farm, is reunited with Daddy.
© *June 15, 1925*

LITTLE ORPHAN ANNIE daily strip by Harold Gray. Mrs. Pewter fashions Annie's famous dress, which she wears from then on. © November 16, 1927

LITTLE ORPHAN ANNIE daily strip by Harold Gray. An outstanding example of Gray's authentic depiction of rural America. © July 22, 1929

LITTLE ORPHAN ANNIE daily strip by Harold Gray. After being stranded at sea, Annie is rescued by Daddy, who brings her back to civilization.
© November 13, 1930

LITTLE ORPHAN ANNIE daily strip by Harold Gray. Annie and Sandy hit the road again. © September 22, 1936. Courtesy of Rob Stolzer

LITTLE ORPHAN ANNIE Sunday page by Harold Gray. Annie and Daddy do a little Christmas shopping with their meager savings. © 1934. Courtesy of Peter Maresca

LITTLE ORPHAN ANNIE daily strip by Harold Gray. During the Depression years, Annie became increasingly involved in mystery and intrigue, as this example from the "Shanghai" sequence demonstrates. © October 31, 1938

LITTLE ORPHAN ANNIE daily strip by Harold Gray. It appears as if Annie might have walked her last road in this cliffhanger. © January 16, 1939

LITTLE ORPHAN ANNIE daily strip by Harold Gray. Punjab, Wun Wey, and the Asp became regular members of the cast in the 1930s. © May 17, 1939

LITTLE ORPHAN ANNIE daily strip by Harold Gray. Annie unwittingly helps her friend Panda blow up a German submarine, in this wartime episode. © June 6, 1942

MINUTE MOVIES two-tiered daily strip by Ed Wheelan. These comic strip serials were directed by Art Hokum and costarred the handsome Dick Dare, the lovely Hazel Dearie, the sinister Ralph McSneer, and the bumbling Fuller Phun. *November 18, c. 1928. © George Matthew Adams Syndicate, Inc. Courtesy of the Art Wood Collection of Cartoon and Caricature, Prints and Photographs Division, Library of Congress*

HAIRBREADTH HARRY daily strip by Charles W. Kahles. The artist's original HAIRBREADTH HARRY Sunday page debuted in 1906. A daily strip version was launched by the Ledger Syndicate in 1923. *© 1923 Ledger Syndicate, Inc. Courtesy of Sandy Schechter*

TO BE CONTINUED

Although storytelling was an important element of the comics from the beginning, the adventure strip took its modern form in the mid-1920s. *Hairbreadth Harry* and *Minute Movies,* which started as parodies of stage and film melodramas, popularized the cliffhanger approach, while *The Gumps* and *Little Orphan Annie* raised the levels of suspense and pathos in the funnies. George Storm's juvenile adventure strips, *Phil Hardy* and *Bobby Thatcher,* added the element of danger to the mix, and by the end of the decade, Roy Crane incorporated all of these ingredients in *Wash Tubbs,* the first fully developed "blood and thunder" strip.

BOBBY THATCHER daily strip by George Storm. The illustrator on PHIL HARDY, which debuted in 1925, Storm started his own juvenile adventure strip in 1927. *© 1929 McClure Syndicate, Inc. Courtesy of Editor & Publisher*

HAIRBREADTH HARRY original hand-colored Sunday page by Charles W. Kahles. A classic episode featuring the hero, Harry; the fair damsel, Belinda Blinks; and the villain, Rudolph Rassendale. © April 29, 1928, Ledger Syndicate, Inc. Courtesy of the Library of Congress. Gift of Jessie Kahles Straut.

roy crane

ROY CRANE—Self-caricature done for a 1925 Christmas card.
Courtesy of Art Wood
All Wash Tubbs and Captain Easy comic strips © NEA Service, Inc.

A MAJOR CONTRIBUTOR to the development of the adventure strip, this talented cartoonist created two classic features over the course of a career that spanned six decades. His experiments in storytelling and rendering influenced a generation of artists who expanded the horizons of the comics medium.

Royston Campbell Crane was born in Abilene, Texas, on November 22, 1901. His parents encouraged their only child's artistic interests, and when Roy was fourteen he took the C. N. Landon mail-order cartoon course. In 1920, he studied at the Chicago Academy of Fine Arts and then succumbed to youthful wanderlust, riding the rails through the Southwest and sailing to Europe on a freighter.

In 1922, he jumped ship in New York and got a job at the *New York World*, where he worked as H. T. Webster's assistant. After one false start, a panel titled *Music to the Ear*,

Crane sold a strip to his old correspondence instructor, Charles N. Landon, who also happened to be the comics editor of the Newspaper Enterprise Association.

Wash Tubbs, which starred a diminutive, skirt-chasing grocery clerk who resembled comedian Harold Lloyd, debuted on April 21, 1924. Crane soon ran out of daily jokes involving his character's preoccupations with get-rich-quick-schemes and pretty girls, so he sent him off to the South Seas on a treasure hunt. Five months into its run, *Wash Tubbs* had evolved into a picaresque adventure strip, blending continuing stories and hilarious high jinks. Over the course of the next few years, Wash picked up a sidekick, Gozy Gallup; repeatedly tangled with a brutish sea captain, Bull Dawson; and finally, in 1929, crossed paths with a handsome soldier of fortune named Captain Easy.

Although Crane had introduced dangerous villains and a dashing hero into his feature, it continued to combine thrills and laughs. "*Wash Tubbs* remained a boisterous, rollicking, fun-loving strip full of last minute dashes, free-for-all fisticuffs, galloping horse chases, pretty girls and sound effects—Bam, Pow, Boom, Sok, Lickety-whop," Robert C. Harvey wrote in *The Art of the Funnies.* "When Crane's characters ran, they ran all out—knees up to their chins. When they were knocked down in a fight, they flipped backwards, head over heels."

During the 1930s, Crane began experimenting with various shading techniques to create more atmospheric backgrounds in his strip. For a time, he used pebble board, which gave a rich texture to the drawings when a soft crayon was applied. He then switched to Craft-Tint Double Tone paper, which provided two different types of patterns when a chemical solution was painted on. Crane used these tools to render realistic jungles, deserts, oceans, and mountains. The characters who cavorted in this evocative scenery were still drawn in a conventional "big-foot" style, giving the strip a distinctive look.

Crane's next major feature, *Buz Sawyer,* which was launched by King Features on November 1, 1943, represented the final phase in his stylistic evolution. It combined fast-paced adventure stories, inspired by the dramatic events of World War II, with authentically illustrated military equipment and real locations, which Crane researched during trips around the world.

Crane continued to refine the storytelling and art in *Buz Sawyer,* with the help of talented assistants including Ralph Lane, Hank Schlensker, Ed Granberry, and Clark Haas, until he passed away in 1977. His career traced all of the major milestones in the development of the adventure strip genre, leaving other artists a well-marked trail to the uncharted territories of artistic discovery.

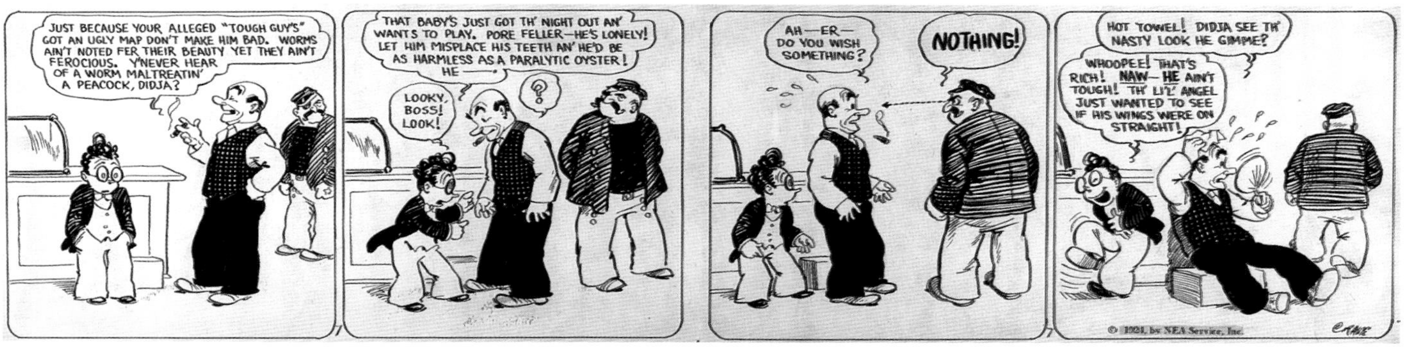
JUST BECAUSE YOUR ALLEGED "TOUGH GUY'S" GOT AN UGLY MAP DON'T MAKE HIM BAD. WORMS AIN'T NOTED FER THEIR BEAUTY YET THEY AIN'T FEROCIOUS. Y'NEVER HEAR OF A WORM MALTREATIN' A PEACOCK, DIDJA?
THAT BABY'S JUST GOT TH' NIGHT OUT AN' WANTS TO PLAY. PORE FELLER—HE'S LONELY! LET HIM MISPLACE HIS TEETH AN' HE'D BE AS HARMLESS AS A PARALYTIC OYSTER! HE——
LOOKY, BOSS! LOOK!
?
AH—ER— DO YOU WISH SOMETHING?
NOTHING!
HOT TOWEL! DIDJA SEE TH' NASTY LOOK HE GIMME?
WHOOPEE! THAT'S RICH! NAW—HE AIN'T TOUGH! TH' LI'L' ANGEL JUST WANTED TO SEE IF HIS WINGS WERE ON STRAIGHT!

***WASH TUBBS* daily strip by Roy Crane. Wash worked in a grocery store during the first months of Crane's new feature.** © 1924. Courtesy of All Star Auctions

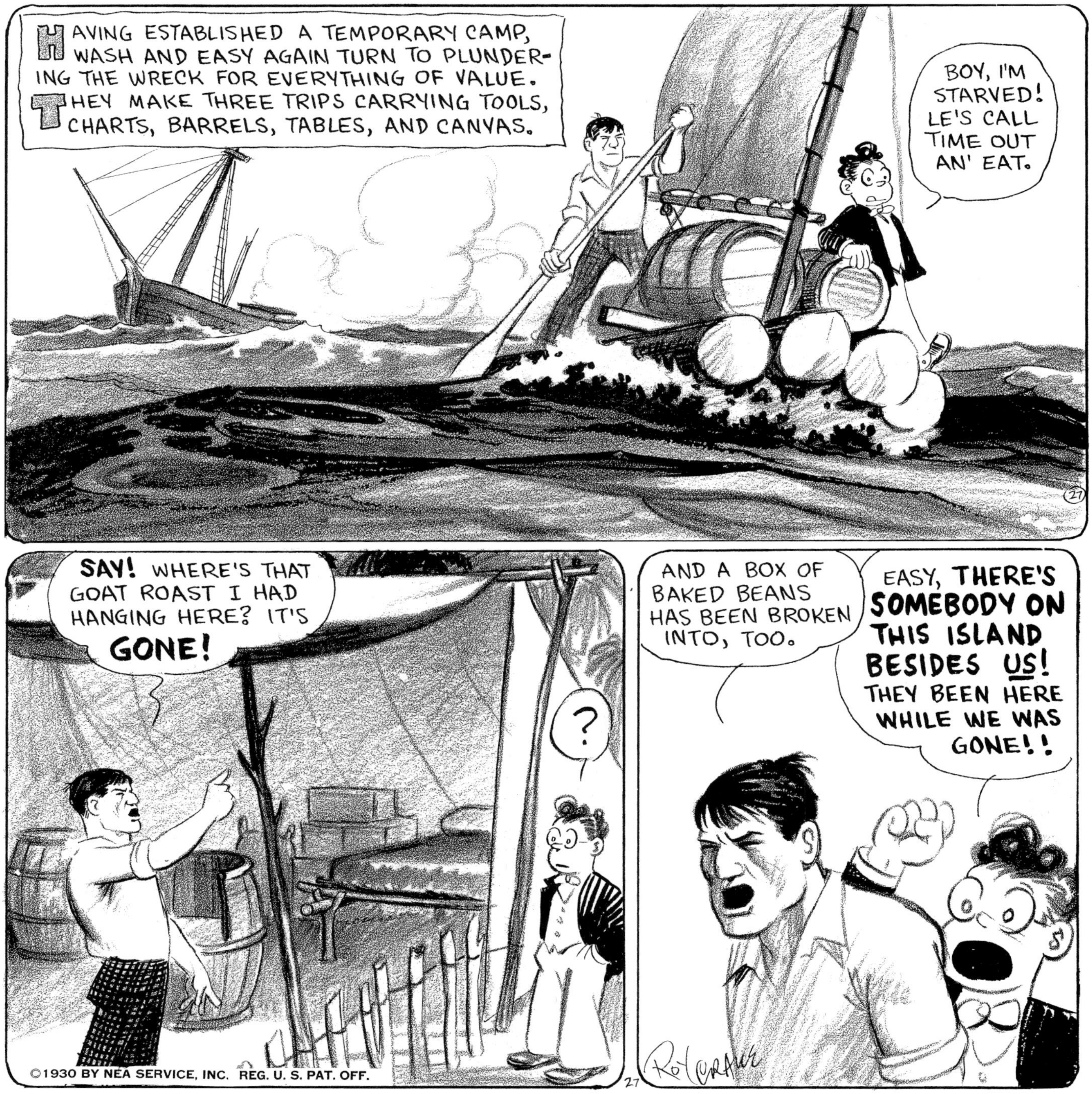
HAVING ESTABLISHED A TEMPORARY CAMP, WASH AND EASY AGAIN TURN TO PLUNDERING THE WRECK FOR EVERYTHING OF VALUE. THEY MAKE THREE TRIPS CARRYING TOOLS, CHARTS, BARRELS, TABLES, AND CANVAS.
BOY, I'M STARVED! LE'S CALL TIME OUT AN' EAT.
SAY! WHERE'S THAT GOAT ROAST I HAD HANGING HERE? IT'S GONE!
?
AND A BOX OF BAKED BEANS HAS BEEN BROKEN INTO, TOO.
EASY, THERE'S SOMEBODY ON THIS ISLAND BESIDES US! THEY BEEN HERE WHILE WE WAS GONE!!
©1930 BY NEA SERVICE, INC. REG. U. S. PAT. OFF.
ROY CRANE

***WASH TUBBS* daily strip by Roy Crane. The artist experimented with crayon pencil on pebble board to render scenery and atmosphere in this famous episode. Wash and Easy, who had just become partners, are stranded at sea.** © 1930. Courtesy of the International Museum of Cartoon Art

WASH TUBBS hand-colored Sunday strip by Roy Crane. Before the CAPTAIN EASY Sunday page debuted in 1933, WASH TUBBS ran as the topper companion to J. R. Williams's OUT OUR WAY Sunday feature. © June 12, 1932. Courtesy of the Sheldon Memorial Art Gallery, Howard Collection of American Popular Art

WASH TUBBS daily strip by Roy Crane. After his introduction in 1929, Captain Easy's tough-guy persona proved to be the catalyst in the strip, as these three examples from the early 1930s demonstrate. © July 12, 1932. Courtesy of the Sheldon Memorial Art Gallery, Howard Collection of American Popular Art

WASH TUBBS daily strip by Roy Crane. © 1933. Courtesy of Rob Stolzer

WASH TUBBS daily strip by Roy Crane. © 1934. Courtesy of Russ Cochran

WASH TUBBS Sunday page panel and spot illustration by Roy Crane. The artist's patented visual storytelling technique blended humor, drama, heroics, and pretty girls. © c. 1936. Courtesy Illustration House (above) and Frank Pauer (right)

WASH TUBBS daily strip by Roy Crane. A superlative example of the special effects Crane produced using Craft-Tint Double Tone paper.
© February 3, 1940. Courtesy of Frank Pauer

CAPTAIN EASY recolored Sunday page by Roy Crane. Easy had his own separate adventures in the Sunday continuities. This is the debut episode.
© July 30, 1933. Courtesy of Syracuse University and American Color

the thirties

THEY'LL DO IT EVERY TIME daily panel by Jimmy Hatlo. Reading the Sunday funnies had become a weekly ritual in most American homes.

"It would storm just as I got my laundry out."

METROPOLITAN MOVIES daily panel by Denys Wortman. Mopey Dick and the Duke, the two tramps in Wortman's feature, built a ramshackle home in a shantytown during the dark days of the Depression. c. 1932. © United Feature Syndicate, Inc.

THE ROARING TWENTIES ENDED IN A PANIC. ON TUESDAY, OCTOBER 29, 1929, FIVE DAYS AFTER "BLACK THURSDAY," 16.4 MILLION SHARES WERE TRADED ON THE FLOOR OF THE NEW YORK STOCK EXCHANGE. WHEN THE BELL SOUNDED, $15 BILLION IN MARKET VALUE HAD BEEN WIPED OUT. A MONTH LATER, STOCK LOSSES HAD DOUBLED AND THREE MILLION AMERICANS WERE OUT OF WORK.

By mid-1932, the cumulative worth of Wall Street investments was 11 percent of what it had been at its peak in 1929. In the first three years after the crash, hourly wages dropped 60 percent, eighty-six thousand businesses failed, more than five thousand banks closed their doors, industrial output was cut in half, and unemployment reached fifteen million. To make matters worse, the most devastating drought in American history reduced the Great Plains to a dust bowl. On March 4, 1933, President Herbert Hoover sighed dejectedly, "We are at the end of our string. There is nothing more we can do." It was his last day in office.

The Great Depression caused catastrophic social disruption. Former bankers sold apples on street corners and stood in breadlines. Shantytowns of the dispossessed, derisively called "Hoovervilles," sprang up on the outskirts of major cities across the country. Marriage and childbirth rates declined while crime and suicide soared. Despondent fathers, unable to find jobs, stayed at home while their wives and children looked for work. Farmers abandoned their parched land and headed west for California in a massive wave of migration. An army of World War I veterans descended on Washington, D.C., and angrily—but unsuccessfully—demanded early payment of their promised bonus for wartime service.

The new president, who took over for Hoover on that gray, chilly day in March 1933, offered hope for a better future. "The only thing we have to fear is fear itself," Franklin Delano Roosevelt assured Americans in his inaugural address. "The people of the United States have not failed. . . . They want direct, vigorous action."

FDR delivered on his promises. In the first one hundred days of the new administration, fifteen major bills were passed. The "New Deal" for the nation provided financing for farmers and home buyers, created jobs, guaranteed bank deposits, and established an "alphabet" of government agencies and initiatives (NRA, WPA, CCC, TVA) that helped get the country back on its feet. Roosevelt sold these programs to the American public via his direct "fireside chats," broadcast on network radio. He was reelected in 1936, and by 1939 the gross national product was $91 billion—a 60 percent increase in six years. The New York World's Fair of 1939, which looked toward "the World of Tomorrow," symbolized to many the end of the crisis.

"When the spirit of the people is lower than at any other time, during this Depression," Roosevelt observed in 1936, "it is a splendid thing that for just fifteen cents an American can go to a movie . . . and forget his troubles." At that time, theaters were selling more than eighty million tickets a week, as the Hollywood dream factory worked overtime to provide escapist entertainment. Movie audiences delighted in the lovable antics of Shirley Temple, the elegant footwork of Fred Astaire and Ginger Rogers, and the madcap mayhem of the Marx Brothers. *The Wizard of Oz* and *Gone With the Wind,* both released in 1939, broke box office records. Mickey Mouse, Felix the Cat, Betty Boop, and Popeye starred in both animated films and newspaper comic strips.

The 1930s were also the golden years of radio. By the end of the decade, 85 percent of the nation's households owned a receiver. The comedy of George Burns and Gracie Allen, the swing music of Benny Goodman, and the drama of *The Shadow* filled the airwaves. The opening lines of the famous theme song "Who's that little chatterbox? The one with pretty auburn locks?" signaled the start of *Adventure Time with Orphan Annie,* a popular after-school program, which aired on the NBC radio network from 1931 to 1943. In addition to uplifting moralistic tales, Annie offered her young fans premium prizes in exchange for coins wrapped in metal foil seals, obtained from jars of Ovaltine malted milk mix. Radio programs starring comic characters continued to proliferate during the decade, and one syndicate reported in 1936 that it had fourteen features being prepared for adaptation to the broadcast medium.

Newspaper comics provided cheap thrills for children of all ages. Readers could travel to the jungles of darkest Africa, the wide-open spaces of the Wild West, or the farthest reaches of outer space in the panels of their favorite features. Tarzan, Red Ryder, and Buck Rogers were among the many comic strip heroes who provided a welcome diversion for weary Americans. Direct references to the Depression were avoided, for the most part, on the funnies pages.

Comics offered more than escapism, however. In many of the humorous family features, a picture of domestic stability was portrayed, insulated from poverty, unemployment, and homelessness. Any challenge to this order usually came from within the extended cast of friends, neighbors, and relatives and was often trivial in nature. The characters would solve their problem in a clever or humorous way, and, sooner or later, things would return to normal. It was only a matter of time before another mini-crisis intruded on the harmony of the group and the cycle would begin again. The relatively untroubled life of families in the funnies must have been comforting to readers during the Depression.

Adventure strips served a similar function but accomplished it in a different way. Danger was more life-threatening in these features and posed seemingly insurmountable challenges for the protagonists. The heroes, who were male in most of the strips, would take control of the situation, often acting independently of the law, to battle the threat to the established order. In some cases, the characters required superhuman powers to defeat their enemies, and the stories were morality plays of good versus evil. The heroes rarely had to deal with the day-to-day problems of earning a living or raising a family and were always victorious in the end. These fantastic scenarios, which were a departure from the established humor formula, must have been equally reassuring to Depression readers, who felt powerless to cope with the real-life challenges they faced on a daily basis.

Newspaper circulation continued to climb during the decade, reaching a high of 41.5 million in 1937, but profits were down due to the loss of advertising revenue. Smaller papers struggled to survive and either folded or were

MAW GREEN companion feature by Harold Gray. This strip ran at the bottom of the LITTLE ORPHAN ANNIE Sunday pages during the 1930s.

WILLIAM RANDOLPH HEARST—Portrait by William Downes of "the Chief" at the peak of his power. *1935. Courtesy of Editor & Publisher*

absorbed by one of the chains. *Editor & Publisher* reported that between 1924 and 1934, groups owning more than one newspaper had doubled, from 31 to 63. These organizations controlled 361 daily papers, which accounted for 37.6 percent of the total circulation.

The Hearst empire, the largest of the chains, reached its peak in 1935, with twenty-six daily and seventeen Sunday papers in nineteen cities (representing 13.6 percent of the total daily circulation and 24.2 percent of the Sunday circulation of the country), thirteen magazines, eight radio stations, two motion picture companies, four syndicates, and two wire services. The Chief, who also owned two million acres of real estate, valued at $56 million, and a vast collection of art and antiques, had an estimated personal wealth of $220 million. Financial hardship finally caught up with the organization in 1937, when many holdings, including nine daily papers and five Sunday editions, had to be liquidated to pay off debts. Hearst, who had supported FDR during his first term, withdrew his support by the mid-1930s, calling the president's economic program the "Raw Deal."

The syndicates also went through a period of growth and consolidation during the decade. United Feature Syndicate, which was founded in 1919, purchased the Metropolitan Newspaper Service on March 15, 1930, and absorbed the World Feature Service (the former syndicate department of the *New York World* newspapers) on February 28, 1931. These acquisitions added many established features to the syndicate's stable, including *Ella Cinders, Tarzan, The Captain and the Kids,* and *Fritzi Ritz.* Among the other changes in the early 1930s were the sale of Central Press Association to King Features,

the addition of comics to the roster of the Associated Press, and the merger of the North American Newspaper Alliance, the Associated Newspapers, and the Bell Syndicate into a single organization.

"These recent syndicate consolidations," claimed Monte Bourjaily, general manager of United Feature Syndicate in 1930, "are a salutary sign of the ambition to make better newspapers. The syndicate's job, as well as the newspaper's, is to inspire readers to turn off their radios to read, and to stay at home with their paper rather than to go off to the talkies."

Reader surveys were increasingly used to determine the popularity of comic strips and led directly to a new development in the field: color advertising in the Sunday funnies. Professor George Gallup, who taught at Drake, Northwestern, and Columbia universities, released his pioneering study of newspaper readership in 1930. He discovered that "more adults read the best comic strip in a newspaper on an average day than the first rate banner story." After conducting extensive interviews and analyzing the statistics, Gallup broke down his findings into categories based on gender and income. The results showed that comic strips ranked right behind the picture pages in overall popularity among his projected group of two million readers. Gallup argued that newspaper editors needed to apply scientific methods, rather than intuition, to determine varying degrees of interest among their target audience. This knowledge was also essential to the selling and placing of advertisements in the newspaper.

These findings led to the formation of Hearst Comics in 1931, a division of the company organized to develop color advertisements for the Sunday comic sections. The first successful initiative of the new group was a series for General Foods' Grape-Nuts Flakes cereal, which debuted in forty-nine papers on May 17, 1931. The comic-style ads, which starred "Egbert Energy" and "Suburban Joe," were produced by Hearst Comics and the Young & Rubicam advertising agency. General Foods reported a dramatic increase in Grape-Nuts sales as a direct result of this campaign.

John K. Jessup, a copywriter for the J. Walter Thompson agency, speculated about the future of comic advertising at a meeting on March 12, 1932. "I think advertising must admit that it will have to make use of a modified form of comic strip," explained Jessup. "Only by sponsoring a comic strip can it probably take full advantage of the strip's popularity." The leading comic section advertisers in the early 1930s were Lever Brothers (Lifebuoy, Rinso, and Lux soaps) and General Foods (Grape-Nuts, Postum, Post Toasties, Jell-O, and Minute Tapioca).

A group of 30 newspapers formed another agency, the Comic Weekly Corporation, in May 1932 to sell advertising space in their comic sections. Other organizations were soon

LITTLE ALBY advertisement for General Foods' Grape-Nuts Flakes. An early ad campaign in the Sunday comics. October 14, 1934, Omaha Bee-News. Courtesy of Mark Johnson

established, and by 1934 comic advertising was bringing in more than $9 million in additional revenue to 188 newspapers. During this period of phenomenal growth, *Puck—The Comic Weekly,* which was distributed to the seventeen Hearst Sunday papers with a combined circulation of five million, featured ads from fifty major companies, promoting seventy-five products, at a rate of $16,000 per page. By 1937, 300 newspapers were generating more than $17 million in comic section advertising revenue.

The demand for comic-style ads led to the growth of "advertising service studios," which specialized in this type of art. Thomas Johnstone, a former manager of the *New York World*'s Press Publishing Company, had one of the largest stables of artists in the business. In the mid-1930s, Johnstone's studio produced campaigns for Lux Soap, Chase and Sanborn Coffee, Nestlés Chocolate, Shell Gasoline, Ivory Soap, and Fleischmann's Yeast, and his artists earned between $100 and $1,200 per page for advertising work. King Features Syndicate set up its own service in 1937, making all of its top talents available. Fees varied according to the reputation of the artists, but their names and characters could not be used in any advertisements.

The success of comic advertising also affected the makeup of the Sunday funnies. Comic sections increased in size from four or eight pages to twelve, sixteen, twenty-four, or even

thirty-two pages to accommodate advertisements. Strips were also produced in different formats to create more space. In addition to the traditional full-page size, the syndicates offered half-page and tabloid sizes. These formats allowed newspapers to double the number of comics without increasing their newsprint costs. Advertisers preferred to purchase half-page display ads to run on the same page as popular features in the half-page format.

In February 1935, *Puck—The Comic Weekly* introduced a tabloid-sized section, featuring reformatted versions of established comics as well as new creations, including *Betty Boop* by Bud Counihan, *Hejji* by Theodor Geisel (Dr. Seuss), and *The Kewpies* by Rose O'Neill. The experiment was abandoned six months later. A Hearst official explained to *Editor & Publisher* that "many of the comics, some of which had been running as long as 38 years, could not be squeezed down to the smaller size and still do justice to the art work." It would prove to be a brief respite for artistic integrity. In the coming years, the size in which comic strips were printed would continue to shrink, and it became increasingly rare for a feature to occupy a full-size newspaper page.

Fortune magazine, in an April 1933 article, "The Funny Papers," reported, "Of 2,300 U.S. dailies, only two of any importance (*New York Times* and *Boston Transcript*) see fit to exist without funnies. U.S. Funny Paper, Inc. grosses about

$6,000,000 a year. Some twenty comic-strip headliners are paid at least $1,000 a week for their labors."

Cartoonists' incomes were derived from weekly fees paid by newspapers for their creations, which ranged from $3 to $300 per paper. A modestly successful strip that appeared in 150 papers, and earned an average of $10 per paper, could bring in $1,500 a week. After the standard fifty-fifty split with the syndicate, a cartoonist in this category could earn $39,000 a year, not counting additional revenue from secondary sources.

The *Fortune* article listed Bud Fisher, Sidney Smith, and George McManus as the top earners, each with a weekly income of $1,600. A dozen other artists were also included in the list, with weekly salaries of more than $1,000 each. These estimates were actually lower than many previous figures but included only money earned directly from newspaper syndication. Licensing could increase annual earnings substantially. Clare Briggs, for example, reportedly made an additional $100,000 in 1928 for his Old Gold cigarette ads. In the depths of the Depression, these salaries were astronomical. Adjusting for inflation, $1,600 a week in 1933 would be almost $1 million a year in contemporary dollars.

Money could not prevent tragedy, however. Sidney Smith, creator of *The Gumps,* signed a new three-year contract, worth $450,000, on Saturday, October 19, 1935. After celebrating at his country home in Genoa City, Wisconsin, Smith drove a group of friends back to Chicago. As he returned to the farm early Sunday morning, Smith's small sedan collided head-on with another car, spun off the road, and crashed into a telephone pole. Smith fractured his skull and died instantly. The fifty-eight-year-old cartoonist, who was known for his fast driving, left valuable real estate holdings and personal property, as well as a $350,000 insurance policy, to his widow and two children.

Arthur Crawford, manager of the Chicago Tribune–New York News Syndicate, which distributed *The Gumps* to 350 newspapers, announced on October 26 that Stanley Link, who had worked as Smith's assistant for ten years, would continue drawing the strip, with Blair Walliser as the writer. But Link apparently was unable to agree on terms with the syndicate, and Gus Edson was then named as Smith's successor. The first episode that Edson drew appeared on December 16, 1935.

In 1938, Edson remembered that "it was a grand moment" when Captain Patterson informed him he was taking over the popular feature. "But still I could not help but feel somewhat shaky at the thought of trying to fill the shoes of such a famous comic artist," he added. "I felt no differently, I suppose, than any baseball player would if called upon to pinch hit for Babe Ruth." Edson continued *The Gumps* until the syndicate finally retired the strip on October 17, 1959.

The most successful features were valuable properties, and syndicates were not inclined to end a strip when a cartoonist

POPEYE promotional drawing by E. C. Segar. THIMBLE THEATRE STARRING POPEYE was named the "fastest selling comic in 1936."
© November 14, 1936, King Features Syndicate, Inc. Courtesy of Editor & Publisher

died. E. C. Segar, creator of *Thimble Theatre Starring Popeye,* succumbed to leukemia on October 13, 1938, at the age of forty-three. At that time, Segar was earning $100,000 a year, the strip was appearing in five hundred newspapers, and more than six hundred licensed Popeye products were on the market. King Features quickly announced that *Popeye* would be continued. Doc Winner, a syndicate staff artist who had ghosted the feature during Segar's illness, took over initially and was succeeded in mid-1939 by the team of Tom Sims (writer) and Bela "Bill" Zaboly (illustrator).

Other long-running features, which had dwindling lists of subscribers and limited licensing programs, were terminated after the creator retired or died. *Happy Hooligan* ended on August 14, 1932, when Frederick B. Opper was finally persuaded to put down his pen. The "Dean of American Cartoonists" passed away on August 27, 1937, at the age of eighty. King Features wisely decided to discontinue *Krazy Kat* after George Herriman died on April 25, 1944.

In most cases, comics and their creators had remarkable longevity. *Editor & Publisher* reported in 1938 that there were thirty-one comics still being syndicated that had been around since before 1920. Among the durable survivors were *The Katzenjammer Kids* (1897), *Little Jimmy* (1904), *Hairbreadth Harry* (1906), *Mutt and Jeff* (1907), *Toonerville Folks* (1908), *Slim Jim* (1910), *Polly and Her Pals* (1912), *Bringing Up Father* (1913), *Krazy Kat* (1913), *Abie the Agent* (1914), *Freckles and His Friends* (1915), *The Gumps* (1917), *The Bungle Family* (1918), *Toots and Casper* (1918), *Harold Teen* (1919), *Barney Google* (1919), *Thimble Theatre* (1919), and *Gasoline Alley* (1919).

All of these features were of the traditional "funny paper" type. During the 1930s, a new genre—the adventure strip—

was beginning to challenge the humor strip in popularity. Writers, readers, and cartoonists began to debate the relative merits of the two competing styles.

In the May 1936 issue of *Forum* magazine, John Ryan vehemently attacked the new breed of comics for portraying "sadism, cannibalism, bestiality. Crude eroticism. Torturing, killing, kidnapping, monsters, madmen, creatures which are half-brute, half-human. Raw melodrama; tales of crimes and criminals; extravagant exploits in strange lands on other planets, pirate stories. . . . Vulgarity, cheap humor and cheaper wit. Sentimental stories designed for the general level of the moronic mind. Ugliness in thought and expression. All these, day after day, week after week, have become the mental food of American children young and old."

"As the mother of a couple of little boys," Mrs. A. T. Lindem wrote to the editor of the *Minneapolis Journal* in 1936, "I wish to register a protest against the unwholesomeness and dangerous influence of some of the comic strips which could more truthfully be called 'crime strips.'" Some of the criticism of the adventure genre, made by concerned parents and educators, was reminiscent of the protests voiced by anti-comics crusaders in the early years of the twentieth century.

A poll of adult comic readers, published in the April 1937 issue of *Fortune* magazine, listed the fourteen favorite strips, in order of preference, as *Little Orphan Annie, Popeye, Dick Tracy, Bringing Up Father, The Gumps, Blondie, Moon Mullins, Joe Palooka, Li'l Abner, Tillie the Toiler, Dan Dunn, Gasoline Alley, Henry,* and *Out Our Way.* Only *Dick Tracy, Joe Palooka,* and *Dan Dunn* could be called "adventure strips."

Ham Fisher, the creator of *Joe Palooka,* came to the defense of his fellow "blood and thunder" artists. "Many of the present comics are so admirably written and drawn that their appeal is more to adults than in the past," argued Fisher. "Many of them

OUT OUR WAY daily panel by J. R. Williams. "The Worry Wart" tries his hand at cartooning. © 1936 NEA Service, Inc. Courtesy of Bill Blackbeard

today hold the place that another generation gave to their favorite short story writers."

The adventure strip introduced a new look to the medium. Realistically rendered characters and settings were the essential ingredients of the emerging genre. "The advent of illustrators on the comics page marked the last stage in the development of the modern comic strip," wrote Robert C. Harvey in *The Art of the Funnies.* This graphic style added another dimension to the story strip.

Hal Foster, who was an experienced commercial illustrator before he took a job as the artist on the new *Tarzan of the Apes* feature in 1929, started the trend toward realism in the comics. The drawings for the ten-week, daily newspaper "comic strip" series were done in the style of book illustrations, with text adapted from Edgar Rice Burroughs's novel set in type beneath each picture. After the initial run of the feature, from January 7 to March 16, 1929, Foster returned to his career as an advertising artist.

Tarzan was a success, and Metropolitan Newspaper Service hired Rex Maxon to replace Foster and continue the daily feature. A Sunday page was launched on March 15, 1931, and Foster was persuaded six months later to come back; he illustrated the weekly installments from September 17, 1931, to May 2, 1937.

After a year of on-the-job training, Foster began to flourish as a graphic storyteller. He experimented with close-ups, long shots, and variable panel sizes. His figures moved with power and grace. He added realistic detail to his backgrounds, costumes, and architecture and adapted a technique of contrasting black and white, known in painting as chiaroscuro, to create dramatic lighting effects. Foster's work would influence many of the artists who followed him in the adventure strip genre.

Frustrated with the quality of the *Tarzan* scripts he had to illustrate, and dissatisfied with the meager pay he received ($75 to $125 a week), Foster decided to create his own feature. As early as 1934, he drew a prototype of the historical strip he envisioned, but he tore it up because he felt it lacked authenticity. By 1936, he had finished six months of *Derek, Son of Thane.* Incredibly, United Feature Syndicate, which was then distributing *Tarzan,* turned down Foster's submission. William Randolph Hearst had admired Foster's work on *Tarzan,* and he quickly signed the artist up after his executives looked at the samples. The renamed strip, *Prince Valiant in the Days of King Arthur,* debuted in eight newspapers on February 13, 1937.

Foster's epic feature brought a new level of artistic excellence to the medium. With the freedom to write original stories and develop distinctive characters, Foster created a fantastic world of knights and maidens, adventure and romance, and made it believable with historical detail and majestic scenery.

For more than six decades, *Prince Valiant* has provided a refined taste of classic graphic literature in the Sunday comics.

Alex Raymond also brought the talents of an illustrator to the adventure strip genre. During the early 1930s, Raymond, who was influenced by such artists as John LaGatta, Franklin Booth, and Matt Clark, worked in the King Features bullpen as a ghost artist on *Tim Tyler's Luck* and *Blondie.* He was eventually enlisted to illustrate three features that were designed to compete with *Buck Rogers, Tarzan,* and *Dick Tracy. Flash Gordon, Jungle Jim,* and *Secret Agent X-9* were all released by King Features in January 1934. Raymond left *Secret Agent X-9* in late 1935 and focused all of his creative energies on the *Flash Gordon* Sunday pages (with *Jungle Jim* as the "topper," or companion, strip). He perfected a distinctive dry brush technique to render the elegant figures of Flash Gordon and Dale Arden, and he experimented with innovative page layouts to depict the fantastic world of Mongo. Later in the decade, he switched to a more precise pen-and-ink method, which complemented the bold blacks in his balanced compositions. Although fans and students of Raymond's work differ over their preferred period of his stylistic evolution, they all agree that he was an accomplished artist and that his influence was pervasive.

Milton Caniff was another artist whose graphic innovations were to have a major impact on the field of the story strip in the 1930s. Caniff's first successful feature, *Dickie Dare,* which the Associated Press launched on July 31, 1933, began as a strip about a twelve-year-old boy who encountered such classic figures as Robin Hood, General Custer, and Captain Kidd in his imaginative fantasies. Eventually Dickie stopped daydreaming and teamed up with a real-life sidekick, Dynamite Dan Flynn, sailing the high seas in search of adventure. Caniff's juvenile story strip, which was drawn in a style similar to Lyman Young's *Tim Tyler's Luck,* attracted the attention of Captain Patterson of the Chicago Tribune–New York News Syndicate.

Patterson gave the young cartoonist a week to develop a new adventure strip and suggested an opening story line in which a young protagonist and a dashing adventurer cross paths with a lady pirate in the exotic Far East. Caniff came

TERRY AND THE PIRATES promotional drawing by Milton Caniff. This creation by Caniff had all the essential ingredients of the modern action-adventure strip. © *July 17, 1937, Tribune Media Services, Inc. All rights reserved. Reprinted with permission. Courtesy of Editor & Publisher*

back with a batch of samples. The Captain was impressed but decided to change the title from *Tommy Tucker* to *Terry and the Pirates*. The daily strip began on October 22, 1934, and a Sunday page was added on December 9.

Terry and the Pirates initially looked very much like *Dickie Dare*, but Caniff matured as an artist during the first year of the feature. At the time, he shared a studio in Manhattan with his old friend Noel Sickles, who was drawing *Scorchy Smith* for the Associated Press. Sickles was experimenting with a new technique, in which he boldly applied ink with a brush to create dramatic shapes and shadows. Caniff adapted this approach to his own work, blending cinematic composition, atmospheric effects, and realistic rendering with violent action, sex appeal, and dramatic suspense. Caniff was also progressing as a storyteller. The characters in *Terry and the Pirates*, in contrast to the predictable behavior of most adventure strip heroes, had multifaceted personalities, leaving readers to wonder how they would react in various situations. The plots were fast-paced and the dialogue was snappy.

Caniff became the most influential artist in the comic strip field during the 1930s, and his style was widely admired and imitated. The pioneering efforts of Hal Foster and Alex Raymond reached fruition in the work of Caniff. In the space of six years, the adventure strip had evolved into its definitive form.

The debate between the advocates of the adventure and humor genres was, for the most part, irrelevant. The comic pages during the 1930s were an eclectic mix of unique creations, many of which did not fall into either of these categories. Cartoonists experimented with endless variations on the established formulas.

Dick Tracy, which could be called an "adventure strip," featured hard-hitting action in an urban setting that closely resembled Chicago. But Chester Gould's classic detective comic, which debuted on October 4, 1931, was drawn in a style that was both realistic and uniquely expressive. The epic battle of good versus evil was symbolized by the contrast between Tracy's square-jawed profile and the hideously deformed faces of Gould's grotesque gallery of villains. Buildings, vehicles, and devices, on the other hand, were rendered with the meticulous attention to accuracy and detail of a mechanical draftsman. The success of the original cops-and-robbers comic inspired a long list of Depression-era crime strips, including *Dan Dunn, Radio Patrol, Secret Agent X-9, Red Barry,* and *Charlie Chan.*

Thimble Theatre was another creation that defied categorization. E. C. Segar's feature was originally a spoof of movie serials when it debuted on December 19, 1919. Throughout the 1920s, the strip chronicled the adventures of the Oyl clan—Nana, Cole, Olive, and Castor, along with Olive's boyfriend, Ham Gravy. Popeye first appeared on January 17, 1929, and was initially just one of the many oddball characters who made regular guest appearances in the strip. But the cantankerous sailor with the corncob pipe, bulging forearms, and squinting mug soon took over the show, as his uncompromising integrity won the allegiance of millions of newspaper readers. Segar blended humor, philosophy, violence, and surrealism in his rambling continuities, which often lasted for months. Among the many memorable pen-and-ink performers in *Thimble Theatre* were J. Wellington Wimpy, the Sea Hag, Alice the Goon, Toar, Poopdeck Pappy, Swee'pea, and Eugene the Jeep.

Blondie, which started on September 8, 1930, as a late entry in the Jazz Age pretty-girl genre, was the most successful family feature in the comics by the end of the decade. The star of the strip, Blondie Boopadoop, fell in love with Dagwood

BLONDIE promotional drawing by Chic Young. This illustration appeared in an advertisement a week before the debut of the strip. © August 30, 1930, King Features Syndicate, Inc. Courtesy of Editor & Publisher

Bumstead, a millionaire's son whose parents threatened to disinherit him after he told them of his intention to marry the flighty flapper. In protest, Dagwood went on a twenty-eight-day hunger strike in January 1933. The Bumsteads finally gave in, and one of the most memorable weddings in comic strip history took place on February 17, 1933. Dagwood gave up his family fortune and settled down to a life as the domestic Everyman, babysitting for his growing brood, crashing into the mailman, and catching hell from his boss, Mr. Dithers. Alex Raymond was Chic Young's assistant during the early 1930s and is credited with giving Blondie her sexy figure and fashionable attire. The rest of the characters were designed in a more conventional cartoon style, and, for a time, semi-realistic rendering and humorous caricature coexisted in the strip.

Al Capp's *Li'l Abner*, which debuted on August 13, 1934, was also a blend of different drawing techniques, which changed as the strip evolved. In the early episodes, Abner had a correctly proportioned physique, but over the course of time his head and feet grew in size. Daisy Mae developed a voluptuous figure, and Mammy and Pappy Yokum became shorter and more cartoon-like. Many of the other characters had exaggerated features—big noses, flappy ears, bulging eyes—attached to normal bodies. The overall effect was one of distorted naturalism, which perfectly matched Capp's savage satire of the human condition.

The personalities of the main cast were in place from the beginning. Mammy Yokum was the boss, Pappy was her straight man, Abner was the fool, and Daisy Mae was his love-struck pursuer. "While the *Li'l Abner* characters themselves are broad burlesques in the tradition of my ideals," Capp explained, "the situations in which I plunge 'em are macabre, horrible, thrilling and chilling in the new 'suspense continuity' tradition." His secret was to "throw comedy characters into melodramatic situations and to show them solving monstrous tribulations in a simple-minded way." He had discovered a unique combination of comedy and suspense, humor and adventure, and would capitalize on this successful formula for forty-three years.

The 1930s was a remarkably fertile period for comic creators. The funnies pages resembled a three-ring circus, with daredevils, clowns, jugglers, and animal acts all performing simultaneously. The syndicates released dozens of new features that exploited the full range of thematic possibilities and graphic techniques.

Joe Palooka (1930) by Ham Fisher starred a naive boxing champ and his ambitious manager, Knobby Walsh. *Mickey Mouse* (1930) by Floyd Gottfredson featured the cartoon screen star and his faithful sidekicks in rollicking adventure tales. *Alley Oop* (1933) by V. T. Hamlin, which initially had a prehistoric setting, later introduced the concept of time

travel to the comics. *Henry* (1934) by Carl Anderson and *The Little King* (1934) by Otto Soglow were performed in pantomime. *Mandrake the Magician* (1934) and *The Phantom* (1936) were both created by Lee Falk and are classics of the story strip genre. *Oaky Doaks* (1935) by R. O. Fuller provided a humorous take on knighthood. *Smokey Stover* (1935) by Bill Holman was a screwball comedy about a fireman and was jam-packed with cryptic sayings and corny puns. *Smilin' Jack* (1936) by Zack Mosley was an aviation strip created by a licensed pilot. *Nancy* (1938) by Ernie Bushmiller officially became a new feature when the spike-haired moppet usurped the starring role from her aunt Fritzi Ritz. *Red Ryder* (1938) by Fred Harmon was the most successful of the cowboy comics.

The *Superman* newspaper comic strip, which was released by the McClure Syndicate on January 16, 1939, represented

SUPERMAN *promotional drawing by Wayne Boring. The Caped Crusader strikes a powerful pose in an advertisement for the comic strip.*

JOE PALOOKA *promotional drawing by Ham Fisher. This drawing was published not long after Great Britain declared war on Germany.*
© October 28, 1939, McNaught Syndicate, Inc. Courtesy of Editor & Publisher

another new development in the adventure genre. Booklets featuring graphic stories had been around since the mid-nineteenth century, but it was not until 1933 that the modern comic book took on its definitive form. Harry Wildenberg, an employee for Eastern Color Printing Company, came up with the idea of folding a newspaper page in half, and then again into quarters, to come up with a magazine-size booklet. Wildenberg obtained the rights from a handful of newspaper syndicates to reprint their strips and got an order from Proctor & Gamble to produce a promotional giveaway. A million copies of *The Funnies on Parade,* a thirty-two-page, full-color comic book, were published and distributed, free of charge, in the spring of 1933. When Eastern successfully experimented with selling some issues of another promotional comic book, *Famous Funnies: A Carnival of Comics,* later that year, an industry was born.

Comic book publishers soon began hiring artists to create original material for the growing market instead of reprinting newspaper comic strips. In 1936, the syndicates started releasing their own strip reprint collections in the new format. Then *Superman* debuted in *Action Comics* No. 1, dated June 1938, and the age of superheroes was under way. Within a few short years, the newsstands were overflowing with comic books starring costumed characters. Their circulation reached an all-time high in the early 1950s, when close to 1.3 billion comic books were being sold annually. At the end of the 1930s and throughout the next decade, these developments had a powerful influence on the newspaper comics business, as the syndicates

felt increasing pressure to compete with the new medium.

World events would also have a profound impact on the American comics industry. The economic hardships of the Depression led to the rise of fascist dictatorships in Germany, Italy, and Spain, and these so-called Axis powers soon formed a military alliance. Japan expanded into Manchuria in 1931 and invaded China in 1937; Italy seized Ethiopia in 1935. The Nazis took back the Rhineland in 1936, marched into Austria in 1938, and annexed Czechoslovakia in 1939. After Adolf Hitler's forces attacked Poland on September 1, 1939, Great Britain and France declared war on Germany.

It was only a matter of time until the United States would be forced to enter the global conflict. As the nation prepared for war, newspaper publishers, syndicate executives, and cartoonists looked toward an uncertain future. "We believe that the comic strips will swing more than ever to outright humor, that continuity will be lightened, that the more sorrowful aspects of some strips will be eliminated," predicted Arthur Crawford, general manager of the Chicago Tribune–New York News Syndicate, in September 1939. "Our experience has indicated that readers continue to follow the strips in time of disaster and national crisis."

Cartoonists and their characters would play an important part in the war effort. The funnies were destined to provide inspiration, education, and welcome relief to civilians on the home front and soldiers in combat. The escapism of the Depression years was coming to an end.

hal foster

THE "FATHER OF THE ADVENTURE STRIP" produced two classic creations: *Tarzan*, which debuted on January 7, 1929, and *Prince Valiant*, which began on February 13, 1937. He is credited with introducing realistic rendering, historical accuracy, and dramatic composition to the comics medium.

Harold Rudolf Foster was born in Halifax, Nova Scotia, on August 16, 1892. His father died when Harold was four years old, and his stepfather moved the family to Winnipeg, Manitoba, in 1905. As a teenager, he began teaching himself how to draw by studying the work of Edwin Austin Abbey, Howard Pyle, Arthur Rackham, and N. C. Wyeth. His first job was with the Hudson Bay Company in 1910; his many duties included illustrating women's undergarments for the mail-order catalog.

In 1919, after earning a reputation as "the best wrinkle artist in Winnipeg," Foster set out on a thousand-mile bicycle trek to Chicago. He eventually became one of the top commercial artists in the Windy City, working on accounts for Northwest Paper Company, Union Pacific Railroad, and *Popular Mechanics* magazine.

In 1927, an enterprising advertising executive, Joseph Neebe, secured the rights for a syndicated newspaper adaptation of Edgar Rice Burroughs's *Tarzan of the Apes*. Neebe was turned down by the premier illustrator of the *Tarzan* novels, J. Allen St. John, so he hired Foster instead. After the initial ten-week series was completed, Foster continued his advertising career but returned to do the *Tarzan* Sunday page starting in 1931.

Although Foster initially felt that comics were beneath his abilities, he soon found inspiration in his adopted medium and experimented with new techniques in storytelling and composition. He also became increasingly frustrated illustrating other writers' scripts. When he decided to create his own feature, he looked back in time for his subject matter.

Foster adapted the traditional romantic epic of Arthurian legend and compressed ten centuries of history into one era. "If I drew [King Arthur] as my research has shown, nobody would believe it," he explained. "I cannot draw King Arthur with a black beard, dressed in bearskins and a few odds and ends of armor that the Romans left when they went out of Britain, because that is not the image people have." Although the story is set in the fifth century, during the Roman occupation, the castles, costumes, and customs in *Prince Valiant* were more typical of the period after the Norman conquest in 1066.

The focus of the strip was primarily on sword and sorcery in the early years, but as the feature evolved, romantic and domestic drama complemented the action sequences. Prince Valiant married Aleta on February 10, 1946; his first son, Arn,

PRINCE VALIANT—Full-figure portrait by Hal Foster. *c. 1940*
All Tarzan comic strips © United Feature Syndicate, Inc.
All Prince Valiant comic strips © King Features Syndicate, Inc.

was born on August 31, 1947, followed by twin daughters in 1951 and another son in 1961. As his father got older, young Arn began taking on the more dangerous assignments. "You have to write a story the way you would compose music," Foster said. "You know, high notes and low notes. You have violence one week, and the next story will be the children and home, probably the adventure of one of the children. Then you can get into the blood and thunder again."

Foster claimed that until he went into semiretirement in 1970, he spent fifty-three hours a week on each full-page episode of *Prince Valiant*. He frequently designed spectacular panels filled with battling warriors, galloping horses, towering castles, and panoramic scenery. No other newspaper artist had the space to work in or the talent to fill it.

"It's true I've brought traditional art and illustration technique to the funnies, but it wasn't done consciously," he told interviewer Bill Crouch in 1974. "This has always been my style. Some people dissect their art in formal terms but I've never done that with my work."

He retired in 1979 and passed away three years later. A gentleman until the end, Hal Foster earned his reputation as the "Prince of Illustrators."

AFTER THREE YEARS OF ADVENTURING UP AND DOWN THE WORLD PRINCE
VALIANT AT LAST COMES HOME...COMES HOME AS THE RAGGED BALLAD
SINGER OF A KING WHO INTENDS TO TAKE FAIR THULE BY TRICKERY!
HE GAZES DOWN UPON THE SCENE OF HIS CHILDHOOD AND REMEMBERS
HOW IT HAD ONCE BEEN BETRAYED TO SLIGON. HE WONDERS IF HE CAN
PREVENT THE DOOM THAT VALGRIND IS PREPARING FOR IT.
NEXT WEEK — An Old Friend.

PRINCE VALIANT *single panel from a Sunday page by Hal Foster. Val returns to his boyhood home of Thule.* © 1943. Courtesy of Illustration House

TARZAN original hand-colored Sunday page by Hal Foster. A presentation piece colored by Foster and given to the family of Edgar Rice Burroughs, the creator of Tarzan, as a gift. © January 1, 1933. Courtesy of Jack Gilbert

TARZAN original Sunday page by Hal Foster. This page followed the one on the previous page. Both are from Foster's famous "Egyptian" sequence.
© January 8, 1933. Courtesy of Jack Gilbert.

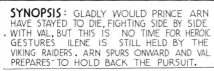

Prince Valiant

SYNOPSIS: GLADLY WOULD PRINCE ARN HAVE STAYED TO DIE, FIGHTING SIDE BY SIDE WITH VAL, BUT THIS IS NO TIME FOR HEROIC GESTURES. ILENE IS STILL HELD BY THE VIKING RAIDERS. ARN SPURS ONWARD AND VAL PREPARES TO HOLD BACK THE PURSUIT.

"I WISH THE GODS HAD MADE YONDER BRAVE FOOL MY FRIEND INSTEAD OF MY SWORN ENEMY."

THE JEWELLED HILT OF THE "SINGING SWORD" FITS SNUGLY IN HIS HAND, AS VAL MARCHES RESOLUTELY TO HIS FATE

THE NORTHMEN ARE BEWILDERED AT SUCH FOOLHARDY COURAGE, SUSPECTING A TRICK— BUT ONE HUGE VIKING—

A CAPTAIN, STEPS FORWARD SAYING, "MY TWO-EDGED AXE WILL SOLVE THIS RIDDLE."— VAL'S BLADE SWISHES SOFTLY, WAITING—

BUT ERE THE AXE CAN FALL, THE "SINGING SWORD" SHRIEKS EXULTANTLY, AS THE KEEN EDGE BITES THROUGH SHIELD AND HELMET AND A WARRIOR'S SOUL GOES WINGING TO VALHALLA.

"COME CLOSER," TAUNTS VAL, "MY BEAUTIFUL SWORD IS THIRSTY,'" AND HALF A HUNDRED HARDY VIKINGS CROWD FORWARD.

AGAIN AND AGAIN THE TERRIBLE SWORD RISES AND FALLS, GLEAMING WET IN THE SUNLIGHT, AND ABOVE THE ROAR OF THE WATERS AND THE CLASHING OF ARMS CAN BE HEARD VAL'S RINGING BATTLE-CRY, "FOR ILENE."

= NEXT WEEK =
THE EXECUTIONER

HAL FOSTER
71 6-19-38

PRINCE VALIANT recolored Sunday page by Hal Foster. The "singing sword," which Prince Arn of Ord had just given to Val, was forged by the same sorcerer who made King Arthur's Excalibur. © June 19, 1938. Courtesy of Russ Cochran and American Color

Prince Valiant

IN THE DAYS OF KING ARTHUR
BY HAROLD R FOSTER

433 A.D.
THULE REGAINED
SAVE THIS STAMP

SYNOPSIS: THE FRIAR UTTERS A FEW WORDS AND CLARIS IS NO LONGER A MENACE TO THE THRONE AND ALFRED BECOMES A MARRIED MAN ··· CUPID HAS MADE A SIMPERING IDIOT OF THE BOISTEROUS, TALL ROGUE WHOSE RINGING LAUGH AND CLASHING SWORD HAD KEPT THULE BUSY.

VAL IS DISGUSTED ~ A GOOD FIGHTING MAN HAS BEEN SPOILED TO MAKE JUST ANOTHER HUSBAND.

VAL RIDES HOMEWARD THROUGH A SUNNY, PEACEFUL LAND.

YES, A PEACEFUL LAND NOW ··· WHERE HEARTY YOUNG WARRIORS WEAR THEIR ARMOR ON A PEG.

FOR THE KING IS ALMOST TOO LENIENT FOR HIS TIMES AND ONLY ORDERS SUCH MURDERS AND EXECUTIONS AS ARE FOR THE PUBLIC GOOD, NEVER FOR PRIVATE PLEASURE — AND HIS PEOPLE GRUMBLE AT THE LACK OF ENTERTAINMENT.

EACH MORNING VAL TRAINS WITH THE OTHER KNIGHTS IN THE PALACE COURTYARD.

THE AFTERNOONS ARE SPENT MUCH AS HANDSOME PRINCES SPEND THEM EVERYWHERE.

ROME
SPQR
FEARS THE COMING OF ATTILA
SAVE THIS STAMP

VAL'S EVENINGS ARE MOST INTERESTING, SCHOLARS, POETS, TRAVELERS AND PHILOSOPHERS GATHER IN HIS ROOMS FOR DISCUSSION AND HE LEARNS MANY CURIOUS THINGS.
112 - 4 - 2 - 39

EVERY SATURDAY A GAY TOURNAMENT IS HELD AFTER WHICH THE SURVIVORS FEAST MERRILY.

HAL FOSTER

NEXT WEEK
KNIGHT ERRANT

IN FACT, IT IS AN IDEAL KINGDOM WHERE JUSTICE, PROSPERITY AND PEACE REIGN — AND VAL IS BORED.

1939, King Features Synds   World rights reserved

SAVE THIS STAMP

455 A.D.
SAXONS GAIN FOOT HOLD IN EUROPE

PRINCE VALIANT Sunday page by Hal Foster. A magnificent example of Foster's artistry featuring castles, horses, fair maidens, and jousting.
© April 2, 1939. Courtesy of Howard Lowery.

alex raymond

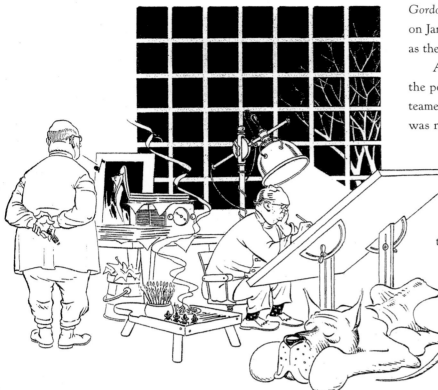

ALEX RAYMOND—Caricature by Jim Raymond from Comics and Their Creators. *1942*
All Secret Agent X-9, Jungle Jim, and Flash Gordon comic strips © King Features Syndicate, Inc.

THE ILLUSTRATOR OF FOUR MAJOR FEATURES during a relatively brief twenty-six-year career, this versatile artist left his mark on comics history. He influenced many of the top story strip creators and set a new level of artistic excellence in the field.

Alexander Gillespie Raymond was born on October 2, 1909, in the affluent suburb of New Rochelle, New York. While attending the Grand Central School of Art in Manhattan, he got a job as an order clerk at a Wall Street brokerage, but he gave up that career path after the stock market crash of 1929.

Raymond started assisting Russ Westover, a family friend and former neighbor, on *Tillie the Toiler* in late 1929 and was soon working in the King Features art department. Between 1930 and 1933, he did backgrounds and enhanced the female characters in *Blondie* for Chic Young and also ghosted *Tim Tyler's Luck* for Lyman Young, Chic's brother. During this period, Raymond's style evolved from a conventional, semi-caricatured approach, typical of the early juvenile adventure strips, to the fluid, polished look he would soon call his own.

When King Features president Joseph Connolly asked his artists to come up with strip ideas to compete with *Buck Rogers* and *Tarzan*, Raymond submitted samples for *Flash Gordon* and *Jungle Jim*. His famous double feature debuted on January 7, 1934, with *Flash* as the main attraction and *Jim* as the topper strip.

At the same time, King Features signed a contract with the popular pulp-fiction writer Dashiell Hammett and teamed him up with Raymond on *Secret Agent X-9*, which was released on January 2, 1934. This handsome detective feature, designed to compete with *Dick Tracy*, initially looked promising, with gorgeous women, violent action, and a tough-talking hero. But Hammett did not adapt well to the comic strip medium, and Raymond eventually decided to concentrate all of his efforts on his *Flash/Jim* page. By late 1935, Leslie Charteris was writing the scripts for *Secret Agent X-9* and Charles Flanders had taken over as the artist, beginning a long line of contributors to the feature, which was renamed *Secret Agent Corrigan* in 1967 and lasted until 1996.

Flash Gordon starred "a Yale graduate and renowned polo player" and his glamorous paramour, Dale Arden. The romantic adventures of these star-crossed lovers provided the recurring story line for the futuristic epic, which combined swords and horses with ray guns and spaceships in a curious hybrid of science fiction and costume drama. The melodrama unfolded on the planet Mongo, ruled by the evil Ming the Merciless.

Late in 1934, Don Moore was hired by King Features to write *Flash Gordon*. Having recently completed a four-year stint as the editorial director for *Argosy–All Story Weekly,* Moore continued to recycle tired clichés from the pulp-fiction genre for his *Flash Gordon* scripts. Raymond's artwork transcended the contrived plots and stilted dialogue, transforming the strip into a stylish adventure fantasy with mythic overtones.

Flash Gordon was one of the most popular adventure heroes of the 1930s, starring in more than 150 newspapers, a radio show, and a series of movie serials. Raymond was frequently compared to Hal Foster for his artistic accomplishments; by the early 1940s, the work of these two adventure strip masters was beginning to look remarkably similar.

Raymond enlisted in the Marines during World War II, relinquishing *Flash Gordon* to his assistant Austin Briggs. When he returned, he launched his own detective strip, *Rip Kirby,* on March 4, 1946. Ten years later, not quite forty-seven years old, Raymond died after crashing a sports car into a tree near his home in Connecticut. It was a tragic end to an illustrious career.

SECRET AGENT X-9 daily strip by Alex Raymond. Dashiell Hammett's scripts called for dangerous women, ruthless thugs, and a dashing hero, who in this episode was operating under the alias "Dexter." © June 9, 1934. Courtesy of Craig Englund

SECRET AGENT X-9 daily strip by Alex Raymond. A dramatic nighttime scene, a beautiful girl, a startling revelation, and an explosive conclusion are blended seamlessly in this outstanding example of Raymond's black-and-white artistry. © January 26, 1935. Courtesy of Bruce Hamilton

JUNGLE JIM Sunday page by Alex Raymond. Both of Raymond's weekly features were done in the tabloid format for a six-month period in 1935.
© May 26, 1935. Courtesy of Russ Cochran

FLASH GORDON recolored Sunday page by Alex Raymond. The influence of the pulp-art genre on Raymond's style is evident in this famous episode. © June 2, 1935. Courtesy of Russ Cochran and American Color

FLASH GORDON/JUNGLE JIM Sunday page with matching topper by Alex Raymond. The artist's elegant brushwork is used to dramatic effect as Flash gradually becomes visible in an episode from the "Witch Queen" sequence. © September 8, 1935. Courtesy of Ricardo Martinez

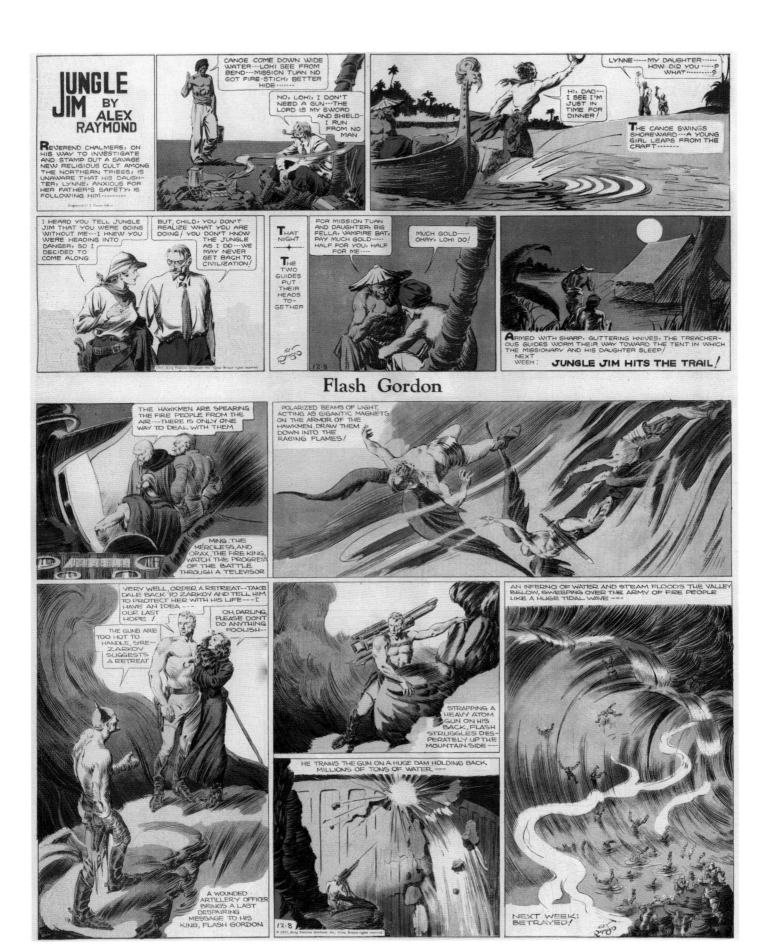

FLASH GORDON/JUNGLE JIM newspaper page by Alex Raymond. Before the paper shortages of World War II, the top artists had full pages to display their talents. © December 8, 1935. Courtesy of Peter Maresca.

FLASH GORDON Sunday page by Alex Raymond. Lost in the untamed forest of Arboria on the distant planet of Mongo, Flash and Dale are saved by a bolt of lightning. © January 31, 1937. Reproduced from a King Features proof

FLASH GORDON Sunday page by Alex Raymond. Flash crosses swords with Ming the Merciless.
© August 14, 1938. Reproduced from a King Features proof

SCORCHY SMITH daily strip by Noel Sickles. © October 18, 1935, the Associated Press. Courtesy of Art Wood

LIGHT AND SHADOW

Although his career in the comics was brief, Noel Sickles is credited with introducing a revolutionary approach to realistic rendering in his work on *Scorchy Smith* from 1933 to 1936. "I did *Scorchy* on a 3-ply Strathmore sheet," Sickles explained. "The first step in inking was with a #3 Winsor-Newton brush and I'd do only the shadows in the figures and backgrounds. The outline inking was done with a 170 or 303 pen point." This "chiaroscuro technique" created a cinematic effect and had a profound influence on Sickles's studio mate, Milton Caniff, as well as many other artists who would follow in the adventure strip genre.

ADVENTURES OF PATSY daily strip by Mel Graff. The artist adopted the style of his Associated Press colleagues Caniff and Sickles for his strip, which debuted on March 11, 1935. Patsy was a female Dickie Dare. © December 2, 1935, the Associated Press

milton caniff

A TIRELESS VOLUNTEER who devoted his talents and energies to numerous organizations, including the Boy Scouts of America, the U.S. Air Force, and the National Cartoonists Society, the "Drawing Board Patriot" was the best ambassador the comics profession ever had. He was also the most influential artist in the adventure strip genre.

Milton Arthur Paul Caniff was born in Hillsboro, Ohio, on February 28, 1907. His father worked as a printer, and Milt started his lifetime association with the "inky-fingered fraternity" at the age of fourteen when the *Dayton Journal* hired him as an office boy. He also developed a passion for acting when he performed as an extra in a few Hollywood two-reel comedies during annual trips his family made to California.

Caniff attended Ohio State University from 1926 to 1930 and pursued a full schedule of extracurricular activities that included working in the art department of the *Columbus Dispatch,* acting in a local stock theater company, and drawing cartoons for the college yearbook and humor magazine. He once considered pursuing a career on the stage, but his mentor, cartoonist Billy Ireland, advised him, "Stick to the ink pots kid, actors don't eat regularly."

After graduation, Caniff started a commercial art studio in Columbus with his friend Noel Sickles, but the Associated Press soon made him an offer to come to New York. Caniff worked at the AP from 1932 to 1934 and drew a variety of features, including a single-column, captioned cartoon, *Puffy the Pig;* a three-column panel, *The Gay Thirties;* a daily comic strip, *Dickie Dare;* and occasional spot illustrations and caricatures.

Mollie Slott, assistant manager of the Chicago Tribune–New York News Syndicate, showed some samples of *Dickie Dare* to her boss, Captain Joseph Medill Patterson, and a meeting between the powerful publisher and the young cartoonist was set up. Patterson asked Caniff to create an adventure strip for his syndicate, and the result was *Terry and the Pirates,* which debuted on October 22, 1934.

As Caniff developed his artistic and storytelling skills, the strip soared in popularity, reaching its peak during the war years. Between 1934 and 1945, he received more than ten thousand letters from his loyal readers, and in 1944 he was earning an estimated annual income of $70,000 from four hundred newspaper clients. He had also become increasingly frustrated that he did not own and control his creation. In 1945, it was revealed that Caniff was abandoning *Terry and the Pirates* after his contract with Patterson's syndicate expired at the end of 1946, to launch a new adventure strip. *Steve Canyon* debuted on January 13, 1947, and ran

MILTON CANIFF—Self-caricature from Comics and Their Creators. *1942*
All Terry and the Pirates comic strips © Tribune Media Services, Inc. All rights reserved.
Reprinted with permission

until June 5, 1988, shortly after Caniff's death on April 3 of that year.

Caniff, who described himself as "an armchair Marco Polo," rarely had the opportunity to visit the exotic locales he brought to life in the panels of *Terry and the Pirates* and *Steve Canyon.* Instead he relied on an extensive "morgue" of magazines, newspaper clippings, and books filled with photographs of foreign countries, military equipment, costumes, uniforms, and numerous other items he depicted in the strip.

"Every detail must be accurate because there is always a man or woman who has been to the place you are portraying," Caniff advised aspiring cartoonists. "Remember that many people can draw well, but there are few who combine the talent with the ability to spin a gripping yarn," he continued. "Develop the two, slighting neither, and you may have the secret of a magic carpet that will send you and your readers soaring in expanses of fancy that would make the *Arabian Nights* seem like Forty Winks."

Caniff followed his own advice and created two masterpieces of comic strip storytelling in *Terry and the Pirates* and *Steve Canyon.* No cartoonist ever perfected all of the elements of the art form as well as the "Rembrandt of the Comic Strip."

The strips on this page show Caniff's evolving style from 1934 to 1937.
TERRY AND THE PIRATES introductory strip by Milton Caniff. TERRY looked very much like DICKIE DARE, in the beginning. © 1934. Courtesy of Bruce Hamilton

TERRY AND THE PIRATES daily strip (subtitled "Show Stopper") by Milton Caniff. A classic Caniff cliffhanger.
© September 11, 1935. Courtesy of the Milton Caniff Collection, The Ohio State University Cartoon Research Library

TERRY AND THE PIRATES daily strip (subtitled "The Mask Falls for the Briefest Moment") by Milton Caniff. The Dragon Lady reveals her true feelings for
Pat while he is sleeping. © October 24, 1936. Courtesy of Art Wood

TERRY AND THE PIRATES daily strip (subtitled "Strip Wheeze") by Milton Caniff. This noncanonical strip, which was not part of any story, was probably
used for promotional purposes by newspapers. © September 7, 1937. Courtesy of the Sheldon Memorial Art Gallery, Howard Collection of American Popular Art

TERRY AND THE PIRATES *daily strips by Milton Caniff. A sampling of Caniff's fully matured work, these daily episodes, starring Normandie and Burma, were painted with a blue wash to indicate where Ben Day adhesive shading was to be applied.* © February 27 and June 11, 1937, and January 5 and June 8, 1938. Courtesy of the Art Wood Collection of Cartoon and Caricature, Prints and Photographs Division, Library of Congress

TERRY AND THE PIRATES Sunday page by Milton Caniff. This nighttime gun battle with Pat, Terry, and the Dragon Lady is an example of Caniff at the peak of his artistic abilities. © August 27, 1939. Courtesy of Bruce Hamilton.

TERRY AND THE PIRATES daily strip sequence by Milton Caniff. Raven Sherman, an American heiress who was providing aid to the Chinese, dies after being pushed out of the back of a truck. © October 13, 14, 15, and 16, 1941. Courtesy of the Milton Caniff Collection, The Ohio State University Cartoon Research Library

TERRY AND THE PIRATES Sunday page by Milton Caniff. Terry and Dude Hennick say farewell to Raven in the mountains of China.
© October 19, 1941. Courtesy of the Milton Caniff Collection, The Ohio State University Cartoon Research Library

BUCK ROGERS Sunday page by Dick Calkins (artist) and Phil Nowlan (writer). The Sunday BUCK ROGERS stories starred Buddy Deering, Wilma's teenage brother. Sunday Oregonian. © May 8, 1932, John F. Dille Company. Courtesy of Peter Maresca

BUCK ROGERS daily strip by Dick Calkins (artist) and Phil Nowlan (writer). The costars of the daily episodes were Buck Rogers and Wilma Deering.
© 1932 John F. Dille Company. Courtesy of Francisco Lopez

BLASTOFF *Buck Rogers,* which debuted on January 7, 1929, was not the first comic strip to entertain readers with adventures in outer space, but it did launch the 1930s science fiction genre. Although the artwork was crude and the dialogue was wooden, the rocket ships, ray guns, and robots in *Buck Rogers* became standard equipment in many subsequent creations. In addition to newspaper strips like *Brick Bradford* (1933) and *Flash Gordon* (1934), many of the early comic book creators also borrowed gadgets and concepts from Calkins and Nowlan's pioneering effort.

BUCK ROGERS bottom half of a Sunday page by Dick Calkins (artist) and Phil Nowlan (writer). This example is one of the few pieces of original artwork to survive from the early period of this influential strip. © 1932 John F. Dille Company. Courtesy of Francisco Lopez

THE PHANTOM Sunday page by Lee Falk (writer) and Ray Moore (artist). The origin story of "the Ghost Who Walks."
© December 29, 1940, King Features Syndicate, Inc. Courtesy of King Features Syndicate

THE PHANTOM daily strip by Lee Falk (writer) and Ray Moore (artist). **The first costumed superhero in the funnies began his career on February 17, 1936.** © March 25, 1937, King Features Syndicate, Inc. Courtesy of Francisco Lopez

MANDRAKE THE MAGICIAN recolored Sunday page by Lee Falk (writer) and Phil Davis (artist). Falk's magician crimefighter made his debut on June 11, 1934. © April 4, 1937, King Features Syndicate, Inc. Courtesy of Francisco Lopez and American Color.

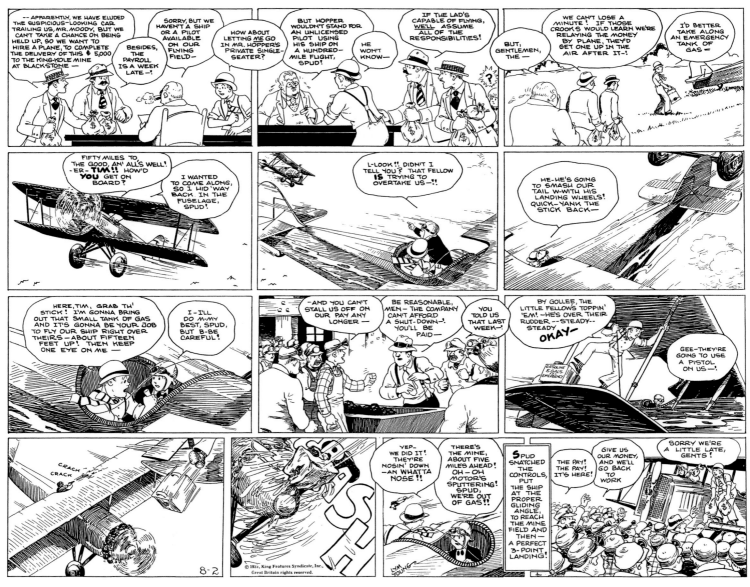

TIM TYLER'S LUCK Sunday page by Lyman Young. Tim saves the day by piloting an airplane. © August 2, 1931, King Features Syndicate, Inc. Courtesy of Francisco Lopez

FLY BOYS AND KID HEROES

Charles Lindbergh's transatlantic airplane flight in 1927 inspired a wave of aviation features, many of which starred young male daredevils. The juvenile story strip genre broadened its horizons during the 1930s to embrace exotic adventures in faraway lands, science fiction, and crimefighting.

DICKIE DARE daily strip by Milton Caniff. Dickie dreams he's fighting mutineers aboard an English vessel in Caniff's juvenile adventure strip, which debuted on July 31, 1933. © October 2, 1933, the Associated Press. Courtesy of Art Wood

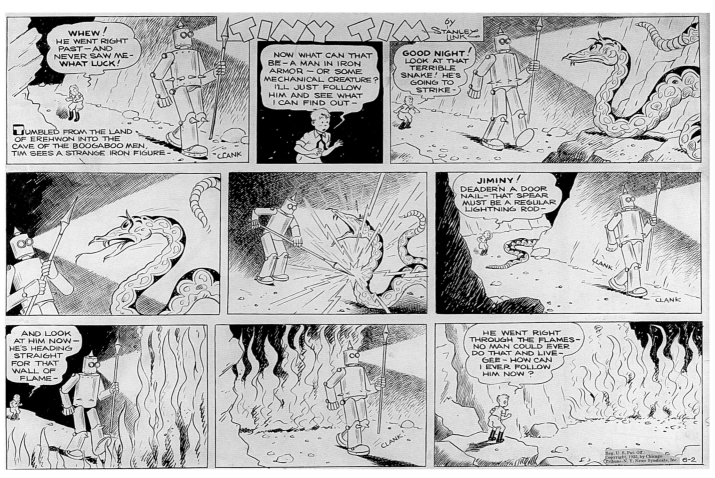

TINY TIM Sunday page by Stanley Link. Link, who ghosted many of Chester Gump's adventures in the 1920s, started his own kid strip in 1931.
© June 2, 1935, Tribune Media Services, Inc. All rights reserved. Reprinted with permission. Courtesy of All Star Auctions

MING FOO Sunday page by Brandon Walsh (writer) and Nicholas Afonsky (artist). The companion feature to LITTLE ANNIE ROONEY starred a juvenile hero, Joey Robbins; his Oriental sidekick, Ming Foo; and a crusty sailor, Tom Trout. © October 9, 1938, King Features Syndicate, Inc. Courtesy of King Features Syndicate

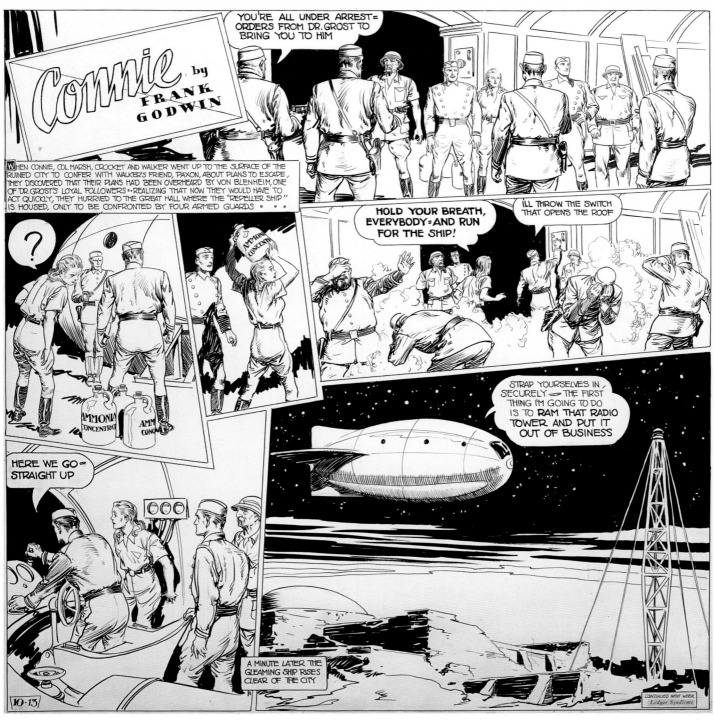

CONNIE Sunday page by Frank Godwin. Constance Courage, the star of Godwin's elegantly illustrated feature, was one of the few heroines in the adventure strip genre. © October 13, 1940, Ledger Syndicate, Inc. Courtesy of Jack Gilbert

CONNIE daily strip by Frank Godwin. CONNIE was a conventional pretty-girl strip when it debuted on November 13, 1927, but during the 1930s the stories became more fantastic. © 1935 Ledger Syndicate, Inc. Courtesy of All Star Auctions

SMILIN' JACK Sunday page by Zack Mosley. This long-running aviation strip started as a Sunday feature called ON THE WING on October 1, 1933, and ended on April 1, 1973. A licensed pilot, Mosley drew his airplanes with technical accuracy. © March 22, 1936, Tribune Media Services, Inc. All rights reserved. Reprinted with permission. Courtesy of Jim Scancarelli.

SMILIN' JACK daily strips by Zack Mosley. The daily strip version of Smilin' Jack began on June 15, 1936. Jack, who grew his trademark mustache after this episode, operated a commercial aviation business. © June 22 and September 9, 1936, Tribune Media Services, Inc. All rights reserved. Reprinted with permission. Courtesy of All Star Auctions (above) and Sandy Schechter (below)

JOE PALOOKA daily strip by Ham Fisher. Joe tries to impress Ann Howe in this early episode. © March 7, 1933, McNaught Syndicate, Inc. Courtesy of Russ Cochran

COMIC HEAVYWEIGHT

One of the most successful sports features of all time was Ham Fisher's *Joe Palooka,* which debuted on April 19, 1930, and continued until November 4, 1984. In addition to the naive prizefighter, the cast included Joe's brash manager, Knobby Walsh; his wealthy girlfriend, Ann Howe; and Smokey, his personal assistant and closest friend.

The plots frequently culminated in exciting boxing bouts, but they also dealt with Joe's romantic exploits and adventures in foreign countries. Although Fisher came up with most of the stories, he was not a talented artist and employed a succession of ghosts, including Phil Boyle, Al Capp, and Mo Leff.

JOE PALOOKA daily strips by Ham Fisher. Joe defends his heavyweight title and gets a hero's welcome. © February 11 and August 20, 1938, McNaught Syndicate, Inc.
Courtesy of the Art Wood Collection of Cartoon and Caricature, Prints and Photographs Division, Library of Congress

JOE PALOOKA Sunday page by Ham Fisher. Joe was a fighter with a heart of gold and could never turn down a request to support a charitable cause.
© 1932 McNaught Syndicate, Inc. Courtesy of Peter Maresca

TAILSPIN TOMMY *daily strip by Glenn Chaffin (writer) and Hal Forrest (artist). One of the first aviation strips, TAILSPIN TOMMY debuted on May 21, 1928, the year after Lindbergh's historic flight.* © 1933 Bell Syndicate, Inc. Courtesy of Russ Cochran

BRICK BRADFORD *daily strip by William Ritt (writer) and Clarence Gray (artist). The early episodes of Ritt's creation, which began on August 21, 1933, dealt with mythological themes, before venturing into time travel.* © June 21, 1935, Central Press Association, Inc. Courtesy of Francisco Lopez

MICKEY FINN *daily strip by Lank Leonard. The Irish flatfoot made his first appearance on April 6, 1936, and continued to walk the beat until December 21, 1975. In this early episode, he has not yet joined the police force.* © 1936 McNaught Syndicate, Inc. Courtesy of Morris Weiss

RED RYDER *daily strip by Fred Harmon. One of the most popular and enduring cowboy comics, RED RYDER was launched as a Sunday feature on November 6, 1938, and a daily strip on March 27, 1939.* © May 2, 1939, NEA Service, Inc. Courtesy of Gary Ernest Smith

RED RYDER Sunday page by Fred Harmon. Red's longtime companion was Little Beaver, a ten-year-old orphaned Navajo.
© 1941 NEA Service, Inc. Courtesy of Peter Maresca

chester gould

THE "MASTER SLEUTH OF THE COMICS" provided vicarious thrills to newspaper readers who wanted to see thugs like Al Capone brought to justice. "I have always been disgusted when I read or learn of gangsters and criminals escaping their just dues under the law," claimed the creator of the square-jawed flatfoot in 1934. "And for that reason I invented in Dick Tracy a detective who could either shoot down these public enemies or put them in jail where they belong."

Chester Gould, was born in Pawnee, Oklahoma, on November 20, 1900. His father, who was a printer for the *Pawnee Courier-Dispatch,* wanted him to be a lawyer, but the boy's first love was drawing. After winning a cartoon contest sponsored by *The American Boy* magazine in 1917, Chester mailed in $20 for twenty lessons from the W. L. Evans School of Cartooning in Cleveland. He attended Oklahoma A&M University from 1919 to 1921 but graduated from Northwestern in 1923 with a degree in business.

Gould was still more interested in becoming a cartoonist, and he attended classes at the Chicago Academy of Fine Arts and worked in the art department of the *Chicago American* while finishing college at night. Determined to sell a comic strip of his own, he doggedly sent samples of his work to newspapers and syndicates, claiming to have created more than sixty different ideas between 1921 and 1931. He managed to have a few features published, including *Fillum Fables* (1924), *Radio Cats* (1924), and *The Girl Friends* (1931), but none of them caught on.

Joseph Medill Patterson of the Chicago Tribune–New York News Syndicate finally responded favorably to one of Gould's submissions. On August 13, 1931, the determined cartoonist received a telegram: "YOUR PLAINCLOTHES TRACY HAS POSSIBILITIES STOP WOULD LIKE TO SEE YOU WHEN I GO TO CHICAGO NEXT STOP PLEASE CALL TRIBUNE OFFICE MONDAY ABOUT NOON FOR AN APPOINTMENT = JM PATTERSON."

In the sample Gould had sent to Patterson, Plainclothes Tracy, a modern-day Sherlock Holmes, battled Big Boy, a thinly disguised caricature of Chicago mob boss Al Capone. Patterson changed the name of the lead character to "Dick Tracy" and suggested an opening story line in which Tracy joined the police force after his girlfriend's father was brutally shot down by robbers. Gould followed Patterson's advice and turned out two weeks of strips in two days.

Dick Tracy debuted on October 4, 1931, and the public responded immediately to the raw violence in the hard-hitting strip. Gould later recalled, "At that time, no cartoon had ever shown a detective character fighting it out face to face with

CHESTER GOULD—Self-caricature with his most famous villains. *August 14, 1944,* Life *magazine. Courtesy of the International Museum of Cartoon Art*

crooks via the hot lead route." Three years after its debut, *Dick Tracy* was appearing in 90 newspapers; a decade later, Gould's list had grown to 250 daily and 125 Sunday clients.

In *Dick Tracy: The Official Biography,* Jay Maeder summed up the unique appeal of Gould's creation: "His strip was defined by fast-action story lines that could kick the breath out of you, arrestingly stylized artwork that was both super-realistic and weirdly cartoonish, a famous rogues' gallery of villains, an unrelievedly grim Calvinist conscience that informed every move every one of its characters ever made—and always the pathological mayhem. The strip was a dark and perverse and vicious thing, sensationally full of blood-splashed cruelty from its first week, the single most spectacularly gruesome feature the comics had ever known; there has never been another newspaper strip so full of the batterings, shootings, knifings, drownings, torchings, crushings, gurglings, gaspings, shriekings, pleadings and bleatings that Chester Gould gleefully served up as often as he possibly could."

Gould was described in 1944 as an "affable, well-adjusted man who drinks bourbon neat, smokes nine good cigars a day and plays poker whenever he gets the chance." Although he was criticized later in his career for glorifying violence, he continued to produce his ghoulishly entertaining creation until he retired in 1977.

DICK TRACY daily strip by Chester Gould. A corrupt politician takes his own life. © December 28, 1931. Courtesy of the International Museum of Cartoon Art

DICK TRACY daily strip by Chester Gould. Tracy proposes to his girlfriend, Tess Trueheart—but he didn't marry her until Christmas Eve, 1949.
© December 30, 1931. Courtesy of Matt Masterson

DICK TRACY daily strip by Chester Gould. Junior and Dick go to visit the mother of slain gangster Giorgio Spaldoni. © May 10, 1934. Courtesy of Matt Masterson

DICK TRACY daily strip by Chester Gould. Tracy walks into a trap at Boris Arson's headquarters. © January 19, 1935. Courtesy of Matt Masterson

DICK TRACY Sunday page by Chester Gould. Dick meets his future charge, Junior, for the first time. © September 8, 1932, Detroit Free Press. Courtesy of Peter Maresca

DICK TRACY Sunday page by Chester Gould. Tracy goes after Stud Bronzen's human-smuggling operation with his bare fists.
© March 13, 1938. Courtesy of Matt Masterson

DICK TRACY daily strip by Chester Gould. Dick is lost in a blizzard trying to rescue an abducted child, Johnny Wreath. © March 23, 1943. Courtesy of Matt Masterson

DICK TRACY daily strip by Chester Gould. A dramatic chase scene with 88 Keyes, a gold-digging bandleader. © May 29, 1943. Courtesy of Matt Masterson

DICK TRACY daily strip by Chester Gould. Mrs. Pruneface tracks Tracy in the rain. © July 17, 1943. Courtesy of Matt Masterson

DICK TRACY daily strip by Chester Gould. Tracy is trapped in one of Gould's ghoulish "Near-Deathtraps." © August 10, 1943. Courtesy of Matt Masterson

DICK TRACY daily strip by Chester Gould. The demise of Flattop Jones, a hired killer. © May 16, 1944. Courtesy of Matt Masterson

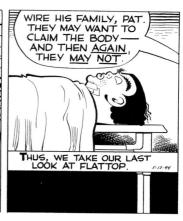

DICK TRACY daily strip by Chester Gould. The final appearance of Gould's most famous 1940s villain, on a slab in the city morgue.
© May 17, 1944. Courtesy of the International Museum of Cartoon Art

DICK TRACY daily strip by Chester Gould. Tracy fights the Brow, a notorious Axis spy. © September 22, 1944. Courtesy of Matt Masterson

DICK TRACY daily strip by Chester Gould. A violent shoot-out with Measles. © February 27, 1945. Courtesy of Matt Masterson

RADIO PATROL Sunday page by Eddie Sullivan (writer) and Charlie Schmidt (artist). Sergeant Pat, Stutterin' Sam, Molly Day, and Pinky Pinkerton plan a Christmas dinner. © December 25, 1937, King Features Syndicate, Inc. Courtesy of Francisco Lopez

RADIO PATROL daily strip by Eddie Sullivan (writer) and Charlie Schmidt (artist). The success of DICK TRACY spawned many other crime strips. RADIO PATROL, the first feature to star uniformed policemen, debuted on April 16, 1934. © December 25, 1934, King Features Syndicate, Inc. Courtesy of Francisco Lopez

JIM HARDY daily strip by Dick Moores. A former assistant to Chester Gould on DICK TRACY, Moores created his own strip, which starred an ex-convict, on June 8, 1936. © July 24, 1936, United Feature Syndicate, Inc.

RED BARRY Sunday page by Will Gould. The artist, who was no relation to Chester, introduced his fast-talking, hard-hitting crimefighter to newspaper readers on March 19, 1934. © May 5, 1935, King Features Syndicate, Inc. Courtesy of Francisco Lopez

CURLEY HARPER Sunday page by Lyman Young. Curley started out as a college athlete in the companion feature to TIM TYLER'S LUCK on March 31, 1935, and eventually became an investigative reporter. © September 18, 1938, King Features Syndicate, Inc. Courtesy of Francisco Lopez

DAN DUNN daily strip by Norman Marsh. Dan, a square-jawed detective with a trench coat and fedora hat, was the most blatant rip-off of DICK TRACY.
© March 16, 1938, Publishers Syndicate. Courtesy of Russ Cochran

DAN DUNN daily strip by Norman Marsh. This strip was launched on September 25, 1933, and ended on October 3, 1943, a year and a half after its creator reenlisted in the Marines. © April 9, 1938, Publishers Syndicate. Courtesy of Bill Janocha

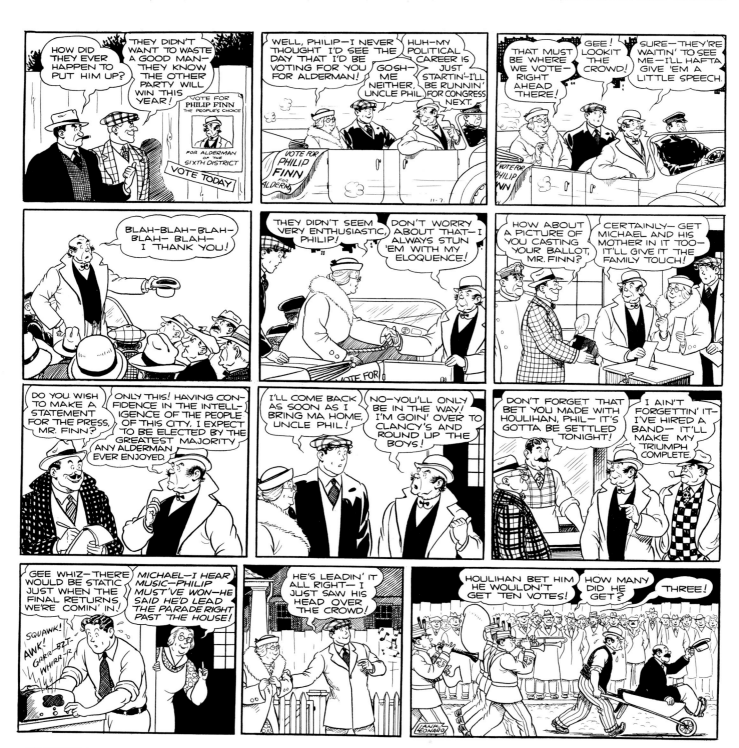

MICKEY FINN Sunday page by Lank Leonard. The Sunday version of Leonard's strip debuted on May 17, 1936, with NIPPIE as the topper strip.
© November 7, 1937, McNaught Syndicate, Inc. Courtesy of Jim Scancarelli

CHARLIE CHAN *Sunday page by Alfred Andriola. The comic strip adaptation was launched as a Sunday page on October 30, 1938, and continued until May 31, 1942.*
© November 17, 1940, McNaught Syndicate, Inc. Courtesy of Francisco Lopez

CHARLIE CHAN—*Portrait by Alfred Andriola. The Oriental sleuth initially starred in a series of six novels by Earl Derr Biggers, beginning in 1925.* © September 10, 1938, McNaught Syndicate, Inc. Courtesy of Editor & Publisher

CHARLIE CHAN *daily strip by Alfred Andriola. The artist, a former assistant to Milton Caniff, produced his strip with the help of Charles Raab and others.*
© August 18, 1939, McNaught Syndicate, Inc. Courtesy of All Star Auctions

SKYROADS *daily strip by Russell Keaton. Created by two pilots, Lieutenant Lester Maitland and Dick Calkins, in 1929, this aviation strip was drawn by* Russell Keaton *in the 1930s.* © 1938 John F. Dille Company. Courtesy of Bill Janocha

DON WINSLOW OF THE NAVY *daily strip by Frank V. Martinek (writer) and Leon Beroth (artist). Designed in 1934 as a recruiting tool by Martinek, a former navy intelligence officer,* DON WINSLOW *featured suspenseful espionage stories and authentic detail.* © February 25, 1938, Bell Syndicate, Inc. Courtesy of Bill Janocha

MYRA NORTH, SPECIAL NURSE *daily strip by Ray Thompson (writer) and Charles Coll (artist). This blonde-haired registered nurse, who began her adventures in 1936, managed to attend to her medical duties while fighting criminals and spies.* © 1937 NEA Service, Inc. Courtesy of Bill Janocha

SCORCHY SMITH *daily strip by Bert Christman. A talented artist who took over* SCORCHY SMITH *from Noel Sickles in 1936, Christman left the strip in 1938 to fly airplanes for the navy and was killed in combat in 1942.* © June 3, 1938, the Associated Press. Courtesy of Bill Janocha

e. c. segar

POPEYE, THE PERPETUALLY SCOWLING, grammatically challenged sea dog with superstrength, became a hero to millions of Americans during the worst days of the Depression for his stubborn integrity and no-punches-pulled approach to problem solving. The spinach-eating sailor made his first appearance in the *Thimble Theatre* comic strip after it was a decade old. Nine years later, the man who created him passed away at the height of his career.

Elzie Crisler Segar was born in the small town of Chester, Illinois, on the banks of the Mississippi River, on December 8, 1894. At the age of twelve, he went to work at the Chester Opera House, where he ran the projector, accompanied the pianist on drums, and drew with chalk on the sidewalk in front of the theater to promote the shows. In the spring of 1916, he completed the W. L. Evans correspondence course in cartooning, and soon afterward he left for Chicago to pursue his fortune.

The legendary cartoonist Richard F. Outcault helped Segar obtain employment at the *Chicago Herald,* where he was given his first strip assignment, *Charlie Chaplin's Comic Capers.* In 1917, he started his own feature, *Barry the Boob,* about a bumbling soldier in the European war. Soon after, the *Herald* went bankrupt and was taken over by William Randolph Hearst. Segar ended up working for Hearst's *Chicago American,* where he created a local interest feature entitled *Looping the Loop.* His cartoons attracted the attention of Hearst's editor, Arthur Brisbane, and he was summoned to New York, where King Features launched *Thimble Theatre* on December 19, 1919.

Initially modeled after Ed Wheelan's *Midget Movies,* Segar's strip featured a cast of pen-and-ink performers who spoofed popular films and plays. Segar soon gave up on the original premise and began weaving stories around the continuing adventures of Olive Oyl, her endlessly scheming brother Castor, and her boyfriend Harold Hamgravy (whose name was later changed to Ham Gravy). Segar's writing and drawing skills matured as his cast expanded and the plots stretched out in length; by the end of the decade, however, *Thimble Theatre* was appearing in only a half-dozen newspapers.

In 1929, Castor Oyl plotted to make a fortune at a gambling casino on Dice Island with the help of Bernice the Whiffle Hen, a bird who guaranteed good luck when the three hairs on her head were rubbed. After buying a boat, Castor went down to the docks and hired a sailor, with a squint in one eye and a corncob pipe, to man the vessel. Segar initially intended for Popeye to be another incidental character in the strip, but readers responded to his feisty

E. C. SEGAR—*Self-caricature from an advertisement for the W. L. Evans School of Cartooning.* **1917,** Cartoons magazine. Courtesy of Illustration House
All Thimble Theatre comic strips © King Features Syndicate, Inc.

personality almost immediately. As the list of newspapers subscribing to *Thimble Theatre* continued to grow, Popeye became a national celebrity, starring in a series of animated films produced by the Fleischer Studio and endorsing hundreds of products, all of which earned millions of dollars in licensing fees.

Until his death on October 13, 1938, at the age of forty-three, Segar offered up a masterful blend of comedy, fantasy, satire, and suspense in *Thimble Theatre Starring Popeye* (renamed in 1931). He introduced a string of memorable characters to play off his hero's idiosyncrasies, including the parasitic sidekick J. Wellington Wimpy (1931), archrival Bluto (who appeared only briefly in the strip during 1932), adopted "infink" Swee'pea (1933), and long-lost Poopdeck Pappy (1936).

Segar also popularized a lexicon of comic expressions in the strip. Popeye's signature sayings, "I yam what I yam an' tha's all I yam" and "Blow me down!" became classic catchphrases, as were Wimpy's "I will gladly pay you Tuesday for a hamburger today" and "Let's you and him fight." Among the many words Segar added to the popular vernacular were "jeep" and "goon."

Bud Sagendorf, who was hired as Segar's assistant a little more than a year after Popeye was introduced, described his employer as "short of stature, slight of frame, mild-mannered and somewhat introverted." During the 1930s, Segar lived in Santa Monica, California, eighteen miles away from George Herriman. According to Sagendorf, the two cartoonists, who even looked alike, never met. Although they shared a mutual professional admiration, they were each too shy to impose on the other.

THIMBLE THEATRE and THE FIVE FIFTEEN promotional drawing by E. C. Segar. More than seven years before the debut of Popeye, Segar drew the cast of his two comic features in this advertisement for the W. L. Evans School of Cartooning. © November 25, 1921. Courtesy of Bruce Hamilton

THIMBLE THEATRE STARRING POPEYE daily strip by E. C. Segar. Popeye, Olive Oyl, and Merlock Jones are on board the Blue Squid in an episode from the fourth month of the "Eighth Sea" continuity. © September 5, 1932. Courtesy of Bruce Hamilton

THIMBLE THEATRE STARRING POPEYE daily strip by E. C. Segar. Bluto, the star villain in the Fleischer Studio's animated POPEYE films, appeared only briefly in Segar's strip, during 1932. © September 22, 1932. Courtesy of Jerry Dumas

THIMBLE THEATRE STARRING POPEYE daily strip by E. C. Segar. King Blozo appears in the first day of the "Long Live the King" story, during which Segar dabbled in political commentary. © November 14, 1932. Courtesy of Bruce Hamilton

THIMBLE THEATRE Sunday page by E. C. Segar. Popeye breaks out of jail to fight Kid Jolt. One of the few existing original Sunday pages with the matching SAPPO topper feature. © December 21, 1930. Courtesy of Illustration House

THIMBLE THEATRE STARRING POPEYE daily strip by E. C. Segar. After being rescued by Popeye, Toar, a nine-hundred-pound prehistoric caveman, shows his appreciation with a kiss. © May 8, 1935. Courtesy of Bruce Hamilton

THIMBLE THEATRE STARRING POPEYE daily strip by E. C. Segar. Wimpy launches the good ship Hamburger. © June 10, 1935. Courtesy of Bruce Hamilton

THIMBLE THEATRE STARRING POPEYE daily strip by E. C. Segar. Swee'pea, who was left on Popeye's doorstep on July 28, 1933, is as fearless as his adopted father. © February 21, 1936. Courtesy of Craig Englund

THIMBLE THEATRE STARRING POPEYE daily strip by E. C. Segar. Olive asks all-knowing Eugene the Jeep some probing questions.
© June 2, 1936. Courtesy of Bruce Hamilton

THIMBLE THEATRE STARRING POPEYE daily strip by E. C. Segar. Six mermaids follow Poopdeck Pappy from Barnacle Island.
© November 20, 1936. Courtesy of Bruce Hamilton

THIMBLE THEATRE STARRING POPEYE original pen-and-ink Sunday page by E. C. Segar, with color overlay. This classic Sunday page features two of Wimpy's most quotable phrases and ends with Popeye's signature saying. © *November 19, 1933. Courtesy of Bruce Hamilton*

THIMBLE THEATRE STARRING POPEYE daily strip by E. C. Segar. Popeye is flummoxed by the Sea Hag. © *January 11, 1937. Courtesy of Bruce Hamilton*

THIMBLE THEATRE STARRING POPEYE daily strip by E. C. Segar. Wimpy toots up a hamburger on the Sea Hag's magic flute. The orange stains are from rubber cement used to attach the Ben Day shading. © *November 26, 1937. Courtesy of Bruce Hamilton*

THIMBLE THEATRE STARRING POPEYE recolored Sunday page by E. C. Segar. A number of newspaper editors refused to run this gruesome episode.
© October 1, 1933. Courtesy of Bruce Hamilton and American Color

THIMBLE THEATRE STARRING POPEYE daily strip by E. C. Segar. Popeye lectures his ninety-nine-year-old father on the virtues of dignity. © September 18, 1937.
Courtesy of Bruce Hamilton

THIMBLE THEATRE STARRING POPEYE daily strip by E. C. Segar. A strip from the last story Segar worked on, which he was unable to finish due to deteriorating health. © August 15, 1938. Courtesy of Bruce Hamilton

chic young

BLONDIE BOOPADOOP AND DAGWOOD BUMSTEAD got off to a rocky start. The son of a tycoon, Dagwood was just one of Blondie's many boyfriends. After announcing his intention to marry the blonde-haired gold digger, bumbling Bumstead could not obtain his parents' approval for the proposed union. To protest, he went on a twenty-eight-day hunger strike. This episode gave the struggling feature the boost it needed. By the time the couple wed on February 17, 1933, *Blondie* was on its way to becoming the most popular comic strip in America, a position it maintained for five decades. Blondie and Dagwood's creator was no overnight success either.

Murat Bernard Young was born in Chicago on January 9, 1901, but grew up in St. Louis. After graduating from high school, he returned to his birthplace and enrolled at the Art Institute of Chicago. In 1921, he created his first comic strip, *The Affairs of Jane,* for the Newspaper Enterprise Association, but it lasted only six months. He tried another pretty-girl feature, *Beautiful Bab,* for the Bell Syndicate in 1922. That effort survived for four months. Undaunted, Young sold *Dumb Dora* to King Features in 1924. He continued this strip for six years, until the syndicate turned down his request for a bigger salary.

Blondie, Young's fourth feature with a female lead, was launched by King Features on September 8, 1930. After a modest start, sales of the strip stalled, and it was eventually canceled in Hearst's flagship paper, the *New York American.* Apparently, readers struggling with the hardships of the Depression were no longer entertained by the screwball antics of a ditzy flapper and her rich boyfriends. In desperation, Young and the syndicate decided to have Blondie fall in love with one of her suitors and get married. As a final twist, her new husband would get disinherited and the couple would be condemned to a life of middle-class drudgery.

The solution worked; sympathetic readers identified with Blondie and Dagwood's struggles, and Young's feature started to pick up new subscribers. The wedding was an event worthy of national media attention, and circulation continued to climb after Baby Dumpling (named "Alexander" after Young's assistant Alex Raymond) was born on April 15, 1934.

Within a few short years, all of the supporting players and recurring scenarios were in place. Dagwood worked at J. C. Dithers and Company while his boss's wife, Cora, went shopping with Blondie. Next-door neighbors Herb Woodley and Tootsie joined the cast, and the Bumstead family grew to include Cookie, who was born in 1941, and Daisy the dog, who had five puppies later that same year. Dagwood was forever oversleeping, crashing into the mailman, and chasing

CHIC YOUNG—Self-caricature. *c. 1945. Courtesy of the International Museum of Cartoon Art*
All Blondie comic strips © King Features Syndicate, Inc.

after his bus. He sought relief from this daily routine by snoozing on the couch, soaking in the bathtub, or raiding the icebox for the ingredients to his famous sandwich.

In 1938, Columbia Pictures produced the first of twenty-eight *Blondie* movies, starring Penny Singleton and Arthur Lake. A successful radio show and two television series followed during the next three decades. Licensed products, including books, games, greeting cards, dolls, clothing, cosmetics, and various other household items, brought in additional income.

By 1948, Young was earning an annual salary of $300,000 and *Blondie* was appearing in 1,136 daily and Sunday papers. It was the number one strip in the business.

When asked to describe his creation, the modest cartoonist mused, "It is difficult to define *Blondie* as a continuity strip, but I do use the greatest, simplest, and most interesting continuity of all, the continuity of life itself, and add a little humor, the spice of life."

"I prefer to call *Blondie* a streamlined gag strip," he added, "whose happenings are true and have occurred in almost every home. You, see I am catering to the average American family."

It took a few false starts, but Chic Young had discovered the secret to success on the funnies pages.

BLONDIE daily strip by Chic Young. Dagwood introduces Blondie to his wealthy father in the debut episode of Young's feature.
© September 8, 1930. Courtesy of Craig Englund

BLONDIE daily strip by Chic Young. The Bumsteads come up with a plan to show their son the folly of his marital plans. © September 22, 1930. Courtesy of Art Wood

BLONDIE daily strip by Chic Young. Mrs. Bumstead tricks Dagwood into dating other girls. © August 20, 1931. Courtesy of Craig Englund

BLONDIE daily strip by Chic Young. Blondie and Dagwood are apart on Christmas Day. © December 25, 1931. Courtesy of Craig Englund

BLONDIE daily strip by Chic Young. Dagwood was sick in bed a few days before he started his famous hunger strike. © December 31, 1932. Courtesy of David Applegate

Dagwood went on a hunger strike in January 1933 to force his parents to grant him permission to marry Blondie.
BLONDIE daily strip by Chic Young. The first episode of the twenty-eight-day protest. © *January 3, 1933. Courtesy of Craig Englund*

BLONDIE daily strip by Chic Young. The doctor makes a prediction. © *January 5, 1933. Courtesy of Craig Englund*

BLONDIE daily strip by Chic Young. A missing goldfish. © *January 14, 1933. Courtesy of Craig Englund*

BLONDIE daily strip by Chic Young. The end is near. © *January 25, 1933. Courtesy of Craig Englund*

BLONDIE daily strip by Chic Young. The Bumsteads give in, and the hunger strike is over. © *January 30, 1933. Courtesy of Craig Englund*

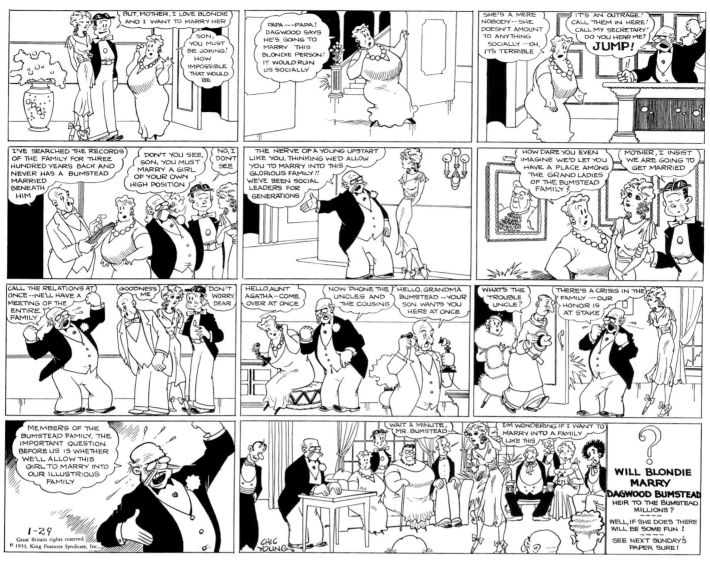

BLONDIE Sunday page by Chic Young. The entire Bumstead clan opposes Blondie and Dagwood's marriage. © January 29, 1933. Courtesy of Craig Englund

BLONDIE daily strip by Chic Young. The historic wedding of Blondie and Dagwood. © February 17, 1933. Courtesy of the Library of Congress

BLONDIE daily strip by Chic Young. Newlywed Blondie has a jealousy problem. © May 16, 1933. Courtesy of Craig Englund

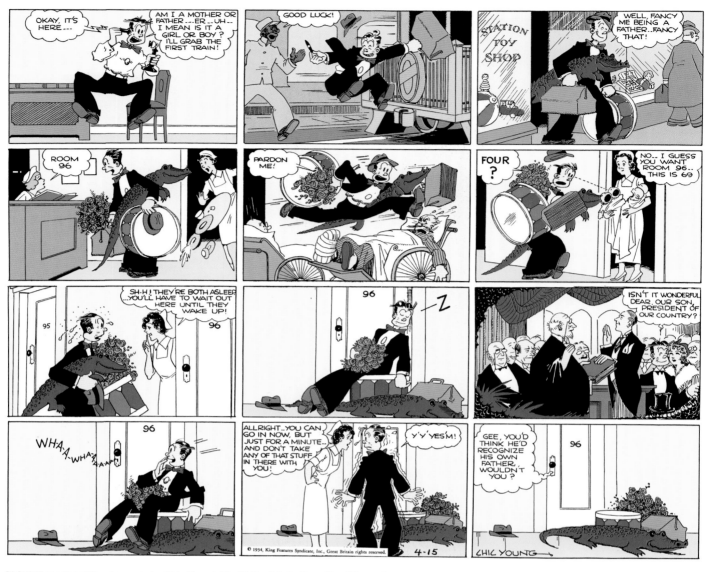

BLONDIE recolored Sunday page by Chic Young. The birth of Baby Dumpling (Alexander). © April 15, 1934. Courtesy of Craig Englund and American Color

BLONDIE daily strip by Chic Young. Baby Dumpling comes home. © April 27, 1934. Courtesy of Richard Marschall

BLONDIE daily strip by Chic Young. Blondie and Dagwood take the baby on vacation. © July 24, 1934. Courtesy of Craig Englund

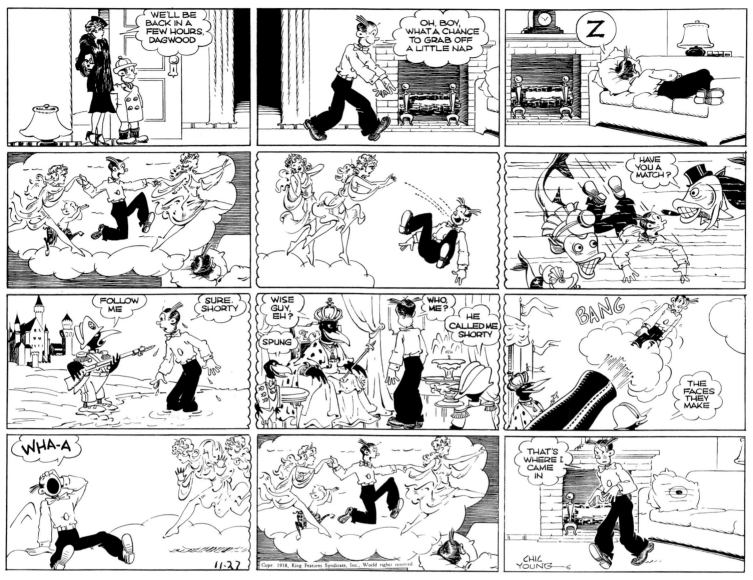

BLONDIE Sunday page by Chic Young. Dagwood has a wild dream while napping on the couch. © *November 27, 1938. Courtesy of the Library of Congress*

BLONDIE daily strip by Chic Young. The secret to Dagwood's sandwich is revealed. © *October 9, 1944. Courtesy of the Library of Congress*

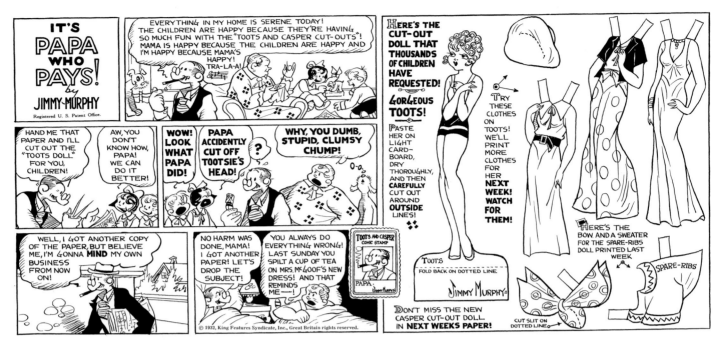

IT'S PAPA WHO PAYS! topper strip for TOOTS AND CASPER Sunday page by Jimmy Murphy. Cutout dolls were popular during the 1930s.
© 1932 King Features Syndicate, Inc. Courtesy of the International Museum of Cartoon Art

PAPER DOLLS Pretty girls continued to grace the funnies pages during the 1930s, as the flapper look gave way to more sophisticated styles and comic strip females tried to keep up with the glamour queens of the movies. Starring roles ranged from dangerous femme fatales to demure domestic divas, complementing the working girl and college coed parts that predominated in the 1920s. A new crop of illustrators, influenced by the work of John Held Jr. and Russell Patterson, joined the ranks of newspaper comic artists.

THE VAN SWAGGERS topper strip for TILLIE THE TOILER Sunday page by Russ Westover. Readers were invited to send in fashion designs.
© 1934 King Features Syndicate, Inc. Courtesy of the International Museum of Cartoon Art

A SPORTING DECISION illustration by Ethel Hays. One of the most successful women cartoonists of the 1920s and 1930s, Hays drew a daily panel, FLAPPER FANNY, for the Newspaper Enterprise Association, as well as illustrations for the Sunday newspapers. © January 13, 1935, Everyweek magazine. Courtesy of the International Museum of Cartoon Art

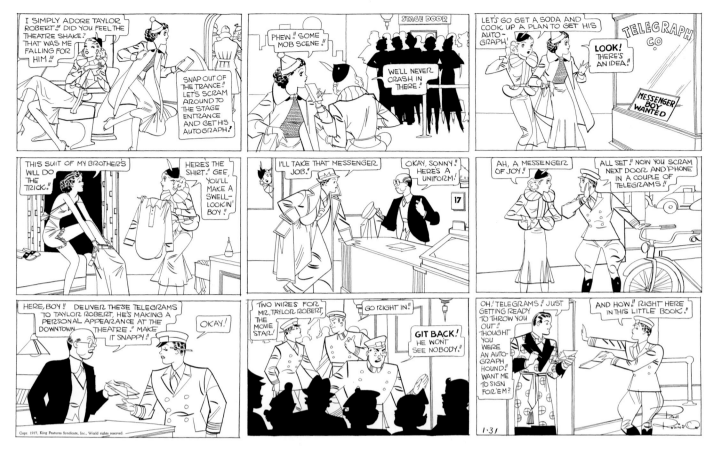

ETTA KETT Sunday page by Paul Robinson. Etta dresses in her brother's suit to get an autograph from a handsome movie star.
© January 31, 1937, King Features Syndicate, Inc. Courtesy of the International Museum of Cartoon Art

OH, DIANA daily strip by Don Flowers. Diana speaks out for women's rights. © April 15, 1936, the Associated Press. Courtesy of the International Museum of Cartoon Art

OH, DIANA daily strip by Don Flowers. The artist also did a daily panel, MODEST MAIDENS, for the Associated Press.
© May 12, 1938, the Associated Press. Courtesy of Jim Scancarelli

GAGS AND GALS Sunday page by Jefferson Machamer. He worked as an artist for Judge magazine in the 1920s before creating a comic strip, PETTING PATTY, in 1928 and a syndicated Sunday-page feature, GAGS AND GALS, in 1935. © April 18, 1937, King Features Syndicate, Inc. Courtesy of Richard Marschall

DUMB DORA daily strip by Bill Dwyer. Chic Young's 1925 flapper strip was taken over by Paul Fung in 1930 and Bill Dwyer in 1932 before ending in 1934. This example was ghosted by Dwyer's friend Milton Caniff. © September 6, 1932, King Features Syndicate, Inc. Courtesy of Bill Janocha

al capp

Any resemblance to any actual character, living or dead, is purely accidental! — *Al Capp*

AL CAPP—Self-caricature from Comics and Their Creators. 1942
All Li'l Abner comic strips © Capp Enterprises, Inc.

THE CREATOR OF ABNER, MAMMY AND PAPPY YOKUM, and
Daisy Mae Scragg wrote in 1977, "I knew all my characters
from Strip One. In forty-three years, there was never any
basic change in them." *Li'l Abner*, which debuted on August
13, 1934, and continued until November 13, 1977, was syndicated to nine hundred newspapers at the peak of its popularity
and inspired a Broadway musical, a feature film, an amusement
park (Dogpatch U.S.A.), and a soft drink (Kickapoo Joy Juice).

Alfred Gerald Caplin (who later changed his name to
Capp) was born in New Haven, Connecticut, on September
28, 1909. His parents, who were Russian Jews, struggled to
support their four children, and the family moved frequently.
At the age of nine, after losing his leg in a trolley car accident,
Alfred decided to become a cartoonist. He took classes in
figure drawing and perspective at the Pennsylvania School
of Fine Arts, the Boston Museum School, and the Designers
Art School but never graduated from high school.

In 1932, Capp got his first job drawing a syndicated
panel, *Mister Gilfeather,* for the Associated Press in New
York, but he quit after six months and went home to Boston.
The following year, he returned to Manhattan, where he
was hired by Ham Fisher to work on the *Joe Palooka* comic
strip. When Fisher left on a six-week vacation, Capp wrote
and drew a series of six Sunday pages in which Joe Palooka
and his manager, Knobby Walsh, traveled to Kentucky to visit
a backwoods boxer named Big Leviticus and his family. Shortly
after this story ran in November 1933, Capp quit and finished

preparing twelve weeks of samples for his own hillbilly strip.
In later years, Fisher would accuse his former employee of
stealing his characters, but Capp had, in fact, "ghosted" the
Big Leviticus sequence.

King Features liked Capp's idea but wanted him to make
some changes, so he sold it to United Feature Syndicate, as it
was, for less money. *Li'l Abner* debuted inauspiciously in eight
papers, but the twenty-five-year-old cartoonist had a formula
he knew would make the strip successful.

"My family of innocents is surrounded by a world of super-
average people," Capp explained years later. "This innocence
of theirs is indestructible, so that while they possess all the
homely virtues in which we profess to believe, they seem
ingenuous because the world around them is irritated by them,
cheats them, kicks them around. They are trusting, kind, loyal,
generous, and patriotic. It's a truly bewildering world in which
they find themselves."

Although Capp's political leanings changed over the years,
readers never had any trouble distinguishing the heroes from
the villains in *Li'l Abner*. Corrupt politicians, con men, snobs,
fools, and whiners were among the phonies skewered by his
caustic pen. Capp's targets were selfishness, pretension, and
ignorance, and his weapon was satire.

The driving force behind the strip was the attraction
between Abner and Daisy Mae. The scantily clad mountain
girl, who became more voluptuous as the years went by,
was madly in love with the handsome hillbilly, but Abner
was equally consumed with the urge to escape from her clutches.
In November 1937, Capp introduced an event in which the
unattached females of Dogpatch chased the available men and,
according to tradition, could marry any bachelor they caught.
Sadie Hawkins Day was observed annually in the strip for
many years, as well as on college campuses across the country.

On March 29, 1952, Abner finally gave in to Daisy Mae's
charms and married her. "Something went out of the strip with
the wedding," wrote comic historian Ron Goulart, "and the
domesticated Abner was not the man he had been before
the fateful day when Marryin' Sam tied the knot."

Li'l Abner continued to be one of the most popular comics
in America throughout the rest of the 1950s and early 1960s,
but it began losing papers after Capp's political satire became
increasingly vitriolic and he was convicted of sexually harassing
a twenty-year-old college coed in 1972. The man who John
Steinbeck claimed, in 1952, "may very possibly be the best
writer in the world today" died in 1979, two years after he
put down his pen. There has never been another cartoonist
quite like him.

LI'L ABNER *daily strip no. 1 by Al Capp. The debut appearance of Capp's lovable hillbilly.* © August 13, 1934. *Courtesy of Craig Englund*

LI'L ABNER *daily strip no. 23 by Al Capp. The country boy visits the big city in the strip's first continuity.* © 1934. *Courtesy of Sandy Schechter*

LI'L ABNER *daily strip by Al Capp. Abner tries to make Daisy Mae jealous.* © February 29, 1936. *Courtesy of Bill Janocha*

LI'L ABNER *daily strip by Al Capp. Fantastic Brown prepares for a shotgun wedding between Abner and his daughter.* © March 11, 1936. *Courtesy of Craig Englund*

LI'L ABNER daily strip by Al Capp. After the first episode in 1937, Sadie Hawkins Day became an annual tradition. © November 20, 1937. Courtesy of Denis Kitchen

LI'L ABNER daily strip by Al Capp. Romantic misunderstandings were a perennial problem until Abner and Daisy Mae got hitched in 1952.
© October 25, 1938. Courtesy of Denis Kitchen

LI'L ABNER daily strip by Al Capp. The artist used bold lettering, judicious blacks, heavy panel borders, and innovative layouts to make his strip stand out on the comics pages. © 1939. Courtesy of Denis Kitchen

LI'L ABNER daily strip by Al Capp. Daisy Mae comes to Abner's rescue. © April 23, 1940. Courtesy of Denis Kitchen

LI'L ABNER recolored Sunday page by Al Capp. Cinder-Abner stars in a fairy-tale takeoff. The ADVICE FO' CHILLUN topper warns kids about jumping off moving vehicles. This was how Capp lost his leg. © July 10, 1938. Courtesy of Bruce Hamilton and American Color

LI'L ABNER daily strips by Al Capp. In this superhero spoof, Abner was hired to masquerade as the Flying Avenger.
© June 7 and 26, 1941. Courtesy of the Art Wood Collection of Cartoon and Caricature, Prints and Photographs Division, Library of Congress

LI'L ABNER daily strips by Al Capp. It looks as if Daisy Mae has finally caught Abner in another Sadie Hawkins Day race.
© September 25 and November 15, 1943. Courtesy of the Art Wood Collection of Cartoon and Caricature, Prints and Photographs Division, Library of Congress

LI'L ABNER Sunday page by Al Capp. FEARLESS FOSDICK by Lester Gooch was Capp's parody of Chester Gould's DICK TRACY. The indestructible detective was a regular guest in the strip for many years. © May 30, 1943. Courtesy of the Swann Collection, Prints and Photographs Division, Library of Congress

ALLEY OOP promotional drawing by V. T. Hamlin. The Sunday page
debuted on September 9, 1934. © July 21, 1934, NEA Service, Inc. Courtesy of
Editor & Publisher

PREHYSTERIA Vincent Hamlin's caveman
comic, *Alley Oop*, was launched by the Newspaper
Enterprise Association on August 7, 1933. After six
years of adventures in the Stone Age land of Moo,
Hamlin sent his star on a journey through time.
Among the many places Oop visited were ancient
Troy, Cleopatra's Egypt, and the Spanish Main.
Ralph B. Fuller's *Oaky Doaks*, which took place "when
knighthood was in flower," was another strip that
reinterpreted history with a humorous spin.

ALLEY OOP daily strip by V. T. Hamlin. In addition to Oop, the original cast included his girlfriend Oola and sidekick Foozy, King Guzzle, Queen
Umpateedle, and Dinny the stegasaurus. © 1933 NEA Service, Inc. Courtesy of Gary Ernest Smith

ALLEY OOP daily strip by V. T. Hamlin. The artist was adept at rendering both atmosphere and action with his distinctive crosshatch technique.
© April 27, 1934, NEA Service, Inc. Courtesy of Gary Ernest Smith

ALLEY OOP Sunday page by V. T. Hamlin. An amateur paleontologist, Hamlin provided scientific facts about dinosaurs in the DINNY'S FAMILY ALBUM companion feature. © November 11, 1934, NEA Service, Inc. Courtesy of Peter Maresca.

ALLEY OOP Sunday page by V. T. Hamlin. A swashbuckling pirate sequence from the later time-travel period. © July 13, 1941, NEA Service, Inc. Courtesy of Gary Ernest Smith

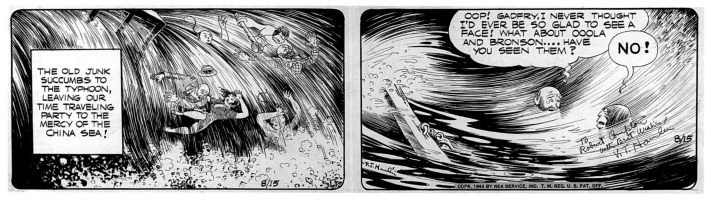

ALLEY OOP daily strip by V. T. Hamlin. Oop and friends are swept into the surging ocean by a typhoon in this example of Hamlin's fluid brushwork.
© August 15, 1945, NEA Service, Inc. Courtesy of All Star Auctions

OAKY DOAKS Sunday page by R. B. Fuller. This feature debuted as a daily strip on June 17, 1935, and as a Sunday page six years later. In this episode, the bumbling knight matches his limited wits with the evil sorceress Witch Hazel. © April 30, 1944, the Associated Press. Courtesy of the Art Wood Collection of Cartoon and Caricature, Prints and Photographs Division, Library of Congress

SMOKEY STOVER Sunday page by Bill Holman. This wacky weekly feature, which debuted on March 10, 1935, and continued until 1973, was filled with visual puns and nonsensical sayings. © August 25, 1940, Tribune Media Services, Inc. All rights reserved. Reprinted with permission. Courtesy of the International Museum of Cartoon Art

SMOKEY STOVER promotional drawing by Bill Holman. The frenetic fireman answers the alarm. © November 19, 1938, Tribune Media Services, Inc. All rights reserved. Reprinted with permission. Courtesy of Editor & Publisher

SCREWBALL STRIPS

The madcap humor of the Marx Brothers was mirrored on the funnies pages by a number of comic features during the 1930s. These creations blended slapstick chaos, wacky characters, and an abundance of puns and sight gags. Rube Goldberg paved the way for this type of comedy with his various strips and panels in the teens and twenties, and Bill Holman further refined the tradition with his 1935 Sunday feature, *Smokey Stover*. Gene Ahearn, Milt Gross, George Swanson, and Harry Hershfield were also practitioners of the screwball school of comics.

SMOKEY STOVER daily strip by Bill Holman. This feature ran as a daily strip for only a brief time during the 1930s. © December 30, 1938, Tribune Media Services, Inc. All rights reserved. Reprinted with permission. Courtesy of Jim Scancarelli

BOOB McNUTT Sunday page by Rube Goldberg. This weekly page included two companion features, **BILL** and **BOOB McNUTT'S ARK**, which provided additional outlets for his prolific imagination. © January 21, 1934, Star Company. Courtesy of the International Museum of Cartoon Art

***ABIE THE AGENT** Sunday page by Harry Hershfield. Abie was a car salesman when the strip started in 1914. By the 1930s, he was the boss of his own company.* © August 3, 1930, International Feature Service, Inc. Courtesy of Russ Cochran

***ABIE THE AGENT** daily strip by Harry Hershfield. The artist lost a court battle with Hearst in 1931 and did not draw his feature for four years, until the dispute was finally resolved in 1935.* © December 18, 1931, International Feature Service, Inc. Courtesy of Bill Janocha

THE SQUIRREL CAGE Sunday page (companion feature to ROOM AND BOARD) by Gene Ahearn. The bearded hitchhiker, who uttered the nonsensical phrase "Nov shmoz ka pop," is a favorite with comic trivia buffs. © December 19, 1937, King Features Syndicate, Inc. Courtesy of Sandy Schechter

OUR BOARDING HOUSE consecutive daily panels by Gene Ahearn. When Ahearn switched syndicates from the Newspaper Enterprise Association to King Features in 1936, his famous phony, Major Hoople, became Judge Puffle in the feature, renamed ROOM AND BOARD. © June 12 and 13, 1935, NEA Service, Inc.
Courtesy of the Art Wood Collection of Cartoon and Caricature, Prints and Photographs Division, Library of Congress

COUNT SCREWLOOSE OF THE NUT HOUSE hand-colored Sunday page by Milt Gross. The Count was a screwball with delusions of grandeur who escaped from an insane asylum on a weekly basis, only to return after encountering the lunacy of the real world. Gross's most famous feature debuted in the New York World on February 17, 1929, and was syndicated by King Features, beginning in 1930. © February 22, 1931, King Features Syndicate, Inc. Courtesy of Bill Alger

DAVE'S DELICATESSEN Sunday page by Milt Gross. The artist launched this zany feature, which shared a page with COUNT SCREWLOOSE, on June 7, 1931. © August 9, 1931, King Features Syndicate, Inc. Courtesy of Sandy Schechter

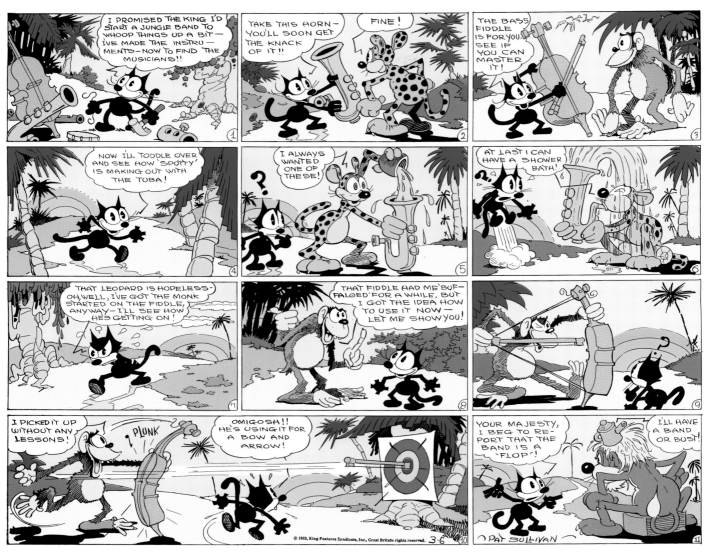

FELIX THE CAT recolored Sunday page by Pat Sullivan. The newspaper strip, which debuted on August 14, 1923, was drawn by Felix's animator, Otto Messmer, until 1955. © March 6, 1932, King Features Syndicate, Inc. Courtesy of Russ Cochran and American Color

CARTOON CROSSOVERS

Many of the top animated movie stars and newspaper comic characters were adapted to other mediums in the late 1920s and 1930s. *Felix the Cat* and *Mickey Mouse* were among the most successful comic strip spin-offs to be licensed from film studios, while Betty Boop's career as a syndicated siren was relatively short. E. C. Segar's Popeye had his own animated series during the 1930s, and a number of other pen-and-ink personalities, including the Toonerville Folks, the Katzenjammer Kids, Henry, Little Jimmy, Barney Google, and Krazy Kat, also made screen appearances.

BETTY BOOP daily strip by Bud Counihan. The boop-oop-a-doop girl starred in her own comic strip from July 23, 1934, to November 27, 1937.
© October 31, 1934, King Features Syndicate, Inc. Courtesy of the International Museum of Cartoon Art

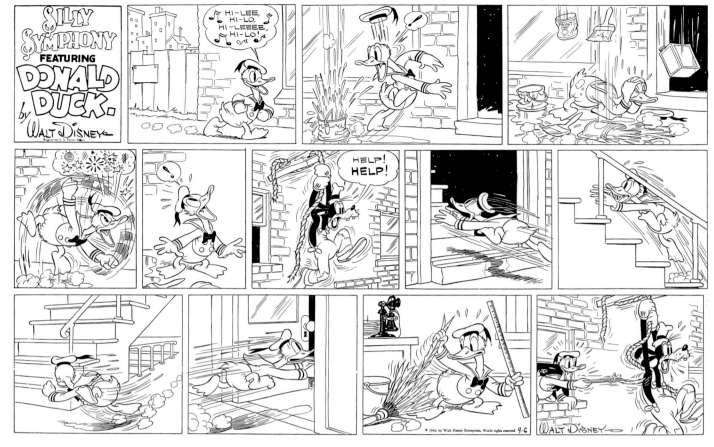

SILLY SYMPHONY Sunday page, starring Donald Duck, by Al Taliaferro. The artist was a master at capturing Donald's manic energy.
© September 6, 1936, Disney Enterprises, Inc. Distributed by King Features Syndicate, Inc. Courtesy of Bruce Hamilton

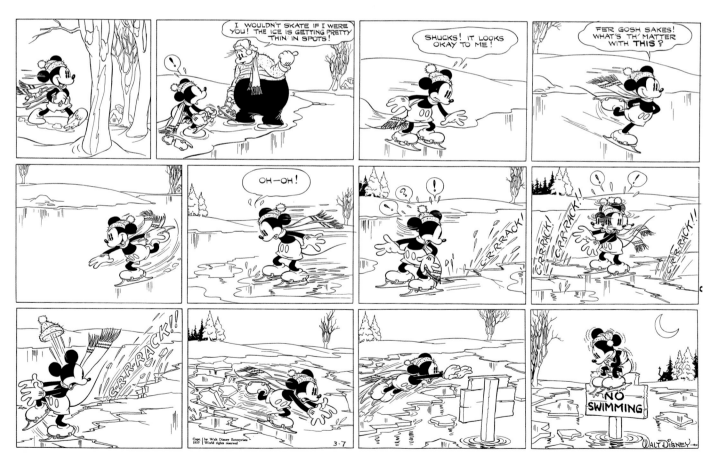

MICKEY MOUSE Sunday page penciled by Floyd Gottfredson and inked by Ted Thwaites. Mickey usually performed visual sight gags on Sunday.
© March 7, 1937, Disney Enterprises, Inc. Distributed by King Features Syndicate, Inc. Courtesy of Bruce Hamilton

MICKEY MOUSE *daily strip from the "Blaggard Castle" story, penciled by Floyd Gottfredson and inked by Ted Thwaites. This episode was inspired by the animated film short* THE MAD DOCTOR. *© February 3, 1933, Disney Enterprises, Inc. Distributed by King Features Syndicate, Inc. Courtesy of Bruce Hamilton*

MICKEY MOUSE *daily strip, with Peg Leg Pete, penciled by Floyd Gottfredson and inked by Ted Thwaites. Mickey's nemesis made his first strip appearance in 1930. © March 16, 1934, Disney Enterprises, Inc. Distributed by King Features Syndicate, Inc. Courtesy of Rob Stolzer*

MICKEY MOUSE *daily strip from the "Bad Bandit of Inferno Gulch" sequence, penciled by Floyd Gottfredson and inked by Ted Thwaites. Mickey, astride his faithful nag, Steamboat, is confronted by the masked Bat Bandit. © June 6, 1934, Disney Enterprises, Inc. Distributed by King Features Syndicate, Inc. Courtesy of Bruce Hamilton*

DISNEY EVERY DAY

Mickey Mouse was less than two years old when he became the star of a comic strip on January 13, 1930. The original gags were written by Walt Disney and drawn by animator Ub Iwerks. Floyd Gottfredson, a gifted cartoonist and writer who would work on the feature for forty-five years, took over the daily strip in May 1930 and began producing extended humorous adventure stories. A

Mickey Sunday page, also drawn by Gottfredson, debuted on January 10, 1932. Donald Duck made his first newspaper appearance, illustrated by Al Taliaferro, in the topper strip, *Silly Symphony,* on September 16, 1934, and was given his own feature beginning in 1938. Other Disney characters, including Snow White, the Three Little Pigs, and the Ugly Duckling, also made guest appearances in *Silly Symphony* during the 1930s.

MICKEY MOUSE *daily strip, with color overlay, from the "Seven Ghosts" story, penciled by Floyd Gottfredson and inked by Ted Thwaites. This was the first sequence to feature Mickey, Donald, and Goofy in costarring roles. © October 8, 1936, Disney Enterprises, Inc. Distributed by King Features Syndicate, Inc. Courtesy of Bruce Hamilton*

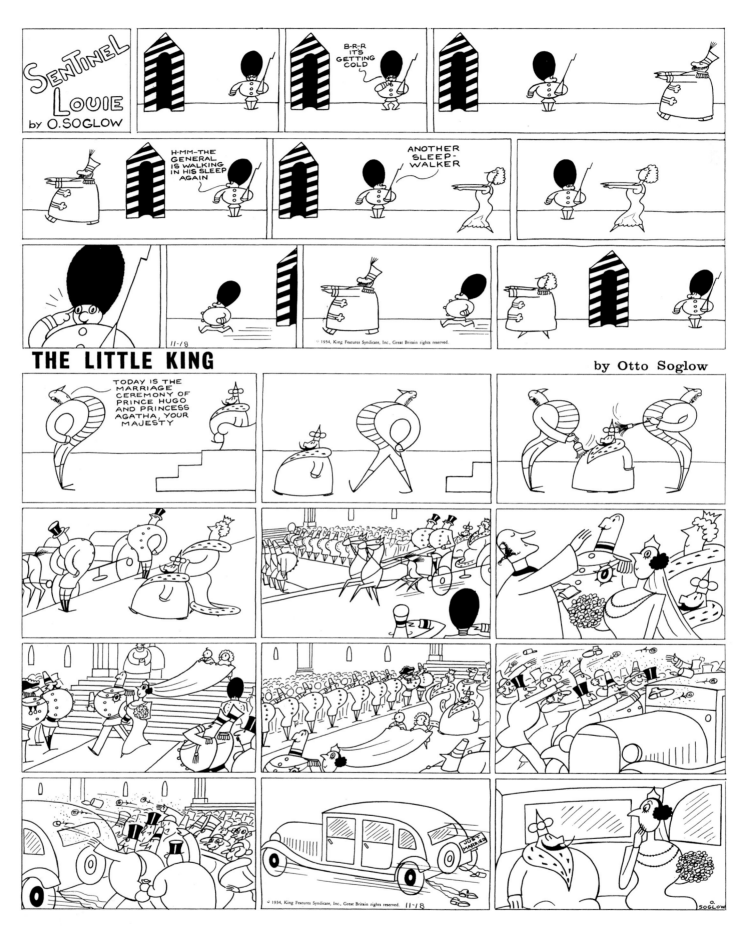

THE LITTLE KING Sunday page, with **SENTINEL LOUIE** topper, by Otto Soglow. This speechless monarch first appeared in the pages of The New Yorker in 1931 before making his newspaper debut in 1934. © November 18, 1934, King Features Syndicate, Inc. Courtesy of Howard Lowery.

BRUTUS Sunday page by Johnny Gruelle. The creator of *RAGGEDY ANN AND ANDY* produced another comic strip feature, which starred a domestic everyman named Brutus Dudd, from November 17, 1929, to February 27, 1938. © August 28, 1932, New York Tribune, Inc. Courtesy of Bill Janocha.

THE HOME OF RIGHT AROUND HOME—Self-portrait by Dudley Fisher. In 1935, Fisher introduced his bird's-eye-view page in the Columbus Dispatch; three years later, it went into national syndication as RIGHT AROUND HOME. June 30, 1945, *Editor & Publisher. Courtesy of Jack Gilbert*

MYRTLE consecutive daily strips by Dudley Fisher. The daughter in the RIGHT AROUND HOME family starred in her own spin-off strip beginning on May 26, 1941. © August 22 and 23, 1941, King Features Syndicate, Inc. Courtesy of King Features Syndicate

RIGHT AROUND HOME original hand-colored Sunday page by Dudley Fisher. The crowded compositions by Fisher gradually shifted from rural to suburban scenes and were inspired by his own Ohio neighborhood. © September 18, 1938, King Features Syndicate, Inc. Courtesy of Jack Gilbert.

PETE THE TRAMP daily strip by C. D. Russell. Pete was a fixture in Judge magazine before his newspaper debut on January 10, 1932.
© January 22, 1936, King Features Syndicate, Inc. Courtesy of Sandy Schechter

APPLE MARY daily strip by Martha Orr. The artist's Depression-era grandmother, who first appeared on October 29, 1934, was later transformed by Allen Saunders and Ken Ernst into the matronly busybody Mary Worth. © December 27, 1937, Publishers Syndicate. Courtesy of the International Museum of Cartoon Art

BIG CHIEF WAHOO daily strip by Allen Saunders (writer) and Elmer Woggon (artist). Saunders's first successful creation began as a western parody in 1936 before it evolved into an adventure strip, renamed STEVE ROPER, in 1947. © January 23, 1937, Publishers Syndicate. Courtesy of Bill Janocha

ABBIE AN' SLATS daily strip by Al Capp (writer) and Raeburn Van Buren (artist). Capp's second feature, which debuted on July 7, 1937, starred a tough city kid and his spinster aunt, and it showcased the talents of Van Buren, an accomplished illustrator. © October 9, 1939, United Feature Syndicate, Inc. Courtesy of Gill Fox

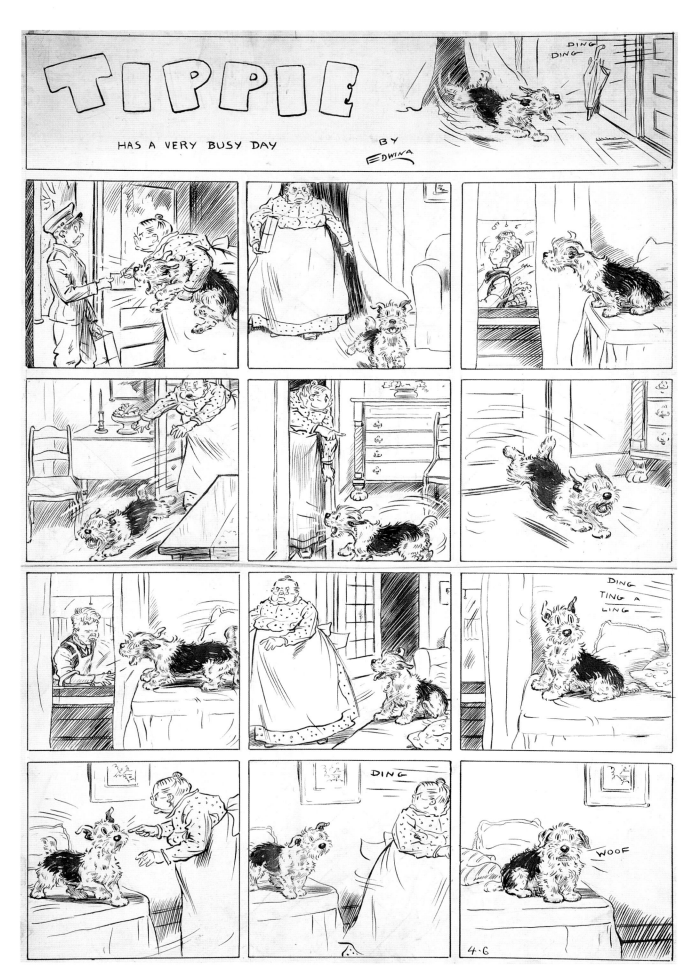

TIPPIE Sunday page by Edwina Dumm. One of the most endearing canines in the comics debuted in the daily strip CAP STUBBS in 1918 and became the star of his own Sunday page in 1934. © April 6, 1935, King Features Syndicate, Inc. Courtesy of Illustration House

NAPOLEON

By Clifford McBride

(c) Arthur J. LaFave

12-22-35

NOW TO FASTEN MY WHISKERS ON AND I'LL BE OFF TO THE WIDOW SMITH'S WITH THIS LOAD OF FOOD AND PRESENTS! BOY, I CAN JUST IMAGINE TH' EXPRESSIONS ON THOSE FIVE KIDS' FACES!

I HOPE I CAN GET OUT OF THE YARD WITHOUT NAPOLEON MISTAKING ME FOR A BURGLAR!

NOW LOOK WHAT YOU DID YOU BIG BONEHEAD! YOU'VE RUINED MY CHRISTMAS AND SIX OTHER PEOPLE'S! WHAT ARE YOU GOIN' TO DO ABOUT IT?

NAPOLEON Sunday page by Clifford McBride. The ungainly pooch, Napoleon, and his portly owner, Uncle Elby, first appeared in McBride's weekly gag feature during the 1920s before becoming costars of their own daily comic strip on June 6, 1932. © December 22, 1935, Arthur J. LaFave. Courtesy of Russ Cochran

THE KEWPIES Sunday page by Rose O'Neill. *A pioneer in the early years of the funnies, O'Neill created her comic cupids in 1905. After gaining popularity in the leading women's magazines, THE KEWPIES was first launched as a newspaper feature in 1917 and revived as a Sunday page in 1935.* © February 1, 1936, Rose O'Neill. Courtesy of Illustration House

SKIPPY Sunday page by Percy Crosby. This kid, who habitually wore the same checkered cap, shorts, and bow tie, first appeared in Life magazine in 1923 before a daily comic strip was released on June 23, 1925. The Sunday page followed on October 7, 1926. © December 29, 1935, Percy L. Crosby/King Features Syndicate, Inc. Courtesy of Mort Walker

CHILD PHILOSOPHERS

Although the younger generation of funnies folk still had a relatively carefree existence during the Depression, the problems of the real world were starting to have an effect. Certain characters, such as Little Orphan Annie and Skippy, displayed a strong instinct for survival and often engaged in extended monologues, talking to themselves or their juvenile and canine companions with adult sophistication. More inclined to face their challenges with a spunky independence, kids in the comics were starting to grow up.

SKIPPY daily strip by Percy Crosby. SKIPPY reached the peak of its popularity in the mid-1930s, but the strip declined as Crosby struggled with mental illness, and it ended on December 8, 1945. © November 13, 1937, Percy L. Crosby/King Features Syndicate, Inc. Courtesy of the International Museum of Cartoon Art

LITTLE FOLKS introductory strip by "Tack" Knight. A former assistant to Gene Byrnes on REG'LAR FELLERS, Knight produced this kid strip from 1930 to 1933. © 1930 Tribune Media Services, Inc. All rights reserved. Reprinted with permission. Courtesy of Illustration House

MUGGS AND SKEETER daily strip by Wally Bishop. Muggs was a ten-year-old boy who maintained his comic strip career for forty-seven years. © August 18, 1931, Central Press Association, Inc. Courtesy of Russ Cochran

CAP STUBBS AND TIPPIE daily strip by Edwina Dumm. Her low-key feature, which ran for forty-eight years, was about the simple relationship between a boy and his dog. © October 16, 1933, George Matthew Adams Service, Inc. Courtesy of Frank Pauer

HENRY daily strip by Carl Anderson. The artist was sixty-seven years old when his bald-headed boy first appeared in The Saturday Evening Post in 1932. Hearst signed Anderson up two years later to do a comic strip starring the silent kid. © July 4, 1935, King Features Syndicate, Inc. Courtesy of Russ Cochran

LITTLE ANNIE ROONEY Sunday page by Brandon Walsh (writer) and Nicholas Afonsky (artist). Afonsky, who illustrated the Sunday page from 1934 to 1943, was the most gifted artist to work on this feature. © August 2, 1935, King Features Syndicate, Inc. Courtesy of the International Museum of Cartoon Art

LITTLE ANNIE ROONEY daily strip by Brandon Walsh (writer) and Darrell McClure (artist). This obvious imitation of LITTLE ORPHAN ANNIE was scripted for most of its thirty-seven-year run by Walsh, a former ghostwriter on THE GUMPS. © April 1, 1931, King Features Syndicate, Inc. Courtesy of Sandy Schechter

LITTLE ANNIE ROONEY daily strip by Brandon Walsh (writer) and Darrell McClure (artist). McClure, who took over as the artist on the LITTLE ANNIE ROONEY daily strip on October 6, 1930, and drew both versions after Afonsky died in 1943, continued the feature until April 16, 1966.
© December 25, 1941, King Features Syndicate, Inc. Courtesy of the International Museum of Cartoon Art

SKEETS Sunday page by Dow Walling. The artist produced this charming Sunday feature from 1932 to 1951. © February 19, 1933, New York Tribune, Inc. Courtesy of Bill Janocha

FRITZI RITZ daily strip by Ernie Bushmiller. *After only two months on the scene, Nancy was already getting the last laugh.*
© October 10, 1933, United Feature Syndicate, Inc. Courtesy of Sandy Schechter

GAG GIRL Fritzi Ritz's niece was first introduced in Ernie Bushmiller's strip in August 1933. Over the course of the next five years, the spike-haired moppet gradually usurped the starring role, and in 1938, the name of the feature was officially changed to *Nancy*. By 1948, Bushmiller's brainchild was one of the top strips in the business, with 450 newspaper clients.

NANCY promotional drawing by Ernie Bushmiller. *Nancy was once described as a chipmunk with a case of the mumps.* December 18, 1937, Editor & Publisher.
© United Feature Syndicate, Inc.

NANCY daily strip by Ernie Bushmiller. *The artist used his visual ingenuity to help Nancy solve problems.*
© August 1, 1941, United Feature Syndicate, Inc. Courtesy of Matt Masterson

NANCY daily strip by Ernie Bushmiller. *Nancy's pal Sluggo made his debut on January 24, 1938.* © September 5, 1942, United Feature Syndicate, Inc. Courtesy of Gill Fox

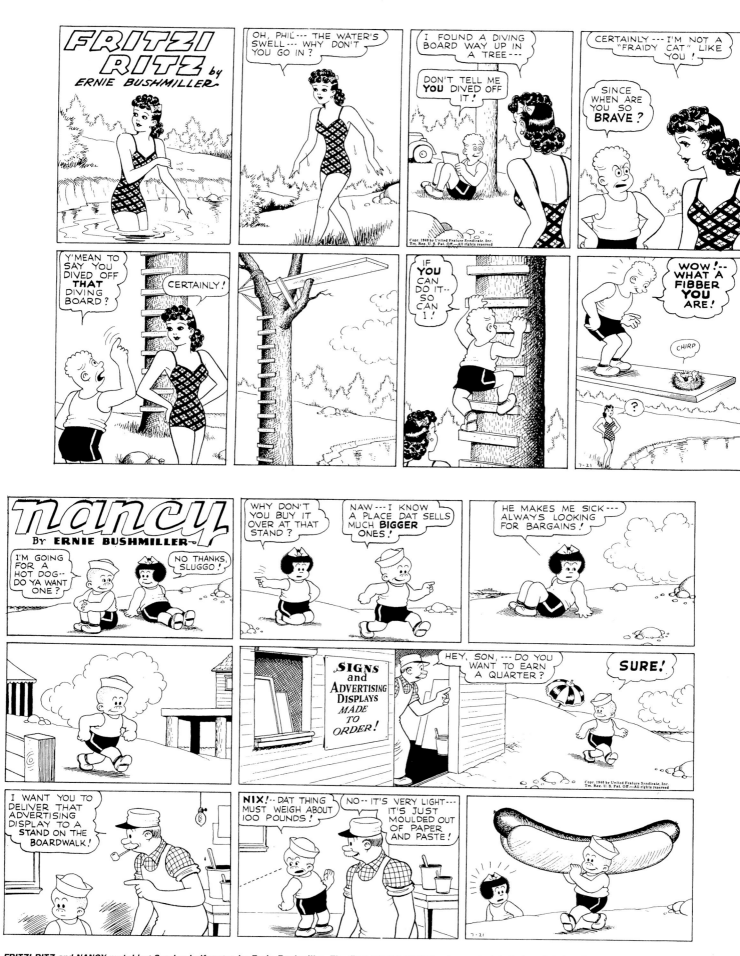

FRITZI RITZ and NANCY matching Sunday half-pages by Ernie Bushmiller. The first FRITZI RITZ Sunday page debuted on October 6, 1929, and was joined by the PHIL FUMBLE topper strip in 1930. When Nancy got her own Sunday feature in 1938, Phil got kicked upstairs to the new FRITZI RITZ half-page.
© July 21, 1940, United Feature Syndicate, Inc. Courtesy of Howard Lowery

THE THRILL THAT COMES ONCE IN A LIFETIME daily panel by H. T. Webster. An early comic art collector is born.
© October 2, 1937, New York Tribune, Inc. Courtesy of Rob Stolzer

the
forties

"Can't you read those comics a bit louder? I'm stuck back here in
the kitchen all day and never know what's going on in the world."

THE NEIGHBORS daily panel by George Clark. This newspaper feature was done in the modern style of magazine
gag cartooning. © April 21, 1941, Tribune Media Services, Inc. All rights reserved. Reprinted with permission. Courtesy of Editor & Publisher

SNUFFY SMITH—Special drawing by Billy DeBeck. A rare political statement by the creator of BARNEY GOOGLE.
© October 12, 1940, King Features Syndicate, Inc. Courtesy of Editor & Publisher

MERICA WATCHED AND WAITED WHILE THE WAR IN EUROPE ESCALATED. ON MAY 10, 1940, THE GERMAN ARMY LAUNCHED A BLITZKRIEG THROUGH THE NETHERLANDS, BELGIUM, AND LUXEMBOURG, AND BY JUNE IT WAS OCCUPYING FRANCE. THE GERMAN AIR FORCE BEGAN BOMBING COASTAL TOWNS ALONG THE ENGLISH CHANNEL IN JULY, AND THE LUFTWAFFE COMMENCED A MASSIVE AERIAL ASSAULT AGAINST BRITAIN'S CITIES ON AUGUST 13, 1940. ROMANIA, YUGOSLAVIA, AND GREECE ALSO FELL TO THE AXIS POWERS, AND, ON JUNE 22, 1941, THE LARGEST INVASION FORCE IN HISTORY, THREE MILLION STRONG, MARCHED INTO THE SOVIET UNION ON AN EIGHTEEN-HUNDRED-MILE FRONT.

The tide began turning against isolationists in the United States. According to a poll taken in December 1939, 67.4 percent of American citizens opposed getting involved in the conflict; six months later, 67.5 percent supported some form of aid to the European allies. On December 17, 1940, President Roosevelt introduced his "Lend-Lease" plan, which proposed the loan of supplies in exchange for future compensation. On February 4, 1941, Ohio Congressman John Vorys criticized FDR's program in a speech to the House of Representatives. "Our policy now is like that of Popeye's friend [Wimpy]—'let's you and him fight,'" declared Vorys. The Lend-Lease Act passed the House by a vote of 260 to 165 in March and immediately provided for $7 billion in food, tanks, trucks, planes, guns, ammunition, and other vital supplies, which were shipped to Britain in

1941. The "arsenal of democracy" was gearing up for America's entry into the war.

Within three days after the Japanese surprise attack on the U.S. naval base at Pearl Harbor, Hawaii, on December 7, 1941, Germany and Italy also declared war on the United States. A sleeping giant had been awakened.

In 1939, only 2 percent of the nation's industrial output was military-related. In the year after Pearl Harbor, war production quadrupled; by 1944, the defense budget accounted for 45 percent of the gross national product. The standing army, which numbered 188,000 volunteers in 1939, swelled to more than a million soldiers in the year after the Selective Training and Service Act was signed into law on September 16, 1940. Women filled positions that men left behind, and by 1943, sixteen million women had jobs outside the home.

Americans on the home front contributed to the cause in many ways. They bought $135 billion in War Bonds, grew their own food in Victory Gardens, and volunteered for civil defense duty. Children collected used metal and rubber to be recycled into armaments. Rationing of gasoline and groceries became a sacrifice that citizens learned to live with. The United Service Organizations (USO) recruited forty-five hundred actors and performers, including Bob Hope, Bing Crosby, and Duke Ellington, to put on shows for GIs around the world. Hollywood producers turned out propaganda and training movies for the military, and more than twenty-nine thousand volunteers from the film industry served in the armed forces.

Cartoonists also did their part, by creating special drawings for government agencies, making personal appearances for war veterans, and providing morale-boosting messages in their features. Popeye became the official "spokescharacter" for the U.S. Navy, in a series of recruitment ads that began appearing in newspapers in July 1941. Al Capp created a special, color Sunday-page feature for the Treasury Department in 1942: *Small Fry*, which was later renamed *Small Change*, persuaded readers to buy War Bonds and was distributed to newspapers free of charge. Little Orphan Annie's Junior Commando movement, which was inspired by a plotline in Harold Gray's strip in the summer of 1942, organized more than a hundred thousand youngsters nationwide into small local groups to round up newspapers, scrap metal, old tires, and kitchen grease to be used as raw materials for the munitions factories. A troupe of cartoonists that included Milton Caniff, Gus Edson, Ernie Bushmiller, and Rube Goldberg gave chalk talks to wounded GIs recuperating in home-front hospitals.

"The knights of the drawing board are doing their bit to help Uncle Sam speed the day of victory over the Axis," lauded *Editor & Publisher* on September 19, 1942. "The nation's syndicate cartoonists whose material appears in newspapers over the land have enlisted for the duration to aid in doing the job of keeping up the morale of the fighting men and the folks at home."

Many comic strip characters signed up for active duty. Joe Palooka was one of the first to enlist, on November 29, 1940, soon after the draft became official. His creator, Ham Fisher, was a loyal FDR supporter and had visited Fort Dix in New Jersey to gather background material prior to the episode in which Joe marched into a U.S. Army recruiting office. For the next six years, Fisher's simpleminded boxing champ served his country valiantly, although he never rose above the rank of private first class.

Milton Caniff's Terry Lee became a flight officer in the U.S. Army Air Force, and Pat Ryan rose to the rank of lieutenant in the navy. Roy Crane's Captain Easy was a captain in army intelligence. Russ Westover's Tillie the Toiler joined

TERRY LEE—Character portrait by Milton Caniff. Terry enlisted in the Army Air Force on October 17, 1942. © October 18, 1943, Tribune Media Services, Inc. All rights reserved. Reprinted with permission

the Women's Army Auxiliary Corps. Frank King's Skeezix served as a corporal in army ordnance. Billy DeBeck's Snuffy Smith was accepted by the army on November 13, 1940, and Barney Google enlisted in the navy in September 1941. Don Winslow of the navy and Sergeant Stony Craig of the Marines were already signed up when the war started and continued to serve in active duty.

Other comic strip stars did their part on the home front. Secret Agent X-9 tracked spies for the Federal Bureau of Investigation in Washington, D.C., and Dick Tracy did undercover work for naval intelligence. Freckles and his friends rolled bandages for the Red Cross, assisted at a military canteen, sold bonds and stamps, and volunteered for civil defense duty. Nancy and Sluggo collected scrap metal. Meanwhile, Blondie and Dagwood, Maggie and Jiggs, Andy and Min, and many of the other comic strip couples continued with business as usual on the nation's funnies pages.

Cartoonists also saw active duty. Alex Raymond turned *Flash Gordon* over to his assistant, Austin Briggs, and joined the Marines in February 1944. Zack Mosley, the creator of *Smilin' Jack,* was a submarine spotter for the Civil Air Patrol in Florida. Gus Arriola launched *Gordo* on November 24, 1941, two weeks before the attack on Pearl Harbor. He had to discontinue the strip on October 28, 1942, after he enlisted in the army. Arriola did animation work for the First Motion Picture Unit during the war and resumed the *Gordo* Sunday page on May 2, 1943, but he could not restart the daily strip until June 24, 1946. Bert Christman, who took over *Scorchy Smith* from Noel Sickles in 1936, enlisted as a navy pilot in 1938 and, after Pearl Harbor, was flying with the American Volunteer Group of aviators. His plane was shot down in Burma on January 23, 1942, and Christman was killed by machine gun fire before he could reach the ground in his parachute.

Most of the established creators remained at home for the duration, but a handful of servicemen earned their cartooning stripes overseas during the war. Bill Mauldin, who was eighteen years old when he enlisted in 1940, started drawing cartoons for the *45th Division News.* He experienced the grim realities of frontline combat in Italy and France and was wounded at Salerno in 1943. His most famous wartime series, *Up Front,* starred two weary, unshaven foot soldiers, Willie and Joe, and appeared in the *Army Times, Stars and Stripes,* and two book collections. United Feature began distributing it as a syndicated panel on April 17, 1944, and Mauldin won the Pulitzer Prize in 1945 for his uncompromising cartoons.

In one of his books, *The Brass Ring,* Mauldin claimed that he was once reproached by General George Patton. Angry about the cartoonist's honest portrayal of an infantryman's life in the foxholes and trenches, Patton bellowed at Mauldin, "You know as well as I do that you can't have an army without respect for officers. What are you trying to do, incite a goddamn mutiny?" Mauldin told Patton he was only drawing what he had observed and refused to change his approach.

After he returned home on June 15, 1945, Mauldin adapted his two dog-faced GIs to a newspaper panel, initially titled *Sweatin' It Out,* for United Feature Syndicate. "I began with these guys when they were inducted, went through training with them, saw them fight in Italy and France," Mauldin explained. "Now they're coming home pooped out and are going to have to find out how to be civilians. They might even acquire wives." The feature was criticized as being too political for a syndicated panel and ended after Mauldin's contract with United Feature expired in 1949.

George Baker worked at the Disney Studio for four years before he was drafted into the army in June 1941. After Baker's

THE SAD SACK promotional drawing by Sergeant George Baker. From an advertisement for the first syndicated release of Baker's wartime strip.
© December 2, 1944, Consolidated News Features, Inc. Courtesy of Editor & Publisher

winning entry in a cartoon contest was published in *Life* magazine, *Yank,* the new army weekly, requested regular submissions from him. "I had to devise an average soldier," Baker remembered. "The state of mind of a soldier was more authentic and real to me than his outer appearance. So therefore my character looked resigned, tired, helpless and beaten." The title Baker chose for his new feature was a shortened version of "a sad sack of s . . . ," which was military slang for a loser.

The Sad Sack premiered on June 17, 1942, and was immediately a hit with GIs. Simon and Schuster published book collections of Baker's cartoons in 1944 and 1946, and Consolidated News Features obtained the right to syndicate *The Sad Sack* to thirty newspapers for twenty-two weeks, beginning in December 1944. At the end of the war, Bell Syndicate took over the distribution, and on May 5, 1946, Sad Sack became a civilian. The newspaper Sunday page lasted until the mid-1950s, but a comic book adaptation, published by Harvey Comics from 1949 to 1982, was more successful after Sad Sack reenlisted in 1951. Fred Rhoades, a Marine veteran who drew *Gizmo & Eightball* for *Leatherneck* magazine during the war, took over the *Sad Sack* comic book in 1954.

Special publications for military personnel, ranging from large-circulation periodicals to single-page camp newsletters, proliferated during the war. In addition to world and local news, photos, editorials, letters, and pinups, most of them included cartoons. *Stars and Stripes,* a daily tabloid newspaper of eight to sixteen pages with a circulation of more than a million, featured Mauldin's *Up Front*, Baker's *The Sad Sack*, Caniff's *Male Call*, Dave Breger's *G.I. Joe*, Dick Wingert's *Hubert*, and Leonard Sansone's *The Wolf*. *Yank*, a twenty-four-page weekly magazine with a circulation of about 2.5 million, also printed the cartoons of Mauldin, Baker, and Breger. *Leatherneck*, a monthly produced by the Marine Corps in Washington, D.C., offered *Hashmark* by Fred Lasswell and *Gizmo & Eightball* by Fred Rhoades.

In the summer of 1942, the army set up the Camp Newspaper Service in New York to distribute features to more than three thousand GI publications. This military-run operation sent out weekly proof sheets and mats to bases around the world. Among the established features that the syndicates provided free of charge were *Gasoline Alley*, *Smilin' Jack*, *Blondie*, *Nancy*, *Li'l Abner*, and *Joe Palooka*.

Caniff, who was unable to be on active duty because of phlebitis, was determined to help boost the morale of the troops. In addition to creating special drawings for many government campaigns and making appearances at veteran hospitals, he began producing a special weekly *Terry and the Pirates* strip for the Camp Newspaper Service in October 1942. After a newspaper editor in Florida complained about a nearby military base violating the paper's territorial exclusivity in regard to *Terry* by publishing the strip in the base's newsletter, Caniff decided to develop a different weekly feature expressly for distribution to the armed services. *Male Call*, which its creator described as a "two-minute furlough," debuted on January 24, 1943, and did not include any of the characters from *Terry and the Pirates*. Instead, it starred a sexy, brunette femme fatale who had a thing for men in uniform.

"Miss Lace is probably the most delectable pen-and-ink creation of all time, the camp follower of every fighting man's dreams," Bill Mauldin remembered. "Milton Caniff produced in her a confection of femininity which put all the 'pin-ups' in the shade, and he never realized a nickel's profit from her." An estimated fifteen million GIs looked forward to her weekly appearances from 1943 to 1946.

While military publishing thrived, the war closed many foreign markets for the major newspaper syndicates. King Features, which had twenty-six overseas bureaus, was hit the hardest. After the Nazis invaded Belgium, the Netherlands, and France, American comics were banned in most newspapers in those countries. Publishers in England were forced to cancel features due to paper shortages. Currency exchange restrictions, the closing of shipping lanes, and the loss of advertising revenue further restricted business. The syndicates tried to compensate by expanding their sales efforts in South America.

Shortages of materials, including newsprint and ink, also hurt business on the home front. On February 16, 1942, the

"Here y'are, men, latest copies of 'Stars and Stripes' an' 'Yank'!"

PRIVATE BREGER panel by Lieutenant Dave Breger. The Allied invasion forces were provided with entertaining reading matter.
© c. 1944, King Features Syndicate, Inc.

Atlanta Constitution and the *Atlanta Journal* announced that they were both cutting their daily comics by half, from two pages to one, to conserve paper. "All of your favorites will remain, more than a dozen comic adventure strips and panels," the papers assured their readers, " but war has struck in the midst of these amusing people and we break the bad news this morning." *Jane Arden* and *Mary Worth's Family* were among the strips that were canceled.

The syndicates quickly responded to this threat by offering their comics in reduced sizes. On April 20, 1942, United Feature Syndicate began distributing its daily strips in a four-column width, as well as in the standard five- and six-column formats (one column is approximately two inches wide). A special committee of the American Society of Newspaper Editors (ASNE) reported on February 16, 1943, that 70 percent of the nation's daily papers were running comics in the four-column size. The committee also proposed that the legibility of the comics could be maintained by shortening the balloons and eliminating complicated art detail, and it predicted that the five- and six-column widths would be a thing of the past after the next government cut in newsprint supply.

Newspapers were also demanding a reduction in the size of color comics to half-page and one-third-page formats to conserve paper and ink. The ASNE committee proposed that the standard width of a Sunday comics page should be cut back. King Features announced in March 1943 that many of its

This is it

BUZ SAWYER promotional drawing by Roy Crane. Buz and his sidekick, Rosco Sweeney, in an advertisement for Crane's new adventure strip.
© January 1944 King Features Syndicate, Inc. Courtesy of Editor & Publisher

strips, including *Blondie, Thimble Theatre Starring Popeye, Mickey Mouse, Bringing Up Father,* and *Barney Google and Snuffy Smith,* were being offered in a one-third-page size.

Early in 1944, Fred Ferguson, president of the Newspaper Enterprise Association, looked forward to the end of the war but speculated that "even with more newsprint available, I don't see why the newspapers would want to return to a six-column comic strip. The artists have got over the hump of adjusting their work, and they've succeeded admirably in fitting into smaller spaces. As a matter of fact, with more tightly written balloons, the material has improved." Comic strips would never be restored to their prewar dimensions.

After the hostilities ended and the foreign markets were reopened, international distribution of comics became a growth industry. "We never did any promotion in the South American and European countries," claimed Mollie Slott, assistant manager of the Chicago Tribune–New York News Syndicate, "but the war and the GIs' enthusiasm for comics has opened up a big field for us there."

Cartoonists also sought new opportunities. In 1943, Roy Crane announced that he had signed a contract with King Features to create a new adventure strip. Crane's assistant, Leslie Turner, took over *Wash Tubbs/Captain Easy* in May 1943, which continued to be distributed by the Newspaper Enterprise Association. When *Buz Sawyer* debuted on

November 1, 1943, Crane's lead character was a navy pilot on the aircraft carrier *Tippecanoe.* Buz and his buddy, Rosco Sweeney, were shot down and stranded on a tropical island in their first months of duty and continued fighting on the Pacific front throughout the war. When Emperor Hirohito capitulated on August 15, 1945, Buz and Rosco had just escaped from a Japanese submarine and were on their way to participate in a bombing raid over Tokyo. Crane rushed out a special strip explaining that "the current story sequence began before the Jap surrender," and he requested the readers' patience while the continuity reached its conclusion. *Tim Tyler's Luck, Jungle Jim,* and *Superman* were among the other adventure strips that were caught in the middle of war stories when the fighting stopped.

Caniff also decided during the war to launch a new feature for a competing syndicate. In January 1945, when the story got out that he had signed a contract with Marshall Field, publisher of the *Chicago Sun* and *PM,* Caniff was still obliged to continue *Terry and the Pirates* for the Chicago Tribune–New York News Syndicate until October 1946. "I'm a lame duck," he admitted. "That makes me anxious to do the best job I can on *Terry.*" Field guaranteed Caniff $525,000 for five years and full ownership of a strip he had yet to conceive. King Features, the selling agent, claimed in an advertisement on May 19, 1945, that 63 newspapers had agreed to carry

Caniff's new creation "sight unseen." By the time *Steve Canyon* debuted on January 13, 1947, a total of 234 subscribers had been convinced that Caniff's new strip would be a winner.

As comic books gained in popularity during the late 1930s and early 1940s, newspaper syndicates searched for ways to respond to the challenge. In April 1940, the Chicago Tribune–New York News Syndicate produced a sixteen-page oblong color booklet, measuring $10^1/_2$ by $8^1/_2$ inches, that was inserted in the *Sunday Tribune* comic section. Readers got twice as many comics for their money, and sales of the *Tribune* increased by one hundred thousand issues. Early editions of that syndicate's *Sunday Comics Magazine* contained such recycled features as *Texas Slim* by Ferd Johnson and *Bobby Make-Believe* by Frank King, but eventually it added new creations, including *Streamer Kelly* by Jack Ryan, *Mr. Ex* by Bert Whitman, and *Brenda Starr, Reporter* by Dale Messick.

Victor Fox, a former accountant for Detective Comics, claimed that no matter how hard the syndicates tried to imitate the comic book format, they would not succeed unless they offered juvenile readers "thriller" stories. Fox had started his own publishing company and boasted that his monthly and bimonthly magazines had a total circulation of more than five million. The Fox Feature Syndicate also provided Sunday-page and daily strip versions of many of their comic book features, including *The Blue Beetle, The Green Mask, Spark Stevens,* and *Red Dexter.* Fox announced in May 1940 that he would be making available to newspapers a sixteen-page comic magazine that featured many of his adventure heroes; however, there is no evidence the Fox booklet was ever produced.

The Register and Tribune Syndicate of Des Moines, Iowa, jumped on the newspaper insert bandwagon on June 2, 1940. Its sixteen-page *Comic Book Section* featured three complete stories and was initially distributed to five newspapers, including the *Washington Star, Baltimore Sun,* and *Philadelphia Record.* The seven-page lead story starred a masked detective, named the Spirit, and was written and drawn by Will Eisner. The original stories for the backup strips, *Lady Luck* and *Mr. Mystic,* were also developed by Eisner but drawn by other artists.

"I decided my leading figure wouldn't be what we call a costume character," Eisner remembered in 1941. "I gave him a mask, as a sort of fillip to his personality. And he had to be on the side of the law, of course, but I believed it would be better if he worked a little outside of the law." Eisner's comic-noir character stalked the mean streets of Central City,

THE SPIRIT comic page by Will Eisner. The "splash page" was an Eisner innovation.
© January 12, 1941, and 1974 by Will Eisner

which closely resembled the gritty urban milieu of the cartoonist's New York home.

The most successful of the comic book insert features, *The Spirit* appeared as a daily strip from October 13, 1941, to March 11, 1944. The comic book version, which sold more than five million copies a week, lasted until September 28, 1952. Although the syndicates continued to introduce thriller features throughout the 1940s, strips starring costumed crime fighters were, for the most part, short-lived on the funnies pages.

In November 1945, *Editor & Publisher* hosted a luncheon at the Hotel Astor in New York City for a group of prominent women comic artists. Among the attendees were Edwina Dumm (*Cap Stubbs and Tippie*), Hilda Terry (*Teena*), Tarpe Mills (*Miss Fury*), Odin Waugh (*Dickie Dare*), Dale Messick (*Brenda Starr*), and Virginia Clark (*Oh, Diana*).

"The occasion was historic," *Editor & Publisher* claimed. Not only was it the first major gathering of female cartoonists, "but it also marked the return of women to the same proportionate position in the field as in the very early days when Kate Carew drew *The Angel Child.*"

Other female pioneers from the first decades of the funnies included Rose O'Neill (*The Kewpies*), Grace Drayton (*Dimples*),

Nell Brinkley (*The Adventures of Prudence Primm*), and Ethel Hays (*Flapper Fanny*). Although Martha Orr's *Apple Mary*, which debuted on October 29, 1934, was a modest success in the Depression years, the percentage of women cartoonists declined during the ascendancy of the adventure strip.

"No woman cartoonist has ever broken into the front lines of comic strips," claimed Amram Schoenfeld in 1930. "The newspaper cartoon is a form of art in which women do not seem to be entirely at home," he continued, "the comic strip apparently demanding a type of humor and technique which is essentially masculine."

This sexist attitude was typical in the male-dominated funnies business of the 1930s. During World War II, however, as women became essential to the workforce, opportunities also opened up in the comics industry. In fact, one of the most powerful syndicate executives at that time was Mollie Slott, assistant manager of the Chicago Tribune–New York News Syndicate.

Slott had been hired by the Tribune Syndicate in 1914 as a secretary and had risen through the ranks of the company during the 1920s. In her first seven years, she worked for six different managers, learning aspects of the business from each of them. Slott ran the office during the periods between bosses, while the search was on for a new executive to replace the previous one. She became indispensable to the running of the syndicate operation.

In 1933, Captain Patterson summoned Slott to New York from the *Tribune* offices in Chicago. She adapted well to the change and had a major influence on the selection of many new strips, including *Smilin' Jack*, *Terry and the Pirates*, and *Smokey Stover*. She also convinced Patterson to take a chance with *Brenda Starr*.

Dale Messick, who changed her name from Dalia to disguise her gender when submitting her work by mail, initially presented a strip about a woman bandit to the syndicate. Patterson, who reportedly claimed that he had once hired a woman cartoonist and was determined not to do so again, rejected Messick's idea outright. But when Slott looked at the samples, she saw potential in the young woman's work. At Slott's suggestion, Messick turned her heroine into a feisty, red-haired newspaper reporter and named her after the famous debutante Brenda Frazier. Patterson reluctantly added *Brenda Starr, Reporter* to the syndicate's lineup but refused to carry it in his flagship paper, the *New York Daily News*—and it did not appear there until after his death in 1946. The strip debuted on June 30, 1940, in the *Tribune*'s sixteen-page comic book insert as a Sunday-only feature; a daily version was added on October 22, 1945. Messick was one of the first women to succeed in the story strip genre, and she continued to produce *Brenda Starr*, with the help of a team of talented assistants, until her retirement in 1980.

On March 27, 1942, an exhibition entitled "The Comic Strip, Its Ancient and Honorable Lineage and Present Significance" opened at the American Institute of Graphic Arts in New York City. The National Arts Club hosted a dinner on April 6, honoring two dozen of the comic artists whose work was included in the display. Dr. Emanuel Winternitz from the Metropolitan Museum of Art spoke at the event, praising the comic strip as a work of art. Among the cartoonists in attendance were Milton Caniff, Billy DeBeck, H. H. Knerr, Alex Raymond, Rube Goldberg, and Harry Hershfield.

"The funnies are being taken seriously as art after all these years," reported *Editor & Publisher*. "The exhibit, and the plans for its tour of the larger cities, certainly is a tribute to the knights of the drawing board who have for years and today continue to bring happiness into the homes of the vast newspaper reading public."

Events within the comics pages also made headlines during the first half of the decade. On October 16, 1941, Raven Sherman, a major character in Milton Caniff's *Terry and the Pirates*, died after being pushed out of the back of a moving truck. Readers reacted emotionally to the loss and sent letters and telegrams, expressing both sympathy and outrage, to the syndicate's offices. Students at colleges across the country held

BRENDA STARR *promotional drawing by Dale Messick. The cast of Messick's strip is introduced.* October 31, 1941, San Francisco Call-Bulletin. © Tribune Media Services, Inc.
All rights reserved. Reprinted with permission. Courtesy of Trina Robbins

mock funerals for the fictitious American heiress who had been using her money to supply medical aid to the Chinese.

"I am not certain how the dastardly idea to kill off Raven generated in my mind," Caniff reminisced in 1979. "Perhaps a letter from a reader which said, 'You are always having people fighting, but not one ever gets killed, or even badly hurt,' lighted the macabre spark. More likely it was simply a promotion device with which I hoped to publicize *Terry and the Pirates*."

A publicity gimmick in another popular comic strip set off a different response from readers. Chic Young announced on April 13, 1941, that Blondie was expecting her second child, and King Features offered a $100 prize for the best name. The syndicate received 431,275 submissions. Among the many unusual names readers sent in for the baby girl were Daggy-Doo, Tad Pole, Bottle Neck, and Zephyr. Beatrice Barken of Cleveland had the winning entry: Cookie.

A strike of the New York Newspaper and Mail Deliverers in July 1945 led to a series of events that dramatically revealed how indispensable comics were to daily life in the city. The seventeen hundred union workers, who were demanding an exorbitant pension package, refused to deliver papers throughout the metropolitan area, forcing readers to stand in long lines outside the publishers' offices to pick up each day's edition.

Mayor Fiorello LaGuardia felt he had to do something to appease the masses. On Sunday, July 8, 1945, with newsreel cameras rolling, the mayor went on the radio and read the latest installment of *Dick Tracy*. "Crash, goes the big heavy pot over Wetwash Wally's head the minute he opens the door," bellowed the mayor into the microphone, vocalizing the violent conclusion to Chester Gould's Sunday page.

As the strike dragged into its second week, LaGuardia took to the airwaves again on July 15, this time bringing readers up-to-date on developments in *Little Orphan Annie*. "Don't be a crook! That's the moral!" the mayor exclaimed, emulating the melodramatic tone of Harold Gray's closing lines.

The strike ended on the following Tuesday. After seventeen days without newspapers, readers were finally able to catch up with the story lines in their favorite comic strips. New Yorkers had survived the crisis, with the help of their charismatic leader.

In the five decades since the Yellow Kid made his first appearance, the funnies, which began as an experiment in newspaper publishing, had become an essential element of American life. Comic strip characters were everywhere. They starred in live action and animated films, stage plays and radio programs. Their adventures were retold in books and inspired hit songs. Their faces were used to sell thousands of products.

Comic strip creators did more than entertain. They made significant contributions to the folklore and language of popular culture. Terms like "jeep," "hot dog," palooka," and "dingbat" were introduced in the comics, as well as such immortal phrases as "Leapin' Lizards," "I yam what I yam," and "great balls o' fire." Sadie Hawkins Day was celebrated as a national holiday, and Superman was revered as an American hero.

The social changes of the first half of the twentieth century were also recorded in the funnies pages. As newspapers increased their circulation and the comics were adapted to other forms of entertainment, cartoon art became the visual language of the mass media. Cartoonists invented symbols and ideas that were universally recognizable to this vast audience. At the same time, they also made observations that were fresh and meaningful to their readers. As a result, the best of their work reflected what was currently humorous and of vital concern on the day it was published. In re-creating fads and fashions, technological progress, historical events, and social changes, cartoons can reveal far more than the written word alone.

The newspaper business has faced many challenges in the postwar years, but the comics remain a vital part of the entertainment industry. Cartoonists have preserved the past with their drawings and continue to enrich our cultural legacy. It is impossible to understand American history in the twentieth century without an appreciation and understanding of the newspaper comic strip.

THE COMICS GO TO WAR

Many funnies characters were already in uniform before the Japanese attack on Pearl Harbor on December 7, 1941; after America retaliated, the conflict continued to have a dramatic impact on the content of the comics. Although many strip stars signed up for active duty, relatively few saw actual combat. The harsh realities of training and fighting were, for the most part, depicted in the cartoons produced specifically for the troops by GI artists such as Bill Mauldin, Dave Breger, and George Baker.

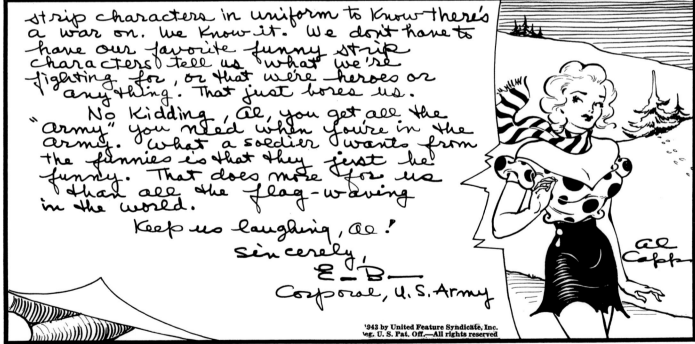

LI'L ABNER daily strip by Al Capp. A letter from an army corporal helped Capp explain to his readers why Abner was staying home.
© December 25, 1943, Capp Enterprises, Inc. Courtesy of Art Wood

BARNEY GOOGLE AND SNUFFY SMITH Sunday page by Billy DeBeck. After Snuffy joined the army, his fellow "yardbirds" came up with this catchy tune.
© October 19, 1941, King Features Syndicate, Inc. Courtesy of the International Museum of Cartoon Art

BARNEY GOOGLE AND SNUFFY SMITH daily strip by Billy DeBeck. Snuffy takes an important message from Winston Churchill.
© 1941 King Features Syndicate, Inc. Courtesy of Art Wood

JOE PALOOKA daily strip by Ham Fisher. Joe was fighting against the Nazis in Yugoslavia when he encountered a female partisan fighter in this wartime episode. © August 14, c. 1942, McNaught Syndicate, Inc. Courtesy of Jim Scancarelli

BARNEY BAXTER Sunday page by Frank Miller. Barney and Gus battle a Japanese fleet sailing toward the Suez Canal.
© January 3, 1943, King Features Syndicate, Inc. Courtesy of Peter Myer

BUZ SAWYER daily strip no. 15 by Roy Crane. An early example of Crane's second major comic strip creation. © 1943 King Features Syndicate, Inc. Courtesy of Jim Scancarelli

BUZ SAWYER daily strip by Roy Crane. Buz hears the news of the Japanese surrender. © August 28, 1945, King Features Syndicate, Inc. Courtesy of King Features Syndicate

BUZ SAWYER daily strips by Roy Crane. The war veteran returns home. © October 4 and 5, 1945, King Features Syndicate, Inc. Courtesy of King Features Syndicate

TILLIE THE TOILER Sunday page by Russ Westover. Tillie joined the Women's Army Auxiliary Corps before her boyfriend, Mac, signed up. © September 6, 1942, King Features Syndicate, Inc. Courtesy of the International Museum of Cartoon Art

VESTA WEST Sunday page by Ray Bailey. Vesta gets a letter from a friend who is serving with the Women's Army Auxiliary Corps.
© April 4, 1943, Tribune Media Services, Inc. All rights reserved. Reprinted with permission. Courtesy of the International Museum of Cartoon Art

TERRY AND THE PIRATES daily strip by Milton Caniff. Terry is far from home on Christmas Day.
© December 25, 1943, Tribune Media Services, Inc. All rights reserved. Reprinted with permission. Courtesy of Bruce Hamilton

DRAFTIE daily strip by Paul Fogarty (writer) and William Juhre (artist). Lem and Oinie do their part in this wartime feature.
© March 27, 1944, John F. Dille Company. Courtesy of Bill Janocha

TIM TYLER'S LUCK Sunday page by Lyman Young. Tim and his buddies were still fighting the Japanese after the war had ended.
© September 30, 1945, King Features Syndicate, Inc. Courtesy of King Features Syndicate

"Th' hell this ain't th' most important hole in th' world. I'm in it."

"Wisht somebody would tell me there's a Santa Claus."

UP FRONT daily panels by Bill Mauldin. The artist won the Pulitzer Prize for his war cartoons in 1945.

"You'll git over it, Joe. Oncet I wuz gonna write a book exposin' th' Army after th' war, myself."

V-E Day
"Th' hell with it. I ain't standin' up till he does!"

TERRY AND THE PIRATES daily strip by Milton Caniff. The artist drew a strip for the Camp Newspaper Service that initially starred Burma.
© October 18, 1942, Tribune Media Services, Inc. All rights reserved. Reprinted with permission. Courtesy of the Milton Caniff Collection, The Ohio State University Cartoon Research Library

MALE CALL daily strip by Milton Caniff. Miss Lace, who replaced Burma, received many letters from adoring GIs. © October 10, 1943, by Milton Caniff. Courtesy of Art Wood

MALE CALL daily strip by Milton Caniff. The female anatomy was a Caniff specialty. © August 20, 1944, by Milton Caniff. Courtesy of the Milton Caniff Collection, The Ohio State University Cartoon Research Library

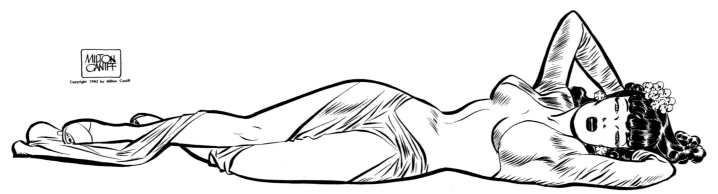

MALE CALL daily strip by Milton Caniff. Some of Caniff's ideas, such as this one, were rejected. © 1943 by Milton Caniff. Courtesy of the Milton Caniff Collection, The Ohio State University Cartoon Research Library

ENLISTED MAN'S RAG

THE SAD SACK cartoons by Sergeant George Baker. Two examples of Baker's popular series, which ran in Yank magazine during the war. © c. 1942, Sad Sack Inc.

SEX HYGIENE

G.I. JOE cartoon by Lieutenant Dave Breger. The artist showed the humorous side to daily life at an army base. © c. 1942, Yank magazine.
Courtesy of the International Museum of Cartoon Art

"Stars and Stripes newspaper? I think I gotta news item for you."

PRIVATE BREGER ABROAD daily panel by Lieutenant Dave Breger.
Private Breger calls the Star and Stripes with a big scoop.
© October 4, 1943, King Features Syndicate, Inc. Courtesy of King Features Syndicate

"Gee . . . ' I was always SURE I'd be dancin' with joy when I left the Army . . . but . . . I feel kinda funny instead . . ."

PRIVATE BREGER ABROAD daily panel by Lieutenant Dave Breger.
The last episode before Private Breger's return to civilian life.
© October 20, 1945, King Features Syndicate, Inc. Courtesy of King Features Syndicate

SUPERMAN *daily strip by Jerry Siegel and Joe Shuster. This wartime episode was probably drawn by Wayne Boring.*

HAVE YOU SEEN

Wonder Woman ?

KING FEATURES SYNDICATE

TO THE RESCUE Costumed crimefighters and adventure heroes continued to invade the funnies pages during the war years. Superman battled the Nazis, and strips starring Batman and Wonder Woman were launched. Comic heroines joined their male counterparts as the strong-armed Rosie the Riveter became a national icon for female empowerment. Soldiers, aviators, cowboys, ape-men, and space rangers dominated the genre, and even journalists joined the ranks of adventure strip characters.

WONDER WOMAN *promotional drawing for the syndicated strip written by William Moulton Marsten and illustrated by H. G. Peter. The newspaper strip lasted only a year.*

BATMAN AND ROBIN *debut strip by Bob Kane. Artists on this strip, which ran for three years, included Jack Burnley and Dick Sprang.*

SUPERMAN *recolored Sunday page by Wayne Boring. An episode of Superman's "Service for Servicemen" campaign.*

BATMAN AND ROBIN recolored Sunday page by Bob Kane. The first page of the BATMAN Sunday feature.

MISS FURY Sunday page by Tarpe Mills. Marla Drake dons her black leopard-skin costume to fight the Nazis. © 1943 Bell Syndicate, Inc. Courtesy of Peter Maresca

SPARKY WATTS daily strip by Gordon "Boody" Rogers. A former assistant to Zack Mosley on SMILIN' JACK, Rogers created this superhero spoof in the early 1940s. © July 31, 1940s, Frank Jay Markey Syndicate. Courtesy of Craig Yoe

THE SHADOW daily strip by Vernon Greene. A comic strip starring the mystery man popularized in pulp fiction and radio began in 1940.
© 1940s Ledger Syndicate, Inc. Courtesy of the International Museum of Cartoon Art

FLASH GORDON daily strip by Austin Briggs. Alex Raymond's assistant drew the FLASH GORDON daily strip from its debut on May 27, 1940, until June 1944.
© October 23, 1943, King Features Syndicate, Inc. Courtesy of Bill Janocha

JOHNNY HAZARD daily strip by Frank Robbins. This wartime adventure feature started on June 5, 1944, the day before D-Day.
© December 27, 1944, King Features Syndicate, Inc. Courtesy of Jim Scancarelli

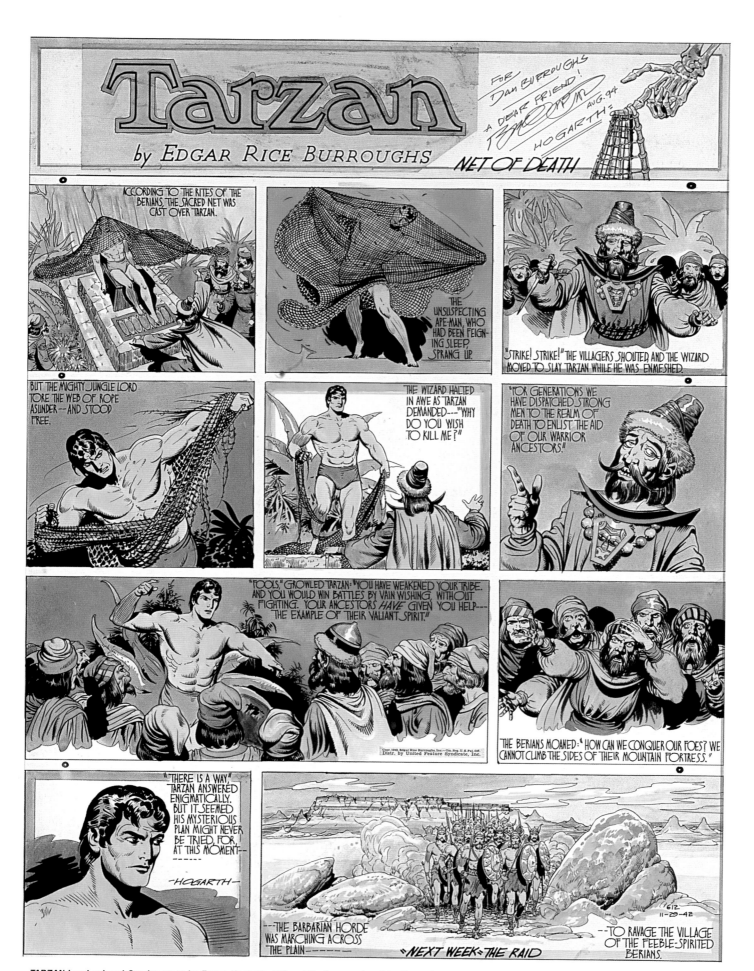

TARZAN *hand-colored Sunday page by Burne Hogarth. This original was colored by Hogarth and presented to Danton Burroughs, the son of Tarzan's creator, in 1994. Hogarth illustrated the feature from 1937 to 1950, with the exception of two years between 1945 and 1947.*
© November 29, 1942, United Feature Syndicate, Inc. Courtesy of Bruce Hamilton

KING OF THE ROYAL MOUNTED Sunday page by Zane Grey (writer) and Jim Gary (artist). Sergeant King was a Canadian Mountie who always got his man. He was frequently accompanied by Betty Blake and her brother Kid. © January 23, 1944, King Features Syndicate, Inc. Courtesy of King Features Syndicate

KING OF THE ROYAL MOUNTED consecutive daily strips by Zane Grey (writer) and Allen Dean (artist). This northwestern adventure strip was scripted by the famed western novelist Zane Grey. The Sunday page was launched on February 17, 1935, and a daily version followed a year later.
© March 9 and 10, 1937, King Features Syndicate, Inc. Courtesy of King Features Syndicate

BRONCHO BILL Sunday page by Harry O'Neill. One of the earliest western features, BRONCHO BILL debuted in 1928 as YOUNG BUFFALO BILL and was produced by O'Neill until 1950. © May 4, 1941, United Feature Syndicate, Inc. Courtesy of Jack Gilbert.

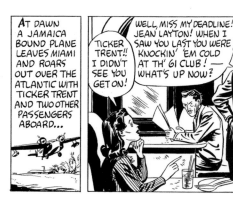

FOREIGN CORRESPONDENT daily strip by Charles Raab. An acquaintance and admirer of Milton Caniff, Raab worked on TERRY AND THE PIRATES, CHARLIE CHAN, and ADVENTURES OF PATSY before trying to launch his own creation, FOREIGN CORRESPONDENT, in 1943.
c. 1943. Courtesy of the International Museum of Cartoon Art

FLYING JENNY story recap strip by Russell Keaton. This feature, which debuted in October 1939, was the first strip to star a female aviator.
© November 6, 1939, Bell Syndicate, Inc. Courtesy of Denis Kitchen

HAP HOOPER, WASHINGTON CORRESPONDENT daily strip by William Laas (writer) and Jack Sparling (artist). Hap, who made his first appearance on January 29, 1940, worked as a newspaper reporter and hunted spies during the war. © May 12, 1942, United Feature Syndicate, Inc. Courtesy of Ethan Roberts

INVISIBLE SCARLET O'NEIL daily strip by Russell Stamm. A former assistant to Chester Gould, Stamm introduced Scarlet, who had the ability to become invisible, to newspaper readers on June 3, 1940. © March 17, 1942, Chicago Times, Inc. Courtesy of Russ Cochran

BRENDA STARR Sunday half-page by Dale Messick. This lady reporter, who made her first appearance on June 30, 1940, was a fiery redhead with a short temper. © June 1, 1941, Tribune Media Services, Inc. All rights reserved. Reprinted with permission. Courtesy of Sandy Schechter

MARY WORTH Sunday page by Allen Saunders (writer) and Ken Ernst (artist). Ernst and Saunders renamed APPLE MARY in 1944, after the feature had been transformed into the prototypical modern soap opera strip. © December 17, 1944, Publishers Syndicate. Courtesy of Russ Cochran

BARNABY—The first four daily strips by Crockett Johnson. This streamlined strip, which debuted in the liberal New York tabloid PM on April 20, 1942, starred a little boy and his imaginary fairy godfather, Mr. O'Malley. It was embraced by artists, writers, and intellectuals but lasted only a decade.
© April 20, 21, 22, and 23, 1942, Field Publications

COMIC RELIEF

Launching a feature in the midst of a world war was a risky proposition, but the syndicates were still determined to develop new talent in the early 1940s. Although the serious mood of the nation was more conducive to adventure and story strips, daily laughs were also needed. A handful of creators came up with features that had little to do with the armed services but contributed to the cause by providing a welcome respite from the grim realities of the global conflict.

THE FOLLOWING MORNING

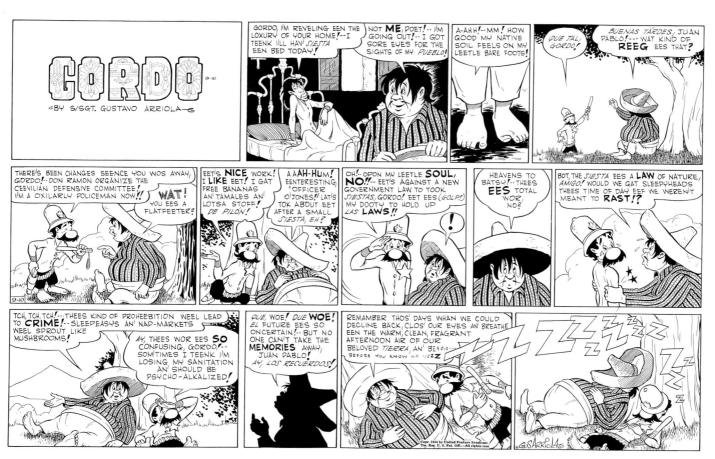

GORDO Sunday page by Gus Arriola. Gordo Lopez, who made his debut on November 24, 1941, was a fat, lazy Mexican dirt farmer from the tiny village of Del Monte. After a six-month hiatus, Arriola managed to continue his Sunday page while serving in the army during the war.
© September 10, 1944, United Feature Syndicate, Inc. Courtesy of the International Museum of Cartoon Art

BUGS BUNNY Sunday page by Roger Armstrong. The star of the Warner Bros. Studio got his own Sunday feature on January 10, 1943. A daily strip followed in 1946. © October 24, 1943, Warner Bros. Entertainment Inc. Courtesy of Russ Cochran

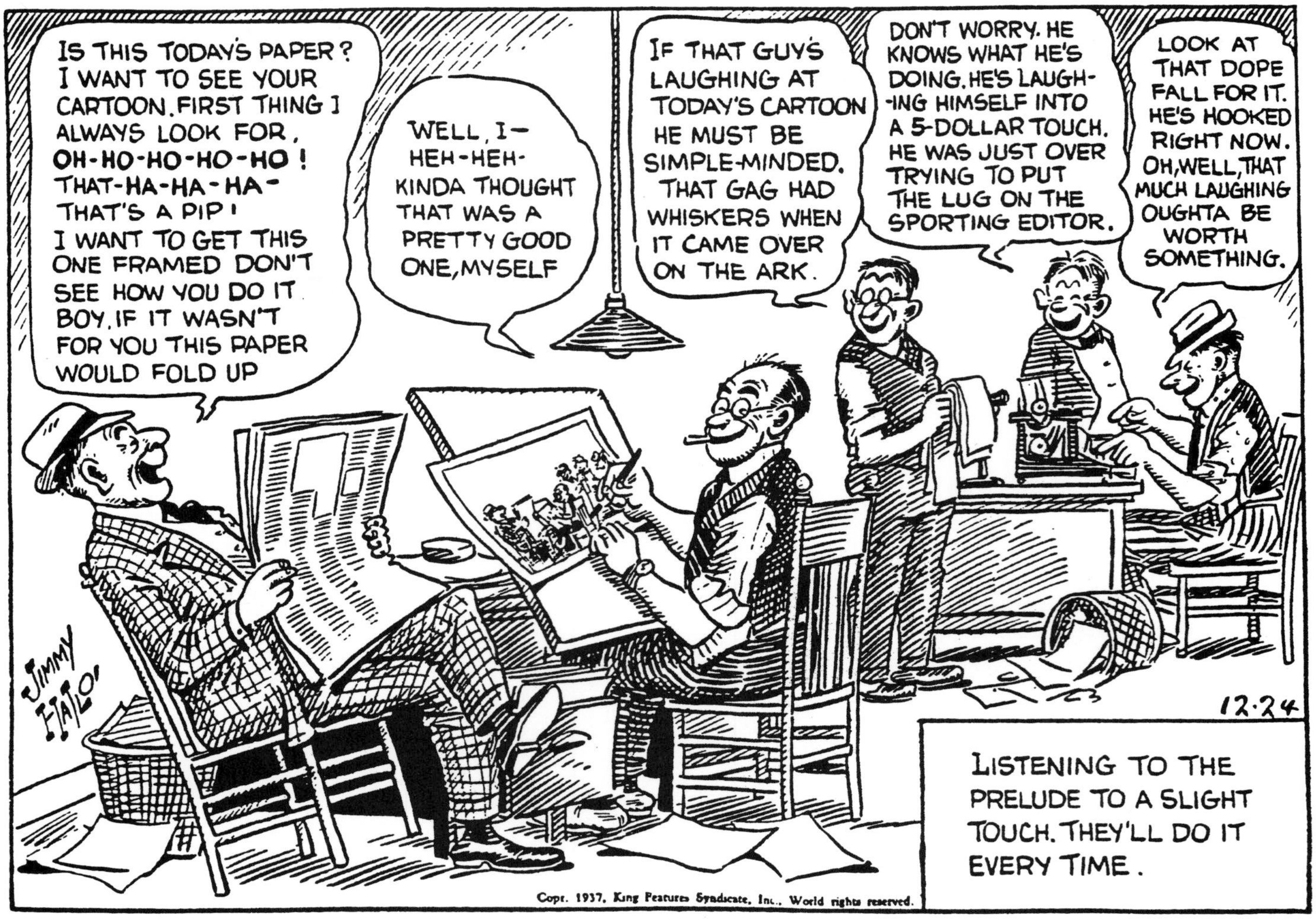
IS THIS TODAY'S PAPER? I WANT TO SEE YOUR CARTOON. FIRST THING I ALWAYS LOOK FOR, OH-HO-HO-HO-HO! THAT-HA-HA-HA- THAT'S A PIP! I WANT TO GET THIS ONE FRAMED DON'T SEE HOW YOU DO IT BOY. IF IT WASN'T FOR YOU THIS PAPER WOULD FOLD UP
WELL, I- HEH-HEH- KINDA THOUGHT THAT WAS A PRETTY GOOD ONE, MYSELF
IF THAT GUY'S LAUGHING AT TODAY'S CARTOON HE MUST BE SIMPLE-MINDED. THAT GAG HAD WHISKERS WHEN IT CAME OVER ON THE ARK.
DON'T WORRY. HE KNOWS WHAT HE'S DOING. HE'S LAUGH-ING HIMSELF INTO A 5-DOLLAR TOUCH. HE WAS JUST OVER TRYING TO PUT THE LUG ON THE SPORTING EDITOR.
LOOK AT THAT DOPE FALL FOR IT. HE'S HOOKED RIGHT NOW. OH, WELL, THAT MUCH LAUGHING OUGHTA BE WORTH SOMETHING.
JIMMY HATLO
12·24
LISTENING TO THE PRELUDE TO A SLIGHT TOUCH. THEY'LL DO IT EVERY TIME.
Copr. 1937, King Features Syndicate, Inc., World rights reserved.

THEY'LL DO IT EVERY TIME* daily panel by Jimmy Hatlo. This popular panel debuted in the** San Francisco Call-Bulletin ***in 1929 and was nationally syndicated beginning on May 4, 1936.
© December 24, 1937, King Features Syndicate, Inc. Courtesy of King Features Syndicate

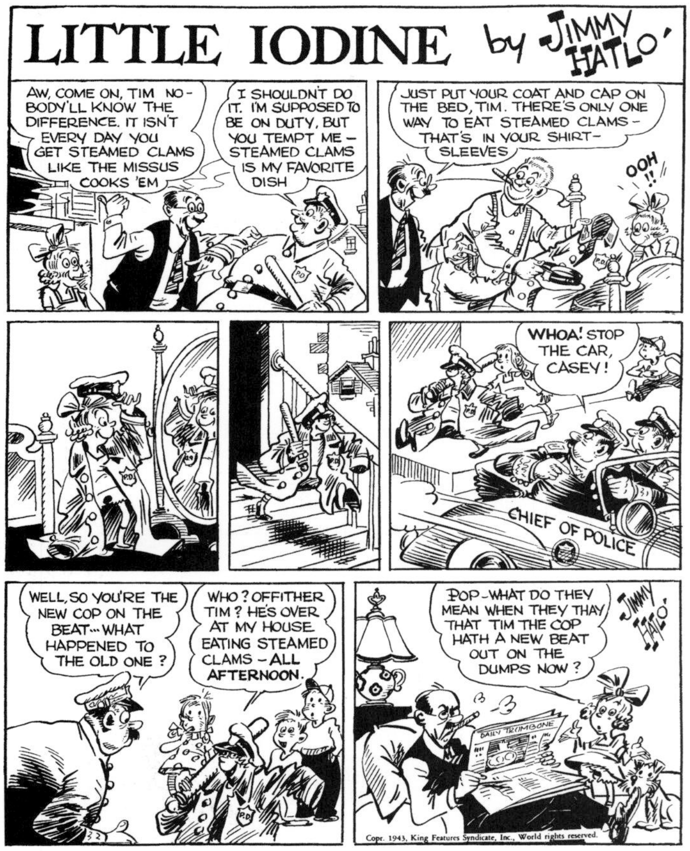
LITTLE IODINE by JIMMY HATLO
AW, COME ON, TIM NOBODY'LL KNOW THE DIFFERENCE. IT ISN'T EVERY DAY YOU GET STEAMED CLAMS LIKE THE MISSUS COOKS 'EM
I SHOULDN'T DO IT. I'M SUPPOSED TO BE ON DUTY, BUT YOU TEMPT ME - STEAMED CLAMS IS MY FAVORITE DISH
JUST PUT YOUR COAT AND CAP ON THE BED, TIM. THERE'S ONLY ONE WAY TO EAT STEAMED CLAMS - THAT'S IN YOUR SHIRT-SLEEVES
OOH !!
WHOA! STOP THE CAR, CASEY!
CHIEF OF POLICE
WELL, SO YOU'RE THE NEW COP ON THE BEAT... WHAT HAPPENED TO THE OLD ONE?
WHO? OFFITHER TIM? HE'S OVER AT MY HOUSE EATING STEAMED CLAMS - ALL AFTERNOON.
POP - WHAT DO THEY MEAN WHEN THEY THAY THAT TIM THE COP HATH A NEW BEAT OUT ON THE DUMPS NOW?
JIMMY HATLO
DAILY TRUMBONE
Copr. 1943, King Features Syndicate, Inc., World rights reserved.

***LITTLE IODINE* daily panel by Jimmy Hatlo. A regular character in *THEY'LL DO IT EVERY TIME*, Hatlo's little brat became the star of her own feature on July 4, 1943.** *© 1943 King Features Syndicate, Inc. Courtesy of King Features Syndicate*

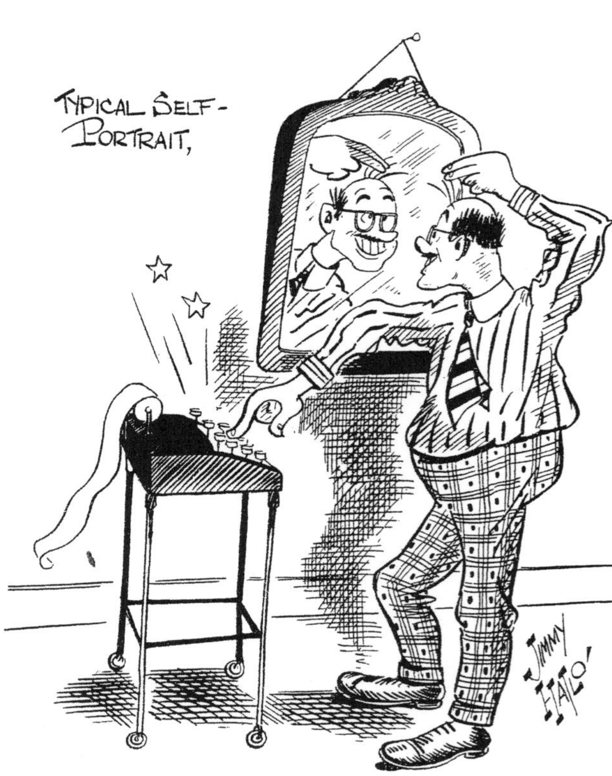
TYPICAL SELF-PORTRAIT,
JIMMY HATLO

JIMMY HATLO—Self-caricature from **Comics and Their Creators.** *© 1942*

THE FLOP FAMILY by SWAN-o

THE FLOP FAMILY daily panel by George Swanson. The creator of SALESMAN SAM and ELZA POPPIN launched a new feature, drawn in his trademark screwball style, on August 29, 1943. © September 26, 1943, King Features Syndicate, Inc. Courtesy of the International Museum of Cartoon Art

FRED LASSWELL—Self-caricature. c. 1945. Courtesy of Mark Cohen

BUNKY Sunday half-page by Fred Lasswell. After Billy DeBeck died on November 11, 1942, his assistant, Fred Lasswell, took over both BARNEY GOOGLE AND SNUFFY SMITH and its companion feature, BUNKY. Wearing his baby bonnet, Bunker Hill Jr. wandered the world with his unsavory companion, Fagin, in search of adventure. © June 6, 1943, King Features Syndicate, Inc. Courtesy of Jim Scancarelli

will eisner

THE SPIRIT WAS THE STAR of a sixteen-page weekly comic magazine that was syndicated to newspapers from 1940 to 1952. The creator of this masked crime fighter was the only artist to successfully adapt the comic book format to the Sunday funnies.

Will Eisner was born in Brooklyn on March 6, 1917, the son of Jewish immigrants. He discovered comics when he worked as a newsboy on Wall Street. "To me art, being a syndicated cartoonist, represented a way out of the ghetto," Eisner remembered.

After graduating from De Witt Clinton High School in the Bronx, he attended classes at the Art Students League. He also worked in a printshop, got a night job at the *New York American,* and was the art director for *Eve* magazine, which folded shortly after he was fired.

In 1936, after selling a few of his strips to a struggling comics magazine, he teamed up with Jerry Iger and opened one of the first successful comic book art shops. With a staff that eventually reached twenty (including Bob Kane, Jack Kirby, and Lou Fine), the shop turned out fifteen comic books a month. In addition to selling their work to publishers like Quality, Fiction House, and Fox, they produced comics in a Sunday-page format for foreign clients.

In 1939, Everett "Busy" Arnold of Quality approached Eisner with an offer to design a comic book for newspaper syndication. Eisner terminated his partnership with Iger and created *The Weekly Comic Book* (also known as *The Spirit Section*), which was distributed by the Register and Tribune Syndicate and debuted on June 2, 1940. Eisner wrote and illustrated the seven-page lead feature, *The Spirit,* and developed the two backup series, *Lady Luck* and *Mr. Mystic.*

Eisner's creation became the testing ground for his experiments in page layout, atmospheric rendering, and dramatic scripting. "Surreal perspectives and lighting effects gave *The Spirit* a compelling aura of mystery," wrote Catherine Yronwode in *The Art of Will Eisner.* "This was augmented by Eisner's seemingly obsessive desire to draw water in all its forms, from rain-swept streets to fog-enshrouded, rotting wharves. The graphic close-ups of brutal violence, carefully off-set by bouts of slapstick comedy and sexual innuendo, left the reader in a constant state of emotional and aesthetic surprise."

A daily comic strip version of *The Spirit* was launched on October 13, 1941, but it was not the ideal vehicle for Eisner's talents, and it ended in 1944. "The problem is that it's such a confining operation," Eisner explained. "I couldn't be as imaginative or do all the things I wanted to do. I'm a great experimenter—I get my kicks from experimenting and breaking

WILL EISNER—Self-caricature. © *1974 by Will Eisner*

down walls—and there was no 'elbow room' in a daily strip. It was like conducting a symphony in a telephone booth."

After serving in the army from 1942 to 1945, Eisner resumed work on *The Spirit,* which other artists had continued in his absence. Between December 23, 1945, and August 12, 1951, Eisner had a hand in all of the weekly episodes and was at the peak of his creative powers. The series ended in 1952, after he turned the work over to assistants.

For the next sixteen years, Eisner operated a commercial studio that produced instructional comics for a wide range of clients, including the Department of Labor and New York Telephone. In 1978, he published *A Contract with God and Other Tenement Stories.* The four illustrated vignettes in the 192-page book were based on Eisner's experiences growing up during the Depression in the Bronx. The sixty-one-year-old cartoonist had discovered a new format—the graphic novel—to further explore the potential for personal expression in the comics medium.

THE SPIRIT—Portrait by Will Eisner. © *1974 by Will Eisner*

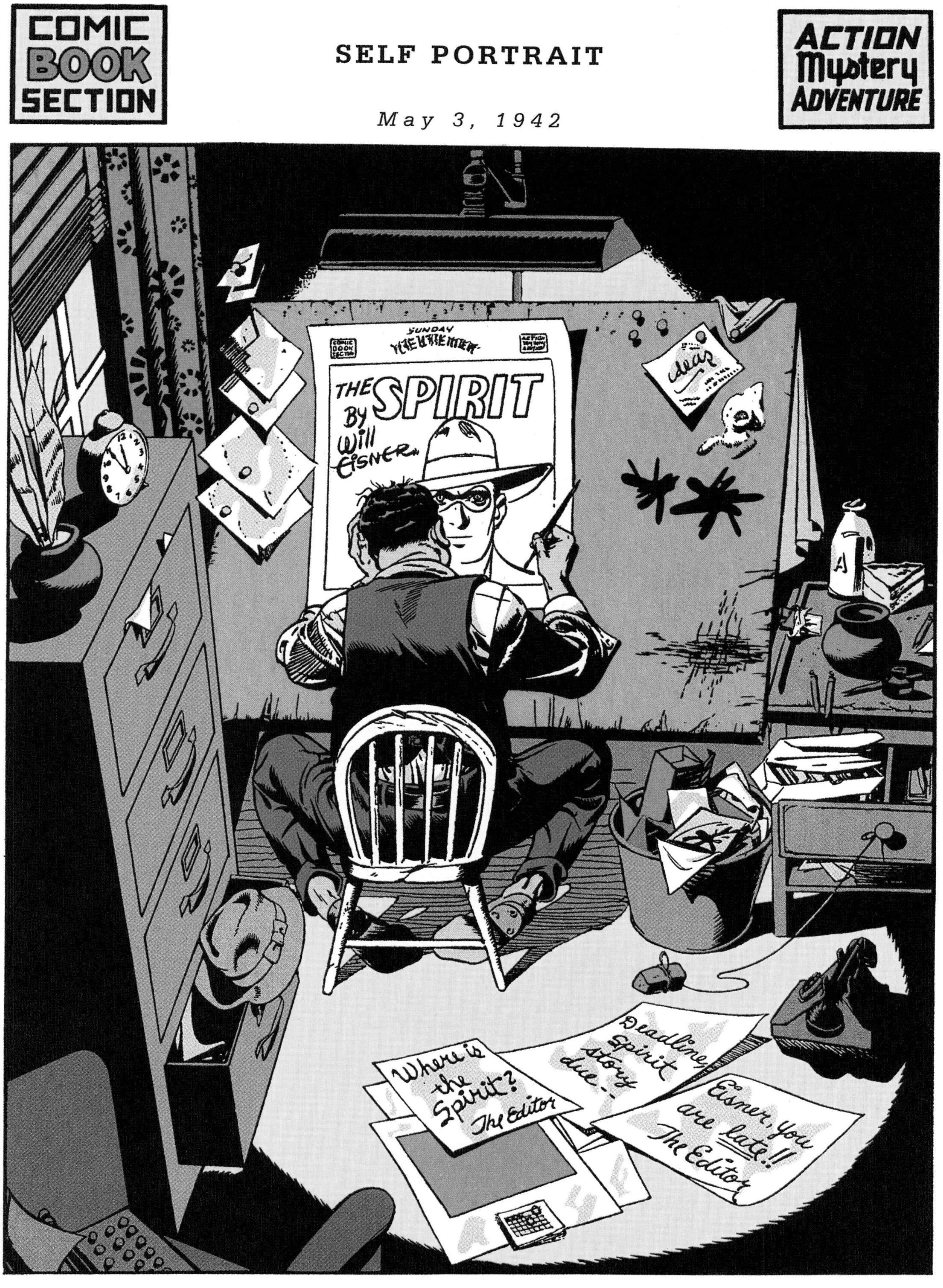
COMIC BOOK SECTION
SELF PORTRAIT
May 3, 1942
ACTION Mystery ADVENTURE
SUNDAY
THE SPIRIT
By Will Eisner
Where is the Spirit? The Editor
Deadline, Spirit story due..
Eisner, you are late!! The Editor

THE SPIRIT comic page by Will Eisner. In one of the last stories he did before joining the army, Eisner pictured himself at the drawing board.

THE ORPHANS

August 25, 1940

THE SPIRIT splash page by Will Eisner. The artist did not want his lead character to be a costumed superhero, but he added the mask to pacify his publisher. © August 25, 1940, and 1974 by Will Eisner. Courtesy of Will Eisner

THE SPIRIT splash page by Will Eisner. "At the Prom" is one of only two known original pages to have survived from Eisner's prewar period. © December 1, 1940, 1974 by Will Eisner. Courtesy of Denis Kitchen

THE SPIRIT daily strip by Will Eisner. While Eisner served in the army from 1942 to 1945, the daily strip was drawn by Jack Cole and Lou Fine.
© December 25, 1943, and 1974 by Will Eisner. Courtesy of Art Wood

ACKNOWLEDGMENTS

The author would like to thank the following individuals and organizations for their invaluable assistance in producing this book:

Individuals: Bill Alger, Rob Andrews, David Applegate, David Astor, Ralph Bakshi, Bob Beerbohm, Ed Black, Bill Blackbeard, John Canemaker, John Carlin, Jim Carlsson, Alfredo Castelli, Russ Cochran, Bill Crouch, Jerry Dumas, Will Eisner, Craig Englund, John Fawcett, Gill Fox, Jim Gauthier, Jack Gilbert, Marty Goldman, Carole Goodman, Ian Gordon, Ron Goulart, Bruce Hamilton, R. C. Harvey, Tom Heintjes, Todd Hignite, Eric Himmel, Jud Hurd, Tom Inge, Bill Janocha, Mark Johnson, Denis Kitchen, Charlie Kochman, Francisco Lopez, Howard Lowery, Joe and Nadia Mannarino, Peter Maresca, Richard Marschall, Ricardo Martinez, Matt Masterson, Patrick McDonnell, Joe McGuckin, Peter Merolo, Peter Myer, Angelo Nobile, Richard Olson, Frank Pauer, Trina Robbins, Ethan Roberts, Jim Scancarelli, Sandy Schechter, Richard Slovak, Gary Smith, John Snyder, Art Spiegelman, David Stanford, Rob Stolzer, Mort and Catherine Walker, Neal Walker, Eugene Walters, Morris Weiss, Doug Wheeler, Jason Whiton, Malcolm Whyte, Mark Winchester, Art Wood, and Craig Yoe.

Syndicates: King Features—Jim Cavett, Mark Johnson, Jay Kennedy, Karen Moy, and Claudia Smith. Tribune Media Services—Jan Bunch and Lee Hall. United Media—Maura Peters.

Organizations and institutions: American Color—Andy Olsen. Boston University—Dr. Howard Gotlieb, Sean Noel, and J. C. Johnson. Cartoon Art Museum—Jenny Robb Dietzen and Andrew Farago. Cartoon Research Library, Ohio State University—Lucy Shelton Caswell and Marilyn Scott. Frye Art Museum—Richard West. Illustration House—Roger Reed and Walt Reed. International Museum of Cartoon Art—Stephen Charla, Alexis Faro, and Jeanne Greever. Library of Congress—Sara Duke. Periodyssey—Richard West. Syracuse University—Carolyn Davis. University of Nebraska Sheldon Memorial Art Gallery—Dan Siedell.

ARTICLES

The following comics-related periodicals were used for general research:

Cartoonews. Published six times a year from April 1975 to 1980 by Jim Ivey, Orlando.

Cartoonist PROfiles. Published quarterly since March 1969 by Cartoonist PROfiles Inc., 281 Bayberry Lane, Westport, CT 06430.

Cartoons Magazine. Published monthly from January 1912 to June 1921 by H. H. Windsor, Chicago.

Circulation. Published from 1921 to 1926 (or later) by King Features Syndicate. Only twelve different issues of this rare magazine are known to exist.

Comic Art. Published quarterly since fall 2002 by Comic Art, 5715 Nottingham Ave., St. Louis, MO 63109.

Comic Book Marketplace. Published (now monthly) since March/April 1993 by Gemstone Publishing, P.O. Box 469, West Plains, MO 65775.

Comic Buyer's Guide. Published weekly since 1971 by Krause Publications, Inc., 700 E. State St., Iola, WI 54990.

The Comics Journal. Published (now monthly) since January 1977 by Fantagraphics Books, Inc., 7563 Lake City Way N.E., Seattle, WA 98115.

Editor & Publisher. Originally titled *The Fourth Estate,* published weekly since 1894 by BPI Communications, Inc. 770 Broadway, New York, NY 10003.

Hogan's Alley. Published (now annually) since autumn 1994 by Bull Moose Publishing Corp., P.O. Box 4784, Atlanta, GA 30362.

Inks. Twelve issues were published, three times a year, between February 1994 and November 1997 by the Ohio State University Press, 1070 Carmack Road, Columbus, OH 43110.

Nemo. Thirty-two issues were published between June 1983 and January 1992 by Fantagraphic Books, Inc. 7563 Lake City Way N.E., Seattle, WA 98115.

The R.F. Outcault Reader. The Official Newsletter of the R.F. Outcault Society. Published quarterly from March 1991 (vol. 1, no. 1) to December 1999 (vol. 9, no. 4). Richard Olson, editor.

The World of Comic Art. Published quarterly from June 1966 to March 1972 by World of Comic Art Publications, P.O. Box 507, Hawthorne, CA 90250.

GENERAL HISTORIES

Alder, Eric. "100 Years of Laughter." *Kansas City Star/ Charlotte Observer,* May 5, 1995.

Caniff, Milton. "Don't Laugh at the Comics." *Cosmopolitan,* November 1958.

Daviss, Bennett. "World of Funnies Is 'Warped with Fancy, Woofed with Dreams.'" *Smithsonian,* November 1987.

DeLeon, Clark. "A Century of Comics." *Philadelphia Inquirer,* April 30, 1995.

Dunn, William. "The Funnies as Fine Art." *The Detroit News Magazine,* March 22, 1981.

Feiffer, Jules (guest editor, special edition). "Comic Rave." *Civilization,* July 1998.

Folkman, David. "The Great Cartoonists of the Century." *Liberty,* winter 1973.

"Funnies Man: Ernie McGee." *Cincinnati Pictorial Enquirer,* Oct. 20, 1957.

Kelly, Walt. "The Funnies Are Relevant." *The Fort Mudge Most* #75, 2001.

Kogan, Rick. "Tales from the Strips." *Chicago Tribune,* Feb. 9, 1995.

Lewis, Boyd. "The Comics—Still Alive at 75." *Chicago Tribune,* Nov. 14, 1971.

Maltin, Leonard. "A Fond Look at the Sunday Funnies." *Diversion,* July 1982.

Marschall, Richard. "Comic Masters." *Horizon,* July 1980.

———. "100 Years of the Funnies." *American History,* October 1995.

Murray, Will (principal historian), and Kim Howard Johnson (contributing writer). "100 Years of Comics" (special edition). *Starlog Millennium 2000 Series,* 2000.

Precker, Michael. "Comic Relief." *Dallas Morning News,* April 8, 1995.

Rizzo, Frank. "AJC Comics Week." *Atlanta Journal-Constitution,* Sept. 21–27, 2003.

"75 Years of American Newspaper Comics." *The American Legion Magazine,* December 1971.

Sheridan, Martin. "Comics and Their Creators." *Literary Digest,* 1930s. Included in this series were short profiles of Gene Ahearn, Merrill Blosser, Robert M. Brinkerhoff, Gene Byrnes, Percy L. Crosby, Billy DeBeck, Bill Dwyer, Vic Forsythe, Rube Goldberg, Milt Gross, Johnny Gruelle, Edgar E. Martin, J. Carver Pusey, Otto Soglow, Cliff Sterrett, H. T. Webster, and J. R. Williams.

Updike, John. "Lost Art." *The New Yorker,* Dec. 15, 1997.

Walker, Brian. "100 Years of the Sunday Funnies: Part 1, 1895–1945." *Collectors' Showcase,* vol. 15, no. 2, April/May 1995.

NOTES

The following articles and books were quoted directly or referred to for specific facts. The listings are by chapter and subject, in order of appearance.

INTRODUCTION

The Yellow Kid: Blackbeard, Bill. "First Balloon Trip to the Rainbow: Outcault's Accidental (and Unnoticed) Invention of the Comic Strip (1896)." *Comic Buyer's Guide* #1143, Oct. 13, 1995.

Canemaker, John. "The Kid from Hogan's Alley." *The New York Times Book Review,* Dec. 17, 1995.

Dreiser, Theodore. "A Metropolitan Favorite: Something About R. F. Outcault, the 'Yellow Kid' and 'Hogan's Alley.'" *Ev'ry Month,* vol. 3, no. 2, Nov. 1, 1896.

Harvey, R. C. "The Origin of a New Species." *Cartoonist PROfiles* #105, March 1995.

Kanfer, Stefan. "From the Yellow Kid to Yellow Journalism." *Civilization,* May/June 1995.

Maeder, Jay. "Polychromous Effulgence: R.F. Outcault." *New York Daily News,* April 25, 1999.

Marschall, Richard. "Shibboleths: Exploding Myths, Looking for New Origins, Redefining Our Terms: The Advent of the Comic Strip." *The Comics Journal* #68, 1982.

McCardell, Roy L. "Opper, Outcault and Company." *Everybody's Magazine,* June 1905.

Olson, Richard D. "R.F. Outcault: The Father of the Comics." *Collectors' Showcase*, vol. 15, no. 2, April/May 1995.

———. "Richard Fenton Outcault's Yellow Kid." *Inks,* vol. 2, no. 3, November 1995.

Outcault, Richard. "How the Yellow Kid Was Born." *New York World,* May 1, 1898.

Reilly, Jim. "The Yellow Kid." *Syracuse Herald American,* April 19, 1992.

Color printing: "Working Colors on Each Other." *American Pressman,* June 1893.

Jimmy Swinnerton: "Sprightly Comics Really Middle-Aged." *Editor & Publisher,* July 21, 1934.

Early comics: Harvey, R. C. "More New Historic Beginnings for Comics." *The Comics Journal* #246, September 2002.

Paviat, Eric. "Proto-Comics: Comics Before Newspaper Strips." *Comic Buyer's Guide* #1129, July 7, 1995.

Robb, Jenny E. "The Lineage of the Newspaper Comic Strip from Hogarth to Howarth." In *Before the Yellow Kid: Precursors of the American Newspaper Comic Strip.* Columbus: The Ohio State University Libraries, 1995.

Wheeler, Doug. "Comic Strips Before the Yellow Kid." *Comic Buyer's Guide* #1525, Feb. 7, 2003.

Wheeler, Doug, Robert L. Beerbohm, and Richard D. Olson. "The Victorian Age Before the Yellow Kid: American Comics of the 19th Century." *The Official Overstreet Comic Book Price Guide* (33rd ed.). Timonium, Md.: Gemstone Publishing, 2003.

Wheeler, Doug, Robert L. Beerbohm, and Leonardo De Sa. "Topffer in America" and "The Myth of the Yellow Kid." *Comic Art* #3, summer 2003.

Hearst and Pulitzer (articles in chronological order): "W.R. Hearst Here." *The Fourth Estate,* Oct. 10, 1895.

"Money Well Spent." *The Fourth Estate,* Jan. 30, 1896.

"The Journal's Rapid Strides." *The Fourth Estate,* Oct. 22, 1896.

Collings, James L. "Personalities and Piracy in Early Syndicate Days." *Editor & Publisher,* June 27, 1959.

Turner, Hy. "This Was Park Row!" *Editor & Publisher,* June 27, 1959.

Yellow journalism: Campbell, Joseph W. *Yellow Journalism: Puncturing Myths, Defining Legacies.* Praeger, 2001.

Winchester, Mark D. "Hully Gee, It's a War!!!" *Inks,* vol. 2, no. 3, November 1995.

THE TURN OF THE CENTURY

Sunday papers (articles in chronological order): "What Americans Read." *The Fourth Estate,* April 19, 1894.

"The Sunday Newspaper" (editorial). *Editor & Publisher,* April 5, 1902.

"Brief Historical Review of American Sunday Journalism." *Editor & Publisher,* Oct. 27, 1917.

Lee, James Melvin. "Story of the First Sunday Newspapers Published in America." *Editor & Publisher,* Oct. 3, 1925.

McCaleb, Kenneth. "Every Exciting Sunday." *Editor & Publisher,* June 27, 1959.

Harvey, R. C. "Fine-Tuning the Form." *Cartoonist PROfiles* #106, June 1995.

Barker, Kenneth S. "The Comic Series of the New York Sunday Herald and the New York Sunday Tribune." *Inks,* vol. 3, no. 2, May 1996.

Beerbohm, Robert L., Doug Wheeler, and Richard D. Olson. "The Platinum Age: 1897–1938." *The Official Overstreet Comic Book Price Guide* (33rd ed.). Timonium, Md.: Gemstone Publishing, 2003.

Syndicates: Lewis, Boyd. "The Syndicates and How They Grew." *Saturday Review,* Dec. 11, 1971.

Marschall, Richard. "A History of Newspaper Syndication." In *The World Encyclopedia of Comics.* Philadelphia: Chelsea House Publishers, 1999.

Protests (articles in chronological order): "Against Sunday Papers." *The Fourth Estate,* April 5, 1894.

"War on Sunday Newspapers." *The Fourth Estate,* July 19, 1894.

"Comic Supplement." *Editor & Publisher,* June 16, 1906.

"Sunday Paper's Sins." *Editor & Publisher,* Nov. 2, 1907.

"Comic Supplement." *Editor & Publisher,* Sept. 19, 1908.

"Defense of Comics." *Editor & Publisher,* Oct. 3, 1908.

Outcault, R. F. "End of Comics: Artist Predicts Passing of the Feature Which He Made Famous." *Editor & Publisher,* Jan. 16, 1909.

"Comic Supplements: League for Their Improvement Discusses Subject at Mass Meeting." *Editor & Publisher,* April 8, 1911.

Bevona, Donald E. "First Sunday Editions Had No Place in Home." *Editor & Publisher,* June 27, 1959.

Nyberg, Amy Kiste. "Percival Chubb and the League for the Improvement of the Children's Comic Supplement." *Inks,* vol. 3, no. 3, November 1996.

Harvey, Robert C. "When Comics Were for Kids." *The Comics Journal* (special edition), winter 2002.

Buster Brown court case (articles in chronological order): "The Buster Brown Affair." *Editor & Publisher,* Dec. 9, 1905.

"Buster Is in Court." *Editor & Publisher,* Feb. 17, 1906.

"'Buster Brown' Injunction." *Editor & Publisher,* March 31, 1906.

Winchester, Mark D. "Litigation and Early Comic Strips: The Lawsuits of Outcault, Dirks and Fisher." *Inks,* vol. 2, no. 2, May 1995.

Early pioneers: Fried, Alan. "Lyonel Feininger: A Kinder, Gentler Comic Strip." *Inks,* vol. 3, no. 3, November 1996.

Gordon, Ian. "Laying the Foundation" (F. M. Howarth). *Hogan's Alley* #9, summer 2001.

Johnson, Mark. "The Two Worlds of Danny Dreamer." *Nemo* #7, June 1984.

———. "The Pioneer and Satire Strip Hairbreadth Harry." *Nemo* #14, August 1985.

———. "Hairbreadth Harry, Our Forgotten Hero." *Battle for Belinda.* Hairbreadth Harry exhibition catalog. Philadelphia: Federal Reserve Bank, 1987.

———. "The Outbursts of Everett True." *Nemo* #26, September 1987.

Lawson, Helen. "The Katzenjammers' Secret" (H. H. Knerr). *Circulation,* vol. 2, no. 9, September 1922.

Marschall, Richard. "The Explorigator: Dreamship of the Universe." *Nemo* #5, February 1984.

———. "George McManus' Pioneer Work of Fantasy: Nibsy the Newsboy." *Nemo* #9, October 1984.

———. "The Forgotten Genius: Gustave Verbeek." *Nemo* #10, December 1984.

———. "The Force Was with Him: The Escapades of Slim Jim." *Nemo* #11, May 1985.

O'Gara, Gil. "Schultze's 'Foxy Grandpa.'" *Comic Buyer's Guide,* Nov. 28, 1986.

Robbins, Trina. "Women and Children First." *Inks,* vol. 2, no. 3, November 1995.

Spiegelman, Art. "Art Every Sunday" (Lyonel Feininger). *The New York Times Book Review,* Oct. 2, 1994.

Straut, Jessie Kahles, and Phil Love. "C.W. Kahles . . . Most Neglected Genius." *Cartoonist PROfiles* #31, September 1976.

First daily strip: Fisher, Bud. "Confessions of a Cartoonist." *The Saturday Evening Post,* four-part article, July 28 and Aug. 4, 11, and 18, 1928.

Harvey, R. C. "Bud Fisher and the Daily Comic Strip." *Inks,* vol. 1, no. 1, February 1994.

Rogers, Bogart. "Hero of San Francisco." *The American Mercury,* December 1954.

Richard F. Outcault: Campbell, Gordon. "The Yellow Kid/Buster Brown." *Cartoonist PROfiles* #51, September 1981.

Hake, Ted. "Buster Brown: America's First Comic Salesman." *Collectibles Monthly,* July 1977.

Hancock, La Touche. "American Caricature and Comic Art." *The Bookman,* November 1902.

Marschall, Richard. "Buster Brown: The Bad Boy Who Made Good." Introduction to *Buster Brown.* Westport, Conn.: Hyperion Press, 1977.

Rudolph Dirks: Blackbeard, Bill. "Max, Maurice and Willie." *Nemo* #2, August 1983.

Dirks, John. "Rudolph Dirks." *Cartoonist PROfiles* #23, September 1974.

Dirks, Rudolph. "Katzenjammer Kids Creator Reveals Rise of Comics." *The Open Road,* January 1950.

Frederick B. Opper: Campbell, Gordon. "Frederick Opper." *Cartoonist PROfiles* #45, March 1980.

Clarke, Penelope. "Mr. Frederick Burr Opper." *Circulation,* vol. 2, no. 9, September 1922.

"F. Opper, Dean of Cartoonists, Dies in Retirement at 82." *Editor & Publisher,* Sept. 4, 1937.

Harvey, R. C. "Who Was Frederick Burr Opper?" *Comics Buyer's Guide* #1154, Dec. 29, 1995.

"Leading Cartoonists of America: Frederick Burr Opper." *Editor & Publisher,* July 19, 1913.

Marschall, Richard. "Opper's Immortal Tramp." Introduction to *Happy Hooligan.* Westport, Conn.: Hyperion Press, 1977.

"Opper of 'The Old Guard.'" *The Dead-Line,* vol. 1, no. 1, September 1917.

Outcault, Richard F. "Opper: Fifty Years a Funmaker." *Circulation,* vol. 5, no. 25, July 1926.

Perry, John. "F. Opper, at 72, Still Working Hard." *Editor & Publisher,* Oct. 12, 1929.

Jimmy Swinnerton: Blackbeard, Bill. "The Man Who Grew Up with the Comics." *Nemo* #22, October 1986.

Campbell, Gordon. "Swinnerton." *Cartoonist PROfiles* #59, September 1983.

"James Swinnerton Dead at 98; Pioneer Newspaper Cartoonist." *New York Times,* Sept. 7, 1974.

Monchak, Stephen J. "Swinnerton Creates New Comic for King Features." *Editor & Publisher,* July 21, 1941.

Phelps, Donald. "Jimmy and Company." *Nemo* #22, October 1986.

Yendis, Beol. "Li'l Ole Bear, M.D." *Circulation,* vol. 5, no. 24, May 1926.

Winsor McCay: Campbell, Gordon. "Winsor McCay." *Cartoonist PROfiles* #46, June 1980.

"Leading Cartoonists of America: Winsor McCay." *Editor & Publisher,* Aug. 2, 1913.

Marschall, Richard. "In His Own Words: Winsor McCay on Life, Art, Animation . . . and the Danger of Greasy Foods." *Nemo* #3, October 1983.

"McCay Leaves Herald." *Editor & Publisher,* June 1, 1911.

"Winsor McCay, Famous Cartoonist and Artist, Dies Suddenly at 63." *Editor & Publisher,* July 28, 1934.

"Winsor McCay: Sketch of the Well-Known Creator of 'Little Nemo.'" *Editor & Publisher,* Dec. 25, 1909.

THE TEENS

Comics business (articles in chronological order): "New Feature Syndicate: M. Koenigsberg Heads New Enterprise." *Editor & Publisher,* Sept. 13, 1913.

Lawler, Will. "The Value of Comics." *Editor & Publisher,* Feb. 21, 1914.

Jackson, Tom. "Katzenjammer Kids: Their Mother Tells E&P Reporter of Hardships." *Editor & Publisher,* June 13, 1914.

"Nation's Laughs Profitable to the Comic Artists." *New York Sun,* May 2, 1915.

Anderson, Isaac. "Why Is a Comic Section?" *Editor & Publisher,* Oct. 27, 1917.

"He Has Originated Hearst Comics for Twenty Years" (Rudolph Block). *Editor & Publisher,* Feb. 8, 1919.

War (articles in chronological order): "New York City Papers Decrease Size to Help Conserve News Print Supply." *Editor & Publisher,* Aug. 5, 1916.

"Two Chief Officers of the Chicago Tribune Enlisted in Nation's Fighting Forces" (Robert McCormick and J. M. Patterson). *Editor & Publisher,* Nov. 10, 1917.

"Donnelly Sees End of Sunday Comics." *Editor & Publisher,* Sept. 14, 1918.

"Premier Cartoonists Work for Liberty Loan." *Editor & Publisher,* Sept. 28, 1918.

"Fontaine Fox Tells His Wife How War Helped Cartoonists." *Editor & Publisher,* Jan. 11, 1919.

"Capt. Joseph Medill Patterson Comes Back from the War to Resume His Important Role in Journalism." *Editor & Publisher,* Feb. 22, 1919.

Animation: Jameson, Martin. "With the Cartoonists in Filmland." *Cartoons,* March 1917.

Cartoonists: "Briggs Brings Skin-nay 'Over' At Last!" *The Dead-Line,* vol. 1, no. 1, September 1917.

Campbell, Gordon. "Briggs." *Cartoonist PROfiles* #53, March 1982.

———. "Fontaine Fox." *Cartoonist PROfiles* #53, March 1982.

———. "Rube Goldberg." *Cartoonist PROfiles* #57, March 1983.

Clark, Arthur "Ted." "The World's Longest Trolley Ride." (Fontaine Fox). *Nemo* #23, December 1986.

———. "Fontaine Fox's Toonerville Trolley." *Cartoonist PROfiles* #113, March 1997.

Corbett James J. "TAD—An Appreciation." *Circulation,* vol. 2, no. 9, September 1922.

Dorgan, T. A. "The Fable of the Sap Who Listened Ahead." *Circulation,* vol. 1, no. 3, July 1921.

Dowhan, Michael W. "Peter Rabbit: Harrison Cady's Masterwork." *Cartoonist PROfiles* #59, September 1983.

"End of the Line" (Fontaine Fox). *Time,* Feb. 21, 1955.

Fox, Fontaine. "A Queer Way to Make a Living." *The Saturday Evening Post,* Feb. 11, 1928.

"Fox Longs for Old Newspaper Days." *Editor & Publisher,* Nov. 9, 1929.

Goldberg, Rube. "Seriously Speaking of Comic Artists." *Circulation,* vol. 2, no. 12, April 1923.

———. "It Happened to a Rube." *The Saturday Evening Post,* Nov. 10, 1928.

———. "Comics, New Style and Old." *The Saturday Evening Post,* Dec. 15, 1928.

"How Sid Smith Got His Own Goat." *The Dead-Line,* vol. 1, no. 1, September 1917.

Ivey, Jim. "Cartooning's Renaissance Man: The Many Comic Inventions of Rube Goldberg." *Nemo* #24, February 1987.

Johnson, Mark. "Squirrel Food" (Gene Ahearn). *Nemo* #25, April 1987.

Kramer, Hilton. "Laughter That Is Close to Tears" (Rube Goldberg). *New York Times,* Jan. 16, 1977.

Langreich, William P. "How the Comickers Regard Their Characters." *Cartoons,* two parts, April and May 1917.

"Leading Cartoonists of America" (profile series). *Editor & Publisher:* Fontaine Fox, May 3, 1913; Rube Goldberg, May 31, 1913.

"Little Tragedies of a Newspaper Office" (profile series). *Editor & Publisher:* Clare Briggs, Aug. 4, 1917; Gene Byrnes, Dec. 29, 1917; Percy Crosby, Nov. 24, 1917; Billy DeBeck, Sept. 22, 1917; Clare Dwiggins, Feb. 16, 1918; Paul Fung, Sept. 8, 1917; Jimmy Murphy, June 16, 1917, and Dec. 18, 1919; Cliff Sterrett, July 14, 1917; H. T. Webster, July 7, 1917; Garr Williams, Feb. 23, 1918.

Marschall, Richard. "The Teenie Weenies." *Nemo* #6, April 1984.

McGeehan. W. O. "The World His Stage, The Studio His Prison" (TAD). *Liberty,* 1925.

McIntire, O. O. "TAD: The Balladeer of Broadway." *Cosmopolitan,* 1926.

Medbury, John P. "The Cartoonist's Mirror" (Rube Goldberg). *Circulation,* vol. 1, no. 4, September 1921.

Mellon, Ben. "Oh Min! Call Chester—Here Comes Our Sid" (Sidney Smith). *Editor & Publisher,* Nov. 11, 1922.

"Press and Sports World Laud TAD in Final Tribute to Genius." *Editor & Publisher,* May 11, 1929.

Resnick, David. "Harry Hershfield, 85 Muses: 'Ish Kabibble!" *Editor & Publisher,* Oct. 17, 1970.

Stevens, Parke. "'Abie' with a Past" (Harry Hershfield). *Circulation,* vol. 2, no. 11, March 1923.

Walker, Brian. "A Collection of Cartoons by Thomas Aloysius Dorgan." Exhibition catalog. Port Chester, N.Y.: Museum of Cartoon Art, 1978.

Correspondence courses: Advertisements for the Cartoon School of the Chicago Academy of Fine Arts, the Federal Course in Applied Cartooning, the Landon School of Illustrating and Cartooning, and The W. L. Evans School of Cartooning. *Cartoons,* 1916 to 1918.

Marschall, Richard. "Mail-Order Success!" *Cartoonist PROfiles* #30, June 1976.

Bud Fisher (articles in chronological order): "Big 'Comics' in Court." *Editor & Publisher,* Aug. 7, 1915.

"Fisher's Right to 'Mutt and Jeff' Upheld." *Editor & Publisher,* Sept. 4, 1915.

"Cartoons Are Subject to Barter and Sale." *Editor & Publisher,* Aug. 26, 1916.

Wheeler, John N. "A Captain of Comic Industry." *The American Magazine,* 1916.

"Guarantee of Cartoon Rights in Bud Fisher Suit." *Editor & Publisher,* May 25, 1918.

"Star Company May Reproduce 'Mutt and Jeff' Cartoons." *Editor & Publisher,* June 29, 1918.

Mellon, Ben. "Press Pays Bud Fisher $200,000 Annually for Famous 'Mutt and Jeff' Comics." *Editor & Publisher,* April 17, 1919.

"Hearst-Fisher Case Again." *Editor & Publisher,* May 14, 1921.

"Uphold Artist's Right to Creations." *Editor & Publisher,* July 23, 1921.

"Fisher Owns Mutt and Jeff." *Editor & Publisher,* Nov. 19, 1921.

"Bud Fisher Makes $3000 a Week." *Editor & Publisher,* June 23, 1928.

"Bud Fisher, Comic Strip Pioneer, Dies." *Editor & Publisher,* Sept. 11, 1954.

Hurd, Jud. "Bud Fisher Scrapbooks." *Cartoonist PROfiles* #3, September 1969, and #4, December 1969.

Dunn, Bob. "Said and Dunn" (visit with Fisher). *Cartoonist PROfiles* #22, June 1974.

George McManus: Campbell, Eugene. "Jiggs at Home." *Circulation,* vol. 1, no. 4, September 1921.

Dillon, Philip R. "The Newlyweds." *Editor & Publisher,* Dec. 24, 1910.

"Gag a Day." *Time,* Dec. 10, 1945.

Hurd, Jud. "Bringing Up Father." *Cartoonist PROfiles* #44, December 1979.

Jones, Llewellyn Rees. "Jiggs, The Globe-Trotter." *World Traveler,* May 1926.

"Let George Do It—He Did." *Editor & Publisher,* July 13, 1912.

Marschall, Richard. "The Decorative Art of George McManus." *Nemo* #14, August 1985.

McManus, George. "If This Be Pessimism—." *Circulation,* vol. 2, no. 11, March 1923.

———. "Jiggs and I." *Collier's,* three-part series, Jan. 19 and 26 and Feb. 2, 1952.

Pew, Marlen. "Horse, Hard Work Won Success for McManus." *Editor & Publisher,* Nov. 16, 1935.

Schuyler, Philip. "McManus Gives a Lesson in Comic Art." *Editor & Publisher,* Sept. 27, 1924.

Staunton, Helen M. "McManus Celebrates 1/3 Century of Jiggs." *Editor & Publisher,* Dec. 1, 1945.

George Herriman: Baldwin, Summerfield. "A Genius of the Comic Page." *Cartoons,* June 1917.

Blackbeard, Bill. "The Forgotten Years of George Herriman." *Nemo* #1, June 1983.

Dorgan, T. A. "This Is About Garge Herriman." *Circulation,* vol. 2, no. 11, March 1923.

Herriman, George. "George Herriman." *The Dead-Line,* vol. 1, no. 1, September 1917.

Inge, M. Thomas. "Herriman's Coconino Baron." Introduction to *Baron Bean.* Westport, Conn.: Hyperion Press, 1977.

———. "George Herriman's Early Years." *Cartoonist PROfiles* #96, December 1992.

———. "Was Krazy Kat Black? The Racial Identity of George Herriman." *Inks,* vol. 3, no. 2, May 1996.

Laughlin, Robert. "When the Kat Went Krazy." *Hogan's Alley* #5, spring 1998.

Marschall, Richard. "The Diary of a Deluded Dandy" (Baron Bean). *Nemo* #16, December 1985.

———. "Stumble Inn." *Hogan's Alley* #4, summer 1997.

THE TWENTIES

Comics business: Barker, Kenneth. "Longtime Companions" (topper strips). *Hogan's Alley* #11, summer 2003.

Brisbane, Arthur. "Why Are Comic Pictures Necessary in Sunday Newspapers?" *Circulation,* vol. 1, no. 3, July 1921.

"Editors Paying Less for Features as Syndicate Bill Grows." *Editor & Publisher,* Jan. 19, 1929.

"In Interview Hearst Speaks Plainly of Policies of His Organization." *Editor & Publisher,* June 21, 1924.

Ivey, Jim. "When Comics Wore Toppers." *Nemo* #18, April 1986.

"'Kid' Comics Growing Up, Survey Shows." *Editor & Publisher,* May 19, 1928.

Robb, Arthur T. "30 Group Ownerships Control 150 U.S. Dailies." *Editor & Publisher,* Feb. 16, 1924.

Roche, John. F. "Stock Crash Made Circulations Soar." *Editor & Publisher,* Nov. 2, 1929.

Schoenfeld, Amram. "The Laugh Industry." *The Saturday Evening Post,* Feb. 1, 1930.

Smith, Steven. "The Critic That Walked by Himself" (Gilbert Seldes). *Hogan's Alley* #6, winter 1999.

Williams, Frank H. "Studying Daily Newspaper Comics Will Help Ad Writers." *Editor & Publisher,* March 12, 1921.

Syndicates: "Concentration Trend in Syndicate Field." *Editor & Publisher,* Jan. 15, 1927.

"Editors Hotly Discuss Syndicate Methods." *Editor & Publisher,* May 3, 1924.

Schuyler, Philip. "1927 Sees Decrease in Number of Syndicates." *Editor & Publisher,* Aug. 27, 1927.

"Syndicate Men Declare Editors Are Responsible for Many Abuses in Syndicate Material." *Editor & Publisher,* Jan. 24, 1925.

Radio: Hearst, William Randolph. "Radio No Menace to Press, Says Hearst." *Editor & Publisher,* April 18, 1931.

Ormsbee, Thomas H. "Newspapers Capitalize Radio Craze in Manifold Ways." *Editor & Publisher,* April 22, 1922.

Pew, Marlen. "Radio Discussed as Press Threat or Promise." *Editor & Publisher,* Feb. 9, 1924.

Schuyler, Philip. "What of Newspapers in This Radio Age?" *Editor & Publisher,* April 23, 1927.

Advertising: "Briggs and Fox Agree to Quit Ads." *Editor & Publisher,* March 3, 1928.

Franklin, Hammond Edward. "Old Gold Using 1180 Newspapers." *Editor & Publisher,* June 8, 1930.

Schuyler, Philip. "Celebrities Keen for Advertising Copy Work." *Editor & Publisher,* Oct. 1, 1927.

Adventure strips: Blackbeard, Bill. "Easy Does It: The Gentle Introduction of Adventure into the Comics." Introduction to *The Complete Wash Tubbs & Captain Easy.* Vol. 5, *1930–1931.* New York: NBM, 1988.

Goulart, Ron. "George Storm, Pioneer of the Adventure Strip." *Nemo* #4, December 1983.

———. "To Be Continued: The Rise and Spread of Humorous Continuity Strips." In *What's So Funny? The Humor Comic Strip in America.* Salina, Kan.: Salina Art Center, 1998.

Harvey, Robert C. "The Adventure Strip Arrives . . . with Ruffles and Flourishes." *Cartoonist PROfiles* #107, September 1995.

Captain Patterson: Gilmore, Lucille Brian. "Medill's Grandsons Build on Great Tradition." *Editor & Publisher,* April 26, 1924.

Harvey, Robert C. "The Captain and the Comics." *Inks,* vol. 2, no. 3, November 1995.

Perry, John W. "N.Y. News, Now 15, Holds Grip on Masses." *Editor & Publisher,* June 30, 1934.

Schneider, Walter E. "Fabulous Rise of N.Y. Daily News Due to Capt. Patterson's Genius." *Editor & Publisher,* June 24, 1939.

Cartoonists: "All in a Day's Work" (profile series). *Editor & Publisher,* 1924: Walter Berndt, July 26; Roy Crane, Sept. 13; Percy Crosby, June 7; T. A. Dorgan, March 15; Carl Ed, Nov. 1; Milt Gross, April 26; Ethel Hays, Dec. 4; A. E. Hayward, Dec. 6; John Held Jr., Oct. 25; Charles W. Kahles, Nov. 15; Ken Kling, July 12; Frederick B. Opper, March 22; H. T. Webster, May 3; Garr Williams, March 29; J. R. Williams, Dec. 13.

Beatty, Jerome. "Interpreter of the Timid Soul" (H. T. Webster). *Reader's Digest,* April 1938.

"Bungles Bopped" (Harry Tuthill). *Time,* June 11, 1945.

Campbell, Gordon. "J.R. Williams." *Cartoonist PROfiles* #56, December 1982.

————. "Believe It or Not." *Cartoonist PROfiles* #60, December 1983.

"Clare Briggs, Cartoon Genius, Dies at 54." *Editor & Publisher,* Jan. 11, 1930.

Clark, Neil M. "Sidney Smith and His 'Gumps.'" *American Magazine,* March 1923.

Davis, Elrick. "Yes! They're from Cleveland" (J. R. Williams). *Cleveland Press,* June 5, 1935.

Erwin, Ray. "Walter Berndt Was a 'Smitty' Himself." *Editor & Publisher,* Feb. 8, 1964.

Goulart, Ron. "The Life and Times of Bunker Hill, Jr." *Nemo* #3, October 1983.

Griffith, Bill. "W.E. Hill: An Appreciation." *The Comics Journal* (special edition), summer 2002.

Heintjes, Tom. "Puttin' on the Ritz: Larry Whittington's Fritzi Ritz." *Hogan's Alley* #7, winter 2000.

Howard, Clive. "The Magnificent Roughneck" (Frank Willard). *The Saturday Evening Post,* Aug. 9, 1947.

Hurd, Jud. "The Bungle Family." *Cartoonist PROfiles* #34, June 1977.

Johnston, William. "At School Webster Ranked Lowest in His Class in Drawing." *Editor & Publisher,* March 3, 1923.

Kelly, Frank K. "America's No. 1 Suburbanite" (Gluyas Williams). *Better Homes and Gardens,* November 1947.

Knoll, Erwin. "30 Years with 'Moon'—Willard Still Has D.T.'s." *Editor & Publisher,* June 27, 1953.

Maeder, Jay. "1/8 Sure Thing—Joe and Asbestos." *New York Daily News,* May 29, 2003.

Marschall, Richard. "Gluyas Williams." *Nemo* #3, October 1983.

————. "Hairbreadth Harry Returns to Earth." *Nemo* #16, December 1985.

————. "The Bee's Knees; the Cat's Pajamas—John Held's Flapper Strips." *Nemo* #22, October 1986.

Perry, John W. "Forget the Average Reader—Webster." *Editor & Publisher,* Nov. 2, 1929.

————. "Fox Longs for Old Newspaper Days." *Editor & Publisher,* Nov. 9, 1929.

Pew, Marlen E. "Carl Ed Ends 20 Years as 'Harold Teen' Artist." *Editor & Publisher,* Jan. 21, 1939.

Phelps, Donald. "The Panel Art of J.R. Williams." *Nemo* #3, October 1983.

————. "The Bungle Family's Little Glories of Inanity." *Nemo* #5, February 1984.

————. "Boarding House Days and Arabian Nights." *Nemo* #13, July 1985.

————. "The Tenants of Moonshine." *Nemo* #14, August 1985.

Pritchett, Richard. "The Inimitable Gluyas Williams." *Yankee,* February 1976.

Rath, Jay. "Dwig—Pen-and-Ink Poet." *Nemo* #11, May 1985.

Ripley, Robert. "There Ain't No Such Animal." *The Saturday Evening Post,* Feb. 6, 1932.

Frank King: Brandenburg, George A. "King's Characters Are Now in 3rd Generation." *Editor & Publisher,* Dec. 22, 1945.

Johnson, Mark. "Frank King's Make-Believe World: The Pre-Gasoline Era." *Nemo* #12, June 1985.

King, Frank. "Home Life in the Comics." *Art Instruction Inc.,* 1959. Reprinted in *Drawn Quarterly* #3, May 2000.

"King of the Comics Strips." *Modern Maturity,* December/January 1968.

Marschall, Richard. "Gasoline Alley's Flights of Fantasy." *Nemo* #29, February 1989.

Monchak, Stephen J. "Frank King's 'Skeezix' Marks 20th Anniversary." *Editor & Publisher,* Feb. 8, 1941.

Pew, Marlen. "Readers Congratulate Author on Skeezix' Rise." *Editor & Publisher,* Sept. 24, 1938.

Phelps, Donald. "The Boys of Winter." *Hogan's Alley* #1, autumn 1994.

Cliff Sterrett: Groth, Gary. "The Comic Genius of Cliff Sterrett." *Nemo* #1, June 1983.

Karfiol, Bernard. "Polly as 'Higher' Art!" *Circulation,* vol. 5, no. 25, July 1926.

Marschall, Richard. "The Genius of Cliff Sterrett and Polly and Her Pals." Introduction to *The Complete Polly and Her Pals.* Vol. 1. Abington, Pa.: Remco Worldservice Books, 1990.

Spiegelman, Art. "Polyphonic Polly: Hot and Sweet." Introduction to *The Complete Polly and Her Pals.* Vol. 1. Abington, Pa.: Remco Worldservice Books, 1990.

Billy DeBeck: "Barney Google Man." *Newsweek,* Nov. 23, 1942.

"Barney Google's Birthday." *Newsweek,* Oct. 14, 1940.

DeBeck, Billy. "Open the Golden Gate! Spark Plug is Coming!" *Circulation,* vol. 5, no. 25, July 1926.

"DeBeck Dies." *Time,* Nov. 23, 1942.

Goulart, Ron. "Barney Google": Meet the Man Who Gave Us Spark Plug, Snuffy Smith and Lots of Laughs." *ComicScene* #4, 1988.

Monchak, Stephen J. "Billy DeBeck Marks 20th Year with King." *Editor & Publisher,* Oct. 7, 1939.

Schoenfeld, Amram. "A Portrait in Zowie." *Esquire,* November 1935.

Harold Gray: Barker, Kenneth. "The Life and Love, Friends and Foes, Trials and Triumphs of Little Orphan Annie." *Nemo* #8, August 1984.

Blackbeard, Bill. "Hot Alligator! How Little Orphan Annie Beat the Pants off the Boys at Strip Dice and MCed the First Comic Strip." *The Comics Journal* (special edition), summer 2002.

Marschall, Richard. "The Master." *Nemo* #8, August 1984.

McCracken, Harry. "Annie's Real 'Daddy.'" *Nemo* #8, August 1984.

Phelps, Donald. "Who's That Little Chatterbox?" *Nemo* #8, August 1984.

"There Are Tears and Laughter in this New Chicago Tribune Comic Strip" (advertisement). *Editor & Publisher,* Dec. 20, 1924.

Roy Crane: Crane, Roy. "Roy Crane and Buz Sawyer." *Cartoonist PROfiles* #3, September 1969.

Harvey, Robert C. "A Flourish of Trumpets: Roy Crane and the Adventure Strip." *The Comics Journal* #157, March 1993.

Hurd, Jud. "Roy Crane's Scrapbook." *Cartoonist PROfiles* #5, March 1970; #6, June 1970; #9; March 1971; #13, March 1972.

THE THIRTIES

Comics business (articles in chronological order): "United Feature Syndicate Buys Metropolitan Service from Elser." *Editor & Publisher,* March 15, 1930.

Perry, John P. "Syndicate Mergers an Aid to Dailies." *Editor & Publisher,* April 5, 1930.

"World Feature Service Taken Over by United Feature Syndicate." *Editor & Publisher,* April 11, 1930.

McAdam, Charles V. "Plop! Wham! Zowie!" *College Humor,* February 1931.

Roche, John F. "Syndicate Men Discuss Feature Trend." *Editor & Publisher,* Sept. 3, 1932.

"The Funny Papers." *Fortune,* April 1933.

Robb, Arthur. "Newspaper Groups Doubled in Decade." *Editor & Publisher,* Feb. 17, 1934.

"Comic Weekly Goes to Tabloid Size." *Editor & Publisher,* Dec. 29, 1934.

"Comic Weekly Back to Full Size." *Editor & Publisher,* May 11, 1935.

Bassett, Warren L. "Hearst Wealth Placed at $220,000,000." *Editor & Publisher,* Sept. 28, 1935.

"Syndicates Now in Their Heyday." *Editor & Publisher,* Sept. 26, 1936.

"Funny Strips: Cartoon-Drawing Is Big Business; Effects on Children Debated." *The Literary Digest,* Dec. 12, 1936.

Brown, Robert U. "Syndicate Editors Tell How to Find Comic Strip Popularity." *Editor & Publisher,* Feb. 20, 1937.

Bassett, Warren L. "W.R. Hearst Celebrates his 50th Year as a Newspaper Publisher." *Editor & Publisher,* March 6, 1937.

Monchak, Stephen J. "Readers Expected to Turn to Comic Humor for War Relief." *Editor & Publisher,* Sept. 30, 1939.

Surveys and advertising (articles in chronological order): Mann, Robert S. "Comic Section Advertising Starts: General Foods Using 49 Papers." *Editor & Publisher,* May 16, 1931.

Brandenburg, George A. "Research Shows Reader Preference." *Editor & Publisher,* Jan. 16, 1932.

"To Sell Space in 30 Comic Sections." *Editor & Publisher,* May 7, 1932.

"11 Dailies Unite to Sell Comic Space." *Editor & Publisher,* June 4, 1932.

Clemow, Bice. "Four-Color Comic Advertising Shows Amazing Growth Since 1931." *Editor & Publisher,* Feb. 9, 1935.

"Big Demand for Sunday Feature Copy" and "Sunday Sections Lead Linage Upturn." *Editor & Publisher,* March 28, 1936.

Brown, Robert U. "Comic Art for Advertisers; 'Swing Pictures' Make Debut." *Editor & Publisher,* Feb. 27, 1937.

Mann, Robert S. "Comic, Roto, Color, and Magazines Bring Linage Worth $41,000,000." *Editor & Publisher,* March 27, 1937.

Heintjes, Tom. "Funny Business." *Hogan's Alley #10,* summer 2002.

Longevity (articles in chronological order): "Sidney Smith Dies in Auto Crash." *Editor & Publisher,* Oct. 26, 1935.

"Edson Doing The Gumps." *Editor & Publisher,* Dec. 21, 1935.

Brown, Robert U. "Gus Edson Completing Successful Year as Author of 'The Gumps.'" *Editor & Publisher,* Nov. 21, 1936.

———. "31 Comics Among 62 Features Surviving Before 1920." *Editor & Publisher,* March 19, 1938.

"Segar, Creator of Popeye, Dies on Coast at 43." *Editor & Publisher,* Oct. 22, 1938.

Pew, Marlen. "Filling Sid Smith's Shoes Toughest Job, Says Edson." *Editor & Publisher,* Oct. 29, 1938.

Cartoonists: Andrae, Tom. "The Mouse's Other Master: Floyd Gottfredson's 45 Years With Mickey." *Nemo #6,* April 1984.

Andrae, Tom, Geoffry Blum, and Gary Coddington. "Of Superman and Kids with Dreams. A Rare Interview with the Creators of Superman: Jerry Siegel and Joe Shuster." *Nemo #2,* August 1983.

Andriola, Alfred. "Charlie Chan: A Mystery Strip." Sales brochure. McNaught Syndicate, 1938.

Beatty, Albert R. "Edwina and Her Dogs." *The American Kennel Gazette,* Dec. 1, 1937.

Becattini, Alberto. "A Concise History of Disney Newspaper Strips." *Comic Book Marketplace #95,* October 2002.

Berchtold, William E. "Men of Comics." *New Outlook,* May 1935.

Brown, Robert U. "Ham Fisher Signs Big Contract." *Editor & Publisher,* April 17, 1937.

———. "Carl Anderson at 73 Hits Syndicate Heights." *Editor & Publisher,* March 12, 1938.

Bumbry, Bob. "Joe Palooka Perennial Champ." *Look,* Oct. 14, 1947.

Calkins, Dick. "That Prophetable Guy, Buck Rogers." *Liberty,* 1945.

Coma, Javier. "The Costumes of Tim Tyler, The Disguises of Lyman Young." *Nemo #15,* October 1985.

Cowley, Malcolm. "The Most of John Held, Jr." *The New York Times Book Review,* Nov. 19, 1972.

Crouch, Bill. "Noel Sickles." *Cartoonist PROfiles #29,* March 1976.

Dale, Bert. "Meet Dick Calkins." *The Open Road,* December 1947.

———. "Meet Bill Holman." *The Open Road,* October 1948.

Dunn, Bob. "The Little King by Otto Soglow." *Cartoonist PROfiles #26,* June 1975.

Feiffer, Jules. "Jerry Siegel: The Minsk Theory of Krypton." *The New York Times Magazine,* Dec. 29, 1996.

"Foo!" (Bill Holman). *Newsweek,* May 22, 1961.

Hamlin, Vincent. "The Man Who Walked with Dinosaurs." *Inks,* vol. 3, no. 2, May 1996.

Harvey, Robert C. "Joe Palooka and the Most Famous Food Fight of the Funnies." *The Comics Journal #168,* May 1994.

Hay, Clayton. "Notary Sojac" (Bill Holman). *Seattle Times,* Dec. 26, 1948.

"Henry and Philbert" (Carl Anderson). *Time,* Feb. 11, 1935.

Hurd, Jud. "Lee Falk." *Cartoonist PROfiles #27,* September 1975.

Kaler, Dave. "Percy Leo Crosby." *Cartoonist PROfiles #34,* June 1977.

Kobler, John. "Up, Up and Awa-a-y! The Rise of Superman Inc." *The Saturday Evening Post,* June 21, 1941.

Marschall, Richard. "When Knights Were Bold, But More So Damsels" (Oaky Doaks). *Nemo #20,* July 1986.

———. "Joe Palooka Retains the Title." *Nemo #22,* October 1986.

———. "Ming Foo: Threats and Thrills, Fantasy and Fortune Cookies." *Nemo #29,* February 1989.

Marschall, Richard, and Bill Janocha. "Edwina at 93." *Nemo #25,* April 1987.

Monchak, Stephen J. "Zack Mosley Goes Up to Get Lowdown on Flying." *Editor & Publisher,* June 22, 1940.

Mosley, Zack. "Smilin' Jack and Zack." *AOPA Pilot,* December 1964.

"Nancy, Sluggo and Ernie." *Newsweek,* June 28, 1948.

Neal, Jim. "Zack Mosley Dies, Creator of 'Smilin' Jack.'" *Comic Buyer's Guide #1053,* Jan. 21, 1994.

Pew, Marlen. "Ernie Bushmiller Changes Name of Strip to 'Nancy.'" *Editor & Publisher,* June 11, 1938.

———. "FDR 'Saves' Joe Palooka from Foreign Legion." *Editor & Publisher,* July 2, 1938.

———. "NEA's 'Alley Oop' to Have Modern Locale." *Editor & Publisher,* April 1, 1939.

Phelps, Donald. "Wild Blue Yonder" (Zack Mosley). *Nemo #7,* June 1984.

———. "Holman's Legacy to Popular Humor." *The Comics Journal* (special edition), winter 2002.

Philips, McCandlish. "Returning from the 25th Century . . . Buck Rogers." *New York Times,* Dec. 2, 1969.

Poling, James. "Ryder of the Comic Page." *Collier's,* Aug. 14, 1948.

Powers, Grant. "Themselves All Over." *The American Legion Magazine,* July 1939.

Rath, Jay. "Silents Please! The Unspeakable Greatness of Carl Anderson's 'Henry.'" *Nemo #26,* September 1987.

Shutt, Craig. "Man of Strips" (Superman). *Hogan's Alley #5,* spring 1998.

Singer, Charles. "Joe Palooka: Cartoon Champon." *Ring, The Bible of Boxing,* December 1983.

Sprague, Andy. "Remembering Zack Mosley." *Cartoonist PROfiles #110,* June 1996.

Adventure strips: Andriola, Alfred. "The Story Strips." *Cartoonist PROfiles #14,* June 1972, and #15, September 1972.

Brown, Robert U. "Artists Ponder What's Happened to Humor in Comics." *Editor & Publisher,* March 13, 1937.

———. "Humor Tops Adventure Cartoons in Fortune's Popularity Poll." *Editor & Publisher,* March 27, 1937.

Goulart, Ron. "Leaping Tall Buildings, Falling on Faces." *Nemo #2,* August 1983.

Marschall, Richard. "The Class of '34." *Hogan's Alley #1,* autumn 1994.

Monchak, Stephen J. "Fox Sees Adventure Comics in Ascendancy." *Editor & Publisher,* Oct. 7, 1939.

Pew, Marlen. "Protest Against 'Crime Comics.'" *Editor & Publisher,* July 4, 1936.

Hal Foster: "Classic Episodes in Hal Foster's Prince Valiant." Exhibition catalog. Greenwich, Conn.: Museum of Cartoon Art, June 1975.

Crouch, Bill. "Prince Valiant by Hal Foster" (interview). *Cartoonist PROfiles #22,* June 1974.

Cuccolini, Guilio C. "Howard Pyle and the Roots of the Artistry of Hal Foster." *Hogan's Alley #5,* spring 1998.

Harvey, Robert C. "Foster's Tarzan and How it Grew." *The Comics Journal #158,* April 1993.

———. "Fostering the Adventure Strip." *Comic Book Marketplace #89,* March 2002.

Kane, Brian M. "The Making of Hal Foster, Prince of Illustrators—Father of the Adventure Strip." *Comic Book Marketplace #89,* March 2002.

Maley, Don. "Hal Foster Both Lives and Loves the Days of Camelot." *Editor & Publisher,* Jan. 25, 1969.

Monchak, Stephen J. "A Two-Fisted Artist Draws 'Prince Valiant.'" *Editor & Publisher,* April 8, 1939.

"'Prince Valiant' Hero for 25 Years." *Editor & Publisher,* Feb. 3, 1962.

Saba, Arn. "Prince Harold." *Canadian Weekend,* 1979.

———. "Drawing on History: Hal Foster's Last Interview." *The Comics Journal #102,* September 1985.

Schreiber, Fred. "The Master, Hal Foster." *Nemo* #9, October 1984.

Alex Raymond: Cuthbert, Raymond A. "Alex Raymond's Flash Gordon: The Comic Strip as Epic Fantasy." *Comic Book Marketplace* #93, August 2002.

Harvey, Robert C. "Raymond and the Right Stuff." *Comic Book Marketplace* #93, August 2002.

Monchak, Stephen J. "Credit Jules Verne for Raymond's 'Flash Gordon.'" *Editor & Publisher*, Aug. 10, 1940.

Winiewicz, Dave. "Flash Gordon: 1935 to 1936." *Comic Book Marketplace* #93, August 2002.

Milton Caniff: Bainbridge, John. "Significant Sig and the Funnies." *The New Yorker*, Jan. 8, 1944.

Caniff, Milton. "There Had to Be a Choice: 'Stick to Your Ink Pots Kid,' Said the Sage of Scioto." *The Quill*, September 1937.

———. "How to Be a Comic Artist." In *Milton Caniff: Rembrandt of the Comic Strip*. Philadelphia: David McKay, 1946.

———. "Detour Guide for an Armchair Marco Polo." King Features Syndicate publication, 1947.

"Dumas from Ohio." *Newsweek*, April 24, 1950.

Harvey, Robert C. "Of Miscellany and Milt." *The Comics Journal* #128, April 1989.

———. "Spotlighting the Art of Milton Caniff" (special issue). *Comic Book Marketplace* #96, November 2002.

Horak, Carl J. "The 60-Year Impact of 'Terry and the Pirates.'" *Comics Buyer's Guide* #1092, Oct. 21, 1994.

Marschall, Richard. "Of Stout Fellahs and Real Thrills: Milton Caniff's Early Adventure Strip, 'Dickie Dare.'" *Nemo* #15, October 1985.

Saba, Arn. "Milton Caniff: An Interview with One of the Masters of Comic Art." *The Comics Journal* #108, May 1986.

"A Salute to Milton Caniff on the Occasion of the 10th Anniversary of 'Terry and the Pirates.'" *The Magazine of Sigma Chi*, February/March 1945.

Small, Collie. "Strip Teaser in Black and White." *The Saturday Evening Post*, Aug. 10, 1946.

Staunton, Helen M. "Steve Canyon—Milton Caniff Unveils His New Strip." *Editor & Publisher*, Nov. 23, 1946.

Chester Gould: Bainbridge, John. "Chester Gould." *Life*, Aug. 14, 1944.

Brandenburg, George A. "Gould Starts 15th Year with Dick Tracy," *Editor & Publisher*, Oct. 6, 1945.

Collins, Max Allen. "Detective and Determination, Comics and Cadillacs: The Chester Gould Interview." *Nemo* #17, February 1986.

DeHaven, Tom. "Bud, Which Way to the Noble Hotel?" *Nemo* #17, February 1986.

"Dick Tracy: The Art of Chester Gould." Exhibition catalog. Port Chester, N.Y.: Museum of Cartoon Art, October 1978.

"Dick Tracy's Creator a Mild Man; Trims Hedges and Plays Violin." *Editor & Publisher*, July 7, 1934.

Phelps, Donald. "Flat Foot Floogie." *Nemo* #17, February 1986.

Walker, Brian. "Good vs. Evil in Black and White." Dick Tracy exhibition catalog. Rye Brook, N.Y.: Museum of Cartoon Art, November 1990.

Yoder, Robert M. "Dick Tracy's Boss." *The Saturday Evening Post*, Dec. 17, 1949.

E. C. Segar: Blackbeard, Bill. "Enter Popeye: The Sailor Who Saved a Sinking Ship." Introduction to *Thimble Theatre Introducing Popeye*. Westport, Conn.: Hyperion Press, 1977.

———. "E.C. Segar's Knockouts of 1925 (and Low Blows Before and After): The Unknown Thimble Theatre Period." *Nemo* #3, October 1983.

Pew, Marlen. "Segar Recovers, Renews King Features Contract." *Editor & Publisher*, June 4, 1938.

Chic Young: Alexander, Jack. "The Dagwood and Blondie Man." *The Saturday Evening Post*, April 10, 1948.

Boyesil, Ned. "Not So Dumb—Dumb Dora." *Circulation*, vol. 5, no. 24, May 1926.

Bryan, J. "His Girl Blondie." *Life*, Aug. 15, 1942.

Pew, Marlen E. "'Chic' Young Completes 8 Years with King." *Editor & Publisher*, Oct. 1, 1938.

Van Gelder, Lawrence. "Chic Young, Creator of 'Blondie,' Dead." *New York Times*, March 16, 1973.

Al Capp: Caplin, Elliott. "We Called Him Alfred . . ." *Cartoonist PROfiles* #48, December 1980.

Capp, Al. "Innocents in Peril." *The World of Li'l Abner*. New York: Ballantine Books, 1952.

———. "Why I Let Abner Marry." *Life*, March 31, 1952.

———. "My Life as an Immortal Myth." *Life*, April 30, 1965.

"Die Monstersinger." *Time*, Nov. 6, 1950.

"Li'l Abner's Mad Capp." *Newsweek*, Nov. 24, 1947.

Maloney, Russell. "Li'l Abner's Capp." *Life*, June 24, 1946.

Marschall, Richard. "Saying Something About the Status Quo" (Capp's last interview). *Nemo* #18, April 1986.

Pew, Marlen E. "Capp Completes 5 Years with United Features." *Editor & Publisher*, Aug. 6, 1938.

"Playboy Interview: Al Capp." *Playboy*, December 1966.

Safire, William. "Gasp! Sob! Li'l Abner is No More." *New York Times*, Nov. 6, 1977.

Schreiner, Dave. "The Storyteller." Introduction to *Li'l Abner*. vol. 1. Princeton, Wis.: Kitchen Sink Press, 1988.

Shenker, Israel. "Al Capp, Harbinger of the Age of Irreverence, Gives Up Cartoons but Not Irascibility." *New York Times*, Nov. 11, 1977.

———. "Al Capp, Creator of 'Li'l Abner,' Is Dead at 70." *New York Times*, Nov. 7, 1979.

Steinbeck, John. Introduction to *The World of Li'l Abner*. New York: Ballantine Books, 1952.

THE FORTIES

Comics go to war: Black, John. "'Yank,' New Army Paper, Off to Flying Start." *Editor & Publisher*, June 20, 1942.

Caniff, Milton. "Comic Strips at War." *Vogue*, July 15, 1943.

———. "The Comics." In *While You Were Gone: A Report on Wartime Life in the United States*. New York: Simon and Schuster, 1946.

Harvey, Robert C. "Cartoonists at War." *The Comics Journal* #118, December 1987.

———. "Chiaroscuro Kipling and a Bit of Lace." *The Comics Journal* #119, January 1988.

Monchak, S. J. "Popeye Assumes Navy Recruiting Assignment." *Editor & Publisher*, July 26, 1941.

———. "Syndicates Cooperating in Defense Bond Sales." *Editor & Publisher*, Jan. 31, 1942.

———. "Scorchy Smith Creator Dead." *Editor & Publisher*, Feb. 7, 1942.

———. "'Junior Commando' Idea Appeals to U.S. Youth." *Editor & Publisher*, Aug. 21, 1942.

———. "Cartoonists Important Factor in Keeping Nation's Morale." *Editor & Publisher*, Sept. 19, 1942.

———. "Sub Hunting, Drawing Are Mosley's Jobs Now." *Editor & Publisher*, April 3, 1943.

Rhode, Michael. "She May *Look* Clean But . . ." *Hogan's Alley* #8, fall 2000.

Staunton, Helen. "New Comics Furnished to GI Papers Overseas." *Editor & Publisher*, July 8, 1944.

Vaughn, Don. "War-Toons." *The Retired Officer Magazine*, June 1998.

Walker, Jerry. "Comic Artists Cheer Veterans by Chalk Talks." *Editor & Publisher*, Oct. 28, 1944.

GI cartoonists: Campbell, Gordon. "Sad Sack." *Cartoonist PROfiles* #69, March 1986.

Freeman, William M. "George Baker, Creator of Sad Sack Cartoon, Is Dead." *New York Times*, May 9, 1975.

Marschall, Richard. "The World War II Cartoonist Corps." *Nemo* #12, June 1985.

Monchak, Stephen J. "Caniff Drawing Again for Army Papers." *Editor & Publisher,* Jan. 30, 1943.

Rovner, Samuel. "United Signs Mauldin, Army Cartoonist." *Editor & Publisher,* April 1, 1944.

Shutt, Craig. "Sad Sack's Two Commanding Officers." *Hogan's Alley* #7, winter 2000.

Staunton, Helen M. "Mauldin's GIs Return Minus the Whiskers." *Editor & Publisher,* June 16, 1945.

Sweeney, Jim. "World War II Show Includes Mauldin, Caniff, Combat Artists." *The Comics Journal* #170, August 1994.

"Where Are the Cartoonists of WWII?" *American Legion Magazine,* 1951.

Comics business: Bassett, Warren L. "Dailies Are Warned Against Hoarding" (paper shortages). *Editor & Publisher,* June 17, 1941.

Harvey, R. C. "Cushlamochree! Their Creators Abandoned Them!" *Comic Buyer's Guide* #1225, May 9, 1997.

Monchak, Stephen J. "War Closing European Markets to Syndicates." *Editor & Publisher,* May 11, 1940.

———. "Woman Executive Holds Sway Over Ace Syndicate Artists" (Mollie Slott). *Editor & Publisher,* Nov. 2, 1940.

———. "Selling King Abroad Poses Many Problems." *Editor & Publisher,* Nov. 25, 1940.

———. "Syndicates Are Big Business, With 35 Million in Annual Sales." *Editor & Publisher,* Sept. 20, 1941.

———. "Syndicates Are Feeling Effects of War Economy." *Editor & Publisher,* Feb. 15, 1942.

———. "Should Color Comics Pages Be Smaller?" *Editor & Publisher,* May 23, 1942.

———. "Strip Standardization Proposed for Duration." *Editor & Publisher,* Jan. 16, 1943.

Rovner, Samuel. "Syndicate Heads See Good Volume in '44." *Editor & Publisher,* Feb. 5, 1944.

Staunton, Helen M. "Syndicate Heads See Boom Coming in Field." *Editor & Publisher,* Jan. 27, 1945.

———. "Will Comic Strips Return to Former Size?" *Editor & Publisher,* Feb. 10, 1945.

———. "Syndicates Strengthen Europe Bridgehead." *Editor & Publisher,* June 2, 1945.

———. "Comics Reconvert Too, with Jap Surrender." *Editor & Publisher,* Aug. 18, 1945.

———. "Syndicate War Years Foreshadow Expansion." *Editor & Publisher,* Oct. 6, 1945.

Comic books: Monchak, Stephen J. "Format Change Won't Help Comics, Fox Says." *Editor & Publisher,* May 18, 1940.

———. "Syndicates Study New Comic Book Technique." *Editor & Publisher,* June 1, 1940.

———. "R&T Syndicate Offers 16-Page Color Comic Book." *Editor & Publisher,* June 8, 1940.

Comics events: Maeder, Jay. "Special Delivery: LaGuardia Reads the Funnies, July 1945." *New York Daily News,* Aug. 31, 2000.

Monchak, Stephen J. "400,000 Names Submitted for Blondie's Baby." *Editor & Publisher,* May 10, 1941.

———. "Of Caniff's Raven Sherman." *Editor & Publisher,* Oct. 18, 1941.

———. "Art Groups Recognize The 'Funnies' as Art." *Editor & Publisher,* April 18, 1942.

Staunton, Helen M. "Women Comic Artists Entertained by E&P." *Editor & Publisher,* Nov. 10, 1945.

Cartoonists: Coker, Paul. "Gus Arriola Interview." *Cartoonist PROfiles* #16, December 1972.

Feldman, Linda. "Starr Power." *Los Angeles Times,* April 26, 1999.

Frank, Ann. "Starr-Crossed: Between the Lines with Dale Messick." *Fort Lauderdale News/Sun-Sentinel,* Nov. 25, 1979.

Hurd, Jud. "Dale Messick Interview." *Cartoonist PROfiles* #16, December 1972.

Monchak, Stephen J. "United's New Strip Has Mexican Locale" (Gordo). *Editor & Publisher,* Nov. 8, 1941.

———. "Arriola Enlists, United's 'Gordo' Strip Suspended." *Editor & Publisher,* Oct. 3, 1942.

Sujka, Sharon. "Dale Messick Hasn't Missed a Daily 'Brenda Starr' Deadline." *Editor & Publisher,* Nov. 23, 1974.

Will Eisner: Eisner, Will. "The Spirit: How It Came To Be." Preface to *Will Eisner's The Spirit Archives.* Vol. 1. New York: DC Comics, 2000.

Harvey, Robert C. "The Consummate Comic Book." Introduction to *Will Eisner's The Spirit Archives.* Vol. 1. New York: DC Comics, 2000.

Moore, Alan. "The Pioneering Spirit." Foreword to *Will Eisner's The Spirit Archives.* Vol. 1. New York: DC Comics, 2000.

Shutt, Craig. "Eisner's Thwarted Dreams." *Hogan's Alley* #11, 2003.

BOOKS

GENERAL HISTORIES

Appel, John J. *Cartoons and Ethnicity.* Columbus: Ohio State University Libraries, 1992.

Becker, Stephen. *Comic Art in America.* New York: Simon and Schuster, 1959.

Berger, Arthur Asa. *The Comic-Stripped American.* Baltimore: Penguin Books, 1973.

Blackbeard, Bill. *The Yellow Kid.* Northampton, Mass: Kitchen Sink Press, 1995.

Blackbeard, Bill, and Dale Crain, eds. *The Comic Strip Century.* 2 vols. Englewood Cliffs, N.J.: O.G. Publishing Corp., 1995.

Blackbeard, Bill, and Martin Williams, eds. *The Smithsonian Collection of Newspaper Comics.* Washington, D.C.: Smithsonian Institution Press and Harry N. Abrams, 1977.

Brian, Denis. *Pulitzer: A Life.* New York: John Wiley & Sons, 2001.

Briggs, Clare. *How to Draw Cartoons.* New York: Harper & Brothers, 1926.

Carlin, John, and Sheena Wagstaff. *The Comic Art Show: Cartoons and Painting in Popular Culture.* New York: Whitney Museum of American Art, 1983.

Carrier, David. *The Aesthetics of Comics.* University Park, Pa.: Pennsylvania State University Press, 2000.

Castelli, Alfredo. *Waiting for the Yellow Kid.* Lucca, Italy: Museo Italiano del Fumetto, 2003.

Caswell, Lucy. *See You in the Funny Papers.* Columbus: Ohio State University Libraries, 1995.

———. *Historic Virtuoso Cartoonists.* Columbus: Ohio State University Libraries, 2001.

Couperie, Pierre, and Maurice Horn. *A History of the Comic Strip.* New York: Crown Publishers, 1968.

Crafton, Donald. *Before Mickey—The Animated Film: 1898–1928.* Chicago: University of Chicago Press, 1993.

Craven, Thomas. *Cartoon Cavalcade.* New York: Simon and Schuster, 1943.

Dierick, Charles, and Pascal Lefevre, eds. *Forging a New Medium: The Comic Strip in the Nineteenth Century.* Brussels: VUB University Press, 1998.

Duin, Steve, and Mike Richardson. *Comics Between the Panels.* Milwaukie, Ore.: Dark Horse Comics, 1998.

Ellinport, Jeffrey M. *Collecting Original Comic Strip Art.* Norfolk, Va.: Antique Trader Books, 1999.

Emery, Michael, Edwin Emery, and Nancy L. Roberts. *The Press in America.* Boston: Allyn and Bacon, 2000.

Gordon, Ian. *Comic Strips and Consumer Culture.* Washington, D.C.: Smithsonian Institution Press, 1998.

Goulart, Ron. *The Adventurous Decade.* New Rochelle, N.Y.: Arlington House, 1975.

———. *The Encyclopedia of American Comics.* New York: Facts On File, 1990.

———. *The Funnies: 100 Years of American Comic Strips.* Holbrook, Mass.: Adams Publishing, 1995.

Gowans, Alan. *The Unchanging Arts.* Philadelphia: Lippincott, 1971.

Hardy, Charles, and Gail F. Storm, eds. *Ethnic Images in the Comics.* Philadelphia: The Balch Institute for Ethnic Studies, 1986.

Harvey, Robert C. *The Art of the Funnies.* Jackson, Miss.: University Press of Mississippi, 1994.

———. *Children of the Yellow Kid.* Seattle: Frye Art Museum, 1998.

———. *A Gallery of Rogues: Cartoonists' Self-Caricatures.* Columbus: Ohio State University Cartoon Research Library, 1998.

———. *The Genius of Winsor McCay.* Columbus: Ohio State University Libraries, 1998.

Hess, Stephen, and Milton Kaplan. *The Ungentlemanly Art: A History of American Political Cartoons.* New York: Macmillan, 1975.

Hollis, Daniel W. *The Media in America.* Santa Barbara, Calif.: ABC-CLIO, 1995.

Horn, Maurice, ed. *75 Years of the Comics.* Boston: Boston Book and Art, Publisher, 1971.

———. *Comics of the American West.* South Hackensack, N.J.: Stoeger Publishing, 1977.

———. *Women in the Comics.* New York: Chelsea House Publishers, 1977.

———. *Sex in the Comics.* New York: Chelsea House Publishers, 1985.

———. *100 Years of American Newspaper Comics.* New York: Gramercy Books, 1996.

———. *The World Encyclopedia of Cartoons.* Philadelphia: Chelsea House Publishers, 1999.

———. *The World Encyclopedia of Comics.* Philadelphia: Chelsea House Publishers, 1999.

Hurd, Jud. *To Cartooning: 60 Years of Magic.* Fairfield, Conn.: PROfiles Press, 1993.

Inge, M. Thomas. *Comics as Culture.* Jackson, Miss.: University Press of Mississippi, 1990.

———. *Great American Comics.* Columbus: Ohio State University Libraries and Smithsonian Institution, 1990.

———. *Anything Can Happen in a Comic Strip.* Columbus: Ohio State University Libraries, 1995.

Janocha, Bill, ed. *The National Cartoonists Society Album 1996.* New York: National Cartoonists Society, 1996.

Katz, Harry L., and Sara W. Duke. *Featuring the Funnies: One Hundred Years of the Comic Strip.* Washington, D.C.: Library of Congress, 1995.

King Features Syndicate. *Famous Artists & Writers of King Features Syndicate.* New York: King Features Syndicate, 1949.

Koenigsberg, M. *King News: An Autobiography.* Philadelphia and New York: F. A. Stokes Company, 1941.

Kunzle, David. *The History of the Comic Strip: The Nineteenth Century.* Berkeley, Calif.: University of California Press, 1990.

Lent, John A. *Comic Books and Comic Strips in the United States: An International Bibliography.* Westport, Conn.: Greenwood Press, 1994.

Lesser, Robert. *A Celebration of Comic Art and Memorabilia.* New York: Hawthorne Books, 1975.

Lupoff, Dick, and Don Thompson. *All in Color for a Dime.* Iola, Wis.: Krause Publications, 1997.

Maltin, Leonard. *Of Mice and Magic: A History of American Animated Cartoons.* New York: Plume, 1987.

———. *The Great American Broadcast.* New York: Dutton, 1997.

Marschall, Richard. *The Sunday Funnies: 1896–1950.* New York: Chelsea House Publishers, 1978.

———. *What's So Funny: The Humor Comic Strip in America.* Salina, Kan.: Salina Art Center, 1988.

———. *America's Great Comic-Strip Artists.* New York: Abbeville Press, 1989.

———. *American Comic Classics.* Washington, D.C.: U.S. Postal Service, 1995.

Matthews, E. C. *How to Draw Funny Pictures.* Chicago: Frederick J. Drake & Co., 1944.

McGivena, Leo E. *The News: The First Fifty Years of New York's Picture Newspaper.* New York: News Syndicate Co., 1969.

Mott, Frank Luther. *American Journalism: A History, 1690–1960* (3rd ed.). New York: Macmillan, 1962.

Murrell, William. *A History of American Graphic Humor (1865–1938).* New York: Macmillan, 1938.

Nasaw, David. *The Chief: The Life of William Randolph Hearst.* Boston: Houghton Mifflin, 2000.

O'Sullivan, Judith. *The Great American Comic Strip.* Boston: Little, Brown and Company, 1990.

Overstreet, Robert M. *The Official Overstreet Comic Book Price Guide* (33rd ed.). Timonium, Md.: Gemstone Publishing, 2003.

Perry, George, and Alan Aldridge. *The Penguin Book of Comics.* Middlesex, England: Penguin Books, 1971.

Phelps, Donald. *Reading the Funnies.* Seattle: Fantagraphics Books, 2001.

Reitberger, Reinhold, and Wolfgang Fuchs. *Comics: Anatomy of a Mass Medium.* Boston: Little, Brown and Company, 1971.

Robbins, Trina. *Paper Dolls from the Comics.* Forestville, Calif.: Eclipse Comics, 1987.

———. *A Century of Women Cartoonists.* Northampton, Mass.: Kitchen Sink Press, 1993.

———. *The Great Women Cartoonists.* New York: Watson-Guptill Publications, 2001.

Robbins, Trina, and Catherine Yronwode. *Women and the Comics.* Forestville, Calif.: Eclipse Books, 1985.

Robinson, Jerry. *The Comics: An Illustrated History of Comic Strip Art.* New York: G. P. Putnam's Sons, 1974.

———. *Cartoon: A Celebration of American Comic Art.* Washington, D.C.: John F. Kennedy Center for the Performing Arts, 1975.

Seldes, Gilbert. *The Seven Lively Arts.* New York: Harper and Brothers, 1924.

Sheridan, Martin. *Comics and Their Creators.* Boston: Hale, Cushman & Flint, 1942.

Strickler, Dave. *Syndicated Comic Strips and Artists 1924–1995: The Complete Index.* Cambria, Calif.: Comics Access, 1995.

Stromberg, Fredrik. *Black Images in the Comics.* Seattle: Fantagraphics Books, 2003.

Thompson, Don, and Dick Lupoff. *The Comic Book Book.* New Rochelle, N.Y.: Arlington House, 1973.

Thorndike, Chuck. *The Business of Cartooning.* New York: The House of Little Books, 1939.

Turner, Hy B. *When Giants Ruled: The Story of Park Row, New York's Great Newspaper Street.* New York: Fordham University Press, 1999.

Varnum, Robin, and Christian Gibbons, eds. *The Language of Comics: Word and Image.* Jackson, Miss.: University Press of Mississippi, 2001.

Walker, Brian. *The Sunday Funnies: 100 Years of Comics in American Life.* Bridgeport, Conn.: The Barnum Museum, 1994.

Watson, Elmo Scott. *A History of Newspaper Syndicates.* Chicago: The Publishers' Auxiliary, 1936.

Waugh, Coulton. *The Comics.* New York: Macmillan, 1947.

Wheeler, John. *I've Got News for You.* New York: E. P. Dutton, 1961.

White, David Manning, and Robert H. Abel, eds. *The Funnies: An American Idiom.* New York: The Free Press of Glencoe/Macmillan, 1963.

Whyte, Malcolm. *Great Comic Cats.* San Francisco: Pomegranate, 2001.

Wood, Art. *Great Cartoonists and Their Art.* Gretna, La.: Pelican Publishing Company, 1987.

Yoe, Craig. *Weird But True Toon Factoids.* New York: Gramercy Books, 1999.

AUTOBIOGRAPHIES, BIOGRAPHIES, AND RETROSPECTIVE ANTHOLOGIES

Barrett, Robert R. *Tarzan of the Funnies.* Holt, Mich.: Mad Kings Publishing, 2002.

Becattini, Alberto, and Antonio Vianovi. *Profili Caniff—Milton Caniff: American Stars and Strips.* Lucca, Italy: Glamour International, 2001.

———. *Profili Raymond—Alex Raymond: The Power and the Grace.* Lucca, Italy: Glamour International, 2002.

Berger, Arthur Asa. *Li'l Abner: A Study in American Satire.* Jackson, Miss.: University Press of Mississippi, 1994.

Blackbeard, Bill. *Jiggs Is Back.* Berkeley, Calif.: Celtic Book Company, 1986.

Cahn, Joseph M. *The Teenie Weenies Book: The Life and Art of William Donahey*. La Jolla, Calif.: Green Tiger Press, 1986.

Canemaker, John. *Winsor McCay: His Life and Art*. New York: Abbeville Press, 1987.

Caplin, Elliott. *Al Capp Remembered*. Bowling Green, Ohio: Bowling Green State University Popular Press, 1994.

Capp, Al. *The Best of Li'l Abner*. New York: Holt, Rinehart and Winston, 1978.

———. *My Well Balanced Life on a Wooden Leg*. Santa Barbara, Calif.: John Daniel and Company, 1991.

Davidson, Harold G. *Jimmy Swinnerton: The Artist and His Work*. New York: Hearst Books, 1985.

Grandinetti, Fred M. *Popeye: An Illustrated History of E.C. Segar's Character in Print, Radio, Television and Film Appearances, 1929–1993*. Jefferson, N.C.: McFarland & Company, 1994.

Groensteen, Thierry. *Krazy Herriman*. Angoulême, France: Musée de la Band Dessinée, 1997.

———. *Popeye: Est C'Qu'il Est Voilà Tout C'Qu'il Est!*. Angoulême, France: Musée de la Band Dessinée, 2001.

Hall, Patricia. *Johnny Gruelle: Creator of Raggedy Ann and Andy*. Gretna, La.: Pelican, 1993.

Harvey, Robert C. *Accidental Ambassador Gordo*. Jackson, Miss.: University Press of Mississippi, 2000.

Higgs, Mike. *Popeye: The 60th Anniversary Collection*. London: Hawk Books, 1989.

Kane, Brian M. *Hal Foster: Prince of Illustrators—Father of the Adventure Strip*. Lebanon, N.J.: Vanguard Productions, 2001.

Maeder, Jay. *Dick Tracy: The Official Biography*. New York: Plume, 1990.

Marschall, Richard. *Screwball Comics*. Thousand Oaks, Calif.: Fantagraphics Books, 1985.

———. *Daydreams and Nightmares: The Fantastic Visions of Winsor McCay*. Westlake Village, Calif.: Fantagraphics Books, 1988.

———. *The Best of Little Nemo in Slumberland*. New York: Stewart, Tabori & Chang, 1997.

Marschall, Richard, and John Paul Adams. *Milt Caniff: Rembrandt of the Comic Strip*. Endicott, N.Y.: Flying Buttress Publications, 1981.

Marzio, Peter. *Rube Goldberg: His Life and Work*. New York: Harper and Row, 1973.

McDonnell, Patrick, Karen O'Connell, and Georgia Riley de Havenon. *Krazy Kat: The Comic Art of George Herriman*. New York: Harry N. Abrams, 1986.

Robbins, Trina. *Nell Brinkley and the New Woman in the Early 20th Century*. Jefferson, N.C.: McFarland & Company, 2001.

Roberts, Garyn G. *Dick Tracy and American Culture*. Jefferson, N.C.: McFarland & Company, 1993.

Robinson, Jerry. *Skippy and Percy Crosby*. New York: Holt, Rinehart and Winston, 1978.

Sagendorf, Bud. *Popeye: The First Fifty Years*. New York: Workman Publishing, 1979.

Smith, Bruce. *The History of Little Orphan Annie*. New York: Ballantine Books, 1982.

Theroux, Alexander. *The Enigma of Al Capp*. Seattle: Fantagraphics Books, 1999.

Walker, Brian. *The Best of Ernie Bushmiller's Nancy*. Wilton, Conn.: Comicana Books, 1988.

———. *Barney Google and Snuffy Smith: 75 Years of an American Legend*. Wilton, Conn.: Comicana Books/Ohio State University Libraries, 1994.

Walker, Mort. *Backstage at the Strips*. New York: Mason Charter, 1975.

Young, Dean, and Richard Marschall. *Blondie and Dagwood's America*. New York: Harper & Row, 1981.

Yronwode, Catherine. *The Art of Will Eisner*. Princeton, Wis.: Kitchen Sink Press, 1982.

REPRINTS

The publishers that have produced reprint collections of newspaper comic strips and panels are too numerous to list here. Among the more notable reprint series have been: *Alley Oop* (Kitchen Sink Press), *Flash Gordon* (Kitchen Sink Press and Nostalgia Press), *Krazy Kat* (Remco/Kitchen Sink Press, Eclipse, and Fantagraphics), *Li'l Abner* (Kitchen Sink Press), *Little Nemo in Slumberland* (Remco/Fantagraphics), *Little Orphan Annie* (Fantagraphics), *Polly and Her Pals* (Remco/Kitchen Sink), *Popeye* (Fantagraphics), *Prince Valiant* (Fantagraphics and Nostalgia Press), *Tarzan* (NBM), *Terry and the Pirates* (Remco/Kitchen Sink and NBM), and *Wash Tubbs and Captain Easy* (NBM). In 1977, Hyperion Press of Westport, Connecticut, published a series of twenty-two volumes entitled *Classic American Comic Strips*. The books in the series, which were edited by Bill Blackbeard, included collections of *A. Mutt, Abie the Agent, Barney Google, Baron Bean, Bobby Thatcher, Bobo Baxter, Bringing Up Father, The Bungle Family, Buster Brown, Connie, Dauntless Durham of the U.S.A., The Family Upstairs, Happy Hooligan, Jim Hardy, Minute Movies, Napoleon, Polly and Her Pals, School Days, Sherlocko the Monk, Skippy, Thimble Theatre,* and *Winsor McCay's Dream Days*.

DISSERTATIONS AND MANUSCRIPTS

Castelli, Alfredo. "Here We Are Again, 1895–1919: The First 25 Years of American Newspaper Comics." Milan, March 21, 2003.

Davidson, Sol. "Culture and Comic Strips." New York University, 1958.

Nystrom, Elsa. "A Rejection of Order: The Development of the Newspaper Comic Strip in America, 1830–1920." Loyola University of Chicago, 1989.

Young, William Henry. "Images of Order: American Comic Strips During the Depression, 1929–1938." Emory University, 1969.

INDEX

The Picture Folk

MARGARET E. SANGSTER

They're of another world, perhaps,
  The little picture folk;
Just made to carry off a laugh,
  An epigram or joke.
They're of another world that lies
  Across a comic sheet,
And yet, beneath the fun of them,
  Is something real and sweet!

There's "*Polly*" and her many pals,
  There's "*Jerry*" and "*Us Boys*";
There's "*Jiggs*" and "*Maggie*" with their flood
  Of troubles and of joys.
There's "*Barney Google*" and his horse,
  There's "*Casper*" and his wife.
And "*Buttercup*," their infant child,
  And "*This is married life!*"

We read about them steadily,
  We know their tiny ways. . . .
Our hands reach out, in friendliness,
  Across the work-filled days.
They make us chuckle, for they bring
  A kindly sense of cheer;
We follow through their lives until
  We feel them very near!

There's "*Indoor Sports*" and "*Little Jim.*"
  There's "*Freddy*"—he works fast!
There's "*Tillie*" at the typewriter,
  Each moment seems her last. . . . .
The "*Piffles*," "*Happy Hooligan*,"
  "*Our Boss*" and "*Buster Brown*";
And "*Slim*" and "*Helpful Henry*," and
  Some others of renown.

They're of another world, perhaps,
  The little picture folk;
Just built to hang some laughter on,
  An epigram or joke,
But, oh, we love them for they're not
  Like books on musty shelves. . . . .
The reason? In their eyes, we see
  The image of ourselves!

In "*Krazy Kat*" we glimpse a heart
  That suffers and forgives;
In "*Father*"—stout and middle-aged,
  A vague romance still lives.
Ambition—it is "*Abie's*" text,
  They all strive toward some goal—
They may be only make-believes,
  But each one has a soul!

"THE PICTURE FOLK" by Margaret E. Sangster. April 1923, Circulation magazine. Author's collection

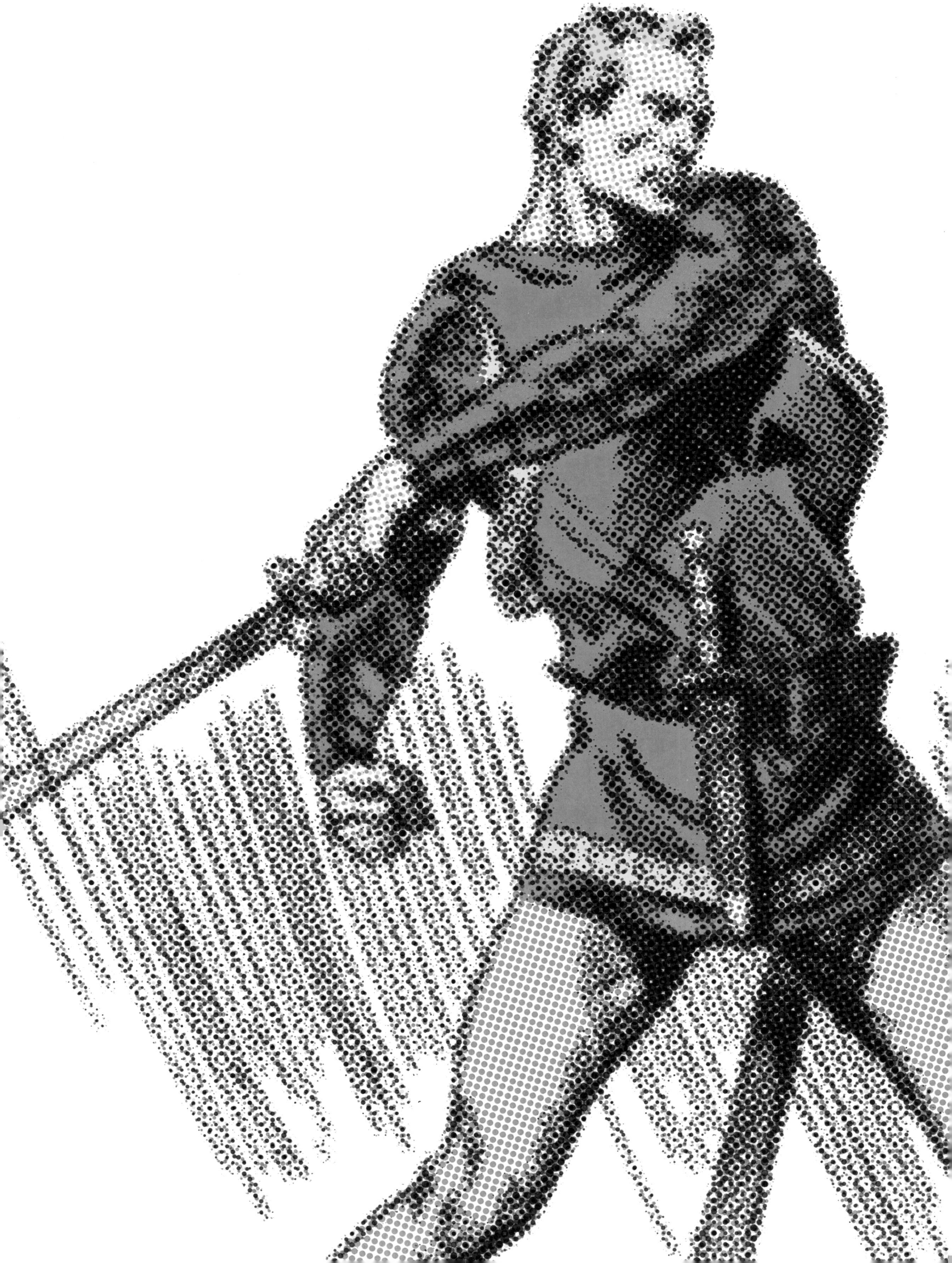

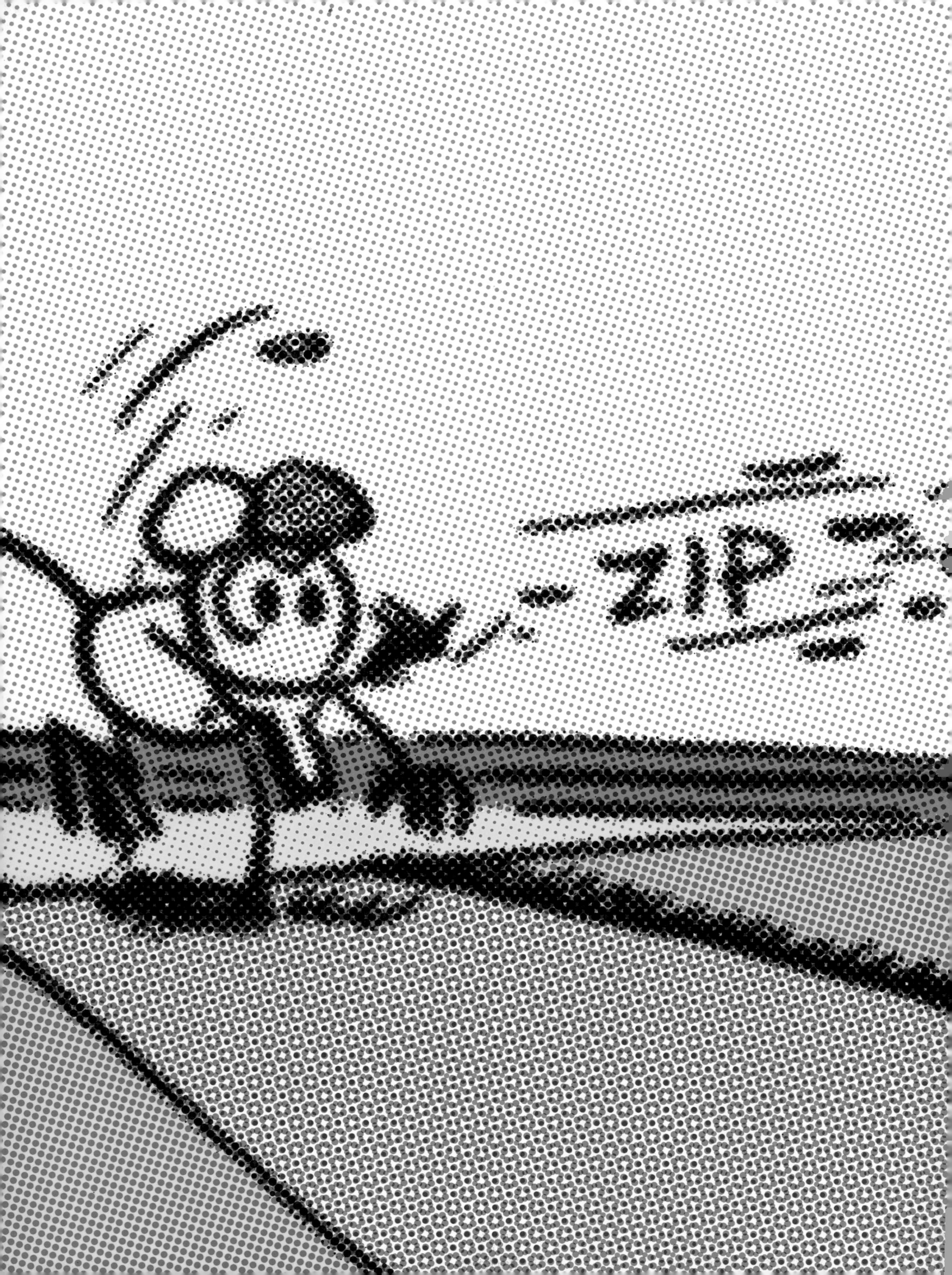
ZIP